COLLECTED WHEEL PUBLICATIONS

VOLUME 9

NUMBERS 116 – 131

BPE

BPS PARIYATTI EDITIONS

BPS Pariyatti Editions
An imprint of Pariyatti Publishing
www.pariyatti.org

Although this is an American edition, we have left any British spelling of words unchanged.

First BPS Pariyatti Edition, 2022
ISBN: 978-1-68172-495-9 (Print)
ISBN: 978-1-68172-157-6 (PDF)
ISBN: 978-1-68172-158-3 (ePub)
ISBN: 978-1-68172-159-0 (Mobi)
LCCN: 2018940050

Contents

WH 116 Practical Advice for Meditators
Bhikkhu Khantipālo 1

WH 117 to 119 Nirvāna, Nihilism and Satori
Douglas M. Burns, MD 35

WH 120 The Kūṭadanta Sutta: On True Sacrifice
Prof. T. W. Rhys Davids 113

WH 121 & 122 The Power of Mindfulness
Nyanaponika Thera 143

WH 123 The Significance of the Four Noble Truths
V. F. Gunaratna 189

WH 124 & 125 Buddhism in South India
Pandit Hisselle Dhammaratana Mahāthera 223

WH 126 The Way of the Noble
T. H. Perera 269

WH 127 Aspects of Reality
Dr. G. P. Malalasekera 289

WH 128 & 129 Aspects of Buddhist Social Philosophy
K. N. Jayatilleke 313

WH 130 & 131 The Buddhist Monk's Discipline
Bhikkhu Khantipālo 351

Key to Abbreviations

A	Aṅguttara Nikāya	Paṭis	Paṭisambhidamagga
Ap	Apadāna	Peṭ	Peṭakopadesa
Bv	Buddhavaṃsa	S	Saṃyutta Nikāya
Cp	Cariyāpiṭaka	Sn	Suttanipāta
D	Dīgha Nikāya	Th	Theragātha
Dhp	Dhammapada	Thī	Therigātha
Dhs	Dhammasaṅgaṇī	Ud	Udāna
It	Itivuttaka	Vibh	Vibhaṅga
Ja	Jātaka verses and commentary	Vin	Vinaya-piṭaka
Khp	Khuddakapāṭha	Vism	Visuddhimagga
M	Majjhima Nikāya	Vism-mhṭ	Visuddhimagga Sub-commentary
Mil	Milindapañha	Vv	Vimānavatthu
Nett	Nettipakaraṇa	Nidd	Niddesa

The above is the abbreviation scheme of the Pali Text Society (PTS) as given in the *Dictionary of Pali* by Margaret Cone.

The commentaries, *aṭṭhakathā*, are abbreviated by using a hyphen and an "a" ("-a") following the abbreviation of the text, e.g., *Dīgha Nikāya Aṭṭhakathā* = D-a. Likewise the sub-commentaries are abbreviated by a "ṭ" ("-ṭ") following the abbreviation of the text.

The sutta reference abbreviation system for the four Nikāyas, as is used in Bhikkhu Bodhi's translations is:

AN	Aṅguttara Nikāya	DN	Dīgha Nikāya
MN	Majjhima Nikāya	Sn	Saṃyutta Nikāya
J	Jātaka story	Mv	Mahāvagga (Vinaya Piṭaka)
Cv	Cullavagga (Vinaya Piṭaka)	SVibh	Suttavibhaṅga (Vinaya Piṭaka)

Practical Advice for Meditators

by

Bhikkhu Khantipālo

WHEEL PUBLICATION NO. 116

Foreword

The following pages were originally intended as new sections to be added to the second edition of my introductory book on the Dhamma, *What Is Buddhism?* However, as many people are greatly interested in the practice of meditation, and as many are also separated from the sources of a living tradition, it is hoped that the following may be of value even apart from the sections of the book which they supplement.

When we consider meditation, we cannot stress too much the importance of having the right reasons for taking it up. Meditation—or, as a better translation of *samādhi*, collectedness—is only one aspect of Buddhist practice, and must, to be successful, go hand in hand with such other practices as generosity, gentleness, non-violence, patience, contentment and humility. If such genuine qualities of the Dhamma neither exist in oneself initially, nor grow through one's practice, then something is drastically wrong, and only a foolhardy person will try to proceed. The practice of collectedness is based upon firm roots of virtue (*sīla*) and cannot succeed in anyone who does not make a real effort to be strict in keeping the precepts.

The signs of "progress" in collectedness are not strange visions, peculiar feelings and the like (though it is conceivable that these may arise also where progress is achieved), but rather an all-round and harmonious growth in the way of Dhamma. If one is without a teacher, then one has to be doubly vigilant, otherwise one will never become aware whether one of Māra's distractions is likely to succeed, or whether one does in fact tread the Middle Practice-Path.

This essay is an extract from *Buddhism Explained*, the second edition (revised and enlarged) of the book formerly known as *What Is Buddhism?* published by The Social Science Press of Thailand.

Bhikkhu Khantipālo

Two Streams in Meditation

Two apparently distinct streams of Buddhist meditation may be discerned, though when meditation is established, these are seen to be complementary.

It may be profitable for some people whose minds are very active and who incline to suffer from distraction to follow with mindfulness the mad monkey-mind's acrobatics. As the mind is really a series of mental events which arise and pass away with incredible rapidity, each of which is a mind complete with supporting mental factors, so at the beginning this kind of mindfulness is really one "mindful" mind watching other "minds" (which are all within one's own mental continuity, of course). One thereby develops the ability to look into the mind and to see where it has gone to. Has it gone to the past, present or future? Has it gone to materiality, or to feelings, or perhaps to cognitions, to volitional activities, or has it gone to consciousness? By this method of "Where has it gone?" the distracted mind slowly comes under the surveillance of the mindful mind, until mindfulness forms a strong foundation for further development. Considerable, though mundane, brilliance of mind is both needed and developed by this practice, which however should be balanced by the tranquillity of the absorptions. When the mind has become calm, one should start to practise for the absorptions (*jhāna*), which will in their turn be the basis for the arising of real insight. This method is called "wisdom leading to calm."

Other methods suited to those whose minds are less disturbed initially, include the classic forty subjects of meditation (see Appendix); and these, together with more developed types of meditation practice, involve the use of a definite object for concentration. This may be one's own body or a part of it, a colour or a picture, a word or a phrase, or abstract contemplation and so forth. All these methods involve some firm but gentle discipline of the mind, in that each time it strays away, it must be gently brought back again (by mindfulness, of course) to concentrate again on the chosen subject.

Some people have the quite mistaken idea that practice of this sort must necessarily lead to tranquillity almost at once. They may be surprised when beginning to practise themselves, since they actually experience more troubles than they had previously. This is, firstly, because they never before really looked into their mind to know the state it has always been in; and secondly, because having taken up a discipline of the mind, it is as though one stirs up with a stick a stagnant pond, or pokes with a stick a fire smouldering under ashes. The wild elephant of the mind, long accustomed to roam in the jungle of desires, does not take readily to taming, or to being tied to the post of practice with the thongs of mindfulness. However, diligence and heedfulness will eventually win for one the fruits of tranquillity.

All these forty subjects are of this second type, in which the calm gained from practice is then used for the arousing of wisdom. They are for this reason called "calm-leading-to-wisdom" methods, and are very important in the present distracted age. For their full explanation one should consult the *Path of Purification* (*Visuddhimagga*), although even the great learning in that book cannot replace the personal contact with a teacher.

Practical Advice for Meditators

Turning from the psychological to the practical aspect, meditation for laypeople may be divided into two categories: that which is done intensively, and that which one practises while going about one's daily life. The meditation practised intensively is also of two sorts: regular daily sitting and occasional retreat practice.

Regular Daily Sitting

We shall first discuss the regular daily period of intensive sitting, which should, where possible, be made every day at the same time. One should guard against its becoming a ritual by earnestness and by being intensely aware of why one has undertaken it. The following suggestions may be found helpful as well.

As to material considerations, the place for meditation should be fairly quiet. If one has a small room which can be used for this purpose, so much the better, and in any case, it is better to meditate alone, unless other members of the household also practise. Where this latter is the case one should make sure that one's mind is pure also in relation to others, for otherwise greed, hatred, and the rest of the robber gang are sure to steal away the fruits of meditation.

Quietness is best obtained by getting up early before others rise; and this is also the time when the mind is clear and the body untired. The sincere meditator therefore keeps regular hours, for he knows how much depends on having just enough sleep to feel refreshed.

After rising and washing one should sit down in clean loose clothing in the meditation place. One may have a small shrine with Buddhist symbols, but this is not essential. Some people find it useful to begin by making the offerings of flowers, incense and light, carefully reflecting while doing so. It is very common in Buddhist countries to preface one's silent meditation by chanting softly to oneself, "*Namo tassa bhagavato arahato sammā-sambuddhassa*," with the Refuges and the Precepts. If one knows the Pali passages in praise of the Buddha, Dhamma and Sangha, these may also be used at this time.[1]

1. See *The Mirror of the Dhamma*, Wheel No. 54 a/b.

Another useful preliminary is a reflection, a discursive recitation, of some truths of the Dhamma, such as:

"Having this precious opportunity of human birth, I have two responsibilities in the Dhamma: the benefit of myself and the benefit of others. All other beings, whether they be human or non-human, visible or invisible, great or small, far or near, all these beings I shall treat with gentleness and wish that they may dwell in peace. May they be happy ... May they be happy.... May they be happy....! I shall help them when they experience suffering, and be glad with them when they are happy. May I develop as well the incomparable equanimity, the mind in perfect balance that can never be upset!

"In looking to the welfare of others, I shall not forget my own progress on the path of Dhamma. May I indeed come to know how, driven here and there by the winds of my kamma, I have suffered an infinity of lives in all the realms of existence! I must also turn my mind to consider how short and fleeting is this life. How mind and body are ever changing, arising and declining from moment to moment. How neither mind nor body belongs to me, neither of them is mine. I must also turn this mind to consider how beset by troubles is this brief life. Having been sired by craving and born out of ignorance, I must realize that death is inescapable, that old age and disease are natural to my condition. I must make efforts to realize for my own good and the good of others that this person called 'myself' is a complex of mentality and materiality wherein no abiding entity such as a soul or self is found.

"May I through this practice experience insight into impermanence, ill and no-self! May I be one who dwells in the Void! And having realized this sublime truth, may I show the way to others!"

When sitting, care should be taken that the body is kept erect, yet relaxed. There should be no strain, but neither should the head droop, nor the lumbar region sag. The body should feel poised and balanced upright. Although the cross-legged positions (such as the lotus posture) are best when the meditator is seated on a fairly soft mat, a chair may be used by those unaccustomed to the lotus posture or else unable to train themselves to sit in that way. Sitting in lotus posture or half-lotus posture will be found much easier if a rather hard cushion is placed so as to raise the buttocks. The knees will then tend to touch the ground and a firm three-pointed sitting (two knees and buttocks) is then attained.

One should sit for the same length of time every day until, as one becomes more proficient in collecting the mind, automatically one will feel like extending the practice. One widely used method for measuring the meditation period is sitting for the length of time taken for a stick of incense to burn down. Having placed the hands in meditation posture relaxed in the lap, the eyes may be closed or left slightly open, according to which is found most comfortable.

Methods used for helping to concentrate the mind are many, and the two main streams in classical meditation have been briefly reviewed in the section above. Other helpful methods include the repetition of a word or phrase and perhaps with it the use of a rosary. If one practises mindfulness of breathing, one may find the use of a word such as "Buddho" or "Arahaṃ" good for quietening the mind. The first syllable is silently repeated when breathing in, and one concentrates on the second during the out-breathing. Also the counting of breath (up to ten, but generally not over this number to prevent the mind wandering) is used as an aid for concentration. But any such aids should be dropped when concentration improves. When the meditation is on a phrase only, a rosary may be used in conjunction, each repetition being marked by one bead.

One's meditation goes well if one finds the mind increasingly absorbed on the chosen meditation subject, but one should not assume that meditation is useless just because for a period, longer or shorter, not much more than sleepiness or distraction is experienced. These hindrances have to be faced; and if they are met, not by irritation or despair, but by quietly observant mindfulness, they can and will be overcome. For success, great persistence and evenness of effort are necessary.

The meditation period may close with some chanting, the usual subject being the well-being of others and the distribution of merits to them. A translation, or the original Pali, of the *Mettā Sutta* (*Discourse on Loving-kindness*)[2] may be chanted at this time and, as

2. See *The Practice of Loving-kindness* (*Mettā*), trans. Ñāṇamoli, Wheel No. 7.

it is not long, can be easily memorized. As methods of chanting vary, it is very helpful if one can obtain recordings, perhaps on tape, of the passages one wishes to learn, recorded by bhikkhus.

While on the subject of chanting, it is very useful to know a few discourses of Lord Buddha in one of the Buddhist classical languages, and to use these for collecting the mind if there should be an occasion when no concentration at all can be attained. At such a time a meditator should not feel depressed but should continue sitting and chant softly to himself. This is what Buddhist monks do twice a day as part of their mental development, and it is useful as well for fostering a more devotional approach necessary as balance with intellectual characters. Another useful method for the overcoming of distraction is walking-practice, which may be done in any passage of the house or in a secluded walk in the garden. A length of twenty or thirty paces will be sufficient, for if longer the mind tends to wander, and if shorter, distraction may be increased. One should walk at the speed one feels to be natural, with the hands clasped, the left in the right, and arms relaxed in front of the body. At the ends of the walk one should turn in a clockwise direction.[3]

Perhaps a few words on devotion would not be out of place here, for this is very important in meditation practice. No one who is not a devoted Buddhist takes up Buddhist meditation, for the simple reason that he does not have the Buddhist ideals in his heart. The taking to heart of the Triple Refuge and the understanding of the Triple Gem are closely linked with Buddhist meditation. A really devoted Buddhist, who puts his whole life into the Dhamma, will have no insurmountable difficulties in meditation practice. Whatever obstacles he comes to, those he leaps over, sustained by devotion. He is prepared for the way to be long and hard because he realizes that he has made it like that. If he finds his way blocked, his meditation failing to progress and he himself without a teacher, he does not waver or falter on the way. He thinks, "I am now experiencing the results of intentional actions (kamma) made by me in the past." And he remembers

3. The tradition of "keeping the right side towards" respected persons and objects has a psychological basis. Also note in English right (for side) and right (good, correct).

Lord Buddha's last words: "Subject to breaking-up are all compounded things. With mindfulness strive on." All difficulties are compounded things and will eventually change; meanwhile much may be done with mindfulness, vigour and devotion.

If one is not too tired after work and if there is the opportunity in the evening, another period of sitting can be undertaken then. In any case, before sleep, it is a wise practice to sit, if only for a few minutes, so as to purify the mind before lying down. One may consider thus: "When I lie down there is no certainty that I shall awake." One may, therefore, be lying down to die, and this is a good reflection to rouse skilful states of mind and banish sensual unskilful ones. If one practises this, "the lying-down to die," it will be a very good preparation for the real event, which is bound to take place at some time in the unknown future. It may even generate the right conditions for the arising of insight allowing one "to die," giving up the grasping at what does not belong to one, that is, the mind and body. At this time also, a Dhamma phrase or word may be used, the repeating of which one eventually falls to sleep. In this way one ends and begins the day with practice of Buddhist teachings. And apart from devotion of one's whole day to them, what could be better?

Retreats

Regarding the second division of intensive practice, that is, when undertaken in retreat, much will depend upon what facilities are available to the earnest student. There are now places in the West where meditation instruction can be sought. The most important thing is to have direct contact with an able meditation master (books serve at the beginning, while even a teacher is later found deficient in some way). After satisfying this one condition, only one other is necessary: one must strive with diligence to practise and realize his teachings. If these two conditions are fulfilled, then one is the most fortunate among human beings.

Many will be without access to a teacher and some may like to try a period of solitary meditation in some quiet part of the country. This should only be attempted if one has already developed a good power of mindfulness. Otherwise what was meant to foster meditation may become a very unprofitable time, perhaps accompanied by the seeming intensification of the mental defilements.

Daily Life

As to the other sort of meditation practice, which is performed in daily life, though much might be written, the following few words may serve as a guide. First, one should not deceive oneself regarding concentration of the mind. It is of no use pretending to oneself or to others that one's daily life is one's meditation—unless of course one has already great powers of concentration. Only the real adept, often one who has sat for many years keeping the monastic discipline, can really perceive ordinary life as meditation; and such a one would be most unlikely to tell others of this fact. Refusing to allow pride an opportunity to distort the real state of mental affairs, one should take stock with fairness and admit one's limitations. This is already a great step forward. The layman who thinks of himself as an Arahat already has blocked off very effectively all real progress; while the honest man has at least the wisdom to be humble.

Much may be accomplished with mindfulness, while without it there is no hope for meditation in daily life. How are quite ordinary events capable of being made into meditation? By mindfulness, which, to begin with, may be defined as *awareness* of the present work in hand. At first great effort has to be made in order to remain mindful of what one is supposed to be doing, nor can one pretend that such mindfulness is pleasant always. To escape from dull and unliked work and situations, we tend to turn either to fantasy worlds, hopes or memories, which are respectively the delusive escapes into the present, future or past. But for one really interested in understanding himself, none of these courses is very rewarding, since they are compounded of delusion with various ingredients, such as fear, craving or ignorance. While in the practice of strict meditation, mindfulness may follow all the wanderings of the mind, in daily life it is better that the mind should be constantly returned to the job in hand. One should not "send" one's mind anywhere, neither to a dream-world nor to the past nor to the future. Lord Buddha compared these periods of time thus:

"The past is like a dream,
The future as a mirage,
While the present is like clouds."

Such a simile may be useful as the mind darts about between dreams, mirages and clouds, all insubstantial, though the ever-changing present, like the clouds in the sky, is the only aspect of time compared to things of greater reality. One may also consider meditation as the exercise of mindfulness which keeps the mind "inside" this body, that is, always focused upon some aspect of it. Of course only the most sincere meditator, who sees the advantage in this to be greater than any pleasure offered by the world, is likely to practise in this way, since this cuts off not only interest in outer objects but also the toying with pleasant or intriguing ideas.

Indeed, with work that is really uninteresting, the way of mindfulness is the only way to convert one's day into something worthwhile. Days pass and bring us nearer to death and an unknown rebirth, while it is now that one has the chance to practise Dhamma. Instead of reacting with aversion or deluded fantasies towards what one does not like (or in other situations indulging one's greed), the Way of Mindfulness constitutes the Middle Practice-Path transcending these ancient patterns of reaction. There is no need to be ruled either by greed or by hatred, nor to be dominated by delusion; but only mindfulness shows the way beyond these.

Constantly bringing the mind back and disengaging it from tangles is the basic practice in everyday life. It is also wise to take advantage of those odd times during work when one waits for something to do, to meet someone, for a bus or train, or any time when one is alone for a few minutes. Instead of turning to a newspaper for distraction, to the television, or to another person for gossip, it is more profitable to "retire inside" oneself. Disengaging attention from exterior objects, take up mindfulness of breathing, or the repetition of some phrase of Dhamma, or significant word such as "Buddho" or "Arahat," doing this until one has again to attend to work. Going inwards as often as possible will be found very useful, strengthening one's sitting practice just as the latter in turn strengthens the ability to turn within.

Mindfulness of breathing is especially good as a concentration method for use during travel and during the times when one is restlessly expecting a bus or a train. Why be agitated or impatient?

A little mindful breathing is just the practice for these moments, since it calms the feverish workings of the mind and the restless movements of the body. One does not have to aimlessly stare out of windows while travelling! Why be a slave of the "eye-dominant" when a little useful practice could take its place? One does not have to listen to the idle chatter of others, so why be a slave to the "ear-dominant"? One cannot shut one's ears, but everyone can withdraw attention to some extent while practising mindfulness.

It is mindfulness also which helps to bring into focus counteractive contemplations. Lust, for instance, is soon dissipated by thoughts of a decaying corpse. The looks which are bestowed on pretty girls (or handsome men) seem ridiculous when it is thought that old ladies and equally ancient men never attract such desire-filled attention. Only when one sees how lust burns up the one who indulges in it, only then does it seem worth relinquishing.

Similarly gluttony, even in a mild form, can be demolished by contemplating the bodily processes connected with food. Chewed food looks a good deal less palatable than when the same stuff before mixing with spittle was nicely laid out on plates. Vomit is just the same substances in the process of change but does not readily arouse greed. Excrement even if placed on the finest gold plate fails to become attractive—yet this is the remnants of the food so eagerly gorged! By the time that one has contemplated food in these three stages, greed has quite disappeared, and one may take food just as a medicine to preserve the body.

Mindfulness is also responsible for becoming sufficiently aware in a moment of anger to turn the mind to other subjects or persons. It is mindfulness that warns one of an approaching situation where anger may arise, and makes it possible to turn aside and dwell in equanimity or, where the Divine Abidings are well developed, in friendliness.

When envy rears its ugly head, mindfulness gives one presence of mind to know "envy has arisen," and if efforts to arouse gladness with others' joy fail, it is mindfulness that helps one dwell in equanimity or, if all else fails, helps turn attention to other objects.

Lord Buddha has truly said, "Mindfulness, I declare, is helpful everywhere."

The social implications of meditation should be obvious from the above. Those who have the strange delusion that Buddhism is a religion of meditative isolation, offering society no social benefits, should understand that a Buddhist believes society can only be changed for the better, and with some degree of permanence, by starting work on himself. Buddhist ideals of society are expressed in a number of important discourses addressed by Lord Buddha to laypeople, and in them the development of the individual is always stressed as a very necessary factor. The advantages of a society in which there are a large number of those dwelling at peace with themselves need hardly be stressed. The development of wisdom and compassion by one man has its effect in leavening the materialistic dough around him. The Buddhist call is therefore *first* to gain peace in one's own heart, when will follow, quite naturally, peace in the world. Trying to obtain peace the other way round will never be practical nor produce a lasting peace, for the roots of greed, hatred and delusion have still a firm grip on the hearts of people. Impractical? Only for those who do not practise. Those who take up the cultivation of mindfulness find out for themselves how it helps to solve life's problems.

Although many journeys to remote and attractive places are now performed with ease, the way leading to Nibbāna still needs effort. But if the way is sometimes drear, with mindfulness the only guiding light, at least from reflection one knows that the goal is glorious and of great worth, not only for oneself but for others as well.

Divine Abidings and Their Perfection
(*Brahma-vihāra*)

The way to that goal leads through what are called the Divine Abidings,[4] which train the deep-rooted emotions from being unskilful into the skilful way of the Dhamma. As has already been emphasized above, the aim of oneself as of all beings is to gain happiness-producing conditions. Therefore one must act in such a way that happiness will result from one's actions. One should, in this case, treat others as they would wish to be treated, for every living being is dear to itself and wishes its own welfare and happiness. One cannot expect to have an isolated happiness arising from no cause or from itself, nor can happiness be expected if one maltreats other beings, human or otherwise. Every being desires life and is afraid of death, this is as true of ourselves as of other creatures.

Only a man who constantly leads an upright and compassionate life is really dear to himself, for he does actions which are of great profit, of great happiness. Other people, although they think that they are dear to themselves, are really their own worst enemies, for they go about doing to themselves what only an enemy would wish for them.

Good conduct depends on a well-trained mind which has gradually been freed from the clutches of greed, hatred and delusion. To hold one's neighbour as dear as one should truly hold oneself is easily said but with difficulty done. It is the particular merit of Lord Buddha's teachings that they always point out how a method is to be translated into experience, the method here being the mental training of the Divine Abidings. When we say "mental," this word should be understood not in the narrow sense of the intellectual processes, but rather to include the full range of the mind-and-heart, intellect and emotions.

There are four states of Divine Abidings: friendliness, compassion, gladness and equanimity. These, especially the first, are very popular meditations in Buddhist countries. What follows is a short explanation of each.

---

4. See Nyanaponika, *The Four Sublime States*, Wheel No. 6.

Friendliness (*mettā*) is an unselfish love which can be extended to everyone. This becomes easy once one has gained the meditative absorptions, when the quality of friendliness becomes an integral part of one's character. In the normal way of things, people only "love" the few people to whom they are especially attached by ties of family, etc. Such is love with sensual attachment, a limited love, and those outside that love are either ignored or disliked. Sensual love, then, is not only linked to attachment (greed), but also to hatred and delusion, so that the person who is content with this love pays a heavy price for it. A love without attachment is scarcely conceivable to many people, but such love is much superior to the former; being without attachment it can become infinite and need not be confined to this or that group of beings. As it can be made infinite, leaving none outside it, so there is no question of the three roots of unskill being linked with it.

Friendliness can be developed gradually in one's meditation period every day, *but if it is really effective* it must show in one's daily life. It makes life easier by turning persons whom one formerly disliked or hated into, at the beginning, those whom one disregards, and then as one's practice becomes stronger, into objects for the arising of loving-kindness. It is Lord Buddha's medicine for the disease of hatred and dislike. Finally, one is warned that it has two enemies: the "near" one is sensual attachment, often miscalled "love," while the "far" enemy to its development is hatred. In the development of friendliness one must beware of these two.

Compassion (*karuṇā*) is taking note of the sufferings of other beings in the world. It overcomes callous indifference to the plight of suffering beings, human or otherwise. Likewise, it must be reflected in one's life by a willingness to go out of one's way to give aid where possible and to help those in distress. It has the advantage of reducing one's selfishness by understanding others' sorrows. It is Lord Buddha's medicine for cruelty, for how can one harm others when one has seen how much they have to suffer already? It has also two enemies: the "near" one is mere grief; while its "far" enemy is cruelty.

Gladness (*muditā*) is to rejoice with others over their success, gains and happiness. It overcomes the grudging attitude to others, and the envy which may arise on hearing of others' joy. It must show in one's life as a spontaneous joy at the very time when one learns that other people have some gain or other, material or immaterial. It has the advantage of making one open-hearted towards others, and does away with secretiveness. A person who develops gladness attracts many friends who are devoted to him, and with them and others he lives in harmony. It is Lord Buddha's medicine for envy and jealousy, which it can inhibit completely. The two enemies of gladness are the merely personal happiness of reflecting on one's own gains—this is the "near" enemy; while the "far" one is aversion to, or boredom with, this gladness.

Equanimity (*upekkhā*) is to be developed to deal with situations where one should admit that it is beyond one's powers to change them. It overcomes worry and useless distraction over affairs which either do not concern one or else cannot be changed by oneself. It is reflected in one's life by an ability to meet difficult situations with tranquillity and undisturbed peace of mind. The advantage to be seen in its development is that it makes one's life more simple by disengaging from useless activity. It is Lord Buddha's medicine for distraction and worry, and its enemies are mere indifference, which is the "near" one; while greed, and its partner resentment, which involve one unskilfully in so many affairs, are its "far" enemies.

The mind well-practised in these four virtues, and then well-trained by their use in daily life, has already gained very much.

Three of the perfections (*pāramī*), or qualities, practised by many Buddhists who aspire to enlightenment may also be outlined here, as they too have an intimate bearing on the practice of meditation.

Patience and Its Perfection
(*Khanti-pāramī*)

Patience is an excellent quality much praised in Buddhist scriptures. It can be developed easily only if restlessness and hatred have already been subdued in the mind, as is done by meditation practice. Impatience, which has the tendency to make one rush around and thus miss many good chances, results from the inability to sit still and let things sort themselves out—which sometimes they may do without one's meddling. The patient man has many a fruit fall into his lap which the go-getter misses. One of them is a quiet mind, for impatience churns the mind up and brings with it the familiar anxiety-diseases of the modern business world. Patience quietly endures—it is this quality which makes it so valuable in mental training and particularly in meditation. It is no good expecting instant enlightenment after five minutes' practice. Coffee may be instant, but meditation is not, and only harm will come of trying to hurry it up. For ages the rubbish has accumulated, an enormous pile of mental refuse, and so when one comes along at first with a very tiny teaspoon and starts removing it, how fast can one expect it to disappear? Patience is the answer, and determined energy to go with it. The patient meditator really gets results of lasting value; the seeker after "quick methods" or "sudden enlightenment" is doomed by his own attitude to long disappointment.

Indeed, it must soon become apparent to anyone investigating the Dhamma that these teachings are not for the impatient. A Buddhist views his present life as a little span perhaps of eighty years or so, and the latest one so far of many such lives. Bearing this in mind, he determines to do as much in this life for the attainment of Enlightenment as possible. But he does not overestimate his capabilities; he just quietly and patiently gets on with living the Dhamma from day to day. Rushing headlong at Enlightenment (or what one thinks it is), like a bull in a china shop, is not likely to get one very far, that is, unless one is a very exceptional character who can take such treatment and, most important, one who is devoted to a very skilful master of meditation.

With patience one will not bruise oneself, but will go carefully step by step along the way. We learn that a Bodhisatta is well aware of this, and that he cultures his mind with this perfection so that it is not disturbed by any of the untoward occurrences common in this world. He decides that he will be patient with exterior conditions—not to be upset when the sun is too hot or the weather too cold. Not to be agitated by other beings which attack his body, such as bugs and mosquitoes. Neither will he be disturbed when people utter harsh words, lies or abuse about him, either to his face or behind his back. His patience is not broken even when his body is subjected to torment, blows, sticks and stones, tortures, and even death itself; he will endure these steadily, so unflinching is his patience. Buddhist monks also are advised to practise in the same way.

In Buddhist tradition the perfection of patience is rather better known than some of the others. This is because a quite outstanding Birth Story illustrates it. The Khantivādin (Teacher of Patience) Birth Story[5] should be read many times and made the object of deep and frequent reflections. Only an exceptionally noble person, in this case Gotama in a previous life, when he was called the Patience-teaching Rishi, can gently exhort a raging and drunk monarch, who, out of his jealous anger, is slowly cutting that person's body to pieces. Such nobility did the Bodhisatta have and such nobility, steadfast endurance and gentleness is required of all who would try to reach the goal of Enlightenment.

5. Jātaka No. 33, see translation issued by the Pali Text Society.

Energy and Its Perfection
(*Viriya-pāramī*)

Just as Enlightenment is inconceivable unless a person has patience, so it is not attainable without effort being made. The Dhamma never encourages the doctrine of fatalism, and true Buddhists never think of events as being rigidly predetermined. Such fatalism is combatted by mindfulness and by energy itself. This perfection is the counterpart of the previous one and, balanced by practice, they ensure that the sincere Buddhist neither passively accepts what he should combat nor rushes around to the disturbance of himself and others when he should have patience. By way of warning it may be mentioned here that in the Buddhist world can be found a number of "methods" which seem to promise the riches of Dhamma all in no time. One hears such remarks as, "What's the use of books and study?" Or even, "The development of calm is a waste of time! One should only develop insight." Such lop-sided approaches do not reflect the wisdom of Lord Buddha, who taught time and again the necessity of a balanced development of mind. Books and their study are useful to some people who wish to gain a good background knowledge of what Lord Buddha really said, before taking up more intensive practice. As for the other assertion, no real insight (only delusive ideas) will arise to the person whose mind has no experience of calm. Such views as these, which are usually based on some peculiar experience of those "teachers" who originate them, are apt to mislead many, since the craving for quick results coupled with the dislike of the necessary hard work are easily stirred up. There must be patience to accept that the conditions required for success of meditation (as outlined here) have to be fulfilled, and the only result, if failing to do so, is straying off the Way. The meditator applies himself steadily to whatever task he has in hand and, coming to the end of it, does not feel tired at all but straightaway takes up a new objective.

It is interesting in this respect that tiredness is of two kinds: that relating to physical exhaustion; and the other kind which is mentally induced and involves the unskilful factors of sloth and torpor. While the former is of course unavoidable, the latter occurs only when the unskilful root of delusion (or dullness) becomes predominant in the mind. This happens when there is a situation which is unpleasant to "me," unwanted, and from which "I" want to escape. People complain that they become much more tired sitting in meditation while practising intensively than they do when, say, they do a bit of heavy reading. When the self feels threatened by a self-revealing event, then this self, rooted in unknowing, throws up a dense fog of torpor proceeding from the root of delusion. On the other hand, many who have practised much meditation remark that they do not have to sleep as long as they did formerly, while energy, when it becomes a perfection as practised by the Bodhisatta, is quite natural and unforced.

This perfection is illustrated by the story of the caravan-leader who saved the merchants, men and animals entrusted to his care, by vigorous action. When others would have given themselves up to death since the caravan had taken a wrong course in the desert and all supplies were exhausted, their leader forced one of them to dig for water, which he found. In this way, in a previous life did Gotama, as the caravan-leader, make effort not only for his own life but also for the welfare of others. Monks are also referred to as "caravan-leaders" in several places in Pali scriptures, showing that it is not only Lord Buddha or a Bodhisatta who is able to guide others. If we deal energetically with our own training, then we too have energy for the advancement of others. Many other stories like the above could be found in Buddhist works showing how necessary is energy, from which spring persistence and determination for the seeing of the truly real, Nibbāna.

Collectedness and Its Perfection (*Samādhi-pāramī*)

Bearing in mind the meanings of this word together with such specialized terms as (mind-) development (*bhāvanā*), absorption (*jhāna*), insight (*vipassanā*), one-pointedness (*ekaggatā*) and meditation exercise (*kammaṭṭhāna*), we may now examine what constitutes perfected collectedness. What especially marks off the good Buddhist's practice, whether he be a Bodhisatta or not, from that of an ordinary meditator (in any religion), is that the latter will most likely become firmly attached to the delights occurring in the upper reaches of the sensual realm, or to the pure joys of the realm of form and, as a result, come to birth in one of these heavenly states. If one gets oneself trapped in one of these bournes, where pleasures and joys are great and sufferings but little, then it is unlikely that one will be able to generate the energy necessary for the perfection of wisdom. Therefore, the good meditator tries to become proficient in the absorptions (so that he can enter them when he likes, which one he likes, remain absorbed for as long as he likes and emerge when he likes), while not being attached to them. But one should note that this applies only to the skilled meditator who has already obtained the absorptions. If one has not reached to these levels, then ardent aspiration, not detachment, will be the correct attitude.

After these absorptions have been attained, they may be reviewed as impermanent, unsatisfactory and devoid of self or soul (*anicca, dukkha, anattā*), at which time detachment from them will naturally arise and insight (*vipassanā*) be experienced. The absorptions (and the powers which may arise in connection with them) are thus, in the Buddhist way of training, never an end in themselves but are always used to promote insight and wisdom, which arise when the collected mind is set the task of examining the mind and body in order to know completely their characteristics.

A story which brings out the meaning of this perfection is told of Kuddalamuni's life. His name means the Mattock-sage and he was thus called because of the difficulty he experienced in freeing himself from attachment to his mattock. Several times leaving his house with intent to meditate in the forest, he was dragged back by the memory of his mattock and his old occupation of farming. One day, reflecting on the inconstancy with which he pursued meditation, he took his mattock and, whirling it round his head, sent it spinning into the depths of the nearby Ganges. Having done this, he burst out in a great cry of joy. The local rajah, who was passing that way with his army, sent a man to enquire why this farmer was so joyful, to which the sage replied by relating his experience. The rajah and many others were much impressed by his reply, and some followed him to take up a meditative life in the forest; after which, we are told, all passed away to experience life in the realm of form. The Mattock-sage, who was none other than Gotama in a past life, exhibited even then another aspect of the perfection of meditation: the ability to train others in meditation after gaining proficiency in it oneself.

Finally, we may add brief notes on some of the dangers to meditation practice.

Dangers to Meditation

While the number of ways a meditator may go astray is legion, the few mentioned below deserve a special mention due to their common occurrence. First, a danger that cannot be stressed enough is the lack of right motivation for the practice of meditation. When the Eightfold Path is described, in its "wisdom" section, standing next to the (at first) intellectual right understanding comes right motivation, thus emphasizing that the emotional roots underlying practice of the Way must be skilful ones: those connected with renunciation (non-greed), goodwill (non-hatred) and non-violence are mentioned. If one approaches Buddhist meditation with neither right understanding regarding *dukkha* and its cessation, nor with right motives, then one's meditation is liable to go seriously astray.

There have, for instance, been those who took up meditation as a way to invest themselves with power, so that they could easily sway or hypnotize disciples. Others have seen it as a quick way to gain both disciples and riches. Fame may also be an unworthy motive. All these, as motives for playing with meditation, may easily lead the unwary into illness, and sometimes mental unbalance. There is nothing worse in Buddhist meditation, where a person's own sure experience is of paramount importance, than a half-baked disciple who sets himself up as a master.

This obviously leads on to a further danger—that of pride, of which there are several forms. One such is the pride of the person who has seen manifestations of light during meditation, and supposes this to be the sign preceding mental absorption. Then there is the pride of one who touches on a mental absorption if only for an instant and as a result assumes that he has become a Noble One, and this can be a very powerful factor in convincing himself if not others. Quite ordinary people who take up meditation may beware of the common "holier-than-thou" attitudes: "I make an effort, whereas you...," or, "*I meditate* every day, whereas you...." Pride is a great obstacle to any progress, and while it is only a Buddha or Arahat who is entirely rid of it, everyone should have the mindfulness to check it.

Related to this is the danger for the person who always looks for so-called progress. He is sure that he is making "progress" because in meditation he sees lights, hears sounds, or feels strange sensations. He becomes more and more fascinated by these as time goes by, and gradually forgets that he started with the aspiration to find the way to Enlightenment. His "meditation" then degenerates into visions and strange happenings, leading him into the realms of occultism and magic. There is no surer way for a meditator to become entangled than this way. Fascinating though all such manifestations may be, they should be rigorously cut down by resorting to bare attention, never permitting discursive thought regarding them and thus avoiding these distractions.

Among "visions" which one may see, whether they be internal (produced from one's own mind) or external (produced by other beings), there may be for some meditators an experience of the fearful, such as the sight of one's own body reduced to bones or inflated as a rotting corpse. If such an experience occurs, or others of a similar nature, one should withdraw the mind from the vision immediately, supposing that one has no teacher. Visions of the fearful variety which occur to some people may be very useful if rightly employed, but without a teacher's guidance they should be avoided.

Another danger is trying to meditate while one is still too emotionally insecure, unbalanced or immature. An understanding of the value of meritorious deeds or skilfulness will come in useful here. As merit purifies the mind, it will be an excellent basis for mind-development, and both the ease with which absorptions are gained and the ease with which insight arises are to some extent dependent upon merit. Meritorious deeds are not difficult to find in life. They are the core of a good Buddhist life: giving and generosity, undertaking the precepts, help and service to others, reverence, listening whole-heartedly to Dhamma, setting upright one's understanding of Dhamma—all these and more are meritorious deeds which bring happiness and emotional maturity. *Merit*, one should always remember, *opens doors everywhere*. It makes possible; it makes opportunities. To have a mind at all times set upon making merit is to have a mind that may be trained to develop absorptions and insight.

Obviously it follows that to try to practise meditation while all the time retaining one's old cravings, likes and dislikes is, to say the least, making one's path difficult if not dangerous. Meditation implies renunciation, and no practice will be successful unless one is at least prepared to make efforts to restrain greed and hatred, check lust and understand when delusion is clouding the heart. How far one carries renunciation, and whether this involves outward changes (such as becoming a monk or nun), depends much on a person and his circumstances, but one thing is sure: inward renunciation, an attitude of giving-up with regard to both unskilful mental events and bodily indulgence, is absolutely essential.

Often connected with the above dangers is another, to be seen in cases where a man suddenly has an opportunity to undertake a longer period of meditation practice. He sits down with the firm resolve, "Now I shall meditate," but though his energy is ever so great and though he sits and sits and walks and walks, still his mind is disturbed and without peace. It may well be that his own strong effort has much to do with his distractions. Moreover, he has to learn that it is necessary to meditate knowing the limitations of his character. Just as any other worker who knows the limits of his strength and is careful not to exhaust himself, so is the able meditator careful. With mindfulness one should know what are the extremes, of laziness and of strain, to be avoided.

It is through straining or forcing meditation practice that many emotionally disturbed states arise. Sudden bursts of intense anger all over insignificant trifles, fierce cravings and lusts, strange delusions and even more peculiar fantasies can all be produced from unwisely arduous practice.

With all these dangers it is a skilled teacher who is most necessary to give advice, so that these and other wrong turnings are avoided and one keeps straight along the way to Nibbāna. Those who are without a teacher should proceed with utmost caution, making sure that their development of mindfulness is very good indeed. If they are mindful and see that, despite their efforts, their meditation practice is making no real difference to their lives in terms of greater internal peace, or externally in relation to others, then it should be apparent that something is wrong. Meditation may be laid aside for some time while making efforts to contact a genuine source of information, preferably a living meditation master, in the meantime giving due attention to unsolved moral problems, which until sorted out will not permit the mind to develop; and making a great effort to live one's life according to Buddhist standards. When quite basic matters of this sort are neglected, one cannot hope to make much progress upon the Middle Practice-Path.

Appendix: 40 Meditation Exercises as Listed in the Path of Purification

If one has no meditation teacher from whom one may request a meditation subject, then one has to rely upon one's knowledge of one's character in order to prescribe for oneself a suitable meditation. There are forty meditation exercises (*kammaṭṭhāna*) noted by the great teacher Buddhaghosa as being suited to certain types of character. For the purposes of meditation, he considers six characters: faithful, intelligent and speculative (in which the skilful roots of non-greed, non-hatred and non-delusion are variously dominant); and greedy, hating and deluded (in which greed, hatred and delusion, the unskilful roots, are dominant). The trouble here is twofold: firstly, very few "pure" types can be found, most people being mixtures of two or more of them—and moreover ever-changing mixtures; and secondly, it is rather difficult to judge which class one's character belongs to since one's own delusion and pride are apt to blur one's judgments. This is but one small matter in which the value of the meditation teacher may be discerned very easily. One may learn much about oneself, however, by being mindful at the time when some unexpected event takes place. At that time one can spot one's reaction and the stains which are present in the mind. Later judgments are not worth very much, since by that time the mind has got round to self-justifications, and other kinds of distortions of the original event.

Below is given the list of the forty meditation exercises with some notes upon their practice, the characters which are benefited and the types of stains combatted by them. The most widely used meditation exercises are starred (*).

Ten Kasiṇas

1. earth
2. water
3. fire
4. air
5. blue
6. yellow
7. red
8. white
9. light*
10. limited space

5 – 8 are recommended for the practice of *hate* characters because of their pure, pleasing colours.

Apart from the possible exception of 5 – 8, no special moral stain is counteracted by these ten kasiṇas. As they are to be developed through the eye, they will not be very suitable for anyone with weak sight (according to Buddhaghosa).

The only one of the ten kasiṇas which seems to be practised much these days is that of light, which some people find arises quite naturally when they begin to concentrate the mind. While Ācariya Buddhaghosa's explanations in the *Path of Purification* tend to stress the importance of using exterior supports for practice (the making of the earth kasiṇa is very minutely described), whenever the writer has heard of them being employed (in Thailand), they are always in the nature of visions (*nimitta*) arising internally and being developed from this basis. It appears that contemplation of an exterior earth, etc., kasiṇa is unknown in Thailand.

Ten Kinds of Foulness (asubha)

11. the bloated (corpse) counteracting delight in beauty of proportions	
12. the livid...	beauty of complexion
13. the festering...	scents and perfumes
14. the cut-up...	wholeness or compactness
15. the gnawed...	well-fleshed body
16. the scattered...	grace of limbs
17. the hacked and scattered...	grace of body as a whole
18. the bleeding...	ornaments and jewellery
19. the worm-infested...	ownership of the body
20. the skeleton...	having fine bones and teeth

11–20 are recommended for *greed* characters.

These and similar lists in the *Satipaṭṭhāna Sutta* reflect the time when disposal of corpses upon charnel-grounds was common. Now, however, even in Buddhist lands they are difficult to find, let alone in Western countries. Teachers in Thailand at the present time stress that one's own body is to be seen in these ways as a vision (*nimitta*) arising in the course of mind-development. As these can be fearful, one should have the instruction of a skilled teacher for dealing with such visions, when they can be of great advantage. It may be stressed here that there is nothing morbid in contemplating such sights, interior or exterior, as these. The body's decay is just something natural, but normally it is not seen because people do not like to admit this. Instead of facing bodily decay and bringing it out into the open, dead bodies are even made to look attractive by embalmers and cosmeticians; and where this cannot be done, they are stowed away in beautiful coffins with bright flowers, etc. Buddhist training makes one look squarely at those aspects of life which normally (that is, with craving) are not considered "nice," and makes one calmly face them in respect of one's own mind and body.

Ten Reflections (anussati) and Stains (kilesa) {counteracted}

21. upon the Buddha*
22. upon the Dhamma
23. upon the Sangha
24. upon virtue (*sīla*)—{counteracts bad conduct (*duccarita*)}
25. upon generosity—{counteracts meanness (*macchariya*)}
26. upon celestials—{counteracts scepticism (*vicikicchā*)}
27. upon death—{counteracts laziness}
28. upon body*—{counteracts lust & sensuality (*kama-raga*)}
29. upon breathing—{counteracts delusion, worry}
30. upon peace—{counteracts disturbance}

21–26. are recommended for *faith* characters,

27. recommended for *intelligent* characters,
28. recommended for *greedy* characters,
29. recommended for *deluded/speculative* characters,
30. recommended for *intelligent* characters.

This group of ten has a more miscellaneous character than the previous two groups. In practising the first three recollections (21–23) one recites the lists of qualities of each one of these.[6] Or if the mind does not become concentrated in this way, one chooses one particular quality and recites that silently and continuously (such as "Buddho" or "Arahaṃ"). Rosaries are used in some places in connection with practice of this sort. The recollections on virtue and generosity are specially good to cultivate in one's old age. One reviews all the meritorious deeds (*puñña*) made by one in the course of life, and recollecting them the mind becomes tranquil and happy, and having such a mental state at the time of death, one is sure to be reborn in very favourable surroundings. One cannot recollect the celestials (*deva*) except by hearsay unless one has seen them. This practice is suitable for those who have increased the range of their minds and so have made contact with other more subtle beings. Death may be recollected by *intelligent* characters since they will not be frightened at the prospects which this practice opens up. It is a great incentive to practise now when one does not know whether even one second from hence, one will be alive. The twenty-eighth recollection—on the body—is for *greedy* characters, who need to develop dispassion regarding the body. This is achieved by the analysis of the body into thirty-two unbeautiful parts, and then by selecting one or more of these and examining it. However, this practice comes to perfection when with insight the body is illuminated and its various components are clearly seen and their nature understood. The mindfulness of breathing is recommended for calming and clearing the mind, and a person of almost any temperament may practise it with benefit, though great care is needed in the subtler ranges of this exercise. The breathing is never forced but observed constantly with mindfulness, the point of concentration being usually the nose-tip or nostrils. However, teachers vary in their practice of it. The recollection of peace, says the great Acariya, is only of certain benefit to those who have already experienced Nibbāna, such as stream-enterers; but others can gain some calm from the contemplation of peacefulness. The peace spoken of here is really

6. See *The Mirror of the Dhamma*, Wheel No. 54 a/b.

Nibbāna, and as one cannot recollect what one has not known if a worldling (*puthujjana*), this is a practice for the Noble Ones (*ariya*).

Four Divine Abidings (Brahma-vihāra)

31. friendliness* ... {counteracts the stain of hatred, dislike}
32. compassion ... {counteracts callous indifference}
33. gladness (with others) ... {counteracts envy}
34. equanimity ... {counteracts worry}

*31 is recommended for hate characters.

Four States of Formlessness (arūpa-bhava)

35.	sphere of	infinite space
36.	" "	infinite consciousness
37.	" "	nothingness
38.	" "	neither-perception-nor-non-perception

These formless absorptions cannot be developed unless one has already perfected the four ordinary absorptions of form. It is said that this group of four may be explored on the basis of the fourth absorption (*jhana*). As few people are likely to have experienced this, we pass on to:

Perception of the Loathsomeness of Food

39. While it is essential for the bhikkhu, who has to rely upon collected food (which is sometimes good and sometimes not), lay people can also benefit from this practice, which Acariya Buddhaghosa notes is for *intelligent* characters, and is designed to lessen, and lead to the destruction of, greed and gluttony.

Defining of the Four Great Elements

40. These are earth (solidity), water (cohesion), fire (temperature) and air (movement), all of which characterize our physical bodies. These elements may be perceived by an analysis based upon the use of mindfulness.[7] This practice is also said to be particularly fitted for the intelligent character.

7. See *The Foundations of Mindfulness*, trans. Nyanasatta, Wheel No. 19, p. 15; and Ledi Sayadaw, *A Manual of Insight*, Wheel No. 31/32, pp. 25, 78.

Those practices not mentioned in connection with character are suited to anyone. As all of these practices are aimed at the lessening and eventual destruction of the stains (*kilesa*), one may appreciate how important they are thought in Buddhist training. Where the stains are present, there the darkness of unknowing holds sway; but where they are not found, there shines forth the wisdom and compassion of Enlightenment.

Nirvāna, Nihilism and Satori

By

Douglas M. Burns, MD

WHEEL PUBLICATION NO. 117/118/119

Introduction

It has been said, and probably correctly, that Buddhism is the least understood and most misunderstood of all major religions. To whatever extent this is true of Buddhist doctrine in general, it is doubly true of the goal toward which that doctrine is directed: Nirvāna.

Nirvāna has been variously explained as Oneness with God, Cosmic Consciousness, deep trance, self-annihilation, Pure Being, non-existence, regression to intrauterine life and a psychedelic ecstasy. Yet none of these explanations agrees with the accounts given by the Buddha and others who are alleged to have realized it. Not only are we confronted with the problem of what Nirvāna is, but arising from this consideration are a number of secondary but important questions: Is Nirvāna really attainable, and if so, is it worth the effort? Just how is it attained, and has anyone in recent history done so? Must we have faith to realize what is yet unknown to us? Is it not a selfish goal or an escapist one? These concerns and others are discussed in detail.

In this writing I have used the Sanskrit word *nirvāna* instead of its Pāli equivalent *nibbāna* because the former is now widely known in the West and familiar to both Buddhists and non-Buddhists. For the same reason I have used the Sanskrit *karma* in preference to the Pāli *kamma*, but the Pāli *dhamma* is used instead of the Sanskrit *dharma*. However, the explanation of Buddhism presented in this writing is based upon the early Theravāda teachings, and unless otherwise indicated all of the references and quotations are attributed directly to the Buddha and his disciples as quoted in the Suttas and Vinaya of the Pāli scriptures. The internal diversity of Mahāyāna Buddhism prohibits any all-inclusive statements as to the similarities and dissimilarities between the two schools regarding their respective views of Nirvāna. But in general it can be said that the Mahāyāna approach is heavily based upon dialectic, metaphysics and mysticism, and hence contrasts sharply with the Theravādin experiential approach as discussed in the following pages.

Chapter IV concerns *satori*, the enlightenment of Zen Buddhism. The relationship between satori and Nirvāna is discussed as well as the relationship of satori to LSD experiences, Christian conversions, and other psychological phenomena.

The references to Pāli scriptures, which follow the quotations and are listed in the bibliography, are numbered in accordance with the volumes of the Pāli Text Society, London. However, not all translations are from this source.

Finally, I wish to express my sincere appreciation to the Venerable Khantipālo of Wat Bovoranives, Bangkok; the Venerable Nāgasena of Wat Benjamabopit, Bangkok; the Venerable Khemānando of Wat Pleng, Dhonburi, Thailand; and to Mr. John Blofeld; all of whom examined the original text of this writing and offered valuable suggestions for its improvement.

Bangkok
1967

I. Cardinal Features of Buddhist Thought

The Realm of Change

To understand the word Nirvāna, one must be acquainted with the other major tenets of Buddhism. For on a conceptual level (but not on an experiential level), Nirvāna is an important part of a well-integrated philosophical system. Thus, to begin our discussion of Nirvāna let us first speak of its antithesis, *saṃsāra*, the so-called "world of becoming." In Buddhism the word *saṃsāra* designates the entire universe of physical and psychological existence: time, space, matter, thought, emotion, volition, perception, karma, and so forth.

The Buddhist version of the beginning of existence is unique among the world's religions. For it teaches that there is no discernible beginning; there never was a Primal Cause which at a given instant in eternity produced or began to produce the universe. Rather, the Buddha taught that every object and condition is the result of other objects and conditions which preceded it; and these in turn are the results of still earlier ones, and so on back into the beginningless past. We live in a world governed by impersonal laws of cause and effect; so it has been throughout all eternity, and so shall it be into the unending future. But while *saṃsāra* may endure forever, not one of its components can do the same. Accompanying the Buddhist doctrine of cause and effect is the equally important teaching of *anicca*, or impermanence. Every living being; every thought, mood and feeling; every hill, mountain and river; is a temporary phenomenon, which in time will give way to new conditions that it has helped to create. The universe then is eternally dynamic, a never-ending process of interacting and interdependent forces and factors, no one of which is eternal, static, immortal, self-formed or self-willed. Within *saṃsāra* it is only the law of change which does not change. The earth and sun themselves will in the course of time perish and be no more, but the Buddha further taught that as old earth-sun systems die out new ones evolve and come into being.[1]

1. Douglas M. Burns, *Buddhism, Science and Atheism* (Bangkok: The World Fellowship of Buddhists, 1965), 47–56.

But cosmology is a relatively insignificant facet of the Dhamma (the teaching of the Buddha). The primary significance of the eternal principles (change, and cause and effect) is the way they relate to the process of human existence: to the hopes, fears, sorrows, and joys which give meaning and purpose to the lives of all conscious beings. This brings us to another important feature of *saṃsāra*, that is, *anattā* or soullessness. The *anattā* doctrine states that all thought, emotion, memory, sensation, perception, and all other forms of our consciousness are temporary, dynamic and interdependent. Without such mental states the notion of oneself can have no meaning, and yet there is not one of these states which alone can be called one's true self, "the real I." One is the composite of all of these, and of no place within these dynamic aggregates does one find some unchanging essence or other stable entity that can be designated as a soul or immutable being.

Buddhism does not deny the existence of the personality; it only states that the personality is compounded and dynamic, a process rather than an entity. Our moods, thoughts, expectations, and emotions change from day to day, hour to hour, minute to minute. Is one at the age of two the same person one finds 10 years later at the age of 12? And is one's 12 year-old self the same person as the 20–year-old self, or the 40 or 60 year-old self? Thus from the Buddhist viewpoint, it is more accurate to say that the two-year-old is a psychophysical phenomenon which in the course of time will be modified by its interactions with other phenomena as well as the interactions of its own internal components. This evolution will result in the respective personalities of ages 12, 20, 40, and so forth.

When asked "Who, Lord, is it who feels?" the Buddha replied:

> It is not a fit question. I am not saying [someone] feels. If I were saying so, the question would be a fit one. But I am not saying that. If you were to ask thus: "Conditioned now by what, Lord, is feeling?" this were a fit question. And the fit answer would be, "Feeling is conditioned by [sense] contact."
>
> S II 13/SN 12:12)

And again he states:

> "He who does the deed and he who experiences [its result] are the same." This, Brahmin, is one extreme. "He who does the deed is not the same as he who experiences." This, Brahmin, is the other extreme. The Buddha, not approaching either of these extremes, teaches a middle doctrine.
>
> S II 76/SN 12:46

The Dhamma teaches that mind and body are interdependent. Neither can come about or endure without the other.[2] When the body dies the mental states which preceded death become the causes of new mental conditions that occur with the birth of a new personality. This is the Buddhist concept of postmortem survival and is termed "rebirth." Those psychological factors preceding death which determine the time, place, and form of the new birth are known as karma (or *kamma* in Pāli).

However, karma (*karma-vipāka*)[3] is not confined to the process of rebirth. Rather it is an ever-present principle of psychological cause and effect: each state of mind is a condition which becomes the cause of other states of mind that will arise in the future. Karma may be classified as wholesome, unwholesome or neutral (*avyākata*), which means that a given mental state is of such a nature that its results will be either pleasant, unpleasant, or neutral (*adukkham-asukha*) respectively. Examples of unwholesome karma are greed and hatred, while wholesome karma is seen in compassion and kindness.[4]

Because one's karma is complex and must act interdependently with other aspects of *saṃsāra*, some of its results will be immediate, while others will be delayed for days, months or years. Or in some cases karma is rendered inoperative by other portions of the

---

2. S II 113–114 /SN 12:67).

3. In proper Pāli usage, *kamma* refers only to volitional actions, that is, causes, while the effects of such actions are termed *vipāka*. However, in Hindu and recent popular Buddhist writings, karma has widely come to mean the whole universal law of cause and effect. Thus I have used the word "karma" in instances where *vipāka* or *karma-vipāka* would technically be correct.

4. Nyanatiloka Mahāthera, "Karma and Rebirth" in *Fundamentals of Buddhism*, Wheel Publication 394/396 (Buddhist Publication Society).

karma of that same personality and thus produces no effect. Thus Buddhism teaches that each man is the product of what he has done or thought in the past, and his present thoughts and actions will determine the future. Though karma is often explained in an ethical context, it must not be confused with social mores or other cultural standards of good and evil, for it operates independently of these. Also, it should not be assumed that karma accounts for all pleasant and unpleasant experience. In addition to one's karma, factors external to oneself act upon personality with pleasant and unpleasant consequences.[5]

Buddhism uses the word "rebirth" to distinguish its position from the Hindu doctrine of reincarnation via an immortal soul. The distinction between the two religious teachings is best illustrated in terms of an analogy. To understand the Hindu position one may imagine a row of various kinds of containers such as a drinking glass, a cup, a bowl, a pot, and so forth. One takes a marble and deposits it in the first container, then lifts it out and puts it in the second, and so on down to the end of the row. The marble represents the soul and the containers the various bodies successively inhabited by the soul. Though each container is different, the marble is essentially unchanged throughout the entire process. To contrast the Buddhist view, imagine that one lights a match and then with the match lights a candle at the same time extinguishing the match. Then with the candle one lights a Coleman lantern (pressure lantern) and extinguishes the candle. Now we ask the question: Is the flame which once burned in the match the same flame now burning in the lantern? One can answer the question either "yes" or "no," both replies being equally appropriate.

While the child is not the same as the adult, the food the child eats, the values he incorporates and the education he receives will strongly determine the nature of his adult existence. And similarly for successive births.

5. A I 173 /AN 3:61.

Life, Living and Empiricism

The above paragraphs briefly describe the Buddhist world view, that is, the conceptual or theoretical framework in which Buddhism has traditionally explained *saṃsāra*. In addition there is the empirical, experiential approach to *saṃsāra* as explained in the following paragraphs. This latter approach is actually the more important, as it transcends any need for faith, dogma and theory. It is possible to explain Buddhism from either an exclusively conceptual, theoretical approach, or from an exclusively experiential one. To give a complete picture, both should be mentioned. It is said that one who pursues Buddhist mental development to its maximum possible degree can have experiential certainty of the theoretical concepts.

Buddhism begins its understanding of *saṃsāra* on a strictly empirical basis, that is, one's immediate conscious experience. Direct experience is the only absolute certainty of which man is capable, and whatever lies beyond experience can only be inferred with varying degrees of probability. For example, no matter how strongly one may believe in God (be it the Moslem Allah, the Hindu Brahma or the Christian Jehovah) one does not have complete certainty that that god exists. But the one thing of which the believer can be sure is that he believes, that is, he experiences the state of mind known as believing. Likewise a scientist may formulate a theory about the structure of a certain molecule. Since he has never seen this molecule (or any molecule), the validity of his theory is a matter of probability, derived from inductive reasoning. The real certainty which the scientist has is first the existence of his idea or belief as to the molecular structure, and, second, the existence of the memories of the facts and observations (which he assumes to be correct) that led to his theory. Finally, any given sensory experience may be either a dream, hallucination, illusion or an actual physical reality, but the one thing of which the recipient can be certain is the conscious experience itself. Or as expressed in the Buddha's own words:

> What, bhikkhus, is everything? The eye and forms, the ear and sounds, the nose and smells, the tongue and tastes, the body and touch, the mind and objects of mind. This, bhikkhus, is called everything. Whoso, bhikkhus, should say, "Rejecting

> this everything, I will proclaim another everything," it would be mere talk on his part, and when questioned he could not make good his boast, and further would come to an ill pass. Why so? Because, bhikkhus, it would be beyond his scope to do so.
>
> S IV 15/SN 35:23

From this it should not be assumed that Buddhism denies the reality of physical existence apart from human awareness. For such is not the case. Nor does the Dhamma state that consciousness is some sort of metaphysical absolute upon which all else is founded. On the contrary, the Buddha clearly stated that human consciousness is dependent upon a physical substrate, that is, a body.[6] Furthermore, while it is true that memory, emotion, sensation and thought cannot exist without consciousness; it is equally true that consciousness cannot exist without at least one of these other four (that is, memory, and so forth). To have consciousness one must be conscious of something. Pure consciousness is not to be found.[7] In other words consciousness is an interdependent phenomenon, as are all other aspects of *saṃsāra*.

However, the most important aspect of conscious existence, the most significant thing in life, is that we have feelings both pleasant and unpleasant. The human mind is far more than a computer which gathers and analyzes information. From the dim awareness of an insect, fish or reptile to the most highly complex and sensitive realizations of humanity, one feature alone is paramount: the pursuit of happiness, pleasure and enjoyment, and conversely the avoidance of pain, sorrow, frustration and fear. Without such feelings there would be no such thing as value, purpose, meaning and significance; motive and incentive could not exist, and there would be no reason to think, speak or act. Man is unique in this regard only in his relative ability to experience a greater diversity and complexity of pleasurable experiences, such as creativity, music and abstract contemplation. Even the most dedicated rationalists and the most self-sacrificing idealists assume

6. *Mahātaṇhāsaṅkhaya Sutta*, M I 259.

7. Nyanatiloka Mahāthera, *Fundamentals of Buddhism*, Wheel Publication 394/396 (Kandy, Sri Lanka: Buddhist Publication Society).

their respective roles because they find some level of satisfaction, happiness or peace of mind in so doing. The Christian and Moslem conceptions of Heaven and Hell are but symbolic simplifications of this pleasure-pain principle.

According to Buddhist doctrine, it is man's thirst for pleasurable experiences that generates new karma (*vipāka*) and perpetuates his existence. Enjoyable experience itself is "kammically" neutral, but what does produce karma (*vipāka*) is our craving (*taṇhā*), the unquenchable yearning for repeated, sensory and emotional stimulations of whatever sorts they may be.

It is craving that sustains our existence. But what does it mean to exist? In terms of experience life is nothing more than each conscious moment: the moments of reading this manuscript, of travelling, of bathing, of studying, of daydreaming, of planning, of worrying, of rejoicing, of striving, of relaxing, of talking, of working. All these and more are life. Each endures for an instant and never again returns exactly the same as before. Which ones do we live for? Which are the ones that justify our desires for continued existence? And conversely how many are of negative value: painful, irritating, disappointing, worrisome, boring, frustrating, empty, or any of the other unpleasant states of mind, all of which Buddhism groups under the one word *dukkha*?

All manifestations of *saṃsāra* come about through cause and effect, and the nature of life is to avoid or minimize *dukkha* while endeavouring to realize a maximum of rewarding or meaningful experiences. Therefore it follows that the key to living is to discover, understand and eliminate those factors which are causes of *dukkha* while at the same time developing and cultivating those which lead to true happiness and well-being.

On the basis of the above, the Buddha repeatedly summarized his doctrine in terms of the Four Noble Truths:

Dukkha is an inherent aspect of *saṃsāra*.

The cause of *dukkha* is *taṇhā*, or misdirected pleasure seeking.

It is possible to realize an end of dukkha.

This end is achieved by means of the Eightfold Path, which is the multidimensional Buddhist practice of spiritual and psychological maturation.

Thus the essence of Buddhism is its way of life. It is the fourth of the Four Noble Truths, that is, the techniques, the practices, the insights and the disciplines that restructure the personality to produce either a relative or a total end of *dukkha*. However, in this writing I wish to give primary concern to the Third Truth, the goal toward which the Fourth Truth is directed.

A study of the Suttas of the Pāli Canon (which are the most authentic existing records of the teachings of the Buddha) reveals that the Buddha taught there are *two* ways in which one can deal with the problem of existence. One is to continually act in such a manner as to create wholesome karma, in other words, to constantly produce conditions which will enhance satisfaction, happiness and well-being. The other is to totally and completely end one's existence within *saṃsāra*, that is, to achieve Nirvāna. The two are not entirely separate paths, for, to a considerable extent, they overlap. The further one progresses towards a complete realization of the former, the closer one will come to attaining the latter. However, the Buddha placed major emphasis and importance on the latter goal, the cessation of one's being in *saṃsāra*. For, while *dukkha* can be minimized within *saṃsāra*, it can never be totally eliminated, and every situation in which one may invest one's hopes, affections and feelings will eventually perish. Furthermore, let us imagine that one acquires an understanding of *saṃsāra* and how to deal with it, and is then able to carry this knowledge over into successive lives for one's continual happiness and prosperity. But even such knowledge itself is created and temporary, and thus like all other creations will eventually perish leaving the personality once again to act blindly towards those laws which mould human destiny.

Thus the Buddhist version of salvation, either of the relative or absolute sort, is something resulting primarily from one's own volitions and can neither be imposed upon one nor granted to one by some external agent. The Buddha's mission was to enlighten men as to the nature of existence and advise them as to how best to behave for their own benefit and the benefit of others. Consequently, Buddhist ethics are not founded upon commandments which men are compelled to follow. From the Buddhist viewpoint each conscious being is an individual free to act as one sees fit. The Buddha only advised men as to which conditions were most wholesome and conducive to long-term benefit. Rather than addressing sinners with such words as "shameful," "wicked," "wretched," "unworthy" and "blasphemous," he would merely say, "You are foolish and acting in such a way as to bring sorrow upon yourselves and others." Often he said, "You yourselves must make the effort. Buddhas are only teachers."[8] Consequently the Buddha did not condemn those who chose to enjoy sensuality and the pleasures of worldly existence. He even advised such persons on how to achieve their ends providing no harm would come to others, but he also cautioned them as to the dangers and reminded them that to maintain such pleasures they must be willing to pay the price: continual effort and diligence. A good example is related in the *Vyaggahapajja Sutta*:

> Once the Exalted One was dwelling amongst the Koliyans in their market town named Kakkarapatta. Then Dīghajānu, a Koliyan, approached the Exalted One, respectfully saluted him and sat on one side. Thus seated, he addressed the Exalted One as follows:
>
> "We, Lord, are laymen who enjoy worldly pleasure. We lead a life encumbered by wife and children. We use sandalwood of Kāsi. We deck ourselves with garlands, perfume and unguents. We use gold and silver. To those like us, O Lord, let the Exalted One preach the Doctrine, teach those things that lead to weal and happiness in this life and weal and happiness in future life."
>
> "Four conditions, Vyagghapajja, conduce to a householder's weal and happiness in this very life. Which four? The accomplishment of persistent effort, the accomplishment of watchfulness, good friendship and balanced livelihood."
>
> "What is the accomplishment of persistent effort?"
>
> "Herein, Vyagghapajja, by whatsoever activity a householder earns his living, whether by farming, by trading, by rearing cattle, by archery, by service under the king, or by any other kind of craft; at that he becomes skilful and is not lazy. He is endowed with the power of discernment as to the proper ways and means; he is able to carry out and allocate [duties]. This is called the accomplishment of persistent effort."
>
> "What is the accomplishment of watchfulness?"

8. Dhammapada 276.

"Herein, Vyagghapajja, whatsoever wealth a householder is in possession of, obtained by dint of effort, collected by strength of arm, by the sweat of his brow, justly acquired by right means; such he husbands well by guarding and watching so that kings would not seize it, thieves would not steal, fire would not burn, water would not carry away, nor ill-disposed heirs remove. This is the accomplishment of watchfulness."

"What is good friendship?"

"Herein, Vyagghapajja, in whatsoever village or market town a householder dwells, he associates, converses, engages in discussions with householders or householders' sons, whether young and highly cultured or old and highly cultured, full of faith, full of virtue, full of charity, full of wisdom. He acts in accordance with the faith of the faithful, with the virtue of the virtuous, with the charity of the charitable, with the wisdom of the wise. This is called good friendship."

"What is balanced livelihood?"

"Herein, Vyagghapajja, a householder knowing his income and expenses leads a balanced life, neither extravagant nor miserly, knowing that thus his income will stand in excess of his expenses, but not his expenses in excess of his income....

"The wealth thus amassed, Vyagghapajja, has four sources of destruction: debauchery; drunkeness; gambling; and friendship, companionship and intimacy with evildoers. ... "

A IV 280–282/AN 8:54

II. The Nature of Nirvāna

We now come to what is one of the most frequently asked questions in Buddhism: What is Nirvāna? In the above paragraphs we have already stated that it is the ending of rebirth, the final termination of one's existence within *saṃsāra*. And in the Pāli Canon we read, "The ceasing of becoming is Nirvāna."[9] The origin of the word itself carries this same implication. One common etymological explanation is that *nir* means "not," and *vāna* can be rendered as "the effort of blowing." This was probably a simile referring to a smith's fire which goes out if not repeatedly blown upon; the implication being the extinction of the fires of greed, hatred and delusion.[10] Thus it is not surprising that many critics of Buddhism have considered Nirvāna to be a sophisticated version of suicide, a goal of self-extinction, complete nihilism and, absolute zero.

Such a conclusion, however, is one-sided and superficial. The Buddha himself rejected and cautioned against the two extremes of philosophical dualism, one extreme being eternalism or existence and the other being annihilationism or non-existence. Though this was usually taught with reference to the existence or non-existence of the personality after death, it is equally appropriate to Nirvāna. The whole tradition of Theravāda Buddhism has emphatically rejected the nihilistic interpretation of Nirvāna and a significant portion of the writings of the famed fifth century Theravādin scholar, Buddhaghosa, was directed at refuting the notion of Nirvāna as non-existence.[11]

Perhaps most significant is that the Buddha and many of his disciples experienced Nirvāna, that is, they were aware of it, as the Buddha said, "here and now in this present life." And in the Suttas we find statements that the Buddha and the other *arahants*[12] "enjoyed the peace of Nirvāna." It is referred to by such terms as "profound," "deep," "hard to see," "hard to comprehend," "peaceful," "lofty," "inaccessible to reason," "subtle," "the true,"

9. S II 117 /SN 12: 68.
10. *Visuddhimagga* XVI 67–74.
11. Ibid.
12. An *Arahant* is one who has fully realized Nirvāna.

"the other shore," "to be known by the wise."[13] In the Dhammapada the Buddha says:

> There is no fire like lust,
> No crime like hatred.
> There is no misery like the constituents of existence,
> No happiness higher than the Peace of Nirvāna.
> Hunger is the worst of diseases.
> Component existence is the worst of distresses.
> Knowing this as it really is (the wise realize)
> Nirvāna the highest bliss.
> Health is the highest gain.
> Contentment is the greatest wealth.
> A trusty friend is the best of kinsmen.
> Nirvāna is the supreme bliss.
>
> Dhammapada 202–204

Arahantship is said to be an irreversible condition, for once achieved it is impossible that one can fall back into lust and delusion. Thus an *Arahant* is completely incapable of greed, anger and egotism, and generates no unwholesome karma. In many respects he (or she) will continue to act, think and feel as any normal person until the time of death, and his demise is sometimes termed *parinirvāna,* the complete cessation of existence in *saṃsāra*, the final end of rebirth. Nirvāna has nothing to do with occult powers or supernatural wonders, and many of the *Arahants* at the time of the Buddha stated that they had no such abilities.[14] While with Nirvāna one is liberated from grief, sorrow, despair, worry, frustration, and all other psychological forms of *dukkha*, one is still subject to physical discomforts until such time as the body passes away. Throughout the Suttas we read of occasions when the Buddha sustained a backache,[15] fell ill with intestinal wind,[16] had his foot pierced by a stone splinter,[17] and so forth, and in each

13. Nyanaponika Thera, *Anattā and Nibbāna* (Wheel Publication No. 11, Buddhist Publication Society).

14. S II 121–123 / 12:70, *Susīmāparibbājaka Sutta*).

15. A IV 358–359 /SN 9:4.

16. S I 174 /SN 7:3.

17. S I 27 /SN 1:8.

instance there was accompanying physical pain. But never was there an emotional reaction or psychological discomfort resulting from the pain.

As best can be determined from the scriptural sources, an *Arahant* is not experiencing Nirvāna in every waking moment but is capable of experiencing it at will. Persons who have had such an experience but are not at all times able to reproduce it and may still fall back into greed, anger and delusion are not designated as *arahants* (though eventually they will become such). They are known as *sotāpanna* or "stream winners," ones who have entered the stream that eventually leads to Nirvāna.

Rather than the end of craving per se, Nirvāna *is that which is realized when craving is ended.* Nirvāna is nothing only in that it is no thing. It is neither matter nor energy, and it has no location in space and time. It is not perceived by the senses, nor is it a thought, concept, mood or emotion. Though an *arahant* is conscious of Nirvāna, it is not consciousness in any sense by which we normally understand that word. It is indivisible, timeless, changeless, unborn, and not compounded; in other words the very antithesis of *saṃsāra*. It is thoroughly apart from *saṃsāra* and thus neither influences nor is influenced by karma. In no way does it interact with *saṃsāra* or intervene in *saṃsāra* in the way Brahma or Jehovah is said to answer prayers or manifest divine intervention.

Much of the above is reiterated in the Buddha's famous "Discourse on the Snake Simile":

> A Noble One who has abandoned the conceit of self, has cut it off at the root, removed it from its soil like a Palmyra tree, brought it to utter extinction, incapable of arising again. Thus is the monk a Noble One who has taken down the flag, put down the burden, become unfettered. When a monk's mind is thus freed, O monks, neither the *devas* with Indra, nor those with Brahma, nor those with Pajāpati, when searching will find on what the consciousness of one thus gone [Tathāgata] is based. Why is that? One who has thus gone is no longer traceable here and now, so I say.
>
> So teaching, so proclaiming, O monks, there are some recluses and brahmans who misrepresent me untruly, vainly, falsely, not in accordance with fact, saying, "A nihilist is the ascetic Gotama; he teaches the annihilation, the destruction, the non-being of an

existing individual." As I am not and as I do not teach, therefore these worthy recluses and brahmans misrepresent me untruly, vainly, falsely and not in accordance with fact when they say, "A nihilist is the ascetic Gotama; he teaches the annihilation, the destruction, the non-being of an existing individual." What I teach now as before, O monks, is suffering and the cessation of suffering.

If for that others revile, abuse, scold and insult the Tathāgata [the Buddha], on that account, O monks, the Tathāgata will not feel annoyance, nor dejection, nor displeasure in his heart. And if for that others respect, revere, honour and venerate the Tathāgata, on that account the Tathāgata will not feel delight, nor joy, nor elation in his heart. If for that others respect, revere, honour, and venerate the Tathāgata, he will think, "It is towards this [mind-body aggregate] which was formerly fully comprehended, that they perform such acts."

(The Buddha then repeats the above paragraph advising the monks to do the same when they too receive blame or praise. He then continues:)

Therefore, monks, relinquish whatever is not yours. Your relinquishment of it will for a long time bring you welfare and happiness. What is it that is not yours? Material shape is not yours. Relinquish it. Your relinquishment of it will for a long time bring you welfare and happiness. Feeling is not yours. Relinquish it. Your relinquishment of it will for a long time bring you welfare and happiness... [And likewise for perception, mental formations, and consciousness.]

Alagaddūpama Sutta, M I 139–141/MN 22

A common source of misunderstanding about the Buddha's use of the word Nirvāna originates from the Hindu usage of the same word. The Hindus give it a positive metaphysical and mystical meaning stating that Nirvāna is Union with Brahma or God, a condition of Oneness with the Cosmic Absolute in which the soul of man merges with the Infinite Soul of the Universe. Such a misconception is furthered by the fact that some centuries after the Buddha, various schools of Mahāyāna Buddhism began to develop along mystical and metaphysical paths unknown to, or even refuted by, the Buddha. Consequently Mahāyāna Buddhist writings often abound with such terms as Buddha Nature, Universal Mind, the *Tri-kāya* and Primordial Buddha. Thus the concept of Nirvāna now has a host of mystical, religious and psychological usages quite different from its original Buddhist meaning.

The Buddha spoke relatively little about Nirvāna, one reason being that there is little which is meaningful that one can say about Nirvāna. Within the Pāli Canon the most detailed dissertation on Nirvāna given by the Buddha is this:

> There is, monks, a realm where there is neither earth, water, fire, nor air, nor the sphere of infinite space, nor the sphere of infinite consciousness, nor the sphere of nothingness, nor the sphere of neither-perception-nor-non-perception, neither this world nor a world beyond, nor sun and moon.
>
> There, monks, I say, there is neither coming to birth nor going nor staying nor passing away nor arising. It is without support or mobility or basis. It is the end of *dukkha* [suffering].
>
> That which is selfless, hard it is to see;
> Not easy is it to perceive the truth.
> But who has ended craving utterly
> Has naught to cling to, he alone can see.
>
> There is, monks, an unborn, a not-become, a not-made, a not-compounded. If, monks, there were not this unborn, not-become, not-made, not-compounded, there would not be an escape from the born, the become, the made, the compounded. But because there is an unborn..., therefore there is an escape....
>
> *Pātaligāma, Udāna* 8.2–3, pp. 80–81

The outstanding feature of this quotation is that it is a series of negatives. Other than the simple affirmation "there is," not one positive description is used. Why not?

The answer is not hard to find. Since Nirvāna is in no way related to anything within normal human experience, we have no words adequate to describe it. Even if we should adopt some word or phrase such as "Ultimate Reality" or "Pure Being" such would more likely than not create an illusion of understanding rather than give any true insight. Such terms would tell us no more about Nirvāna than the word "music" tells to a man born deaf, the word "passion" tells to a young child or the word "beatnik" tells to an Eskimo. Thus the value of negative terms is that they discourage one from holding to verbal symbols which quickly become illusions of reality. Or in the language of Zen, "The finger pointing at the moon must not be confused with the moon itself."

As was explained above, the only true certainty man can have is direct experience. Consequently, the Buddha did not attempt to describe the indescribable. Rather than talk about Nirvāna, the great majority of his teachings were concerned with the techniques of psychological development, which proceed from the empirical data of one's own states of consciousness in the immediate present. If such practices are done properly, the dimensions of one's awareness progressively expand until Nirvāna becomes a reality on the basis of direct experience. When that happens explanations become unnecessary. Attempts at verbal descriptions only lead to useless metaphysical conjectures which may divert one's attention and energies from the practices necessary for true realization. Consequently, when questioned on transcendental matters the Buddha would either show the futility of such inquiries or remain silent. We have for example his encounter with the young Brahman, Udāyi:

> "Well then, Udāyi, what is your own teacher's doctrine?"
>
> "Our own teacher's doctrine, venerable sir, says thus: 'This is the highest splendour! This is the highest splendour!'"
>
> "But what is that highest splendour, Udāyi, of which your teacher's doctrine speaks?"
>
> "It is, venerable sir, a splendour greater and loftier than which there is none. That is the Highest Splendour."
>
> "But, Udāyi, what is that splendour greater and loftier than which there is none?"
>
> "It is, venerable sir, the Highest Splendour greater and loftier than which there is none."
>
> "For a long time, Udāyi, you can continue in this way, saying, 'A splendour greater and loftier than which there is none, that is the Highest Splendour.' But still you will not have explained that splendour. Suppose a man were to say, 'I love and desire the most beautiful woman in this land,' and then he is asked, 'Good man, that most beautiful woman

whom you love and desire, do you know whether she is a lady from nobility or from a Brahman family or from the trader class or Sūdra?,' and he replied 'No,' 'Then, good man, do you know her name and that of her clan? Or whether she is tall, short or of middle height, whether she is dark, brunette or golden-skinned, or in what village or town or city she dwells?,' and he replied 'No,' and then he is asked, 'Hence, good man, you love and desire what you neither know nor see?,' and he answers 'Yes,' what do you think, Udāyi, that being so, would not that man's talk amount to nonsense?"

"Certainly, venerable sir, that being so, that man's talk would amount to nonsense."

"But in the same way, you, Udāyi, say, 'A splendour greater and loftier than which there is none, that is the Highest Splendour,' and yet you have not explained that splendour."

Cūla-Sakuludāyi Sutta, M II 32–33/MN 79

The Buddha had acquired an insight totally unrelated to that of a normal person and which in no way could be equated with any experiences in *saṃsāra*, yet he wished to reveal his discovery. The problem can be described in terms of an analogy. Let us imagine there is a man who has been blindfolded from the moment of birth and thus has never had an experience of light, vision, or colour. But from the words of others he comes to know that there is something which he has never realized. He may then attempt to discover this unknown quality by meditating upon it, which is analogous to the mystical approach of meditating upon God or thinking of Ultimate Being. But at best he can only echo in his mind the words "vision," "colour," and "light," or intensify some subjective impression of what he thinks these things may be. On the other hand our blindfolded man may reason as follows: "There is something which I don't realize and which is beyond me. Since it is beyond me it must be greater than I, and if it is a greater than I, it must be able to help me. 'Oh Vision! Oh Light! Please come to me. Make Yourself known unto me, Thy humble servant.'" This, of course, is the devotional approach. The metaphysical approach, the approach of philosophy, is to attempt to verbally describe vision with positive phrases, skilful similes, and inventive metaphors. But what words can enable a blind man to realize the difference between red and green or to comprehend any other features of visual experience? Words cannot, and to avoid creating misconceptions and illusions it is best to either say nothing at all or give only negative descriptions. Consequently, the Buddha talked about one thing and one thing only, that is, how to take off the blindfold.

In line with the above it should be noted that the Suttas of Theravāda Buddhism make little mention of meditating upon Nirvāna. This strongly contrasts with the Hindu practice of meditating upon Brahma and similar meditations in other schools of mysticism. Buddhist meditation is of two major sorts. One is tranquillity, or *samatha*, in which the practitioner concentrates upon a clay or colour disk, a flame, the thought of equanimity, one's own quiet breathing, or any one of several similar things, all for the sake of stilling the mind.[18] More important than *samatha* is insight meditations, or *vipassanā*, which are based on the development of full awareness of one's actions, thoughts, feeling, and emotions.[19]

The one exception to the preceding paragraph concerns the peace meditation. In the early Pāli writings Nirvāna is often termed "the peaceful," and peace is considered to be one feature of Nirvāna. Peace is also listed among the forty prescribed meditation subjects, and it is thus inferred that meditating upon peace is meditating upon an attribute of Nirvāna. This meditation, however, is but one of forty, and meditation instructors would assign it only to selected students. According to the *Visuddhimagga*, it can be of full benefit only to persons who have already glimpsed Nirvāna.[20]

18. Nyanatiloka Mahāthera, *The Path to Deliverance* (Buddhist Publication Society, 1969), 73–118.
19. Nyanaponika Thera, *The Heart of Buddhist Meditation* (Buddhist Publication Society, 1992).
20. *Visuddhimagga* VIII 245–251.

III. Theories Regarding Nirvāna

Can Nirvāna be explained as a trance state such as occurs in deep hypnosis? Or is it a state of ecstasy as seen in mystical practices or under the effect of psychedelic drugs? Or is it regression of the personality back to prenatal existence? All three of these hypotheses have been used to explain Nirvāna. And while such contentions are distasteful to devout Buddhists, it must be admitted that one cannot flatly and dogmatically reject any one of them unless one has experienced Nirvāna for oneself. For how can we prove that one man's subjective experiences are either identical with, or different from, another's? We cannot. As stated before, the only reality and certainty that one has is one's own immediate states of consciousness, be they of subjective or objective origins. However, on the basis of the available evidence it is possible to throw serious doubt on all three of the above.

Trance

The concept of trance includes a variety and spectrum of different but overlapping states which can be classified into somewhat arbitrary groupings and which sometimes merge imperceptibly into states of ecstasy. The most common and readily observed condition of trance is hypnosis. However, as yet, psychology has no satisfactory explanation for hypnosis. The best that can be done is merely to describe what happens, that is, the subject becomes extremely suggestible to the instructions of others even to the extent of having hallucinations and some degree of control of the autonomic nervous system (which is normally beyond conscious control). Usually there is either partial or complete amnesia for the period of hypnosis, but paradoxically one can often recall detailed events of the past not normally accessible to one's memory. As far as the subject's subjective experience is concerned, there is no characteristic feature of the trance per se. Some subjects find it mildly pleasant, others discomforting and others neutral, and the experience can be different for the same subject on different occasions. Strong emotional reactions and states of euphoria may occur but usually not unless induced by the hypnotist. Hypnosis is an alteration in one's normal state of consciousness, but since we do not know what consciousness is in the first place, it is impossible to explain its deviations and alterations.

Hypnotic trance differs from Nirvāna in several important ways. Hypnosis can be rapidly produced, and produced in a wide variety of different kinds of personalities. It rarely lasts more than a few hours at most, and usually produces no enduring alteration in one's psyche. Nirvāna, on the other hand, can only be achieved by a long period of restructuring the total personality with certain very definite character traits as prerequisites (absence of lust and so forth). It is an irreversible state of which one is fully conscious and is very much a unique experience. In the deepest stages of hypnosis one is unconscious and has total amnesia for the event. Subjectively the hypnotic experience has no unique features of its own.

Another category of trance states, and one quite well known in Buddhism, are the eight absorptions or *jhānas*. In the lower four *jhānas* one is said to be fully conscious but to have shut off awareness of all sensory impressions, stilled discursive and verbal thinking and temporarily abandoned lust, anger, agitation, torpor and doubt. Thus, upon reaching the fourth *jhāna* one dwells in a state of pure equanimity and concentration. Having achieved the fourth *jhāna*, one may then progress to the four *arūpajhānas*. These are states of deep *samatha* meditation (see above), and in their successive orders of attainment they are termed "the sphere of infinite space," "the sphere of infinite consciousness," "the sphere of nothingness" and "the sphere of neither-perception-nor-non-perception."[21] Though years of practice may be required to attain these states, they do not represent the complete abolition of craving nor true insight into one's own nature. They are actually pre-Buddhist practices known to the Hindu faith as well as to Buddhism, and the Buddha himself achieved them before realizing Nirvāna.[22] Though the *jhānas* are taught in Buddhism, and though the lower four are even included in the eighth step of the Eightfold Path, they are, though often helpful, not strictly necessary to the attainment of Liberation. (Highly developed mental concentration, however, is indispensable.)

21. *Ariyapariyesana Sutta*, M I 174–175/MN 26.

22. Ibid., I 164–168.

Ecstasy

Like trance, the states of ecstasy also embrace a wide variety of experiences and occur in such diverse situations as the rites and rituals of cults and primitive societies; acute psychotic reactions; epilepsy; moments of solitude in forests and mountains; artistic absorption; deep contemplation; romance; religious fervour; and the intoxications of various drugs such as LSD-25, mescaline and hashish.[23] Spontaneous cases are not uncommon, but here the word "spontaneous" must be taken to mean that the precipitating factors are not immediately discernible. All of these experiences do not belong to the same order of mental phenomena, but our very limited understanding of such states, the inadequacy of language to fully relate them, the great spectrum of human feelings which seems to lack clearly defined boundaries and the ability of the mind to mix various levels of feelings into one experience, all warrant grouping such phenomena under one heading.

What these states have in common is an intense or unusual feeling of bliss, well-being, or euphoria (though fear or other negative emotions may also be present). All of one's usual preoccupations and emotions are swept aside, and for the moment only the ecstasy itself seems important. One may gain the impression of a new and deeper insight into existence. Atheists and agnostics, in describing the effects of LSD, often use such words as "divine," "mystical" and "religious."

Like hypnosis, these states differ from Nirvāna in their sudden onset, relatively brief duration and (with infrequent exceptions) the lack of any lasting influence upon the personality. Also, like hypnosis, they contrast with Nirvāna by appearing in numerous and diverse types of people, regardless of the extent to which one has relinquished greed, hatred and delusion, or resolved emotional conflicts. The paramount feature of ecstasy is that one is so enamoured in bliss that for the moment all else is either forgotten or seems unimportant or unreal. Consequently, at such times it is almost impossible to make sound and realistic judgments. Thus it is significant that the accounts we have of the

23. Arthur P. Noyes and Lawrence C. Kolb, *Modern Clinical Psychiatry* (Philadephia: W. B. Saunders Co., 1963), 80.

Buddha and the other *arahants* reveal that they were unusually realistic and objective. Were this not the case it is unlikely that Buddhism could have won out over numerous competing systems and could have existed to the present day. The Suttas reveal that it was not only necessary for the Buddha and his chief disciples to maintain the order and discipline of the continually expanding body of monks; they also had to be proficient in lecturing, debating, systematizing the doctrine and managing the affairs of everyday life.

Regression

Another hypothesis about Nirvāna is the psychoanalytic belief that it is a state of regression to intrauterine existence: a psychological return to one's prenatal life; when the fetus floated effortlessly in the timeless, black silence of the amniotic fluid; a time free of frustration, anxiety, sensory impressions or awareness of time-space relationships. Perhaps the major proponent of this hypothesis was the well-known psychoanalyst Dr. Franz Alexander. Two paragraphs from his manuscript, "Buddhistic Training as an Artificial Catatonia," are quoted here:

> From our present psychoanalytical knowledge it is clear that Buddhistic self-absorption is a libidinal, narcissistic turning of the urge for knowing inward, a sort of artificial schizophrenia with complete withdrawal of libidinal interest from the outside world. The catatonic conditions of the Hindu ascetics in self-absorption prove quite clearly the correctness of this contention. The mastery of the world is given up and there remains as an exclusive goal of the libido the mastery of the self. In the older pre-Buddha Yogi practice the aim is clearly a mastery of the body, while the absorption of Buddha is directed toward the psychic personality, i.e. the ego.
>
> The Yoga self-absorption, however, has no therapeutic goal; the mastery of the body is an end in itself. Likewise, in Buddhistic self-absorption the turning of the perceptive consciousness inward is an end in itself, a narcissistic-masochistic affair shown by the fact that the way to it leads through asceticism. Psychoanalysis turns inward in order to help the instincts to accommodate themselves to reality; it

> wishes to effect an alliance between consciousness and instinct, in order to make experience with the outer world useful to the instincts. The Buddhistic theory sets itself an easier task: it eliminates reality, and attempts to turn the entire instinctual life away from the world, inwards, towards itself.[24]

Dr. Alexander's thesis, written with a limited knowledge of Buddhism, was published in 1931. Consequently from the Buddhist position it is easy to refute several of the arguments on which he built his case. For example, he equated the lotus position of Buddhist meditation with the fetal position (in which the entire neck and trunk are curled and the wrists and knees brought up over the face). He believed the sole purpose of yogi meditation to be mastery of the body. He mistakenly believed it is only biological forms of suffering (such as old age, sickness and death) which motivate Buddhist training and not any social or emotional forms. He spoke of the end of the Buddha's doctrine "which came with a tragic crash," but since Buddhism is still very much alive in the world today, it is difficult to know just what historical event Dr. Alexander was referring to. On extremely limited data he analyzed the Buddha's disciple Ānanda as acting under the influence of an unresolved Oedipus complex. But perhaps most important is that his case rests heavily upon explaining Nirvāna as attained via the *jhānas*, and he inferred that Nirvāna is but an intensification of the fourth *jhāna*. As already mentioned, Buddhist doctrine teaches that attaining the *jhānas* is not necessary for the realization of Nirvāna,[25]and the Buddha clearly stated that Nirvāna is of a totally different order of being even up to the eighth, or highest, *jhāna*.

But regardless of the errors in Dr. Alexander's thesis, we are still confronted with his basic hypothesis that Nirvāna is regression to intrauterine life. Several considerations make this assumption appear doubtful.

24. Fransz Alexander, "Buddhistic Training as an Artificial Catatonia," in *The Scope of Psychoanalysis* (New York: Basic Books Publishing Co., Inc., 1961), 75–76.

25. Nyanatiloka Mahāthera, *The Word of the Buddha* (Buddhist Publication Society, 1959), p. 79.

First, Alexander believed that regression can go back to the very moment of conception. Yet it is questionable whether or not such a degree of regression is possible in terms of present-day biological theory. The concept of regression presupposes memory, and on good evidence it is generally assumed that human memory is the product of a matured and highly developed nervous system. Yet even at the time of birth the infant human brain is still undeveloped and largely non-functional. If early prenatal memory is possible, we then have evidence to support the Buddhist belief in a non-physical component of the psyche which is present from the time of conception.

Second, if we assume that Nirvāna is the complete withdrawl of libido from the outside world (that is, a total lack of feeling for persons and things outside oneself), then we are at a loss to explain the great emphasis which the Buddha gave to love, ethics and social improvements. Dr. Alexander himself was aware of this:

> Nowhere in the Buddhistic literature has sufficient account been taken of the deep contradiction between the absorption doctrine and Buddha's practical ethics, so far as I am able to follow. The goal of absorption, Nirvāna, is a completely a-social condition and is difficult to combine with ethical precepts.

However, no contradiction exists if one assumes the Buddhist interpretation of Nirvāna (see Ch. VII). Only if one takes Dr. Alexander's position does a problem arise. Thus it was up to Dr. Alexander and not Buddhism to explain the discrepancy. This he did not do.

While the Buddha advocated a state of non-craving and non-attachment, this did not mean a condition devoid of feeling, sensory perception or other forms of experience. We have, for example, the record of his encounter with Uttara, a disciple of a Brahmin teacher named Parasariya. The Buddha inquires of Uttara as to his teacher's doctrine, to which the latter replies:

> As to this, good Gotama, one should not see material shapes with the eye; one should not hear sounds with the ear. It is thus, good Gotama, that the brahman Parasariya teaches the development of the sense-organs to his disciples.

To this the Buddha replies:

> This being so, Uttara, then according to what Parasariya, the brahman, says, a blind man must have his sense-organ developed; a deaf man must have his sense-organ developed. For a blind man, Uttara, does not see material shape with this eye, nor does a deaf man hear sound with his ear....

He then explains his own position on this matter:

> When a monk has seen a material shape with the eye, there arises what is liked; there arises what is disliked; there arises what is both liked and disliked. He comprehends thus: "This that is liked is arising in me; this that is disliked is arising, and this that arises is because it is constructed, is gross. [But] this is the real, this the excellent, that is to say equanimity." So whether what is arising in him is liked, disliked or both liked and disliked, it is [all the same] stopped in him and equanimity remains.
>
> *Indriyabhāvana Sutta*, M III 298–299/MN 152

An *arahant* is said to be wise, oriented to his environment and compassionate towards others. We need only consider the life and personality of the Buddha himself. Had he vegetated by retreating into purely subjective existence, it would have been impossible for him to produce the very strong and lasting effect which he has made upon world history. Alexander explains this by saying that his withdrawal was not complete: one bond remained unsevered, his spiritual attachment to his disciples. Yet we must remember that, at the time of his enlightenment, the Buddha was living completely alone and had no disciples or companions of any sort. Also, from both the Suttas and the *Vinaya* it is apparent that he made great efforts to assure his doctrine would reach all levels of humanity and last for many generations. After his enlightenment, and the enlightenment of sixty of his followers, he gave his well-known missionary address:

> I am freed, monks, from all fetters both divine and human. You also, monks, are freed from all fetters both divine and human. Wander, monks, for the welfare and happiness of many, out of compassion for the world, for the gain, for the welfare and

> happiness of gods and men. Let not two take the same course. Proclaim the Dhamma excellent in the beginning, excellent in the middle, and excellent in the end, in the spirit and in the letter. Proclaim the life of consummate purity.
>
> S I 105/SN 4:5

If we equate the psychoanalytic concept of libido with the Buddhist concept of *taṇhā* or craving, then it may not be far from wrong to say that withdrawing libido from the world is either the same as Nirvāna or a forerunner of Nirvāna. And if we assume that, because the embryo or fetus has not yet experienced the outside world, it thus has not yet invested libido into this world, then we can understand the rationale behind Dr. Alexander's reasoning: Libido remains invested in the self; hence narcissism. We must remember, however, that Buddhist training requires the withdrawal of libido from oneself as well as from the world of sensory experience, and all states of one's thoughts and feelings must be regarded with the same detached objectivity as is the world at large. At this point, the concept of "withdrawing libido" comes under question, for, into what is it withdrawn? Thus Buddhism does not use such a concept, but rather deals with individual states of mind and the causative factors which produce those states.

Even though the concept of embryonic libido is somewhat problematic, Dr. Alexander's hypothesis does warrant consideration. However, in presenting his case his repeated use of the words "narcissistic," "masochistic" and "schizophrenic" gives a rather distorted and unpleasant flavour to the whole idea. Apparently his use of the word "masochistic" comes from the mistaken notion that Buddhism is a type of asceticism. Actually, the Buddha rejected self-inflicted pain as being spiritually futile, and as unwholesome as sensual indulgence.

The word "schizophrenia" covers a variety of mental disorders and certainly its most common forms do not in any way apply to an *arahant*. Among the prime features of most schizophrenias is a distorted perception of external reality (often with delusions and hallucinations) and a marked confusion and deterioration of logical thinking. Speech is often irrelevant, fragmented and inconsistent. This contrasts sharply with the eloquence, clarity and consistency of the Buddha's logic and oratory. Perhaps most significant was his unusual ability to see through semantic problems and thus resolve matters which were purely linguistic in origin, a feature quite opposite to that of schizophrenic thinking. On a feeling level, schizophrenics are often characterized by great emotional lability, inappropriate responses and difficulty in accepting and handling emotional impulses. Again this stands in sharp contrast to the personality of the *arahants*. It is almost inconceivable that a schizophrenic, at least of the usual sort, could successfully institute, manage and perpetuate a complex and highly organized religious order.

It is the catatonic form of schizophrenia (a condition of prolonged trance-like stupor, immobility and seeming unresponsiveness to the outside world) which Alexander specifically equates with Nirvāna. One may remain in such a state for weeks at a time without changing position, not feeding oneself and not even tending to toilet needs. At such times one is usually indifferent to pinpricks and other forms of pain. But even catatonia manifests in a variety of ways and quite commonly is interspersed with episodes of excitement, rambling speech and hyperactivity. Persons who have recovered from catatonic stupor do not describe any particular mental state as being characteristic of this condition, nor is it necessarily pleasant. Usually thought disorders characteristic of other forms of schizophrenia are also present. Perhaps most important is that descriptions given of the catatonic experience bear little in common with the *arahants*' accounts of Nirvāna. Catatonia is not a condition which one enters voluntarily; rather it is the result of social, psychological and environmental forces which overpower and are beyond one's control. Such a person is a victim of *saṃsāra*, and his stupor is a prison which he cannot leave at will. If the depth and tranquillity of Buddhist meditation is a state of catatonia, then it is a condition of catatonia which one enters and leaves mindfully and willfully at one's own discretion (something unknown in the history of psychiatry). Thus Nirvāna is so different from the usual forms of catatonia that it is doubtful that the word "catatonia" can be applied.

The Practical Solution

As stated at the beginning of this chapter, logically and scientifically one can neither prove nor disprove with complete certainty that Nirvāna either is or is not a condition akin to trance, ecstasy or regression. But putting aside all such speculations, the best information we have about Nirvāna is the Pāli Canon of Theravāda Buddhism. If Nirvāna is real and if any person in history has actually realized Nirvāna then in all probability that person was the Buddha himself. On the basis of the historical record we find the Buddha to be a man who dedicated over forty years of his life to the untiring service of his fellow beings; who was widely respected for his wisdom, compassion and moral character; and who apparently did not display anger, greed or prejudice. He was a man noted for his calm and equanimity, and for his strong influence in the lives of many hundreds of millions of people during the past 2,500 years. Thus on the historical record alone, one can reasonably conclude that whatever Nirvāna may be, most likely it is not undesirable.

IV. Zen Enlightenment

Another category of experience, which appears to belong to a class of its own, is the enlightenment of Zen Buddhism, usually termed *satori*. Since Zen is a school of Buddhism and employs some of the same terminology and concepts as early Buddhism, it is often assumed that Zen enlightenment (*satori*) and Theravāda enlightenment (Nirvāna) are the same. But apparently such is not the case. It is difficult to give a satisfactory account of satori, not only because of the elusive and paradoxical features of Zen, but also because of the different versions of enlightenment and Zen in general, as presented by the various Zen sects and masters of the past 1,400 years. One can quote selected passages of Zen scriptures and other Zen writings to support just about any interpretation of Zen that one may choose to formulate. On the basis of Zen literature, however, satori seems to be very much a product of *saṃsāra* and to contain two essential features. One is a true insight into the nature of things and of oneself beyond intellectual knowing. The other is a total restructuring of the psyche so that even though one remains very much involved in *saṃsāra*, one's whole perception of life and response to life situations are so radically altered that life becomes something quite different than it ever was before.[26] There is in Zen only scant mention of ending one's existence in *saṃsāra*. While Zen has given much concern to freeing oneself from the restrictions of intellectualizing and conceptual thinking, it says much less about altering one's feelings, motives and emotions. One occasionally reads of great Zen masters expressing anger and of persons who have realized satori and yet are more selfish than many who have not.[27] We are told that there are degrees of satori, and one must ripen it and grow in it.[28] The renowned Zen scholar D. T. Suzuki comments on the Zen version of *jhāna* or *dhyāna* in these words: "Dhyāna is not quietism, nor is it tranquillization; it is rather acting, moving, performing deeds, seeing, hearing, thinking, remembering."[29]

One may question whether or not satori is a real experience or merely a philosophical ideal which evolved in the history of Zen thought. Two independent sources of evidence indicate that there is such an experience. One source is the recent electroencephalographic (EEG or brain wave) studies of Zen meditators.[30] The other source is the case histories and testimonies of persons allegedly realizing satori in recent years. Both these areas of study require further investigation before any definite conclusions can be drawn, and probably the characteristic Zen EEG tracings are not akin to the subjective experiences described in the case histories. In other words, they appear to be two unrelated phenomena. Also, it may be that both of these recently-studied phenomena are quite different from

---

26. *Zen Buddhism* by D. T. Suzuki (Garden City, New York: Doubleday & Co., Inc., 1956), p. 84.
27. *The Three Pillars of Zen* by Philip Kapleau (Tokyo: John Weatherhill, Inc., 1965), pp. 103–104.
28. Ibid., p. 228.
29. *Zen Buddhism*, op., cit., pp. 181–182.
30. Akira Kasamatsu and Tomio Hirai, *Folia Psychiatrica et Neurologica Japonica*, Vol. 20, No. 4, "*An Electroencephalographic Study of the Zen Meditation* (*Zazen*)," December 1966, pp. 315–336. (Supplementary data obtained by correspondence with the authors.)

the satori experiences of the Zen masters of old or of those Zen monks residing today in secluded and highly disciplined meditation centers.

Electroencephalographic Studies

The EEG investigations have been conducted in Japan since 1953. The subjects studied included monks with many years of meditation experience as well as non-meditators. Two significant findings have been noted. First, during meditation in a well-lighted room and with eyes open, accomplished Zen practitioners produce a rhythmic slowing of the EEG pattern to cycles of seven or eight per second.[31] Usually this is seen in non-meditators only when the eyes are closed and is termed "alpha wave pattern." As a rule it occurs in meditators with open eyes only during, and for a few minutes following, meditation. However, it has occasionally been seen in non-meditators, and as yet no studies have been done to establish a correlation between this EEG pattern and personality structure. It is known that some meditators who produce this pattern are not free of a normal intensity of sexual impulses. The Zen EEG pattern is distinctly different from those of sleep and hypnotic trance, and the meditators said that during meditation they were free from sleepiness, confusion and other mental disturbances. Normally an EEG cannot reveal a person's exact emotions, and people with identical EEG patterns may be experiencing very different states of thought and feeling. However, it was "fairly constant" that the Zen practitioners described their subjective experiences during meditation as "calm, undisturbed and serene." It is noteworthy that no mention is made of religious, mystical, indescribable, transcendental or otherwise unusual states.

The second finding of the EEG studies revealed an alteration in the Zen practitioner's response to sensory stimuli, which suggests an alteration in the perception of one's environment. In normal persons a sudden sensory stimulus, such as a loud noise, draws attention for a brief period, but if the stimulus is repeated at regular and frequent intervals, one eventually becomes oblivious to

31. This occurs in all areas but is most pronounced in the frontal and central regions of the scalp

it and takes no notice. EEG tracings taken on such occasions reveal that in normal subjects the first stimulus produces an alteration in EEG of seven seconds or more; this duration shortens with each successive distraction (in this case noises produced at 15 second intervals) until the fifth stimulus when virtually no EEG effect is seen. It is different, however, with advanced Zen practitioners. The EEG response to the first stimulus lasts only two to three seconds and then continues to last for two to three seconds for every succeeding stimulus up to the twentieth. This suggests a greater total awareness of one's environment but with fewer strong reactions to individual stimuli. This phenomenon has been observed only during meditation and only in persons experienced in Zen training.[32]

Satori is said to be present both in and out of meditation, and the reports of the EEG studies noted above make no mention of whether or not the subjects had had enlightenment. This writer knows of no EEG investigations of Theravāda meditators, or of Mahāyānists apart from Zen.

Case Studies of the Satori Experience

Perhaps the best published examples in English of alleged satori experiences are those described by Mr. Philip Kapleau in his book, *The Three Pillars of Zen*. Mr. Kapleau presents eight case histories, in the form of personal testimonies, which describe in varying amounts of detail the experiences preceding and during enlightenment. His subjects, including himself and his wife, range from 25 to 60 years of age and include three women and five men. Four are Japanese, three are American and one is Canadian. All are lay people, that is, not monks or priests. In the following paragraphs I shall discuss satori as described and explained in Kapleau's writing. All eight of his cases occured to persons who were practising under the guidance of experienced Zen masters and most, if not all, were tested and affirmed by these masters to be genuine instances of satori. However, the reader should be aware that some reputable and long-experienced Zen practitioners reject the validity of these cases.

32. See note 30.

As a psychiatrist, I find it tempting to speculate on the psychological mechanisms which produced Kapleau's case histories, though such speculations can be hazardous on two counts. First, it may be presumptuous to assume that Western psychology in its present form is fully capable of explaining the satori experience. Perhaps it is capable, but having no close contact with persons claiming satori, I cannot venture to say so. Second, Kapleau's case histories do not furnish enough information to enable one to speculate with certainty as to individual psycho-dynamics and personality structures. Some furnish almost no such information, and it is not the primary purpose of his writing to provide this sort of data.

But while there is insufficient data to analyze most of the individual case histories of Kapleau's series, I feel that collectively there is enough information to formulate a reasonable hypothesis for explaining his examples of satori on psychological grounds. Before presenting such a hypothesis, let us first note the nature of Zen training and its subsequent satori experiences.

All but one of Kapleau's eight cases give clear indication of significant emotional disturbances which resulted in the subjects taking up Zen training. In some cases these were relatively normal reactions to stressful situations such as the death of a loved one, serious illness and the insecurity of life in Japan following the war. Other cases indicated more basic personality disturbances such as alcoholism and psychosomatic symptoms. However, in all accounts of Zen training known to this writer, very little concern is given to uncovering the psychological causes of one's disturbances. The Zen practitioner is repeatedly told to see his "true self," that is, to behold his Buddha Nature, his Oneness with the whole universe; and this must be done by dropping dualistic (that is, subject-object) thinking and abandoning conceptualization. For example, we read of one dialogue between a Zen trainee and a master. The trainee says she has had several insights into herself and "felt extremely elated." She is therefore puzzled that the master has told her that insights are *makyo* (that is, mental distractions such as visions and fantasies). In response to this the master makes no inquiry as to what these insights are but responds, "In themselves they [insights] are not harmful, they may even be beneficial in some measure. But if you become attached to or ensnared by them, they can hinder you."[33]

Perhaps the best example of this apparent indifference to motives and personality traits is displayed in the last case of Kapleau's series. The subject relates that, while her childhood could be called almost "ideal," "even from the first, though, there were recurrent periods of despair and loneliness which used to seep up from no apparent source, overflowing into streams of tears and engulfing me to the exclusion of everything else." This is not the behaviour of a normal child, and though the source may not have been "apparent" it would be naive to assume there was no source at all. Then again: "Within a few months our marriage took place, and almost immediately after, I awoke to find myself a widow. The violent, self-inflicted death of my husband was a shock more severe than anything I had ever experienced."[34] One can only wonder what more had taken place but was left unmentioned. It is extremely unusual for a normal well-adjusted man to commit violent, self-inflicted death shortly after his marriage. And it is also unusual for a normal well-adjusted woman to marry a person predisposed to such action. Later the subject enters Zen training in Japan. We are given detailed accounts of her Zen experiences but in only five words told that during this period she marries again. There is no mention of her feelings towards her fiance, her desires for companionship or the nature of the marital relationship. It is as though these aspects of oneself are a world apart from Zen practice and not directly concerned with "seeing into one's True Nature."

The essence of Zen training is *zazen* or the sitting meditation. One practises this at frequent and regular intervals often for hours at a time, over a period of months or years. On such occasions one sits in the company of others and gazes at a blank wall or other blank object. One is repeatedly subjected to great pressures and persuasions to strive with the utmost efforts to empty the mind, abandon intellectualizing and realize the Oneness of all things. Deliberate humiliations and painful brief beatings may be employed to encourage diligence and effort. One is told not to think about the Oneness or to have any ideas about one's

33. Philip Kapleau, *The Three Pillars of Zen*, Boston, 1965, p. 99.

34. Ibid., p. 255.

yet unrealized Buddha Nature. Nevertheless, the practitioner has already heard much about it and knows something of the enlightenment experiences of others before him.

The reactions to one's initial satori experience vary among different individuals, and it is questionable that all of these "enlightenments" represent the same mental phenomenon. Often persons break out in uncontrollable laughter and/or sobbing. Some do neither. Usually there is a sense of joy, calmness or euphoria and often a feeling of oneness with all things. How enduring these states may be is uncertain and probably varies considerably among different individuals. To determine the real value of such experiences it would be necessary to have long-term follow-up reports at regular intervals. A mystical or uplifting emotional experience can be worthwhile in itself, but if years of arduous training have been required to produce it, one should hope for a reward lasting more than a few days or weeks. In the first case of Kapleau's series (which is also the only case that gives no history of previous emotional stress) we are told only of a 48 hour period in which a Japanese executive breaks out with tears, crying and a loud uncontrollable laughter described as "inhuman." With this are great feelings of peace, happiness and freedom. This is most likely akin to the states of euphoria described earlier; and we are given no previous history of this person, and no report of his condition following the "enlightenment."

What then is the satori experience? Probably it is more than one thing, depending on whose experience we are talking about. Also, it may be presumptuous to assume that one not having had satori can fully account for it. Nevertheless, I feel that two types of phenomena are responsible for most of these experiences and such probably occur in varying degrees and combinations in different instances.

Satori and Conversion

The most striking feature of the recorded satori experience is the strong resemblance to stereotypical Christian conversion and/or salvation experiences. Readers of Buddhist writings are often predisposed to negative impressions of Christian experiences, based mostly upon the extremely emotional and fanatic conversions so often witnessed at evangelistic revivals. But Christian conversions include a much deeper and wider range of experiences than these. William James, in his well-known classic *The Varieties of Religious Experience*, covers this topic with remarkable perspicacity, drawing his material both from numerous personal testimonies and case histories as well as from the psychological studies of other researchers. While each conversion is a unique experience which reflects the convictions and emotional constitution of the person involved, one cannot avoid being impressed by the number of recurrent features in Christian conversions which are equally common in alleged satoris. Usually the moment of conversion is preceded by a duration (often several years) of unhappiness, emotional conflict or a general dissatisfaction with oneself and life in general. Often there has been a great (usually frustrated) striving to find God and to be pure and good. Yet the moment of salvation often comes at the instant one lets go and stops trying: "'Lord, I have done all I can, I leave the whole matter with thee.' Immediately there came to me a great peace...."[35]

Such moments often occur when one's emotions or efforts have built up to a point that might be called a spiritual crisis. While this occurs more or less fortuitously in a Christian life, Zen induces it deliberately. In his own account of zazen meditation Kapleau relates the following:

> Suddenly the sun's streaming into the window in front of me! The rain's stopped! It's become warmer! At last the gods are with me! Now I can't miss *satori*! ... Mu, Mu, Mu! ... Again Roshi [the Zen master] leaned over but only to whisper, 'You are panting and disturbing the others, try to breathe quietly.' But I can't stop. My heart's pumping wildly. I'm trembling from head to toe, tears are streaming down uncontrollably. ... Godo cracks me but I hardly feel it. He whacks my neighbour and I suddenly think, 'Why's he so mean? He's hurting him.' ... More tears. ... Godo returns and clouts me again and again, shouting, 'Empty your mind of every single thought; become like a baby again. Just Mu, Mu! right from your guts!' ... crack, crack, crack! ...[36] [All the spacings are Kapleau's.]

35. *The Varieties of Religious Experience* by William James (London: Longmans, Green & Co., 1952), p. 249.

36. *Three Pillars of Zen*, op. cit., p. 218.

And returning to Christianity we read:

> I have been through the experience which is known as conversion. My explanation of it is this: the subject works his emotions up to the breaking point, at the same time resisting their physical manifestations, such as quickened pulse, and so forth, and then suddenly lets them have their full sway over his body. The relief is something wonderful, and the pleasurable effects of the emotions are experienced to the highest degree.[37]

As in Zen, the Christian experience is direct and immediate. Theology and philosophy fade out of sight at least for the moment, and in their place one may experience what appears to be a new insight into the nature of things:

> My emotional nature was stirred to its depths, confessions of depravity and pleading with God for salvation from sin made me oblivious of all surroundings. I pleaded for mercy, and had a vivid realization of forgiveness and renewal of my nature. When rising from my knees I exclaimed, "Old things have passed away, all things have become new." It was like entering another world, a new state of existence. Natural objects were glorified, my spiritual vision was so clarified that I saw beauty in every material object in the universe, the woods were vocal with heavenly music, my soul exulted in the love of God, and I wanted everybody to share in my joy.[38]
>
> Not for a moment only, but all day and night, floods of light and glory seemed to pour through my soul, and oh, how I was changed, and everything became new. My horses and hogs and even everybody seemed changed.[39]

And now as described by Zen devotees:

> Never before had the road been so roadlike, the shops such perfect shops, nor the winter sky so unutterably a starry sky. Joy bubbled up like a fresh spring. The days and weeks that followed were the most deeply happy and serene of my life.[40]

37. *The Varieties of Religious Experience* op. cit., p. 246.
38. Ibid., p. 244.
39. Ibid., p. 245.
40. *The Three Pillars of Zen*, pp. 266–267.

And from another Zen practitioner:

> Am totally at peace, at peace, at peace.
> Feel numb throughout body, yet hands and feet jumped for joy for almost half an hour.
> Am supremely free, free, free, free, free.
> Should I be so happy?
> There is no common man.
> The big clock chimes—not the clock but Mind chimes. The universe itself chimes.
> There is neither Mind nor universe. Dong, dong, dong!
> I've totally disappeared. Buddha is![41]

Also, as in Zen, Christian experiences can be precipitated by a simple word, a passage of scripture or a non-verbal sensory experience.

It is difficult at this point to assert any essential difference between the Christian and Zen experiences. Both claim a state of certainty, a direct knowing beyond logic and argument. Perhaps the basic differences are the respective vocabularies, religious convictions and cultural settings that determine the manner in which one describes and explains them.

While such religious experiences are usually brief and of little consequence, in both the Zen and Christian traditions one finds examples of profound and long-lasting (often permanent) personality changes, usually for the better. Such instances most often are preceded by an unsatisfactory life pattern of either overt or repressed unhappiness: drunkenness, sensuality, cynicism, insecurity and so forth. Apparently one's inner conflicts build up to such a point that there occurs a radical restructuring of the personality. The old, selfish, guilt-ridden and unrewarding tendencies are repressed and their existence denied. Simultaneously the previously denied or undeveloped feelings of companionship and love are brought into focus. Thus one indeed is reborn and is now manifesting a personality pattern which brings much greater personal rewards and brings a previously unknown sense of purpose in life. James states:

41. Ibid., p. 207.

> Another American psychologist, Prof. George A. Coe, has analyzed the cases of seventy-seven converts or ex-candidates for conversion, known to him, and the results strikingly confirm the view that sudden conversion is connected with the possession of an active subliminal (i.e., unconscious) self. Examining his subjects with reference to their hypnotic sensibility and to such automatisms as hypnagogic hallucinations, odd impulses, religious dreams about the time of their conversion, etc., he found these relatively much more frequent in the group of converts whose transformation had been "striking", "striking" transformation being defined as a change which, though not necessarily instantaneous, seems to the subject of it to be distinctly different from a process of growth, however rapid.[42]

In many instances the fruits of both Zen and Christian experiences are highly beneficial in terms of morality, social productivity and one's internal well-being. Yet these remarkable transformations take place with an almost total lack of insight into oneself. The old, neurotic, unwholesome tendencies are more often repressed than resolved, and thus may manifest in more covert ways such as evangelical fervor, "a hatred for sin," or religious fanaticism. This is more apt to occur in the Christian tradition where the religious experience is made a part of a rigidly defined dogma, and the devotee is often unable to separate the experience itself from such concepts as God, salvation and Bible. One knows of examples of saintly, elderly Christians, self-sacrificing and compassionate, who for decades have won the hearts of many and epitomized Christian virtue. Yet if caught in a discussion where the fallacies of their theological convictions are laid bare, fear, anxiety and even unmasked anger break forth until again repressed in conformity with Christian ideals. This also appears to occur to some extent in Zen. We read, for example, of a dialogue between a highly respected Zen master and a pupil. The student raises a doubt about an extremely unlikely Zen teaching which claims that Zen was the Buddha's highest doctrine and was passed on by special transmission down to the present. After the

42. *The Varieties of Religious Experience*, p. 235.

student asks if this is not really a myth, the master unconditionally replies, "No, it is true. If you don't believe it, that's too bad."[43]

Other features of Zen training can also produce desirable personality changes. There is the factor of suggestion: one hears over and over again what should happen, and eventually it does. The introspective nature of Zen, and especially of meditation, can make one aware of mental changes and states of mind which might otherwise go unnoticed, though be no less present in non-meditators. (This can also apply in part to the claims for success of all of the other numerous and divergent schools of psychotherapy besides Zen.) The move to a new environment (either to a new culture for Westerners or into a monastery for Japanese laymen) can in itself change the person and make old concerns seem unimportant; transplanted to a new world, it is easier to abandon old habits, to form a new identity and to relinquish attachments. The process of growing up and maturing, regardless of religion and practice, must be taken into account, especially when we consider that Zen training often requires several years. And finally there is the fact that Zen training is a long and arduous discipline; just as one who has survived a long journey through a wilderness or scaled a difficult mountain or withstood any prolonged stress, the sheer fact of successful endurance gives one self-confidence and a feeling of worth.

Perceptual Alteration

In addition to the above mentioned causes of Zen experiences, the nature of Zen meditation probably produces an additional state of mind not normally present in Christian conversions. This state can occur either singly or in combination with any of the other Zen experiences already noted.

Recent psychological studies have shown that prolonged concentration on simple visual objects can produce striking temporary alterations of feeling and perception. Perhaps most noteworthy are the studies of Dr. Arthur J. Deikman of Austen Riggs Center, Stockbridge, Massachusetts, U.S.A.[44]

---

43. *The Three Pillars of Zen*, p. 133.

44. *The Journal of Nervous and Mental Disease* Vol. 136, No. 4, "Experimental Meditation" by Arthur J. Deikman. U.S.A., Williams & Walkins Co., April,

Dr. Deikman's subjects were seated in front of a blue vase and instructed:

> Your aim is to concentrate on the blue vase. By concentration I do not mean analyzing the different parts of the vase, or thinking a series of thoughts about the vase, or associating ideas to the vase, but rather trying to see the vase as it exists in itself, without any connections to other things. Exclude all other thought's or feelings or sounds or body sensations. Do not let them distract you but keep them out so that you can concentrate all your attention, all your awareness on the vase itself. Let the perception of the vase fill your entire mind.

It is significant that, of the more than eight persons selected for these studies, apparently none had had any previous exposure to meditation, nor had any contact with mystical literature. Subjects were described as "normal adults in their thirties and forties, well educated and intelligent." After a few introductory sessions of about 10 minutes' duration, the sessions were increased to 30 minutes each and held three times a week. Four of the subjects completed 30 to 40 sessions; one completed 78 sessions; and one was still continuing after 106. Though marked individual variations were noted, most, if not all, subjects experienced perceptual changes relating to the vase, modification of the state of consciousness and a general feeling that the sessions were pleasurable and valuable. Quite commonly the vase became more vivid or luminous; a loss of the third dimension was often noted. Some subjects felt a loss of ego boundaries, a confusion of the subject-object relationship as though they and the vase were merging. Such experiences occurred spontaneously and unexpectedly and were sometimes frightening. The degree of success in achieving such states appeared to correlate with one's ability to relinquish control and accept whatever happens. In general the subjects found it difficult to describe their feelings and perceptions. "It's very hard to put into words," was a frequent comment. This difficulty was due in part to the difficulty of describing their experiences without contradictions.

1963. *The Journal of Nervous and Mental Disease* op, cit., Vol. 142, No. 2, "Implications of Experimentally Induced Contemplative Meditation" by Arthur J. Deikman, 1966, pp. 101–116.

Immediately following the meditation sessions, the subjects were asked to describe the experience and also to look out of the window and describe the way things now appeared to them. A few of their comments are quoted below:

> One of the points that I remember most vividly is when I really began to feel, you know, almost as though the blue and I were perhaps merging, or that the vase and I were. I almost got scared to the point where I found myself bringing myself back in some way from it... .
>
> The building is a kind of very white ... a kind of luminescence that the fields have and the trees are really swaying, it's very nice ... lean way over and bounce back with a nice spring-like movement....
>
> The movements are nice, the brightness is. I would have thought it was a terribly overcast day but it isn't. It's a perception filled with light and movement both of which are very pleasurable. Nobody knows what a nice day it is except me.
>
> I am looking differently than I have ever looked before. I mean it's almost as though I have a different way of seeing. It's like something to do with dimensions. It's as though I am feeling what I am looking at. It's as though I have an extension of myself reaching out and seeing something by feeling it. It's as though somebody added something, another factor, to my seeing.
>
> I've experienced ... new experiences and I have no vehicle to communicate them to you. I expect that this is probably the way a baby feels when he is full of something to say about an experience or an awareness and he has not learned to use the words yet.
>
> It's so completely and totally outside of anything else I've experienced.
>
> It was like a parallel world or parallel time....

The similarities between these descriptions and the descriptions of Zen experiences are so striking that little comment is needed.

Dr. Deikman lists several factors which he believes account for these experiences, three of which warrant discussion here. They are de-automatization, perceptual expansion and reality transfer.

In order to explain de-automatization and perceptual expansion it is first necessary to explain the word "perception" as used in modern psychology. For simplicity, our discussion will be confined to visual perception, but the same principles also apply to auditory, tactile and olfactory perception.

Visual perception is dependent upon, but must be distinguished from, simple visual sensation. Sensation is the patterns of colours which we behold upon opening our eyes. Perception is the way in which we understand or interpret these patterns. Contrary to popular assumption, human visual perception is not innate in visual experience but rather is gradually acquired by learning as the result of repeatedly seeing visual patterns. The best and most convincing illustration of this is noted in the case of persons born blind but who in later life receive eye surgery. For all practical purposes these people obtain instant and near-perfect vision for the first time in what has been a lifetime of total blindness. They are overwhelmed by a mass of confusing colours and shapes, which they are totally at a loss to understand. They are unable to determine the difference in distance, size and quality; between a full moon in the sky, a light bulb on the ceiling or a white ball placed two feet in front of them. They are just as likely to try and reach for a cloud as to reach for a piece of paper near at hand. A pencil seen from its end will not be recognized as the same object seen from its side. But only when the pencil has been examined over and over in one's hands (in the same manner and for the same reason as a very young child) will one come to know that these very different visual patterns actually are the same object, that is, a pencil.[45]

Any person raised in a Western culture who in later life learns to read a non-Romanized language, such as Chinese, Thai, Sanskrit or Arabic, will recall that in the beginning great attention had to be given to the details of shape and form of each letter or character. But once fluency is achieved, one scarcely is aware of individual letters, let alone their details of shape. One can now glance at whole patterns of words and immediately comprehend the meanings; just as one competent in English reads these pages.[46]

45. *Space and Sight* by M. Von Senden (Glencoe, Illi.: Free Press, 1960).

46. Thus perception is dependent upon memory and is inseparable from it. In Theravāda Buddhism mind (*nāma*) is divided into four groups, one of which

Psychology uses the word "automatization" to refer to the natural loss of awareness of the intermediate steps in perception. For example, one does not consciously give attention to the shape of each letter in the words one is reading. Automatization thus increases our mental efficiency by freeing the mind from concern for repetitious details. De-automatization is the undoing of automatization, that is, attention is again focused on minor sensory details. Perceptually, de-automatization puts one's mind momentarily on the same level as a young child. Colours become more vivid; previously unnoticed details hold the attention. Commonplace objects such as boxes, brooms and key chains may seem fascinating and beautiful.[47] Concentrative meditation is not the only way of inducing this phenomenon; sensory deprivation and drugs such as marijuana, peyote and LSD-25 are equally, if not more, effective de-automatizers.

The response of Zen practitioners in meditation to repeated stimuli as shown by an EEG[48] may well be the result of de-

is consciousness. Consciousness in turn is interdependent with the other three (see Ch. I). Of these other three the first is termed sensation or feeling (*vedanā*); the second (*saññā*) means both "memory" and "perception" and is translated into English as either one of these two words, usually the latter. The third group is mental formations (*saṅkhārā*) and includes conceptional formations (thinking), willing, planning. (See *Buddhist Dictionary* by Nyanatiloka Mahāthera, Kandy, Sri Lanka, BPS) The corresponding classification used in Western psychology is sensations, perceptions, and concepts arising in that order. After perceptions have become established, the mind is able to use sound (that is, spoken words) and figures (that is, written words) to serve as symbols to represent respective objects, feelings and abstract relationships; this is the formation of concepts. Thus once conceptualization has developed, it no longer is necessary to see or touch a tree, for example, to know that a tree exists at a given site; the simple sound "tree" will bring to mind the perceptions which occur in actually experiencing a tree. The word *sankhāra* has a range of usages, but as applied to the above aspect of Buddhist psychology it includes conceptualization as understood in Western psychology but also includes aspects of volition and motivation.

47. *The Doors of Perception and Heaven and Hell* by Aldous Huxley (Middlesex, England: Penguin Books, 1959).

48. *The Drug Experience,* edited by David Ebin (New York: The Orion Press, 1961), pp. 368–384.

automatization. However, it cannot at this time be concluded that the phenomena of Deikman's relatively inexperienced meditation subjects are either qualitatively or quantitatively the same as the EEG phenomena observed in Zen monks. Control studies on 22 non-meditators failed to produce these same EEG findings. Also, the degree of EEG change correlated directly with the number of years in practice, and the most striking change (that is, 6–7/second theta waves) was rarely if ever seen in monks with less than 20 years of experience.

Following and dependent upon de-automatization is perceptual expansion. So strong is the process of automatization that it is virtually impossible for one to see visual patterns in their true form, independently of perceptual conditioning. ท, for example, will be seen as the written form of *n* by an American, but to a Thai it is the Siamese equivalent of a *t*. And what does the English-trained mind make of บ, ด or ญ?

The figure below will immediately be recognized as a cube. If one stares at the extreme upper right-hand corner of this cube, some people will perceive this corner as belonging to the front (near) side of the cube; others will see it as belonging to the back (far) side. Most people who stare at the cube for a minute or two will perceive the position of the upper right-hand corner as constantly changing; that is, first it is forward, and then back, and then forward again, and so on. In reality there is no front or back side; in fact there is no third dimension at all. Perception compels us to see a third dimension that is not really there. Under de-automatizing drugs such as hashish and LSD the figure above may appear flat, that is, have no third dimension, and yet a moment later one may see all three possibilities (forward, backward and flat) simultaneously. This is but one example of perceptual expansion.

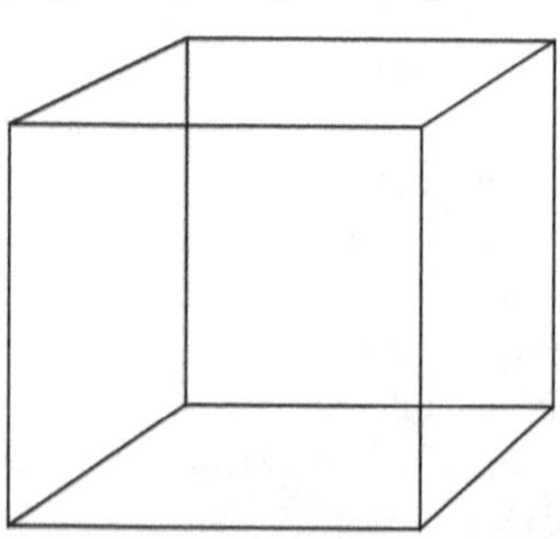

The artistic value of perceptual expansion, whether obtained through drugs or through concentrative meditation, is not to be denied. No doubt it enables an artist to see previously unnoticed patterns and thus can enhance creativity. Also the experience is often accompanied by pleasant and uplifting emotions. However, it is questionable whether or not such experiences have any lasting value in terms of emotional well-being, long-term happiness or adjustment to life problems. The failures of numerous persons who have long tried Zen and/or LSD to resolve emotional and neurotic problems testifies to this fact.[49] Of the two subjects in Deikman's meditation experiments who both practised the longest and got the most striking results, both showed evidence of neurotic conflicts on the basis of personal history and psychological testing, though they were functioning relatively well in their environments. De-automatization experiences, whether induced through chemistry or *zazen*, are quite brief, a few hours at most in the case of drugs and only a few minutes following meditation. Also, we must not forget that normal perception (that is, automatization) has a definite biological value or it would not have evolved. Its presence allows us greater efficiency in dealing with the problems of daily living. The man who quickly reads through a menu will be farther along the road to survival than one who becomes enamoured with the shape and form of the ABCs.

The reader should keep in mind that the above statements regarding meditation are concerned with only one type of meditation, and do not apply to insight meditation (*vipassanā*) as practised in Pāli Buddhism. Nor do these statements apply to the deeper tranquillity practices (*jhāna*), nor to the various discursive meditations.

Dr. Deikman's third factor used to explain the above meditation experiences he terms "reality transfer." This phrase refers to the fact that actual physical reality and the *sensation* or *feeling* of reality are not the same. In the interests of biological

49. This is not to imply that LSD and related drugs have no psychotherapeutic potential at all. There are instances in which they have produced valid psychological insights and thus facilitated personality growth. However, such growth will take place only if one is emotionally and intellectually prepared to confront, understand and make use of the acquired insights.

survival, the normal state of the mind is to invest a feeling of reality into the objects of everyday experience. However, factors which alter the mind (such as hypnosis, LSD, psychotic states and prolonged concentration) can displace this reality sensation. At such times the real world may seem unreal, while subjective states and minor sensory perceptions may appear more real than normal reality.

V. The Occurrence of Arahants

If Nirvāna is real, why are *arahants* so hard to find? Has even one lived within the past century? We are told that at the time of the Buddha over 1,000 of the monks realized Nirvāna. But despite this impressive figure we are also told that the occurrence of *arahants* is rare in the world, and even more rare is the occurrence of an enlightened teacher who warrants the title of "Buddha."[50]

> Few among men are there indeed
> Who cross to the Further Shore.
> The remaining men, most of mankind,
> Run up and down this hither shore.
> But they who Dhamma practise
> In this Dhamma well-expounded,
> It is such among mankind
> Who will reach the Further Shore,
> Who will cross old Death's dominions
> So difficult to cross.
>
> *Dhammapada* 85–86

It goes without saying that the realization of Nirvāna is no easy achievement, for it requires the complete and final abolition of all attachment and craving. What is not fully appreciated, however, is that the desire to remove attachments will not in and of itself effect their removal. Wanting to abandon passion only means that one is in a state of ambivalence, that is, two contradictory or opposing feelings co-exist. We have for example the well-known prayer of St. Augustine:

50. D II 149/DN 16 (*Mahāparinibbāna Sutta,* Ch. V, 23).

> I had begged chastity of Thee, and said, "Give me chastity and continency, only not yet!" For I feared lest Thou shouldest hear me soon, and soon cure me of the disease of concupiscence, which I wished to have satisfied, rather than extinguished.[51]

The problem is compounded by the fact that if the desire to be free of hatred or passion is significantly stronger than the hatred or passion itself, one may unwittingly repress these unwanted feelings so as to hide them from awareness, and thus not realize that they still exist. This brings us to the second major barrier to Nirvāna, which is delusion (*moha*). Delusion and desire are interdependent. It is because of desires of one sort or another that we structure delusions and unconsciously resist their relinquishment. As an example, the desire to be rid of passion is as often as not motivated by a more subtle form of pleasure seeking, which is the egotistical wish to be pure, virtuous and holy. This in turn originates in part from the delusion that one has an Ego, a true unchanging self, something special and unique which is the essence of one's true being. But the level of self-deception goes even deeper than this. In the light of modern science and psychology many persons have come to accept that there is no immortal soul; instead, man is a compounded and highly complex psychophysical phenomenon. However, an intellectual acceptance is something quite different from a thorough emotional acceptance. Quite likely many of the most ardent materialists retain some lingering notion of a soul or even of personal immortality no matter how strongly they may repress such feelings or find them intellectually unpalatable. The same is equally true of great scholars of Buddhist thought, if their scholastic achievements have not been accompanied by successful insight (*vipassanā*) practice. Thus the realization of Nirvāna requires the maximum possible goal of psychoanalysis: a complete laying bare of the subconscious, the total removal of repression, rationalization and all other unconscious defense mechanisms. Ardent discipline, religious dedication and deep faith (no matter how strong they may be) do not guarantee that true insight will be achieved. For quite often discipline, dedication and

---

51. *Confessions*, Book VIII, 17, by St. Augustine (Chicago: Henry Regnery Co., 1948), p. 144.

faith originate from the very factors that obstruct one's progress towards enlightenment. Common among such factors are bigotry, compulsiveness, ethnocentrism, egotism and insecurity. Thus discipline, dedication and faith are double-edged swords. Though they can be assets towards realizing Nirvāna, they must be subjected to close scrutiny and questioning:

> The faults of others are easy to see,
> While hard indeed to see are one's own;
> Like chaff one winnows others' faults,
> Concealing carefully those of one's own;
> Just as a cheating gambler hides
> The ill-thrown dice from others' eyes.
>
> *Dhammapada* 252

But even allowing for the great difficulty in realizing Nirvāna, one might think that among the many millions of Buddhists in the world today at least a few should win the ultimate goal. In this regard two facts must be kept in mind. First, many Buddhist regions are Buddhist in name only. During the past 2,500 years the Dhamma has spread to many lands and become mixed with numerous indigenous beliefs and superstitions, while at the same time its teachings have been radically modified by priests and scholars. Thus many millions of Buddhists have followed and are still following beliefs and practices that are the direct antithesis of the Buddha's teachings. Second, even in nations which have best retained the original teachings, too often these teachings have been either obscured by folklore, mythology and ecclesiasticism, or buried in a deluge of metaphysics, meticulous categorizations and philosophizing. Then again when one does encounter the apparently valid teachings of the Buddha, one occasionally finds that the major emphasis is either upon the correct intonations for chanting these teachings in Pāli (which has been a dead language for two millenniums), or upon scriptural hair splitting, rote memorizing or argumentation.

All of this is not meant to imply that there are very few persons with an extensive and profound grasp of the Dhamma; for such is not the case. The point to be made, however, is that the quoted number of world Buddhists is a figure many times greater than the number of those who truly understand what the Buddha taught. And smaller still is the number of those who both understand and practise.

Persons not usually credulous, and who are in close contact with advanced centers of Buddhist training, have stated that there are indeed *arahants* alive in the world today. This writer can neither deny nor affirm such claims, but two facts must be mentioned. First, the *Vinaya* rules, by which all Theravādin monks are bound, state that a monk must not tell a lay person of his attainment of either *jhāna* or Nirvāna, even though such be true.[52] Second, there are very good reasons for establishing such a rule. One familiar with Asian society need only reflect a moment on what would happen were an *arahant* to make his attainment known. The results would be little short of disastrous. In the minds of uneducated lay Buddhists he would be regarded as a god and in possession of almost limitless supernatural powers. There would be pleas for cures of ailments, requests for prophecies and demands for blessings to protect one from ghosts, ill fortune and injury. Should the announced *arahant* utter any statement contrary to either popular tradition or the letter of Buddhist scriptures, there would be a wail of protests rejecting his claims to enlightenment and accusing him of fraud. Undoubtedly he would be repeatedly approached by fanatics and by persons intent on challenging and testing his claim.

How then can one who has not achieved Nirvāna be assured of the attainment of one who has? This same question was once put to the Buddha:

> The king, the Kosalan Pasenadī, came to visit the Exalted One, and having saluted him, took a seat at one side. Now just then there passed by, not far from the Exalted One, seven ascetics out of those who wore the hair matted, seven of the Niganthas [Jains], seven naked ascetics, seven of the Single Vestment class, and seven Wanderers, all with hairy bodies and long nails, carrying friars' kit. Then the king, rising from his seat, and draping his robe over one shoulder, knelt down on his right knee, and holding forth clasped hands, thrice called out his name to those ascetics: "I am the king, your

52. *Vinaya, Suttavibhanga, Pācittiya* 8.

reverences, the Kosalan Pasenadī." And when they were gone by, he came back to the Exalted One, and saluting him, sat down as before. So seated, he asked the Exalted One: "Are those persons, Lord, either among the world's *arahants*, or among those who are in the Path of arahantship?"

To this the Buddha replied:

> Hard is it, sire, for you who are a layman holding worldly possessions, dwelling amidst the encumbrances of children, accustomed to Benares sandalwood, arrayed in garlands and perfumed unguents, using gold and silver, to know whether those are *arahants*, or are in the Path of arahantship.
>
> It is by life in common with a person, sire, that we learn his moral character; and then only after a long interval if we pay good heed and are not heedless, if we have insight and are not unintelligent. It is by converse with another, sire, that we learn whether he is pure-minded; and then only after a long interval if we pay good heed and are not heedless, if we have insight and are not unintelligent. It is in time of trouble, sire, that we learn to know a man's fortitude and then only after a long interval if we pay good heed and are not heedless, if we have insight and are not unintelligent.

S I 77–78/ SN 3:11

Among the commentaries to the Pāli Canon is the following story:

> At the monastery on the Cittala Hill, there lived an Elder who was a canker-freed Saint [an *arahant*]. As his personal attendant he had a novice who got ordained in his old age. One day that old novice went on alms-round together with the Elder, and carrying the Elder's alms bowl and outer robe, he walked behind him. While they so went, the old novice asked the Elder, "Those who are Saints, how do they look? How can we recognize them?" The Elder said, "There is an old person who carries a Saint's bowl and robe, fulfils all duties towards him, and even goes along with him; yet he cannot recognize Saints. So hard to know, friend, are the Saints!" And not even then did the old novice understand.

Commentary to the *Saṃyutta Nikāya*

At this point one may ask whether or not Buddhism is a satisfactory religion, for it offers salvation to so few. But the problem is not one of "offering" salvation but rather of pointing the way for those who are able and willing to tread the path. What then of persons apparently unable to reach the goal? In this regard we must first remember that Buddhism is empirical; it is dealing with things as they are, not as we would like them to be. A religion which promises universal or easy salvation may be more emotionally satisfying, but in the long run it will tend to be an opiate which diverts our efforts from truly constructive endeavours. But the Buddha was fully aware of the needs and capabilities of the common people. Repeatedly, he gave them instructions for finding comfort and happiness in everyday life.[53] Even those who strive for Nirvāna without fully attaining the goal have not wasted their efforts; for the extent to which one has freed one's mind from greed, hatred and delusion, and developed compassion and equanimity, is the extent to which one finds emotional well-being and peace of mind in the present. Furthermore, such achievements are said to result in good karma, which in turn brings happiness in the future. And in the next birth, which allegedly arises as the result of the present one, one would be that much closer to Nirvāna should one choose to continue the journey. If we consider the great infinity of time as taught in Buddhism and also the fact that Nirvāna is said to be obtainable after several lifetimes of patient endeavour, then perhaps the percentage of beings reaching Nirvāna is much greater than realized. Also, the Buddha is quoted as saying that some persons who make sufficient progress towards Nirvāna will not be reborn in this world. Rather they will continue their existence on some other dimension within *saṃsāra* and in that realm attain the final goal.[54]

53. D III 180–193/DN 31 (*Sigālovāda Sutta*).

54. MN 118/M III 80 (*Ānāpānasati Sutta*).

VI. Aesthetic and Moral Criticisms

Apathy and Negation

As Nirvāna can be realized only by the abolition of desire and craving, it is often viewed as a condition of emotional death, a state of emptiness and apathy. Even in the minds of many Theravādin Buddhists it seems depressing, as if to say one never wins in *saṃsāra*, so the only solution is suicide. Yet suicide of the usual sort is almost invariably preceded by severe and inescapable depression. Before concluding that the quest for Nirvāna is motivated by a deathwish, we should note that the Buddha divided the types of craving one should overcome into three categories. The first two are cravings for sense pleasures and for continued existence. The third craving to be relinquished is craving for annihilation after death.[55]

An *arahant* is not in a state of chronic apathy. In the Suttas the Buddha is often referred to as "the Happy One,"[56] and of the seven states of mind listed as conducive to Nirvāna, the factors of enlightenment, one is happiness and two of the others are tranquillity and equanimity. (The remaining four are mindfulness, investigation of reality, energy and concentration.)[57] The Buddha said:

> Happy is he contented in solitude,
> Seeing the truth he has learned.
> Happy is he who abstains from harming,
> Living restrained towards all that lives.
> Happiness true is freedom from passion
> If senses' cravings are left behind.
> But highest happiness is his
> Who has removed the self-conceit.

Mucalinda, Udāna 2.1

---

55. S V 421/SN 56:11 (*Dhammacakkappavattana Sutta*).

56. D II 93/DN 16 (*Mahāparinibbāna Sutta,* Ch. II, 9).

57. See *The Seven Factors of Enlightenment* by Piyadassi Thera, Wheel Publication No. 1 (Buddhist Publication Society, 1960).

The Buddha's statement "happiness is won by happiness" stands in sharp contrast to the Jain teaching that happiness is won by suffering.[58] Too often Buddhism is misunderstood as a practice of rigid asceticism intended to induce a state of euphoria. In his first sermon the Buddha contradicted this notion by advocating the famed Middle Way, the avoidance of the two extremes: one being sensual indulgence and the other self-torture.[59] And in the *Kassapa-Sīhanāda Sutta* the Buddha asks:

> If a man, O Kassapa, should go naked, and be of loose habits, and lick his hands clean with his tongue, and do and be all those other things you gave in detail, down to his being addicted to the practice of taking food, according to rule, at regular intervals up to even half a month—if he does all this, and the state of blissful attainment in conduct, in heart, in intellect, have not been practised by him, realized by him, then is he far from samaṇaship, far from brahmanship. But from the time, O Kassapa, when a Bhikkhu has cultivated the heart of love that knows no anger, that knows no ill-will—from the time when by the destruction of the deadly intoxications [the lusts of the flesh, the lust after future life and the defilements of delusion and ignorance], he dwells in that emancipation of heart, that emancipation of mind, that is free from those intoxications, and that he, while yet in this visible world, has come to realize and know—from that time, O Kassapa, is it that the *bhikkhu* is called a *saṃana*, is called a *brāhmana*.
>
> *Kassapa-Sīhanāda Sutta*, D I 167 /DN 8

And again he is quoted:

> Now it may well be, Poṭṭhapāda, that you think: "Evil dispositions may be put away, the dispositions that tend to purification may increase, one may continue to see face to face, and by himself come to realize, the full perfection and grandeur of wisdom, but one may continue sad." Now that, Poṭṭhapāda, would not be accurate judgment. When such

58. *The Book of the Gradual Sayings*, Vol. II (AN II), translated by F. L. Woodward (London: The Pali Text Society, 1952), pp. 2–3.
59. S V 421 (*Dhammacakkappavattana Sutta*).

conditions are fulfilled, then there will be joy, and happiness, and peace, and in continual mindfulness and self-mastery, one will dwell at ease.

And outsiders, Poṭṭhapāda, might question us thus: "What then, sir, is that material (or that mental, or that formless) mode of personality for the putting away of which you preach such a doctrine?" And to that I should reply: "Why this very personality, that you see before you, is what I mean."

Poṭṭhapāda Sutta, I 196–197/DN 9

The Buddha never taught that the abolition of all feelings is a prerequisite to Nirvāna. Only those states of mind which are unwholesome (that is, conducive to *dukkha* and undesirable karma) need be abandoned. Usually he classified such states into greed, hatred and delusion. On other occasions they were termed the "five mental hindrances," and enumerated as sensual lust, anger, sloth and torpor, agitation and worry, and sceptical doubt. Sometimes the list was expanded to ten: belief that oneself is an unchanging soul, scepticism, belief in salvation through rules and ceremonies, sensual lust, hatred, craving for existence in a heaven world, craving for the bliss of deep meditation (that is, *arūpajjhāna*, see Ch. III), conceit, restlessness and ignorance.[60]

In place of the unwholesome levels of feeling the Buddha advocated the cultivation and development of the four *brahma-vihāras*: love (*mettā*), compassion, sympathetic joy (that is, the happiness one experiences in perceiving the happiness of others) and equanimity.[61] The first of these four, *mettā*, is usually translated into English as "love" or "loving-kindness," but there is no precise English equivalent. By simultaneously thinking of love, kindness and friendship, we can best understand its meaning.

In Buddhist teaching there is no moral or psychological wrong in encountering and acknowledging an enjoyable experience per se. The pleasures which accompany the sweet taste of sugar, and the beauty of a mountain scene, are not in themselves barriers to

60. S V 61/SN 45:8, 8:9–10.

61. *The Four Sublime States* by Nyānaponika Thera (Kandy, Sri Lanka: Buddhist Publication Society, 1960).

Nirvāna. But danger arises from the craving or attachment that such experiences may produce. That is, the notion "I must have this. I must re-experience it." Thus the Buddha said:

> If he [an *arahant*] feels a pleasant feeling he knows it is transient, he knows it is not clung to, he knows it has no lure for him ... . [The same is then repeated for painful and neutral feelings.] If he feels a pleasant feeling, he feels that feeling with detachment. If he feels a painful feeling, he feels that feeling with detachment.
>
> S II 82/SN 12:51

Referring to the place at which he first realized Nirvāna, the Buddha spoke:

> Pleasant indeed and delightful is the forest grove with a flowing river of clear water, a pleasant and delightful ford and a village near by for procuring food. Indeed it is a most suitable place for a noble youth intent on spiritual exertion.
>
> *Ariyapariyesana Sutta*, M I 167/MN 26

And on an occasion shortly before the Buddha's demise:

> So the Exalted One proceeded to the Cāpala Shrine, and when he had come there he sat on the mat spread out for him, and the Venerable Ānanda took his seat respectfully beside him. Then the Exalted One addressed the Venerable Ānanda, and said: "How delightful a spot, Ānanda, is Vesāli, and how charming the Udena Shrine, and the Gotamaka Shrine, and the Shrine of the Seven Mangoes, and the Shrine of Many Sons, and the Sarandada Shrine and the Cāpāla Shrine!"
>
> *Mahāparinibbāna Sutta*, Ch. III, D II 102/DN 16

And at another time he is quoted:

> Now I, Bhaggava, being of such an opinion, certain recluses and brahmins have falsely, emptily, mendaciously and unfairly accused me, saying, "Gotama, the recluse, is all wrong, and so are his monks." He has said, "Whenever one has attained the stage of deliverance entitled the Beautiful [*subha*, a condition below both Nirvāna and *arūpajjhāna*], one then considers all things as repulsive." But this, Bhaggava, I have not said. What

I do say is this: "Whenever one attains the stage of deliverance, entitled the Beautiful, one is then aware, 'Tis lovely!'"

Pātika Sutta, D III 34/DN 24

This same appreciation of beauty was also expressed by others among the *arahants*. There is, for example, a poem attributed to Sabbaka after his enlightenment:

Whene'er I see the crane, her clear bright wings
Outstretched in fear to flee the black storm cloud,
A shelter seeking, to safe shelter borne,
Then doth the river Ajakaraṇī give joy to me.
Who doth not love to see on either bank
Clustered rose-apple trees in fair array
Behind the great cave (of my hermitage)
Or hear the soft croak of the frogs, well rid
Of their undying mortal foes, proclaim:
"Not from the mountain streams is't time today
To flit. Safe is the Ajakaraṇī.
She brings us luck. Here is it good to be."

Theragāthā, *Psalms of the Brethren* IV 196

And Kassapa, another of the *arahants*, is allegedly the author of the following:

Those upland glades delightful to the soul,
Where the *kareri* spreads its wildering wreaths,
Where sound the trumpet-calls of elephants,
Those rocky heights with hue of dark blue clouds,
Where lies embosomed many a shining tarn
Of crystal-clear, cool waters, and whose slopes
The "herds of Indra" cover and bedeck ...
Here is enough for me who fain would dwell
In meditation rapt, mindful and tense.

Theragāthā, *Psalms of the Brethren* XVIII 261.4

However, it is only the hand that has no wound that can safely handle poison. Not uncommonly, we mistakenly consider ourselves free of addictions simply because we have not been sufficiently separated from the objects of gratification to experience the full intensity of our desires. Cigarette smoking is one obvious example. Thus for one treading the path to Nirvāna, a considerable amount of renunciation and discipline is imperative.

This brings us to another feature of the Dhamma which has given many the impression that it is life-negating, depressing and morbid. There are those passages of scripture which refer to the body or the world in general as "disgusting" or "impure," or else advocate the development of "disgust." This is especially characteristic of the cemetery meditations that occur in *satipaṭṭhāna* practice. Here a monk is advised to meditate upon a human corpse in various stages of decay and putrification, "swollen, blue and festering"; or "being eaten by crows, hawks, vultures, dogs, jackals or by different kinds of worms." And with each of these mental pictures the monk "then applies this perception to his own body thus: 'Verily, also my own body is of the same nature: such it will become and will not escape it.'"[62] Likewise one finds meditations on food in which the meditator visualizes the digestion and decomposition of food as it proceeds through the intestines.[63]

The point to remember is that Buddhism is first and foremost a series of techniques for psychological maturation rather than a philosophy about the nature of the world. Furthermore, these techniques must be varied from person to person and also varied from time to time for any one person, depending upon one's particular state of mind.[64] Thus the above meditations are specific techniques intended as antidotes for specific types of craving (in the above instances the cravings of narcissism, immortality, passion and gluttony). Their function is one of negative conditioning. It is like a man who is repeatedly told while under hypnosis that cigarette smoke tastes like ammonia. This produces the post-hypnotic hallucination that cigarettes do taste like ammonia, and he eventually loses his desire for cigarettes. Or again, it is like Pavlov's dog which is given a painful electric shock every time it sees a certain food. In time all desire for that food is lost. When reading of these meditations one often gets a very depressing view of them. But if they induce depression, one has either misperceived

62. M I 58/MN 10 (*Satipaṭṭhāna Sutta*).

63. *Visuddhimagga* XI, 1–26.

64. S V 112–115/SN 46:6.

them or one's present mental condition is not one for which these meditations are intended. In this regard the Buddha has said:

> If in the contemplation of the body, bodily agitation or mental lassitude or distraction should arise in the meditator, then, Ānanda, he should turn his mind to a gladdening subject. Having done so, joy will arise in him.
>
> S V 156/SN 47:10

A Selfish Goal

Is the goal of Nirvāna a selfish one? Perhaps the most common criticism directed against Buddhism, and Theravāda Buddhism in particular, is that one's primary concern is one's own salvation. The whole effort and purpose of the Eightfold Path is self-development and self-purification, that is, one's personal liberation.

In reply to the question "Is Buddhism selfish?" the answer must be "yes" in the sense that every willful action is selfish. Referring to our previous discussion of the pleasure-pain principle (see Ch. I), all human endeavours (unless purely habitual) are motivated by some attempt at achieving happiness, pleasure, love, self-respect, social approval, beauty and other enjoyable experiences; or else actions are motivated by an endeavour to escape sorrow, pain, fear, guilt, humiliation and other forms of *dukkha*. Even great acts of self-sacrifice are but instances of ambivalence in which one level of feeling (for example, love, religious dedication or a wish for self-esteem) wins out over antagonistic and less respected levels. Christianity and Islam, with their great emphases upon Heaven and Hell (regardless of the ways in which Heaven and Hell may be interpreted), provide clear examples of the pleasure-pain principle occurring in high reaches of religious thought.

Compassion originates not as a philosophical or religious ideal but rather as a feeling which motivates us to help others, and is experienced as a very wholesome and rewarding state of mind. In fact loud advocacies of love and compassion as ideals often indicate that they are wanting as realities; the militancy of most Bohemian peace marchers, fundamentalist clergyman and communist and socialist zealots provide clear examples.[65]

---

65. One may postulate that compassion and allied feelings are divinely

If, however, we take the more conventional usage of the word "selfish," which encompasses greed and egotism, but excludes love (*mettā*) and compassion, then the term does not apply to the Buddha's teachings. As several quotations will demonstrate:

> Then, Lohicca, he who would say, "Suppose a *samaṇa* or a *brāhmaṇa* has reached some good state [of mind], then he should tell no one else about it. For what can one man do for another? To tell others would be like the man who, having broken through an old bond, should entangle himself in a new one. Like that, I say, is this desire to declare to others; it is a form of lust." He who should say thus would be putting obstacles in the way of those clansmen who have taken upon themselves the Doctrine and Discipline.... But putting obstacles in their way he would be out of sympathy for their welfare. Being out of sympathy for their welfare, his heart would become established in enmity, and when one's heart is established in enmity, that is unsound doctrine.
>
> *Lohicca Sutta*, D I 228–229/DN 12

When told that it is unbefitting for one who has renounced the world to spend his life exhorting other men, the Buddha replied:

> Whatever the apparent cause, Sakka, whereby
> Men come to dwell together, none doth fit
> The Wise Man's case.
> Compassion moves his mind.
> And if, with mind thus satisfied, he spends
> His life instructing other men, yet he
> Thereby is nowise bound as by a yoke.
> Compassion moves him and sympathy.
>
> S I 206/SN 10:2

willed but such an assumption immediately raises both the question of free will and the question of the origin of less wholesome feelings such as greed and hatred. Starting on an experiential basis, Buddhism acknowledges the reality of such feelings and proceeds from there. It is interesting to note in this regard that close observations of several species of higher animals suggest that love and compassion are not exclusively human. (*National Geographic*, Vol. 128, No. 6, "New Discoveries Among Africa's Chimpanzees" by Jane Van Lawick-Goodall. Washington, D.C.: December, 1965, pp. 802–831. *Arctic Wild* by Louis Chrisler, New York: Harper, 1958.)

And again he said:

> Monks, it is because I observe these two results therein that I am given to dwelling in lonely spots, in solitary lodging in the forest. What two? Observing my own pleasant way of living in this very life, and feeling compassion for future generations. These are the two results.
>
> A I 60/AN 2:9

Once one of the monks lay ill but was ignored by the others, so intent were they on spiritual training. At this time the Buddha admonished them:

> Whosoever, bhikkhus, would wait upon me, whosoever, bhikkhus, would honour me, whosoever, bhikkhus, would follow my advice, he should wait upon the sick.
>
> Mahāvagga VIII 26/Vinaya I 302

And when the Brahmin Sangarava said that the life of a monk was of benefit to but one person, the monk himself, the Buddha replied that one who succeeds in his practice and attains Enlightenment will become a teacher of men and can lead many thousands to the same liberation.[66]

The justification for the Buddha's great emphasis upon self-development and self-purification was explained in the Sermon on the Mount when Jesus said:

> Or how wilt thou say to thy brother, Let me pull the mote out of thine eye; and, behold, a beam is in thine own eye? Thou hypocrite, first cast the beam out of thine own eye: and then shalt thou see clearly to cast the mote out of thy brother's eye.
>
> St. Matthew 7:4–5

It has been said, "Men can be forgiven for the things they have done in the name of evil, but who can forgive that which has been done in the name of good?" The histories of Europe, Ceylon (now Sri Lanka), Mexico and numerous tribal areas provide the most tragic examples of Christian atrocities committed by men

66. A I 167–168/AN 3.60.6.

apparently sincere in the belief that they were serving God. Likewise for the Moslem faith. More recently, communists with apparently genuine convictions of the rightness of the socialist state have been equally ruthless. A more subtle but common occurrence of this same phenomenon is seen in the everyday process of child raising. Parents, convinced that their particular habits, ideals, mores and customs are the best, too often attempt to mould their children into the same patterns. Sometimes the persuasions are deliberate, direct and suppressive; other times unconscious, covert and insidious. But in either case it is an attempt by one party to force its ways upon another. Sometimes this is done with relative success and harmony, but sometimes with tragedy and heartache to all concerned. Thus the Buddha advised:

> But, Cunda, that one who himself is in the mire should pull out of the mire another sunk therein—this, verily, is an unheard-of thing. But that one himself clear of the slough should be able to lift out of the slough another foundered therein—such a thing may well be. And that one who himself is not subdued, not disciplined, has not attained the Extinction of Delusion, should cause others to become subdued, and disciplined, to attain to the Extinction of Delusion—such a thing has never been known. But that one, himself controlled, trained, delivered from delusion, should lead others to become controlled and trained, lead them to Deliverance from Delusion—such a thing may very well be.
>
> *Sallekha Sutta*, M I 45 /MN 8

Escapist

Akin to the problem of selfishness is that of escapism. The label "escapist" is one commonly used by critics of Theravāda Buddhism, and, as with selfishness, the problem must first be dealt with in terms of semantics. Again referring to the pleasure-pain principle, half of life is escapist in that it is an attempt to avoid *dukkha* (suffering). A man who takes aspirin does so to escape the pain of his headache, and a large part of obeying customs and rules is done to avoid either reproach and punishment or to avoid one's own feelings of guilt. Thus in this sense of the word, Buddhism is very decidedly escapist, for its primary concern is to free men from *dukkha*. However, in addition to their literal meanings the words "escapist" and "escapism" almost always bear connotations of cowardice or of shirking one's duty. Thus when asked whether or not his religion is escapist, a Buddhist is placed in a position where an answer the affirmative will admit to an unsteated and unwarranted value judgment.

If escapist means shirking one's duty, then let us examine the concept of duty. Duty and obedience receive little mention in the Pāli Canon and are not proclaimed as virtues.[67] In Buddhist teaching each being is free to act as each such being sees fit but should first be aware of the nature and consequences of its actions. Duty is not something which exists in nature but rather is a social construct more or less necessary for the preservation of family, tribe and nation. While in an absolute sense, duty itself may not be real, from an experiential position what is real is the feeling or sense of duty which men acquire through social conditioning. Thus in World War I, the German soldier was compelled by duty to kill Frenchmen, while the Frenchman was equally duty-bound to kill Germans. Likewise in the 1960s when an East German escaped to the West, in the eyes of the West he was a hero who underwent dangers and hardships to realize a better way of life. But from the East German position the same man was an escapist, who for selfish motives fled his duties to the people and the socialist state.

If a man should hold dual citizenship in two countries and finds that he must relinquish one of the two, it is easy to imagine that citizens of the rejected nation might find it difficult to be sympathetic and understanding of his choice. Such a reaction would result from ethnocentrism, provincialism and a lack of familiarity with the world beyond their own. Likewise, when a man experiences Nirvāna and chooses it in preference to *saṃsāra*, how are we, who know only the one world and not the other, able to criticize his decision?

---

67. *Sacred Books of the Buddhists,* Vol. IV, *Dialogues of the Buddha Part III* (D III), translated by T. W. Rhys Davids (London: The Pali Text Society, 1957), p. 181.

For all that is said about one's duty to society, it is unusual to find a man whose primary concern is not his own prosperity and happiness. And when a man does loudly proclaim the virtues of duty, we may question to what extent he is only parroting contemporary mores, attempting to win social approval or reacting to guilt feelings which have resulted from the exploitation of one's fellow men. Psychiatrically it is known that those who most strongly adhere to the concept of duty suffer from compulsive personality structures. Such persons fear their own feelings and spontaneity; thus their compulsiveness, excessive morality and preoccupation with duty are but defences used to control their own mistrusted feelings.[68] It is man's socially acquired sense of shame or guilt followed by his desire to avoid (that is, to escape) this feeling that gives the sense of duty such powerful control over human behaviour.

If there is a higher duty than social mores, it is not duty per se, but compassion. For it is compassion that inspires us to help others regardless of the boundaries of culture, race, nation or species. The virtue performed by compassion is thus spontaneous and genuine, rather than forced, premeditated or dutiful. Again if we consider the decades of tireless service to humanity as lived by the Buddha and the other *arahants*, how can we say they did not perform their "duty" to the world.

VII. The Motive and the Means

Throughout this essay three important matters have come into focus. First is the emphasis which Buddhism gives to experience as the basis of both knowledge and spiritual progress. Second, from this experiential background emerges the pleasure-pain principle as the primary concern of life. Third, Nirvāna can be known and understood only by direct experience, and since it can only be known in this way, neither I nor any of the readers of this essay (unless there be *arahants* among you) have any certainty that it is real.

68. *Modern Clinical Psychiatry*, op. cit., pp. 62–63.

With these facts in mind let us turn our attention to two remaining problems that need consideration concerning Nirvāna. First, why should one deny oneself many of life's comforts and joys and endure years of effort and discipline to attain something which may not exist? Second, if Nirvāna is realized only by the abolition of all cravings and desires, what about the desire for Nirvāna itself, the very thing which makes us seek Nirvāna: is not this also a selfish desire?

The problem is not one of attachment to Nirvāna per se, but rather it is a problem of being attached to the thought or idea of Nirvāna. Thus the Buddha comments on the mind of one who is spiritually untrained and undeveloped:

> He recognizes Nirvāna as Nirvāna. Having recognized Nirvāna as Nirvāna he thinks of Nirvāna; he thinks in [the idea of] Nirvāna; he thinks [of self as] Nirvāna; he thinks, "Nirvāna is mine"; he is satisfied with Nirvāna. What is the reason for this? I say that it is not thoroughly understood by him.

Then in contrast he speaks of an *arahant*, one for whom Nirvāna is a reality:

> He directly knows Nirvāna as Nirvāna. From directly knowing Nirvāna as Nirvāna he does not think of Nirvāna, he does not think in [the idea of] Nirvāna; he does not think [of self as] Nirvāna; he does not think "Nirvāna is mine." He does not delight in Nirvāna. What is the reason for this? I say it is because it is thoroughly understood by him.
>
> *Mūlapariyāya Sutta*, M I 4 /MN 1

Perhaps the two questions above are best answered by letting the Pāli Canon speak for itself. In the Majjhima Nikāya we find the following dialogue between the Buddha and the wanderer, Māgandiya. The latter has made the accusation that the Buddha "is a destroyer of life," to which the Buddha replies:

> "Māgandiya, the eye delights in material shapes, is delighted by material shapes, rejoices in material shapes; it is tamed, watched, guarded and controlled by a Tathāgata, and he teaches a Doctrine for its control. Was it on account of

this, Māgandiya, that you said, 'The recluse, Gotama, is a destroyer of life?'"

"Just on account of this did I say, good Gotama, 'The recluse Gotama is a destroyer of life.'"

(As for eye and material shapes, the same is then repeated for sounds, smells, tastes, touch and mental states. The Buddha then continues:)

"What do you think about this, Māgandiya? Suppose someone formerly revelled in material shapes cognizable by the eye, agreeable, pleasant, desired, enticing, connected with sensual pleasure, alluring. After a time, having known the coming to be and passing away of material shapes and the satisfaction in them, and the peril of them and the way of escape from them as it really is, getting rid of craving for material shapes, suppressing the fever for material shapes, he should live devoid of lust, his mind inwardly calmed. What have you, Māgandiya, to say of him?"

"Nothing, good Gotama."

(And again the same is repeated for sounds, smells and so forth:)

"Now I, Māgandiya, when I was formerly a householder, endowed and provided with five strands of sense-pleasures, revelled in them: in material shapes cognizable by the eye, agreeable, pleasant ... in sounds cognizable by the ear ... in smells cognizable by the nose ... in tastes cognizable by the tongue ... in touches cognizable by the body, agreeable, pleasant, desired, enticing, connected with sensual pleasures, alluring. I had three palaces, Māgandiya, one for the rains, one for the cold season, one for the hot weather. During the four months of the rains, being delighted in the palace for the rains by women musicians, I did not come down from that palace. But after a time, knowing the coming to be and passing away of sense-pleasures, and the satisfaction in them and the peril of them and the way of escape from them as it really is, getting rid of the craving for sense-pleasures, suppressing the fever of sense-pleasures, I lived devoid of lust, my mind inwardly calmed. I saw other beings not yet devoid of attachment to sense-pleasures, who were pursuing sense-pleasures: they were being consumed by craving for

> sense-pleasures, burning with the fever of sense-pleasures. I did not envy them. I had no delight in those things. What was the reason for this? It was, Māgandiya, that there is this delight which, apart from pleasures of the senses, apart from unskilled states of mind, attains and remains in a god-like happiness. Delighting in this delight, I do not envy what is low. I have no delight in that.
>
> *Māgandiya Sutta*, M II 503–505/MN 75

And to the monks he spoke:

> The eye is burning, visible objects are burning, eye-consciousness is burning, eye-contact is burning, also whatever is felt as pleasant or painful, or neither painful nor pleasant, that arises with eye-contact as its essential support, that too is burning. Burning with what? Burning with the fire of craving, with the fire of hate, with the fire of delusion. I say it is burning with birth, ageing and death, with sorrow, with lamentation, with pain, grief and despair.

And likewise for sounds, mental states and so forth:

> Monks, when a noble follower who has heard sees thus, he finds aversion in the eye, finds aversion in forms, finds aversion in eye-consciousness, finds aversion in eye-contact, and whatever is felt as painful or pleasant, or neither painful nor pleasant, that arises with eye-contact for its essential support, in that too he finds aversion.

And again for sounds and so forth:

> When he finds aversion, passion fades out. With the fading out of passion he is liberated. When liberated there is knowledge that he is liberated: he understands: "Birth is exhausted, the holy life has been lived, what was to be done has been done, of this there is no more beyond."
>
> Mahāvagga I 21/Vinaya I 34 /SN 35:28

Another version of the same theme occurs in the Saṃyutta Nikāya. Here the Buddha explains how the causal law of dependent origination leads to birth and suffering. Suffering inspires one to trust in the Dhamma, and this in turn gives rise to joy. Joy results in rapture; rapture produces serenity; and serenity results in happiness, which in turn makes for concentration. From concentration arises the knowledge and vision of things as they really are, and this makes for repulsion. Repulsion creates passionlessness, and passionlessness results in liberation.[69]

Thus the scriptures quite clearly provide the solution to the two questions stated above. One does not realize Nirvāna by becoming obsessed with the quest for a transcendental ideal. The Buddhist approach differs from that of some of the bhakti schools of Hinduism, for in bhakti writings we are told that man finds divinity only when his whole being cries out in fervent emotion for the divine, as one whose head is held under water, craves in desperation for air. In contrast, the Buddhist approach is one of confronting each state of consciousness with the close scrutiny of insight and mindfulness, and in so doing, perceiving the unsatisfactory nature of such states and then relinquishing them for this reason alone. Unwholesome mental conditions are abandoned because of their own inherent defects and dangers, not at the bidding of supernatural revelation nor because a reward is promised in a hypothetical life to come. Nor is there a problem of denying oneself present happiness without any compensation. The rewards are immediate. Each forward step is a goal warranted by its own intrinsic merits; this is so, even though all we can say of Nirvāna is that those who have walked the path before us have said that if we follow the course to its maximum possible realization, then something occurs which is beyond all description, a "something" well worth knowing. Nirvāna is found by fully understanding the pleasure-pain principle, stripping it of the delusions it gives rise to and thus putting oneself beyond its influence.

Thus we have resolved St. Augustine's dilemma (see Ch. V). Desire is not conquered by repression, nor by prayer, nor by ideology; for such techniques do not circumvent our lingering thirst for satisfaction. They cannot resolve the ambivalence which they themselves have created. Rather the solution is given by the Buddha when he says that desire is overcome by foreseeing its result, "penetrating it by insight and seeing it plain."[70] Seeing

69. S II 30–31/SN 12:23.

70. A I 264/AN 3:110.

it plain is seeing its pain, and desire is thus willfully abandoned because of what it is in and of itself.

The essence of Buddhist practice rests upon the empirical facts of *saṃsāra*, one's own experience. Faith in something which nobody has been able to experience and testify to is unnecessary; rather there must be faith in one's ability to master one's cravings and faith in the worth of the effort. An essential aspect of the Dhamma is mindfulness, the first of the seven factors of enlightenment (see Ch. VI). In simplified language it is repeatedly and persistently taking a good hard look at things, especially at oneself and one's own feelings in particular. It is the maximum possible degree of self-honesty and consequently one of the most difficult of all things to achieve.

While mindfulness which results in insight is the keynote of liberation, the problem is really more complicated than that. It is complicated because each human being is complicated. Each of us has many distinct and diverse levels to each one's psyche, and each of these levels must be dealt with in a manner appropriate to it alone. Our states of consciousness are continually changing from hour to hour, minute to minute, second to second. There is no single rule of practice to apply to all persons at all times. Thus the Buddha repeatedly emphasized that training can only be done now, in the immediate present:

> How is the solitary life perfected in detail? It is when that which is past is put away; when that which is future is given up; and when, with regard to present self-states that we have got, will and passion have been thoroughly mastered. It is thus that the solitary life is perfected in detail.
>
> S II 283/SN 36:10

And again:

> Do not hark back to things that passed,
> And for the future cherish not fond hopes:
> The past was left behind by thee,
> The future state has yet to come.
> But who with vision clear can see
> The present which is here and now,

Such a wise one should aspire to win
What never can be lost nor shaken.

Bhaddekaratta Sutta, M III 187/MN 131

With this we are now prepared to discuss one final problem regarding the Dhamma, and that is the apparent contradiction between the ideals of love and compassion, and the ideal of non-attachment. The words "love" and "compassion" do not represent two single entities but rather a whole spectrum of feelings which differ from one another in ways so subtle as to often defy description. Love and compassion can be extremely pleasant and meaningful, and they can be effective antidotes to greed and hatred. Yet at other times they can carry us to unrealistic extremes, or lead to frustration if situations prevent their expression. Thus the correct application of love and compassion (and also of detachment and equanimity) is a matter of judgment and timing, as determined by one's particular state of mind at a given moment. While logically and philosophically compassion and non-attachment may be contradictory ideals, when one comes to actually living and practising the Dhamma, no conflict arises.

Despite the existence of *dukkha* (sorrow and discomfort), which is both inherent in, and generated by, passion and craving, there still remains the obvious fact that there is a level of pleasure in these states (or at least an expectation of pleasure). And it is primarily for this reason that we find it so very difficult to relinquish them. The solution is not one that can be proven by argument, logic or science. It can be proven only by oneself and to oneself, that is, to fully and mindfully note the nature and quality of those pleasures which are associated with lust and greed. One must behold them in their true form, free of any social, religious or personal assumptions as to their merits and demerits. In the same manner one makes the same impartial and penetrative observations of equanimity, happiness and *mettā*. On the basis of their own inherent features these latter pleasures (equanimity and so forth) are seen to be more wholesome, more meaningful and more truly satisfying than the pleasures of passion and greed. Furthermore, the very presence of greed, hatred, jealousy or lust excludes the possibility of the higher feelings existing at that same moment. Thus again one finds a true incentive to abandon desires.

There is no savior but oneself; the Dhamma simply invites us to come and see. It points the way, but we must follow.

To a six-year-old child, adult existence often appears dull, spiritless and uninteresting. He is incapable of appreciating most adult interests, and if deprived of playthings, playmates and stories, he will most likely lapse into apathy or depression. But ten years later he is an adolescent with an entirely different set of values and interests. He no longer cares for the childish things of the six-year-old; yet adult life still looks rather blank and pointless when compared with dancing, dating and drag races. Adult values will come in time and with them a natural loss of interest in adolescent pleasures. Thus the layman who finds it difficult to sympathize with the quietude and solitude of a Buddhist monk may reflect upon how his own life appears in the eyes of younger generations. Buddhism is pointing the way for maturation beyond that of the usual social norms. We advance to progressively higher and higher pleasure levels until we reach a state where even pleasure and happiness are transcended. In the *Cūḷasuññata Sutta*, the Buddha furnishes an explicit example beginning with the village life of a lay person, proceeding through a monk's life of solitude in the forest and then continuing on up through the highest states of *jhāna*, each level being successively relinquished for a more rewarding one, with Nirvāna as the end.[71] And in the Aṅguttara Nikāya the Buddha states:

> There are two kinds of happiness, O monks: the happiness of the householder and the happiness of the ascetic. But the greater of the two is the happiness of the ascetic.
>
> There are two kinds of happiness, O monks: the happiness of the senses and the happiness of renunciation. But the greater of the two is the happiness of renunciation.
>
> A I 80/AN 2:1–2

And from the *Dhammapada*:

> If by forsaking a lesser happiness,
> One may behold a greater happiness,

71. M III 104–108/MN *Cūlasuññata Sutta.*

Let the wise man renounce the lesser
Considering the greater.

Dhammapada 290

The journey to Nirvāna is not a sudden one. A thorough and harmonious restructuring of one's being can only come with time and patient endeavour. Thus we read the Buddha's words:

> Just as, bhikkhus, the mighty ocean deepens and slopes gradually down, hollow after hollow, not plunging by a sudden precipice, even so, bhikkhus, in this Dhamma-discipline the training is gradual, it goes step by step; there is no sudden penetration of insight.

Sona, Udāna 5.5, p. 54

And again:

By degrees, little by little, from time to time,
a wise man should remove his own impurities,
as a smith removes the dross from silver.

Dhammapada 239

VIII. The Buddhist Institution

In the preceding chapters, our discussion of Nirvāna has led us to touch upon nearly all other features of the Dhamma: karma, rebirth, ethics, insight practice, aesthetics and epistemology. To complete the picture let us say a few words about Buddhism as a social institution. From the time of the Buddha until the present day, Buddhists have fallen into two major groups. By far the larger group is lay people, who for all practical purposes are much like lay people of any other religion, except for their belief in Buddhist tenets. Among the laity, one finds a wide range of individual variations in the extent to which they understand and practise the Dhamma. It is not unusual to meet both male and female lay Buddhists whose knowledge, discipline and meditation excel those of most monks and nuns.

The monks at the time of the Buddha were not priests. That is, they had no ecclesiastical functions, took no part in rites, ceremonies or ritual and were discouraged from practising astrology, fortune-telling and magic. The purpose of instituting the monastic order was twofold. First it was intended to provide an environment and a way of life most conducive to progress towards Nirvāna. It freed one of the usual cares and obligations of lay people and provided maximum opportunity for training, study and meditation. Second, it was a means of preserving and propagating the teaching. A study of the Vinaya Rules, by which all Theravādin Buddhist monks are bound, reveals that these rules are not primarily moral precepts. Rather they are standards of discipline conducive to one's psychological development or else regulations necessary for maintaining the harmony, preservation and integrity of a large and growing social body.

Thus, from its very conception the monastic order had two missions: one was to learn and practise the Dhamma; the other was to preserve this knowledge and give it to all who wished to hear. Though magic and ritual have since become a part of nearly every Buddhist sect, we still find nations, such as Thailand and Sri Lanka, where the original purposes of the order are still recognized as the primary ones. One need not be a monk or nun to realize Nirvāna. The Suttas list at least twenty- one persons who reached the goal while still laymen.[72] But if one seriously intent on spiritual progress can free himself of social obligations, gain family permission (from his parents if young or from his wife if married), and can meet the other standards necessary for admission to the Order (freedom from debt, insanity and contagious diseases)[73] then the life of a monk or nun is the one which provides the best chances for realizing the goal.

72. A III 451/AN 6:131–151). Commentary to the *Dhammapada* 142.
73. Vinaya I 39–71/ Mahāvagga 72–91.

The Kūṭadanta Sutta: On True Sacrifice

A Discourse from the Dīgha Nikāya

Translated by
Prof. T.W. Rhys Davids

WHEEL PUBLICATION NO. 120

Abbreviations

Com.:	Ācariya Buddhaghosa's Commentary to the Dīgha Nikāya called *Sumaṅgalavilāsinī*
Ed.:	BPS Editor
NewSubCom:	New Sub-commentary (*abhinava-ṭīkā*), by Ñāṇābhivaṃsa Mahāthera, written in Burma in the 19th century

From the Introduction

By Prof. T. W. Rhys Davids

Whoever put this Sutta together must have been deeply imbued with a spirit of subtle irony that plays no less a part in the Suttas than it does in so many of the Jātakas. I have already called attention to the great importance of the right understanding of early Buddhist teaching, of a constant appreciation of this sort of subtle humour. Hitherto, it has been (so far as I am aware) entirely overlooked in the Suttas. Every one recognizes it in the Jātaka tales, though. The humour is not at all intended to raise a laugh, scarcely even a smile. The aroma of it pervades the whole of the exposition. It is none the less delightful because of the very serious earnestness of the narrator. The ethical point at issue, however, is apt to be lost sight of precisely because of that earnestness. And just as a joke may be explained but the point of it spoilt in the process, so in the attempt to write about this irony (much more delicate than any joke), one runs great danger of smothering it under the explanatory words. The attempt, nevertheless, must be made.

What is the special point in this fun, a kind of fun quite unknown in the West? It is the piquancy of the contrast between the mock seriousness of the extravagant, even impossible, details, and the real serious earnestness of the ethical tone. The fun of the extravagance can be matched, easily enough, in European and (especially) in American humour. The piquancy of this contrast is Indian, and especially Buddhist.

The whole legend is obviously invented ad hoc. Its details are not meant to be taken seriously as historical fact. The forced twist given to the meaning of the words *vidhā* and *parikkhāro* is not serious. The words could not be used in the new sense assigned. What we have is a sort of pun, a play upon the words, a piece of dialectic smartness, delightful to the hearers then, and unfortunately quite impossible to be rendered adequately in English prose for readers now.

And it is quite open to question whether this does not apply as much to the whole Sutta as to the legend of King Wide-Realm.

The Brahman Kūṭadanta (pointed-tooth) is mentioned nowhere else and is very likely meant to be rather the hero of a tale than an historical character. In that case we would have before us a novelette, an historical romance, in which the Very Reverend Sir Goldstick Sharp-tooth, lord of the manor of Khānumata (cruel enough, no doubt, and very keen on being sure that his "soul" should be as comfortable in the next world as he was, now, in this), makes up his mind to secure that most desirable end by the murder of a number of his fellow creatures in honour of a god, or as he would put it, by celebrating a sacrifice.

In order to make certain that not one of the technical details (for to the accurate performance of all these the god was supposed to attach great weight) should be done wrongly, the intending sacrificer is ironically represented as doing the very last thing any Brahman of position, under similar circumstances, would think of doing. He goes to the *samaṇa* Gotama for advice about the modes of the ritual to be performed at the sacrifice, the requisite utensils, and the altar-furniture.

The Buddha's answer is to tell him a wonderful legend of a King Wide-Realm, and of the sacrifice he offered, truly the most extraordinary sacrifice imaginable. All its marvelous details (each one settled, be it noted, on the advice of a Brahman) are described with a deliberate extravagance, none the less delicious because of the evident earnestness of the moral to be inferred.

The Brahman of our Sutta wants to know the three modes in which the ritual is to be performed. The three "modes" are declared in the legend (§15) to be simply three conditions of mind, or rather one condition of mind at three different times: the harbouring of no regret before, during, or after the sacrifice, at the expenditure involved. And the material accessories required (the altar-furniture, the priest's outfit), what is that? It is the hearty co-operation with the king of four divisions of his people: the nobles, officials, Brahmans, and householders. That makes four articles of furniture, and eight personal qualifications of the king himself. That makes another eight. And four personal qualifications of his advising Brahman make up the total of the sixteen articles required. No living thing, either animal or vegetable, is injured. All the labour is voluntary; and all the world co-operates in adding its share to the largesse of food, on strict vegetarian principles, in which alone the sacrifice consists. It is offered on behalf of not only the king himself but all the gods. The king desires to propitiate, not any god, but living men. And the muttering of mystic verses over each article used, and over mangled and bleeding bodies of unhappy victims, verses on which all the magic efficacy of a sacrifice had been supposed to depend, is quietly ignored.

It is all ironical, of course, and is the very contrary (in every respect) of a typical Vedic sacrifice. And the evident unreality of the legend may be one explanation of the curious fact that the authors of the Jātaka book (notwithstanding that King Wide-Realm's chaplain is actually identified in the Sutta with the Buddha himself in a previous birth) have not included this professedly Jātaka story in their collection. This is the only case, so far discovered, in which a similar omission has been made.

Having thus laughed the Brahman ideal of sacrifice out of court with the gentle irony of a sarcastic travesty, the author or authors of the Sutta go on to say what they think a sacrifice ought to be. Far from exalting King Wide-Realm's procedure, they put his sacrifice at the very bottom of a long list of sacrifices, each better than the other and leading up to the sweetest and highest of all: the attainment of Arahantship.

Here again, except in the last paragraph, there is nothing exclusively Buddhist. That a sacrifice of the heart is better than a sacrifice of bullocks, the ethical more worthy than any physical sacrifice, is simply the sensible, rational, human view of the matter. The whole long history of the development of Indian thought, as carried on chiefly by Brahmans (however much it may have owed in the earliest period to the nobles and others), shows that they, the more enlightened and cultured of the Brahmans, were not only as fully alive to this truth as any Buddhist, but that they took it for granted all along.

Even in the Vedas themselves there is already the germ of this view in the mental attitude as regards Aditi and Varuṇa. In the pre-Buddhistic *Chāndogya*, in the mystic identification of the sacrifice with man,[1] we find certain moral states placed on an equality with certain parts of the sacrificial procedure. Among these moral states, *ahiṃsā*, the habit of causing no injury to any

1. *Chāndogya Upanishad* 111, 16 and 17.

living thing, is especially mentioned. This comes very near to the Hebrew prophet's "I will have mercy and not sacrifice."[2]

The more characteristically Indian point of view is, no doubt (in the words of the old saying long afterwards taken up by the *Mahābhārata*), that it is truth and not mercy that outweighs a thousand sacrifices.[3] But there is a very great probability that the ahiṃsā doctrine, foreshadowed in the *Upanishad*, and afterwards so extravagantly taken up by the Niganṭhas, the Jains of the Buddha's time, was also a part of the earlier Jain doctrine, and therefore not only in germ, but as a developed teaching, pre-Buddhist. Though the Buddhists did not accept this extreme position, there would seem to be no valid reason for doubting the accuracy of the Buddhist tradition that their view of sacrifice was based on a very ancient belief which was, in fact, common ground to the wise, whether inside or outside the ranks of the Brahmans.

Our Sutta is, then, merely the oldest extant expression, in so thorough and uncompromising a way, of an ancient and widely held trend of opinion. On this question, as on the question of caste or social privileges, the early Buddhists took up, and pushed to its logical conclusions, a rational view held also by others. And on this question of sacrifice their party won. The Vedic sacrifices of animals had practically been given up when the long struggle between Brahmanism and Buddhism reached its close. Isolated instances of such sacrifices are known even down to the Mohammedan invasion. But the battle was really won by the Buddhists and their allies. And the combined ridicule and earnestness of our Sutta will have had its share in bringing about the victory.

That they did win is a suggestive fact. How could they have done so if the Indians of that time had been, as is so often asserted of them by European writers, more deeply addicted to all manner of ritual than any other nation under heaven, more superstitious, more averse to change in religious ceremonial? There seems to me no reason to believe that they were very different in these respects from the Greeks or Romans of the same period. On the contrary, there was a well-marked lay feeling, a wide-spread antagonism

---

2. Hosea 6:6, quoted in Matt. 9:13 and 12:7. See also Micah 6:6-8. Prov. 15:8 and 21:13 are, of course, later.

3. *Mahābhārata* I, 3095 nearly = XIII, 1544. Compare XIII, 6073.

to the priests, a real sense of humour, a strong fund of common sense. Above all there was the most complete and unquestioned freedom of thought and expression in religious matters that the world had yet witnessed. To regard the Indian peoples through Brahman spectacles, to judge them from the tone prevalent in the Srauta and Grihya Sūtras, it would seem impossible that this victory could have been won. But it was won. And our views of Indian history must be modified accordingly.

Kūṭadanta Sutta
(Dīgha Nikāya 5)

The Wrong Sacrifice and the Right Sacrifice

1. Thus have I heard. The Blessed One, when going on a tour through Magadha with a great multitude of the brethren, came to a Brahman village in Magadha called Khāṇumata. And there at Khāṇumata he lodged in the Ambalaṭṭhikā park.[4]

Now at that time the Brahman Kūṭadanta was dwelling at Khāṇumata, a place teeming with life, with much grassland and woodland and water and corn, on a royal domain presented to him by Seniya Bimbisāra, the king of Magadha, as a royal gift, a full gift, with power over it as if he were the king.

And just then a great sacrifice was being made ready on behalf of Kūṭadanta, the Brahman. And seven hundred bulls, seven hundred steers, seven hundred heifers, seven hundred goats, and seven hundred rams had been brought to the post for the sacrifice.

2. Now the Brahmans and householders of Khāṇumata heard the news of the arrival of the Samaṇa Gotama. And they began to leave Khāṇumata in companies and in bands to go to the Ambalaṭṭhikā park.

3. And just then Kūṭadanta, the Brahman, had gone apart to the upper terrace of his house for his siesta; and seeing the people go by, he asked his doorkeeper the reason. And the doorkeeper told him.

4. Then Kūṭadanta thought, "I have heard that the Samaṇa Gotama understands the successful performance of a sacrifice with its threefold method and its sixteen accessory instruments. Now I don't know all this, and yet I want to carry out a sacrifice. It would be well for me to go to the Samaṇa Gotama and ask him about it."

---

4. Ambalaṭṭhikā, "the mango sapling." According to Com. to DN 1, it was a shady park, surrounded by a rampart and provided with a rest house. At the entrance stood a young mango tree, after which the park was named. The Com. says that this park was not the same as the one half way between Rājagaha and Nālandā, mentioned in DN 1, but was very similar to it. (Ed.)

So he sent his doorkeeper to the Brahmans and householders of Khānumata to ask them to wait till he could go with them to call upon the Blessed One.

5. But there were at that time a number of Brahmans staying at Khānumata to take part in the great sacrifice.

[And[5] when they heard that Kūṭadanta was intending to visit the Samaṇa Gotama, they went to Kūṭadanta and asked whether that was so.

"That is my intention, Sirs. I propose to call on the Samaṇa Gotama."

"Let not the Venerable Kūṭadanta do so. It is not fitting for him to do so. If it were the Venerable Kūṭadanta who went to call upon him, then the Venerable Kūṭadanta's reputation would decrease and the Samaṇa Gotama's would increase. This is the first reason why you, Sir, should not call upon him, but he upon you."

6. And they laid before Kūṭadanta, the Brahman, in like manner other considerations:

That he was well born on both sides, of pure descent through the mother and through the father back through seven generations, with no slur put upon him, and no reproach, in respect of birth,

That he was prosperous, well to do, and rich,

That he was a Vedic scholar,[6] knowing the mystic verses by heart, one who has mastered the Three Vedas, with the indices, the ritual, the word-analysis [the *Atharva Veda* as a fourth, and the legends as a fifth],[7] learned in the words and in the grammar,

---

5. The passage in square brackets, extending up to paragraph 8 inclusive, has been supplemented here from the preceding text, the Soṇadaṇḍa Sutta, as this stock passage is not repeated in the Pāli editions nor Rhys Davids' English translation of the Kūṭadanta Sutta. Apart from changing the name of the Brahman, only a very few alterations have been made in the translation. (Ed.)

6. A Vedic scholar (*ajjhāyako*). Com. to DN 3: "Because the learned Brahmans no longer meditate [*na jhāyanti*], they are now called 'scholars,' [or] 'just scholars' [*ajjhāyakā tveva*]. Thus, at an earlier age, this expression '*ajjhāyaka*' arose as a word of blame for those Brahmans who were without attainment of the absorptions [*jhāna*]. But now it is used as a word of praise, in the sense of its derivation from the verb *ajjhāyati*, 'to recite,' i.e., for those who recite the [Vedic] mantras." (Ed.)

7. In view of the fact that only three terms precede it, the Com. says that the *Athārva Veda* has to be added here as the fourth. (Ed.)

versed in Lokāyata (nature lore/sophistry)[8] and in the theory of the signs on the body of a great man,[9]

That he was handsome, pleasant to look upon, inspiring trust, gifted with great beauty of complexion, fair in colour, fine in presence, stately to behold,

That he was virtuous, rich in virtue, gifted with rich virtue,

That he had a pleasant voice and pleasing delivery, and was gifted with polite address, distinct, not husky, suitable for making clear the matter in hand,

That he was the teacher of the teachers of many, instructing three hundred Brahmans in the repetition of the mystic verses, and that many young Brahmans, from various directions and various countries, all craving for the verses, came to learn them by heart under him,

That he was aged, old, well advanced in years, long lived, and full of days,

That he was honoured, considered to be important, esteemed worthy, venerated, and revered by Pokkharasādi the Brahman,

That he dwelt at Khāṇumata, a place teeming with life, with much grassland and woodland and corn, on a royal fief granted him by Seniya Bimbisāra, king of Magadha, as a royal gift with power over it as if he were the king.

For each of these reasons it was not fitting that Kūṭadanta, the Brahman, should call upon the Samaṇa Gotama, but rather that the Samaṇa Gotama should call upon him.[10]

---

8. *Lokāyata*: materialist philosophers speculating on the world (*loka*) or nature, and often using sophistry (*vitaṇḍasattha*) in their arguments. (Ed.)

9. The thirty-two Signs (or Marks) of a Great Man (*mahāpurisa-lakkhaṇa*) are of pre-Buddhist origin and partly of a symbolic nature. They are enumerated and explained in the *Lakkhaṇa Sutta* of the Dīgha Nikāya. (Ed.)

10. Com. to DN 4: "[The Brahmans when speaking in that way, did so because they thought:] 'There is none who does not like it when one's praise is spoken. Hence by praising him we might stop him from going to see the Buddha.' [But Kūṭadanta thought:] 'These Brahmans praise me on account of my descent, etc. But it will not be right for me to be taken in by such praise. Should I not counter their speech by proclaiming to them the greatness of the Buddha which may induce them to call on him likewise?'" (Ed.)

7. And when they had thus spoken, Kūṭadanta said to them:

"Then, Sirs, listen, and hear why it is fitting that I should call upon the Venerable Gotama, and not he that should call upon me.

"Truly, Sirs, the Venerable Gotama is well born on both sides, of pure descent through the mother and through the father back through seven generations, with no slur put upon him, and no reproach, in respect of birth.

"Truly, Sirs, the Samaṇa Gotama has gone forth [into the religious life], giving up the great clan of his relations.

"Truly, Sirs, the Samaṇa Gotama has gone forth [into the religious life], giving up much money and gold, treasure both buried and above the ground.

"Truly, Sirs, the Samaṇa Gotama, while he was still a young man, without a grey hair on his head, in the beauty of his early manhood, has gone forth from the household life into the homeless state.

"Truly, Sirs, the Samaṇa Gotama, though his father and mother were unwilling, and wept, their cheeks being wet with tears, nevertheless cut off his hair and beard, and donned the yellow robes, and went out from the household life into the homeless state.

"Truly, Sirs, the Samaṇa Gotama is handsome, pleasant to look upon, inspiring trust, gifted with great beauty of complexion, fair in colour, fine in presence, stately to behold.

"Truly, Sirs, the Samaṇa Gotama is virtuous with the virtue of the Arahats, good and virtuous, gifted with goodness and virtue.

"Truly, Sirs, the Samaṇa Gotama has a pleasant voice, and a pleasing delivery, he is gifted with polite address, distinct, not husky, suitable for making clear the matter in hand.

"Truly, Sirs, the Samaṇa Gotama is the teacher of the teachers of many.

"Truly, Sirs, the Samaṇa Gotama has no passion of lust left in him, and has put away all fickleness of mind.

"Truly, Sirs, the Samaṇa Gotama believes in karma, and in action; he is one who puts righteousness in the forefront [of his exhortations] to the Brahman race.

"Truly, Sirs, the Samaṇa Gotama went forth from a distinguished family, earliest among the Khattiya clans.

"Truly, Sirs, the Samaṇa Gotama went forth from a family prosperous, well to do, and rich.

"Truly, Sirs, people come right across the country from distant lands to ask questions of the Samaṇa Gotama.

"Truly, Sirs, multitudes of heavenly beings put their trust in the Samaṇa Gotama.

"Truly, Sirs, such is the high reputation voiced abroad concerning the Samaṇa Gotama, that he is said to be an Arahat, exalted, fully awakened, abounding in wisdom and righteousness, happy, with knowledge of the worlds, a Blessed One, a Buddha.

"Truly, Sirs, the Samaṇa Gotama has all the thirty-two bodily marks of a Great Being.

"Truly, Sirs, the Samaṇa Gotama bids all men welcome, is congenial, conciliatory, not supercilious, accessible to all, not hesitant in conversation.

"Truly, Sirs, the Samaṇa Gotama is honoured, held of weight, esteemed and venerated and revered by the four classes [of his followers, viz. the brothers and sisters of the Order, laymen and laywomen].

"Truly, Sirs, many gods and men believe in the Samaṇa Gotama.

"Truly, Sirs, in whatsoever village or town the Samaṇa Gotama stays, there the non-humans do the humans no harm.

"Truly, Sirs, the Samaṇa Gotama, as the head of an Order, of a school, as the teacher of a school, is to be acknowledged superior to all the founders of sects. Whereas some Samaṇas and Brahmans have gained a reputation by all sorts of insignificant matters, not so the Samaṇa Gotama. His reputation comes from perfection in knowledge and conduct.

"Truly, Sir, the king of Magadha, Seniya Bimbisāra, with his children and his wives, with his people and his courtiers, has put his trust in the Samaṇa Gotama.

"Truly, Sirs, King Pasenadi of Kosala, with his children and his wives, with his people and his courtiers, has put his trust in the Samaṇa Gotama.

"Truly, Sirs, Pokkharasādi, the Brahman, with his children and his wives, with his people and his intimates, has put his trust in the Samaṇa Gotama.

"Truly, Sirs, the Samaṇa Gotama is honoured, held of weight, esteemed and venerated and revered alike by Seniya Bimbisāra, the king of Magadha, by Pasenadi the king of Kosala, and by Pokkharasādi, the Brahman.

"Truly, Sirs, the Samaṇa Gotama has now arrived at Khāṇumata, and is staying at Ambalaṭṭhikā. But all Samaṇas and Brahmans who come into our village are our guests. And guests we ought to esteem and honour, to venerate and revere. And as he is now come as a guest, he ought to be so treated, as a guest.

"For each and all of these considerations it is not fitting that the Samaṇa Gotama should call upon us, but rather we should call upon him. Only this much do I know of the excellences of the Samaṇa Gotama; but these are not all of them, for his excellence is beyond measure."

8. And when he had thus spoken, those Brahmans said to him, "The Venerable Kūṭadanta declares the praises of the Samaṇa Gotama that, were he to be dwelling even a hundred leagues from here, it would be enough to make a believing man go to call upon him, even had he to carry a bag [with provisions for the journey] on his back. Let us then all go to call on the Samaṇa Gotama together!"

So Kūṭadanta, the Brahman, with a great company of Brahmans, went out to Ambalaṭṭhikā, where the Blessed One dwelt. Having arrived there he exchanged with the Blessed One the greetings and compliments of politeness and courtesy, and took his seat on one side. And as to the Brahman householders of Khāṇumata, some of them bowed to the Blessed One and took their seats on one side; some of them exchanged with him the greetings and compliments of politeness and courtesy and then took their seats on one side; some of them called out their name and family, and then took their seats on one side; and some of them took their seats on one side in silence.]

9. And when Kūṭadanta, the Brahman, was seated there he told the Blessed One what he had heard, and requested him to tell him about success in performing a sacrifice in its three modes and with its accessories of sixteen kinds.

"Well then, O Brahman, listen attentively and I will speak."

"Very well, Sir," said Kūṭadanta in reply and the Blessed One spoke as follows:

10. "Long ago, O Brahman, there was a king by name Wide-Realm [*Mahā Vijita*], mighty with great wealth and large property; with stores of silver and gold; of aids to enjoyment; of goods and corn; with his treasure-houses and his granaries full. Now, when

King Wide-Realm was once sitting alone, the following thought occurred to him: 'I have in abundance all the good things a mortal can enjoy. The whole wide circle of the earth is mine by conquest to possess. It would be well if I were to offer a great sacrifice that should ensure me well-being and welfare for many days.'

"And he had the Brahman, his chaplain, called; and telling him all that he had thought, he said:

'So I would wish, O Brahman, to offer a great sacrifice—let the Venerable One instruct me how—for my happiness and my welfare for many days.'

11. "Thereupon the Brahman who was chaplain said to the king, 'The king's country, Sire, is harassed and harried. There are robbers abroad who pillage the villages and townships, and who make the roads unsafe. Were the king, so long as that is so, to levy a fresh tax, truly His Majesty would be acting wrongly. But if His Majesty might think, "I'll soon put a stop to these scoundrels' game by degradation and banishment, and fines and bonds and death!" their crimes would not be satisfactorily stopped. The remnant left unpunished would still go on harassing the realm. Now there is one method to adopt to put a thorough end to this disorder. Whoever in the king's realm devote themselves to farming and keeping cattle, to them let His Majesty, the king, give food and seed-corn.[11] Whoever in the king's realm devote themselves to trade, to them let His Majesty, the king, give capital.[12] Whoever there be in the king's realm who devote themselves to government service, to them let His Majesty, the king, give wages and food.[13] Then those men, following each his own business, will no longer

11. "Let the king give food and seed-corn." **Com.**: "If what is given is insufficient, you should give them another supply of seed-grain, food, and agricultural implements." (Ed.)

12. "Let ... the king give capital." **Com.**: "You may give the money without witness or receipt [i.e., as a trade subsidy], waiving the repayment of the capital sum [*mūlacchejjavasena*]." (Ed.)

13. "[To those in government service] let ... the king give wages and food." **Com.**: "You may give to them their daily food requirements and a monthly or weekly [*anuposathika*] salary, together with official positions, grants of villages or hamlets, in accordance with each man's skill, type of work, and valour." (Ed.)

harass the realm; the king's revenue will go up; the country will be quiet and at peace; and the populace, pleased one with another and happy, dancing their children in their arms, will dwell with open doors.'[14]

"Then King Wide-Realm, O Brahman, accepted the word of his chaplain, and did as he had said. And those men, following each his business, harassed the realm no more. And the king's revenue went up. And the country became quiet and at peace. And the populace, pleased one with another and happy, dancing their children in their arms, dwelt with open doors.

12. "So King Wide-Realm had his chaplain called, and said: 'The disorder is at an end. Thanks to the provisions advised by the Venerable One, the revenue has increased. The country is at peace. I want to offer that great sacrifice—let the Venerable One instruct me how—for my well-being and welfare for many days.'

'Then let His Majesty, the king, send invitations to whomsoever there may be in his realm who are Khattiyas, vassals of his, either in the country or the towns; or who are ministers and officials of his, either in the country or the towns; or who are householders of substance, either in the country or the towns, saying, "I intend to offer a great sacrifice. Let the Venerable Ones give their sanction to what will be for me happiness and welfare for many days."'[15]

"Then King Wide-Realm, O Brahman, accepted the word of his chaplain, and did as he had said. And they each—Khattiyas, ministers, Brahmans, and householders—made the same reply,

'Let His Majesty, the king, celebrate the sacrifice. The time is suitable, O king!'

---

14. The chaplain's prescriptions for making the country prosperous and content sound quite modern: agricultural and trade subsidies, ensuring a contented civil service, and in §12 making sure of favourable public opinion before undertaking large expenditure. (Ed.)

15. **Com.**: "Those [invited to give their consent to the great sacrifice] will be pleased about it and will say, 'This king does not enforce the sacrifice in the thought that he is the master, but he informs us about it. How well does he act!' Without such information they might not even have shown themselves at the place of the sacrifice." (Ed.)

"Thus did these four, as colleagues by consent, become accessories to furnish forth that sacrifice.

13. "King Wide-Realm was gifted in the following eight ways:

"He was well born on both sides, on the mother's side and on the father's, of pure descent back through seven generations, and no slur was cast upon him, and no reproach, in respect of birth.

"He was handsome, pleasant in appearance, inspiring trust, gifted with great beauty of complexion, fair in colour, fine in presence, stately to behold.

"He was mighty, with great wealth, and large property, with stores of silver and gold, of aids to enjoyment, of goods and corn, with his treasure-houses and his granaries full.

"He was powerful, in command of an army, loyal and disciplined, in four divisions [of elephants, cavalry, chariots, and bowmen], burning up, I think, his enemies by his very glory.

"He was a believer,[16] and a generous giver, a lord of gifts,[17] keeping open house, a flowing spring from where Samaṇas and Brahmans, the poor and wayfarers, beggars, and petitioners might draw, a doer of good deeds.

"He was learned in all kinds of knowledge.

"He knew the meaning of what had been said, and could explain, 'This saying has such and such a meaning, and that such and such.'

"He was intelligent, expert and wise, and able to think out things, present or past or future.[18]

---

16. "A believer" (*saddho*). **Com.**: "He believes that charity bears fruit." (Ed.)

17. "A generous giver" (*dāyako*). **Com.**: "He is a hero [or determined] in giving [*dāna-sūra*]. He does not stop at the mere belief [that giving is good], but can actually renounce [the gift-object]."

18. "Able to think out things, present or past or future" (*paṭibalo atīta-anāgata-paccuppanne atthe cintetuṃ*). **Com.**: "Thinking, 'It is just because of meritorious actions done in the past, that I am now prosperous,' he was able to think out a thing [fact or advantage; *attha*] of the past. 'Doing a meritorious act now, I shall be able to obtain prosperity in the future.' Thus he thought about future advantage. 'Such a meritorious act is customary with good people; furthermore, I have wealth enough to do it, and I have also the intention of giving [*dāyaka-citta*].' Thus he was able to think about the present facts." (Ed.)

"And these eight gifts of his too became accessories to furnish forth that sacrifice.

14. "The Brahman, his chaplain, was gifted in the following four ways:

"He was well born on both sides, on the mother's and on the father's, of pure descent back through seven generations, with no slur cast upon him, and no reproach in respect of birth.

"He was a Vedic scholar who knew the mystic verses by heart, master of the Three Vedas, with the indices, the ritual, the word-analysis [the *Atharva Veda* as a fourth, and the legends as a fifth], learned in the idiom and the grammar, versed in *Lokāyata* [nature-lore] and in the marks on the body of a great man.

"He was virtuous, established in virtue, gifted with virtue that had grown great.

"He was intelligent, expert, and wise; foremost, or at least the second, among those who hold out the ladle.

"Thus these four gifts of his, too, became accessories to furnish forth that sacrifice.

15. "And further, O Brahman, the chaplain, before the sacrifice had begun, explained to King Wide-Realm the three modes:

'Should His Majesty, the king, before starting on the great sacrifice, feel any such regret as: "Great, alas, will be the portion of my wealth used up herein," let not the king harbour such regret. Should His Majesty, the king, when the great sacrifice has been offered, feel any such regret as, "Great, alas, has been the portion of my wealth used up herein," let not the king harbour such regret.'

"Thus did the chaplain, O Brahman, before the sacrifice had begun, explain to King Wide-Realm the three modes.

16. "And further, O Brahman, the chaplain, before the sacrifice had begun, in order to prevent any compunction that might afterwards, in ten ways, arise as regards those who had taken part therein, said: 'Now there will come to your sacrifice, Sire, men who destroy the life of living things, and men who do not; men who take what has not been given, and men who do not; men who act evilly in respect of lusts, and men who do not; men who speak lies, and men who do not; men who slander, and men who do not; men who speak rudely, and men who do not; men who speak about vain things, and men who do not; men who covet, and men who do not; men who have ill-will, and men who do not; men

whose views are wrong, and men whose views are right.[19] Of each of these let them, who do evil, alone with their evil. For them who do well, let Your Majesty offer; for them, Sire, arrange the rites; let the king gratify them; in them shall your heart within find peace.'

17. "And further, O Brahman, the chaplain, while the king was carrying out the sacrifice, instructed and aroused and incited and gladdened his heart in sixteen ways:

'Should there be people who should say of the king, as he is offering the sacrifice, "King Wide-Realm is celebrating sacrifice without having invited the four classes of his subjects, without himself having the eight personal gifts, without the assistance of a Brahman who has the four personal gifts," then would they speak not according to the fact. For, the consent of the four classes has been obtained, the king has the eight, and his Brahman has the four personal gifts. With regard to each and every one of these sixteen conditions the king may rest assured that it has been fulfilled. He can sacrifice, and be glad, and possess his heart in peace.'

18. "And further, O Brahman, at the sacrifice no oxen were slain, nor goats, nor fowls, nor fatted pigs, nor were any kinds of living creatures put to death; no trees were cut down to be used as posts, no Dabbha grasses mown to strew around the sacrificial spot. The slaves, messengers, and workmen employed there were not coerced by rods nor fear, nor carried on their work weeping with tears upon their faces. Whoever chose to help he worked; whoever chose not to help, worked not. What each chose to do he did; what they chose not to do, that was left undone. With ghee, and oil, and butter, and milk, and honey, and sugar only was that sacrifice accomplished.[20]

---

19. These are the Ten Courses of Action (*kammapatha*), unwholesome and wholesome. (Ed.)

20. While the Discourse does not relate in which way the sacrifice was finally performed, the Com. says that it took the form of a large food distribution in the royal city. Outside each of the four city gates, and in the centre of the city, large alms-halls were erected, and from sunrise until nightfall food and drink of a kind suited to the time of the day were distributed to all comers. For the preparation of the food the best ingredients, like ghee, oil, etc., were used. Those who wanted to take the food along with them were allowed to fill their vessels. In the evening, cloth, incense, and flowers were distributed. At

19. "And further, O Brahman, the Khattiya vassals, and the ministers and officials, and the Brahmans of position, and the householders of substance, whether of the country or of the towns, went to King Wide-Realm, taking with them much wealth, and said: 'This abundant wealth, Sire, we have brought here for the king's use. Let His Majesty accept it from our hands!'

'Sufficient wealth have I, my friends, laid up, the produce of taxation that is just. Do you keep yours, and take away more with you!'

"When they had thus been refused by the king, they went aside, and considered thus, one with the other: 'It would not be good for us now, were we to take this wealth away again to our own homes. King Wide-Realm is offering a great sacrifice. Let us too make an after-sacrifice!'

20. "So the Khattiyas established a continual largesse to the east of the king's sacrificial pit, and the officials to the south thereof, and the householders to the north thereof. And the things given, and the manner of their gift, were in all respects like the great sacrifice of King Wide-Realm himself.

"Thus, O Brahman, there was a fourfold co-operation, and King Wide-realm was gifted with eight personal gifts, and his officiating Brahman with four. And there were three modes of the giving of that sacrifice. This, O Brahman, is what is called the due celebration of a sacrifice in its threefold mode and with its accessories of sixteen kinds."

21. And when he had thus spoken, those Brahmans lifted up their voices in tumult, and said,

"How glorious the sacrifice, how pure its accomplishment!" But Kūṭadanta, the Brahman sat there in silence.

Then those Brahmans said to Kūṭadanta, "Why do you not approve the good words of the Samaṇa Gotama as well-said?"

"I do not fail to approve, for he who does not approve as well-said that which has been well-spoken by the Samaṇa Gotama, his head would split in two. But I was considering that the Samaṇa Gotama does not say, 'Thus have I heard,' nor 'Thus behoves it to be,'

several hundred locations in the city, large vessels with ghee, etc., were placed for everyone's use. In accordance with this explanation, the Com. takes the textual words "sacrificial pit" (*yaññāvāṭa*) as signifying alms halls. (Ed.)

but says only 'Thus it was then,' or 'It was like that then.' So I thought, 'For a certainty the Samaṇa Gotama himself must at that time have been King Wide-Realm, or the Brahman who officiated for him at that sacrifice.' Does the Venerable Gotama admit that he who celebrates such a sacrifice, or causes it to be celebrated, is reborn at the dissolution of the body, after death, into some state of happiness in heaven?"

"Yes, O Brahman, that I admit. And at that time I was the Brahman, who, as chaplain, had that sacrifice performed."

22. "Is there, O Gotama, any other sacrifice less difficult and less troublesome, with more fruit and more advantage still than this?"

"Yes, O Brahman, there is."

"And what, O Gotama, may that be?"

"The perpetual gifts kept up in a family where they are given specially to virtuous recluses."

23. "But what is the reason, O Gotama, and what the cause, why such perpetual giving specifically to virtuous recluses, and kept up in a family, are less difficult and troublesome, of greater fruit and greater advantage than that other sacrifice with its three modes and its accessories of sixteen kinds?"

"To the latter sort of sacrifice, O Brahman, neither will the Arahats go, nor such as have entered on the Arahat way. And why not? Because at such sacrifices, beating with sticks and seizing by the throat[21] take place. But they will go to the former, where such things are not. And therefore are such perpetual gifts above the other sort of sacrifice."

24. "And is there, O Gotama, any other sacrifice less difficult and less troublesome, of greater fruit and of greater advantage than either of these?"

"Yes, O Brahman, there is."

"And what, O Gotama, may that be?"

"The putting up of a dwelling place [*vihāra*] on behalf of the Order of all the four directions."

25. "And is there, O Gotama, any other sacrifice less difficult and less troublesome, of greater fruit and of greater advantage than each and all of these three?"

---

21. The attendants, at such a general largesse, says Buddhaghosa, push the recipients about, make them stand in a queue, and use violence in doing so. (**RD**)

"Yes, O Brahman, there is."

"And what, O Gotama, may that be?"

"He who with trusting heart takes his refuge in the Buddha, in the Teaching, and in the Order. That is a sacrifice better than open largesse, better than perpetual alms, better than the gift of a dwelling place."[22]

26. "And is there, O Gotama, any other sacrifice less difficult and less troublesome, of greater fruit and of greater advantage than all these four?"[23]

"When a man with trusting heart takes upon himself the precepts—abstention from destroying life; abstention from taking what has not been given; abstention from evil conduct in respect of lusts; abstention from lying words; abstention from strong,

---

22. **Com.**: "Though a monastery [*vihāra*] is donated just once, there is later on work still to do in connection with it, e.g., thatching and repairing it. But if one has taken the Refuge in the presence of one single bhikkhu, or the Sangha, or the full assembly of bhikkhus, it is taken once for all [*gahitaṃ eva hoti*]. There is no necessity of taking it repeatedly."

"But if one ... single bhikkhu." NewSubCom.: "This is said because that is the customary way for lay devotees (upāsaka) to take the Refuge, and because the act has a greater weight if done in that manner [i. e., if the Refuge is taken from a bhikkhu]. But it is said that if the lay devotees take the Refuge by themselves, it is just as valid."

"Though a monastery ... taking it repeatedly." NewSubCom.: "This is said for people of intelligence. For them, if they are proficient in understanding the significance of the Refuges, etc., the Refuge will be firm and unshakable."

Com.: "Because the merit of Taking Refuge consisting in the readiness to sacrifice even one's life for the Triple Gem bestows heavenly happiness, therefore it is said to be of 'greater fruit and advantage.'" (Ed.)

"The readiness ... for the Triple Gem." NewSubCom.: "Even if someone threatens to take the life of the lay devotee with a sharp sword, saying: 'If you do not give up the Refuge taken by you, I shall kill you!' the lay devotee should reply, 'Never shall I say that the Buddha is not the [truly] Enlightened One; that the Dhamma is not the [true] Teaching; that the Sangha is not the [true] Community of Saints.'"

"Bestows heavenly happiness." NewSubCom.: "This is only an example of the possible good results of Taking the Refuge."

23. **Com.**: "Having heard that, the Brahman thought, 'To give one's life for someone else is hard indeed. Is there not a sacrifice that is less difficult?'"

intoxicating, maddening drinks, the root of carelessness—that is a sacrifice better than open largesse, better than perpetual alms, better than the gift of dwelling places, better than the taking of refuge."[24]

---

24. **NewSubCom.**: "The Precepts are said to be less difficult than Taking Refuge, because one only has to accept them and abstain from the respective item when occasion arises."

Com.: "Abstention [*virati*] is threefold: 1. factual abstention (*sampatta-virati*), 2. abstention by formal acceptance of the Precepts (*samādāna-virati*), 3. abstention by eliminating [the evil tendencies, *setughāta-virati*, lit. killing through the 'bridge', i.e., the Holy Paths].

"1. There is one who, without having formally accepted the Precepts, remembers his birth, clan, family, country, etc., and thinking that it is not befitting for him [to commit transgressions], he does not kill, etc. He avoids [transgressing] when occasion arises and refrains from it entirely. His abstention is called 'factual' [or 'taking place on a given occasion,' *sampatta-virati*].

"2. If one takes upon oneself the Precepts, saying, 'From today, even for the sake of my life, I shall not kill a living being,' or 'I take upon me the abstention [from ...],' this is called abstention by formal acceptance of the Precepts (*samādāna-virati*).

"3. The abstention of Holy Disciples (*ariya-sāvaka*), those connected with the Noble Path [i.e., Right View, etc.] is called abstention by elimination (*setughāta-virati*)."

NewSubCom.: "Elsewhere it is called 'abstention by destruction' [*samuccheda-virati*], [e.g., in Com. to MN 9 and the Atthasālinī]. Seta [bridge] is the Holy Path. The abstention included in it, which destroys the evil states of mind, is called *setughāta-virati*."

Com.: "The first two kinds of abstention have as objects the life-faculty (*jīvitindriya*), etc., i.e., that against which the transgression takes place when there is killing, etc. The third [supra-mundane] abstention has only Nibbāna as its object.

"If one who has taken the Five Precepts as a unit [i.e., using one single term in the formula] breaks one of the Precepts, in that case all of them are broken."

NewSubCom.: "Taken the Five Precepts as a unit," "That is, together (*ekato ekajjhaṃ*), if one says, 'I take upon myself the rule of conduct with its five parts' [or the fivefold moral rule, '*pañcaṅga samannāgataṃ sīlaṃ samādiyāmi*']. But even in that case one has to know that the Precepts are of five [different] types in regard to their functions [*kicca-vasena*]. All five are broken [in the sense that the vow is broken], because they have been taken

27. "And is there, O Gotama, any other sacrifice as difficult and less troublesome, of greater fruit and of greater advantage than all these five?"

"Yes, O Brahman, there is."

"And what, O Gotama, may that be?"

---

together [in a single formula of vow]. But this does not mean that the *sīla* has an [inseparably] fivefold nature. Rather, by what one transgresses, just by that *kamma* alone one is bound (*kamma-baddho*)."

Com.: "If one takes the Precepts [by stating them] singly, he breaks only that Precept against which he has transgressed. In the Abstention by Eliminating, there is no breaking of the Precepts. In a future existence too, a Holy Disciple (*ariya-savaka*) will never kill nor [break another Precept such as) drink alcohol. He will not do so even for life's sake."

NewSubCom.: "Takes the Precepts singly"—"That is, separately, is done by saying, 'I take upon myself the rule of abstention from killing' [*Pāṇātipātā veramaṇī-sikkhāpadaṃ samādiyāmi*]. In the **Com.** to the *Khuddakapātha* it is said that *veramaṇī-sikkhāpadaṃ* forms a compound; but in the text editions [*pāḷipotthakesu*] a *niggahita* is at the end of [the first word] *veramaṇī* and the two words are separate.

"The above statements refer to laymen. In the case of novices [*sama?era*], in whatever way they may have taken the Precepts, if they have violated one, all will be broken, because they have come to 'defeat' [*parajika*].

"These Five Precepts are called a 'sacrifice' (*yañña*), because they are accepted [with the resolve], 'I shall observe them even if I have to sacrifice love of the self and love of life (*attasinehañca jīvitasinehañca pariccojīvā rakkhissāmi*)!'

"Though compared with the Five Precepts, the Taking of the Refuge has the higher rank (through its great results), yet, provided the Five Precepts are based on the Refuges [*saraṇāgamane yeva paṭṭhāya*] their observation is said to have great results."

Com.: "Because, in Taking Refuge, the obtaining of a correct idea about it [lit. the act of straightening one's views (*diṭṭhujuka-kamma*)] is difficult, while, on the other hand, in the acceptance of the Precepts, a mere abstention is required; therefore the latter 'sacrifice' is said to be less difficult and troublesome, whether one takes them in a desultory manner [*yatha tatha*; **NewSubCom.**: 'without much attention and respect'] or carefully and respectfully [*sakkacca?*; **NewSubCom.**: 'no double effort need be made in the latter case']. As there is no gift [to living beings] comparable to the observance of the Five Precepts, they are of great fruit and advantage." (Ed.)

[(Ed.) The answer is a long passage from the *Sāmaññaphala Sutta*, the "*Discourse on the Fruits of Recluseship*" (DN 2), which contains the following sections:

1. The appearance of a Buddha, his preaching, the conversion of a hearer, and the latter's renunciation of the world and ordination as a monk (as in the *Tevijjā Sutta*, translated in the *Wheel* No. 57/58, page 19).

2. The monk's observance of the Precepts (*ibid.*, p. 19 § 42 up to p. 21).

3. His fearlessness and confidence due to his virtue (*ibid.*, p. 22, first para).

4. Sense-control (*ibid.*, p. 22).

5. Mindfulness and full awareness (*ibid.*, p. 23).

6. Contentedness (*ditto*, p. 23).

7. Conquest of the five hindrances (*ibid.*, p. 23 to 24, end of § 75).

After each of the above sections, the *Kūṭadanta Sutta* adds:]

"This, O Brahman, is a sacrifice less difficult and less troublesome, of greater fruit and greater advantage than the previous sacrifices.

"[Now, having abandoned these five hindrances, and] quite detached from sense-objects, detached from unwholesome states of mind, he enters upon and dwells in the first Absorption [*jhāna*], which is accompanied by applied and sustained thought, filled with bliss and happiness, born of seclusion.

"This, O Brahman, is a sacrifice less difficult and less troublesome, of greater fruit and greater advantage than the previous sacrifices."

[Here follows the text of the second, third and fourth Absorptions, with the same concluding paragraph as above. (Ed.)]

[Insight-knowledge] "With his heart thus serene, made pure, translucent, cultured, devoid of all evil, supple, ready to act, firm, and imperturbable, he applies and bends down his mind to that insight that comes from knowledge. He grasps the fact: 'This body of mine is material, it is build up of the four great elements, it springs from father and mother, it is continually renewed by so much boiled rice and juicy food, its very nature is impermanence, it is subject to erosion, abrasion,[25] dissolution and disintegration; and there is this consciousness[26] of mine, too, bound up and dependent on it.'[27]

"Just, O Brahman, as if there were a Veḷuriya gem, bright, of purest water, with eight facets, excellently cut, clear, translucent, without a flaw, excellent in every way. And through it a string, blue or orange coloured, or red, or white, or yellow should be threaded. If a man, who had eyes to see, were to take it into his hand, he would clearly perceive how the one is bound up with the other.

"Similarly, with his heart thus serene ... [the monk] grasps the fact, 'There is this body of mine, which is material ... and

---

25. This is a favourite description of the body. The words for erosion and abrasion (*ucchādana, parimaddana*) are cunningly chosen. They are also familiar technical terms of the Indian shampooer (and masseur), and are so used in DN 2. The double meaning must have been clearly present to the Indian hearer, and the words are, therefore, really untranslatable. (RD) What is meant is probably that the body is so malodorous and fragile that it needs constant attention by shampooing or anointing (*ucchādana*), massaging (*parimaddana*), etc. (Ed.)

26. Consciousness (*viññāṇa*) stands here also for all other mental functions and faculties. (Ed.)

27. Rhys Davids comments:

"In spite of this and similar passages, the adherents of the soul theory (having nothing else to fasten on to) were apt to fasten on to the Buddhist *viññāṇa* as a possible point of reconciliation with their own theory. Even an admirer of the Buddha (one Sāti, a member of the Order) went so far as to tell the Buddha himself that he must, as he admitted transmigration, have meant that the *viññāṇa* did not really depend upon, was not really bound up with, the body, but that it formed the link in transmigration. In perhaps the most earnest and emphatic of all the dialogues (MN 38), the Buddha meets and refutes at length this erroneous representation of his view. But it still survives. I know two living writers on Buddhism who (in blissful ignorance of the Dialogue in question) still fasten upon the Buddha the opinion he so expressly refused to accept. Sāti's belief, however, was that *viññāṇa* is reborn, implying that it is a transmigrating entity." (RD)

Rhys Davids' formulation of Sāti's view does not express the error correctly. See Dependent Origination by Piyadassi Thera (The Wheel No. 15), p. 16 ff. (Ed.)

there is this consciousness of mine, too, bound up therewith, and dependent on it.'

"This, O Brahman, is a sacrifice less difficult and less troublesome, of greater fruit and greater advantage than the previous sacrifices."

[Here follow, according to DN 2, sections on the "Power of producing a mind-made body" (*manomaya-iddhi*) and on the first five Supernormal Knowledges (*abhiññā*).[28] The text of the sixth Supernormal Knowledge, likewise inserted here from DN 2, is as follows: (Ed.)]

"With his heart thus serene ... he applies and bends down his mind to the Knowledge of the Destruction of the Cankers [*āsavakkhaya*]. He knows as it really is: 'This is Suffering ...'; 'This is the origin of Suffering ...'; 'This is the cessation of Suffering ...'; 'This is the Path that leads to the cessation of Suffering ...' He knows as they really are 'These are the Cankers ...'; 'This is the origin of the Cankers ...'; 'This is the cessation of the Cankers ...'; 'This is the Path that leads to the cessation of the Cankers ...' Of him, thus knowing, thus seeing, the heart is set free from the Canker of Sense-desire; is set free from the Canker of [craving for renewed] Existence; is set free from the Canker of Ignorance. In him, thus set free, arises the knowledge of his emancipation, and he knows, 'Rebirth has been destroyed. The Holy Life has been fulfilled. What had to be done has been accomplished. After this present life there will be no beyond.'

"Just, O Brahman, as if in a mountain stronghold there were a pool of water, clear, translucent, and serene, and a man standing on the bank, and with eyes to see, should perceive the oysters and the shells, the gravel and the pebble and the shoals of fish, as they move about or lie within it, he would know: 'This pool is clear, transparent, and serene, and here within are the oysters and the shells, and the sand and gravel, and the shoals of fish are moving about or lying still.'

"Similarly, with his heart thus serene ... [the monk] knows as it really is, 'This is Suffering ...'; 'These are the Cankers ...' Of

28. To these sections no explicit reference is made in the abridgements given in the Pāli texts of the *Kūṭadanta Sutta*. But the commentary mentions these six sections. (Ed.)

him, thus knowing, the heart is set free from the Cankers ... and he knows, 'Rebirth has been destroyed ... After this present life there will be no beyond.'

"This, O Brahman, is a sacrifice less difficult and less troublesome, of greater fruit and greater advantage than the previous sacrifices. And there is no performance of a sacrifice, O Brahman, higher and loftier than this."

28. And when he had thus spoken, Kūṭadanta, the Brahman, said to the Blessed One,

"Most excellent, O Gotama, are the words of your mouth, most excellent! Just as if a man were to set up what has been thrown down, or were to reveal that which has been hidden away, or were to point out the right road to him who has gone astray, or were to bring a light into the darkness so that those who had eyes could see external forms, just so has the truth been made known to me in many a figure by the Venerable Gotama. I, even I, betake myself to the Venerable Gotama as my guide, to the Doctrine and the Order. May the Venerable One accept me as a disciple, as one who, from this day forth, as long as life endures, has taken him as his guide. And I myself, O Gotama, will have the seven hundred bulls, and the seven hundred steers, and the seven hundred heifers, and the seven hundred goats, and the seven hundred rams set free. To them I grant their life. Let them eat green grass and drink fresh water, and may cool breezes waft around them."[29]

29. Then the Blessed One discoursed to Kūṭadanta, the Brahman, in due order;[30] that is to say, he spoke to him of generosity; of right conduct; of heaven; of the danger, the vanity,

29. **Com.**: "Having thus spoken, the Brahman sent a man to the place of sacrifice, saying, 'Go, my man, climb down into the sacrificial pit and release all those animals from their bonds.' The man did so and reported back to the Brahman that the animals had been released. Until the Brahman had received this message, the Blessed One did not preach Dhamma to him. And why not? Because the Brahman's mind was still perturbed. But when he had received the message, his mind brightened at the thought, 'To many animals I have given freedom.' When the Blessed One knew that the Brahman's mind had brightened and was serene, he began his Dhamma instruction." (Ed.)

30. "In due order." This is the Gradual Instruction (*anupubbikathā*), on which see *The Wheel* No. 98/99, p. 50 and Note 26. (Ed.)

and the defilement of lusts; and of the advantages of renunciation. And when the Blessed One became aware that Kūṭadanta, the Brahman, had become prepared, softened, unprejudiced, upraised, and believing in heart, then did he proclaim the doctrine the Buddhas alone have won: the doctrine of suffering, its origin, its cessation, and of the Path. And just as a clean cloth, with all stains in it washed away, will readily take the dye, even so did Kūṭadanta, the Brahman, even while seated there, obtain the pure and spotless Eye for the Truth, and he knew: "Whatsoever has a beginning, in that is inherent also the necessity of dissolution." [31]

30. And then the Brahman Kūṭadanta, as one who had seen the Truth, had mastered it, understood it, dived deep down into it, who had passed beyond doubt, and put away perplexity and gained full confidence, who had become dependent on no other for his knowledge of the teaching of the Master,[32] addressed the Blessed One and said,

"May the Venerable Gotama grant me the favour of taking his meal tomorrow with me, and also the members of the Order with him."

And the Blessed One signified, by silence, his consent. Then the Brahman, Kūṭadanta, seeing that the Blessed One had accepted, rose from his seat, and keeping his right towards him as he passed, he departed thence. And at daybreak he had sweet food, both hard and soft, made ready at the pit prepared for his sacrifice, and had the time announced to the Blessed One: "It is time, O Gotama, and the meal is ready." And the Blessed One, who had dressed early in the morning, put on his outer robe, and taking his bowl with him, went with the brethren to Kūṭadanta's sacrificial pit, and sat down there on the seat prepared for him. And Kūṭadanta the Brahman satisfied the brethren with the Buddha at their head, with his own hand, with sweet food, both hard and soft, till they refused any more. And when the Blessed One had finished his meal, and cleansed the bowl and his hands, Kūṭadanta, the Brahman, took a low seat and seated himself beside him. And when he was thus seated the Blessed One instructed and aroused

31. This passage indicates the attainment of the first stage of Sainthood, Stream-entry (*sotāpatti*). See *The Wheel* No. 98/99, p. 51 and Notes 33–37. (Ed.)
32. Ibid.

and incited and gladdened Kūṭadanta, the Brahman, with religious discourse, and then arose from his seat and departed thence.

The Power of Mindfulness

By

Nyanaponika Thera

WHEEL PUBLICATION NO. 121/122

Introduction

Is mindfulness actually a power in its own right as claimed by the title of this essay? Seen from the viewpoint of the ordinary pursuits of life, it does not seem so. From that angle mindfulness, or attention, has a rather modest place among many other seemingly more important mental faculties serving the purpose of variegated wish-fulfilment. Here, mindfulness means just "to watch one's steps" so that one may not stumble or miss a chance in the pursuit of one's aims. Only in the case of specific tasks and skills is mindfulness sometimes cultivated more deliberately, but here too it is still regarded as a subservient function, and its wider scope and possibilities are not recognized.

Even if one turns to the Buddha's doctrine, taking only a surface view of the various classifications and lists of mental factors in which mindfulness appears, one may be inclined to regard this faculty just as "one among many." Again one may get the impression that it has a rather subordinate place and is easily surpassed in significance by other faculties.

Mindfulness in fact has, if we may personify it, a rather unassuming character. Compared with it, mental factors such as devotion, energy, imagination and intelligence are certainly more colourful personalities, making an immediate and strong impact on people and situations. Their conquests are sometimes rapid and vast, though often insecure. Mindfulness, on the other hand, is of an unobtrusive nature. Its virtues shine inwardly, and in ordinary life most of its merits are passed on to other mental faculties which generally receive all the credit. One must know mindfulness well and cultivate its acquaintance before one can appreciate its value and its silent penetrative influence. Mindfulness walks slowly and deliberately, and its daily task is of a rather humdrum nature. Yet where it places its feet it cannot easily be dislodged, and it acquires and bestows true mastery of the ground it covers.

Mental faculties of such a nature, like actual personalities of a similar type, are often overlooked or underrated. In the case of mindfulness, it required a genius like the Buddha to discover the "hidden talent" in the modest garb, and to develop the vast inherent power of the potent seed. It is, indeed, the mark of a genius to perceive and to harness the power of the seemingly small. Here, truly, it happens that "what is little becomes much." A revaluation of values takes place. The standards of greatness and smallness change. Through the master mind of the Buddha, mindfulness is finally revealed as the Archimedean point where the vast revolving mass of world suffering is levered out of its twofold anchorage in ignorance and craving.

The Buddha spoke of the power of mindfulness in a very emphatic way:

> "Mindfulness, I declare, is all-helpful." (SN 46:59)
> "All things can be mastered by mindfulness." (AN 8:83)

Further, there is that solemn and weighty utterance opening and concluding the *Satipaṭṭhāna Sutta*, the *Discourse on the Foundations of Mindfulness*:

> This is the only way, monks, for the purification of beings, for the overcoming of sorrow and lamentation, for the destruction of pain and grief, for reaching the right path, for the attainment of Nibbāna, namely, the four foundations of mindfulness.

In ordinary life, if mindfulness, or attention, is directed to any object, it is rarely sustained long enough for the purpose of careful and factual observation. Generally it is followed immediately by emotional reaction, discriminative thought, reflection or purposeful action. In a life and thought governed by the Buddha's teaching too, mindfulness (*sati*) is mostly linked with clear comprehension (*sampajañña*) of the right purpose or suitability of an action, and other considerations. Thus again it is not viewed in itself. But to tap the actual and potential *power* of mindfulness it is necessary to understand and deliberately cultivate it in its basic, unalloyed form, which we shall call *bare attention*.

By bare attention we understand the clear and single-minded awareness of what actually happens *to* us and *in* us, at the successive moments of perception. It is called "bare" because it attends to the bare facts of a perception without reacting to them by deed, speech or mental comment. Ordinarily, that purely receptive state of mind is, as we said, just a very brief phase of the thought process of which one is often scarcely aware. But in the methodical development of mindfulness aimed at the unfolding of its latent powers, bare attention is sustained for as long a time as one's strength of concentration permits. Bare attention then becomes the key to the meditative practice of Satipaṭṭhāna, opening the door to mind's mastery and final liberation.

Bare attention is developed in two ways: (1) as a methodical meditative practice with selected objects; (2) as applied, as far as practicable, to the normal events of the day, together with a general attitude of mindfulness and clear comprehension. The details of the practice have been described elsewhere, and need not be repeated here.[1]

The primary purpose of this essay is to demonstrate and explain the efficacy of this method, that is, to show the actual *power of mindfulness*. Particularly in an age like ours, with its superstitious worship of ceaseless external activity, there will be those who ask: "How can such a passive attitude of mind as that of bare attention possibly lead to the great results claimed for it?" In reply, one may be inclined to suggest to the questioner that he should not rely on the words of others, but should put these assertions of the Buddha to the test of personal experience. But those who do not yet know the Buddha's teaching well enough to accept it as a reliable guide may hesitate to take up—without good reasons—a practice that, on account of its radical simplicity, may appear strange to them. In the following a number of such "good reasons" are therefore proffered for the reader's scrutiny. They are also meant as an introduction to the general spirit of Satipaṭṭhāna and as pointers to its wide and significant perspectives. Furthermore, it is hoped that one who has taken up the methodical training will recognize in the following observations certain features of his own practice, and be encouraged to cultivate them deliberately.

---

1. See Nyanaponika Thera, *The Heart of Buddhist Meditation* (Kandy, Buddhist Publication Society, 2005).

Four Sources of Power in Bare Attention

We shall now deal with four aspects of bare attention, which are the mainsprings of the power of mindfulness. They are not the only sources of its strength, but they are the principal ones to which its efficacy as a method of mental development is due.

These four are:

1. the functions of "tidying up" and "naming" exercised by bare attention;
2. its non-violent, non-coercive procedure;
3. the capacity of stopping and slowing down;
4. the directness of vision bestowed by bare attention.

1. The Functions of "Tidying" and "Naming"

Tidying Up the Mental Household

If anyone whose mind is not harmonized and controlled through methodical meditative training should take a close look at his own everyday thoughts and activities, he will meet with a rather disconcerting sight. Apart from the few main channels of his purposeful thoughts and activities, he will everywhere be faced with a tangled mass of perceptions, thoughts, feelings and casual bodily movements, showing a disorderliness and confusion which he would certainly not tolerate in his living room. Yet this is the state of affairs that we take for granted within a considerable portion of our waking life and our normal mental activity. Let us now look at the details of that rather untidy picture.

First we meet a vast number of casual sense-impressions such as sights and sounds, passing constantly through our minds. Most of them remain vague and fragmentary; some are even based on faulty perceptions and misjudgements. Carrying these inherent weaknesses, they often form the untested basis for judgements and decisions on a higher level of consciousness. True, all these casual sense-impressions need not and cannot be objects of focused attention. A stone on the road that happens to meet our glance will have a claim on our attention only if it obstructs our progress or is of interest to us for some reason. Yet if we neglect these casual impressions too often, we may stumble over many stones lying on our road and also overlook many gems.

Besides the casual sense impressions, there are those more significant and definite perceptions, thoughts, feelings and volitions, which have a closer connection with our purposeful life. Here too, we find that a very high proportion of them are in a state of utter confusion. Hundreds of cross-currents flash through the mind, and everywhere there are "bits and ends" of unfinished thoughts, stifled emotions and passing moods. Many meet a premature death. Owing to their innately feeble nature, our lack of concentration or their suppression by new and stronger impressions, they do not persist and develop. If we observe our own minds, we shall notice how easily diverted our thoughts are, how often they behave like undisciplined disputants constantly interrupting each other and refusing to listen to the other side's arguments. Again, many lines of thought remain rudimentary or are left untranslated into will and action, because courage is lacking to accept their practical, moral or intellectual consequences. If we continue to examine more closely our average perceptions, thoughts or judgements, we shall have to admit that many of them are unreliable. They are just the products of habit, led by prejudices of intellect or emotion, by our pet preferences or aversions, by faulty or superficial observations, by laziness or by selfishness.

Such a look into long-neglected quarters of the mind will come as a wholesome shock to the observer. It will convince him of the urgent need for methodical mental culture extending below the thin surface layer of the mind to those vast twilight regions of consciousness we have just visited. The observer will then become aware that the relatively small sector of the mind that stands in the intense light of purposeful will and thought is not a reliable standard of the inner strength and lucidity of consciousness in its totality. He will also see that the quality of individual consciousness cannot be judged by a few optimal results of mental activity achieved in brief, intermittent periods. The decisive factor in determining the quality of consciousness is self-understanding and self-control: whether that dim awareness characteristic of our everyday mind and the uncontrolled portion of everyday activity tends to increase or decrease.

It is the daily little negligence in thoughts, words and deeds going on for many years of our lives (and, as the Buddha teaches, for many existences) that is chiefly responsible for the untidiness and confusion we find in our minds. This negligence creates the trouble and allows it to continue. Thus the old Buddhist teachers have said: "Negligence produces a lot of dirt. As in a house, so in the mind, only a very little dirt collects in a day or two, but if it goes on for many years, it will grow into a vast heap of refuse."[2]

The dark, untidy corners of the mind are the hideouts of our most dangerous enemies. From there they attack us unawares, and much too often succeed in defeating us. That twilight world peopled by frustrated desires and suppressed resentments, by vacillations, whims and many other shadowy figures, forms a background from which upsurging passions—greed and lust, hatred and anger—may derive powerful support. Besides, the obscure and obscuring nature of that twilight region is the very element and mother-soil of the third and strongest of the three roots of evil (*akusalamūla*), ignorance or delusion.

Attempts at eliminating the mind's main defilements—greed, hate and delusion—must fail as long as these defilements find refuge and support in the uncontrolled dim regions of the mind; as long as the close and complex tissue of those half-articulate thoughts and emotions forms the basic texture of mind into which just a few golden strands of noble and lucid thought are woven. But how are we to deal with that unwieldy, tangled mass? Usually we try to ignore it and to rely on the counteracting energies of our surface mind. But the only safe remedy is to face it—with mindfulness. Nothing more difficult is needed than to acquire the habit of directing bare attention to these rudimentary thoughts as often as possible. The working principle here is the simple fact that two thoughts cannot exist together at the same time: if the clear light of mindfulness is present, there is no room for mental twilight. When sustained mindfulness has secured a firm foothold, it will be a matter of comparatively secondary importance how the mind will then deal with those rudimentary thoughts, moods and emotions. One may just dismiss them and replace them by purposeful thoughts; or one may allow and even compel them to

2. Comy to Sn 334.

complete what they have to say. In the latter case they will often reveal how poor and weak they actually are, and it will then not be difficult to dispose of them once they are forced into the open. This procedure of bare attention is very simple and effective; the difficulty is only the persistence in applying it.

Observing a complex thing means identifying its component parts, singling out the separate strands forming that intricate tissue. If this is applied to the complex currents of mental and practical life, automatically a strong regulating influence will be noticeable. As if ashamed in the presence of the calmly observing eye, the course of thoughts will proceed in a less disorderly and wayward manner; it will not be so easily diverted, and will resemble more and more a well-regulated river.

During decades of the present life and throughout millennia of previous lives traversing the round of existence, there has steadily grown within each individual a closely knit system of intellectual and emotional prejudices, of bodily and mental habits that are no longer questioned as to their rightful position and useful function in human life. Here again, the application of bare attention loosens the hard soil of these often very ancient layers of the human mind, preparing thus the ground for sowing the seed of methodical mental training. Bare attention identifies and pursues the single threads of that closely interwoven tissue of our habits. It sorts out carefully the subsequent justifications of passionate impulses and the pretended motives of our prejudices. Fearlessly it questions old habits often grown meaningless. It uncovers their roots, and thus helps abolish all that is seen to be harmful. In brief, bare attention lays open the minute crevices in the seemingly impenetrable structure of unquestioned mental processes. Then the sword of wisdom wielded by the strong arm of constant meditative practice will be able to penetrate these crevices, and finally to break up that structure where required. If the inner connections between the single parts of a seemingly compact whole become intelligible, they then cease to be inaccessible.

When the facts and details of the mind's conditioned nature are uncovered by meditative practice, there is an increased chance to effect fundamental changes in the mind. In that way, not only those hitherto unquestioned habits of the mind, its twilight regions and its normal processes as well, but even those seemingly solid, indisputable facts of the world of matter—all will become "questionable" and lose much of their self-assurance. Many people are so impressed and intimidated by that bland self-assurance of assumed "solid facts," that they hesitate to take up any spiritual training, doubting that it can effect anything worthwhile. The application of bare attention to the task of tidying and regulating the mind will bring perceptible results—results which will dispel their doubts and encourage in them the confidence to enter a spiritual path.

The tidying or regulating function of bare attention, we should note, is of fundamental importance for that "purification of beings" mentioned by the Buddha as the first aim of Satipaṭṭhāna. This phrase refers, of course, to the purification of their minds, and here the very first step is to bring initial order into the functioning of the mental processes. We have seen how this is done by bare attention. In that sense, the commentary to the Discourse on the Foundations of Mindfulness explains the words "for the purification of beings" as follows:

> It is said: "Mental taints defile beings; mental clarity purifies them." That mental clarity comes to be by this way of mindfulness.

Naming

We said before that bare attention "tidies up" or regulates the mind by sorting out and identifying the various confused strands of the mental process. That identifying function, like any other mental activity, is connected with a verbal formulation. In other words, "identifying" proceeds by way of expressly "naming" the respective mental processes.

Primitive man believed that words could exercise a magical power: "Things that could be named had lost their secret power over man, the horror of the unknown. To know the name of a force, a being or an object was (to primitive man) identical with the mastery over it."[3] That ancient belief in the magical potency of names appears also in many fairy tales and myths, where the

3. Anagarika Govinda, *The Psychological Attitude of Early Buddhist Philosophy* (Rider & Co., 1961).

power of a demon is broken just by facing him courageously and pronouncing his name.

There is an element of truth in the "word-magic" of primitive man, and in the practice of bare attention we shall find the power of naming confirmed. The "twilight demons" of the mind—our passionate impulses and obscure thoughts—cannot bear the simple but clarifying question about their "names," much less the knowledge of these names. Hence this is often alone sufficient to diminish their strength. The calmly observant glance of mindfulness discovers the demons in their hiding-places. The practice of calling them by their names drives them out into the open, into the daylight of consciousness. There they will feel embarrassed and obliged to justify themselves, although at this stage of bare attention they have not yet even been subjected to any closer questioning except about their names, their identity. If forced into the open while still in an incipient stage, they will be incapable of withstanding scrutiny and will just dwindle away. Thus a first victory over them may be won, even at an early stage of the practice.

The appearance in the mind of undesirable and ignoble thoughts, even if they are very fleeting and only half-articulate, has an unpleasant effect upon one's self-esteem. Therefore such thoughts are often shoved aside, unattended to and unopposed. Often they are also camouflaged by more pleasing and respectable labels which hide their true nature. Thoughts disposed of in either of these two ways will strengthen the accumulated power of ignoble tendencies in the subconscious. Furthermore, these procedures will weaken one's will to resist the arising and the dominance of mental defilements, and strengthen the tendency to evade the issues. But by applying the simple method of clearly and honestly naming or registering any undesirable thoughts, these two harmful devices, ignoring and camouflage, are excluded. Hence their detrimental consequences on the structure of the subconscious and their diversion of mental effort will be avoided.

When ignoble thoughts or personal shortcomings are called by their right names, the mind will develop an inner resistance and even repugnance against them. In time it may well succeed in keeping them in check and finally eliminating them. Even if these means do not bring undesirable tendencies fully under control at once, they will stamp upon them the impact of repeated resistance which will weaken them whenever they reappear. To continue our personification, we may say that unwholesome thoughts will no longer be the unopposed masters of the scene, and this diffidence of theirs will make them considerably easier to deal with. It is the power of moral shame (*hiri-bala*) that has been mustered here as an ally, methodically strengthened by these simple yet subtle psychological techniques.

The method of naming and registering also extends, of course, to noble thoughts and impulses, which will be encouraged and strengthened. Without being given deliberate attention, such wholesome tendencies often pass unnoticed and remain barren. But when clear awareness is applied to them, it will stimulate their growth.

It is one of the most beneficial features of right mindfulness, and particularly of bare attention, that it enables us to utilize all external events and inner mental events for our progress. Even the unsalutary can be made a starting point for the salutary if, through the device of naming or registering, it becomes an object of detached knowledge.

In several passages of the Satipaṭṭhāna Sutta the function of naming or "bare registering" seems to be indicated by formulating the respective statements by way of direct speech. There are no less than four such instances in the discourse:

1. "When experiencing a pleasant feeling, he knows 'I experience a pleasant feeling,'" etc.;
2. "He knows of a lustful (state of) mind, 'Mind is lustful,'" etc.;
3. "If (the hindrance of) sense desire is present in him, he knows, 'Sense desire is present in me,'" etc.;
4. "If the enlightenment factor, mindfulness, is present in him, he knows, 'The enlightenment factor mindfulness is present in me,'" etc.

In concluding this section, we briefly point out that the *tidying up* and the *naming* of mental processes is the indispensable preparation for fully understanding them in their true nature, the task of insight (*vipassanā*). These functions, exercised by bare attention, will help dispel the illusion that the mental processes are compact. They will also help us to discern their specific nature or characteristics and to notice their momentary rise and fall.

2. *The Non-coercive Procedure*

Obstacles to Meditation

Both the world surrounding us and the world of our own minds are full of hostile and conflicting forces causing us pain and frustration. We know from our own bitter experience that we are not strong enough to meet and conquer all these antagonistic forces in open combat. In the external world we cannot have everything exactly as we want it, while in the inner world of the mind, our passions, impulses and whims often override the demands of duty, reason and our higher aspirations.

We further learn that often an undesirable situation will only worsen if excessive pressure is used against it. Passionate desires may grow in intensity if one tries to silence them by sheer force of will. Disputes and quarrels will go on endlessly and grow fiercer if they are fanned again and again by angry retorts or by vain attempts to crush the other man's position. A disturbance during work, rest or meditation will be felt more strongly and will have a longer-lasting impact if one reacts to it by resentment and anger and attempts to suppress it.

Thus, again and again, we meet with situations in life where we cannot *force* issues. But there are ways of mastering the vicissitudes of life and conflicts of mind without application of force. Non-violent means may often succeed where attempts at coercion, internal or external, fail. Such a non-violent way of mastering life and mind is Satipaṭṭhāna. By the methodical application of bare attention, the basic practice in the development of right mindfulness, all the latent powers of a non-coercive approach will gradually unfold, with their beneficial results and their wide and unexpected implications. In this context we are mainly concerned with the benefits of Satipaṭṭhāna for the mastery of mind, and for the progress in meditation that may result from a non-coercive procedure. But we shall also cast occasional side glances at its repercussions on everyday life. It will not be difficult for a thoughtful reader to make more detailed application to his own problems.

The antagonistic forces that appear in meditation and that are liable to upset its smooth course are of three kinds:

1. external disturbances, such as noise;
2. mental defilements (*kilesa*), such as lust, anger, restlessness, dissatisfaction or sloth, which may arise at any time during meditation; and
3. various incidental stray thoughts, or surrender to day-dreaming.

These distractions are the great stumbling blocks for a beginner in meditation who has not yet acquired sufficient dexterity to deal with them effectively. To give thought to those disturbing factors only when they actually arise at the time of meditation is insufficient. If caught unprepared in one's defence, one will struggle with them in a more or less haphazard and ineffective way, and with a feeling of irritation which will itself be an additional impediment. If disturbances of any kind and unskilful reactions to them occur several times during one session, one may come to feel utterly frustrated and irritated and give up further attempts to meditate, at least for the present occasion.

In fact, even meditators who are quite well informed by books or a teacher about all the details concerning their subject of meditation often lack instruction on how to deal skilfully with the disturbances they may meet. The feeling of helplessness in facing them is the most formidable difficulty for a beginning meditator. At that point many accept defeat, abandoning prematurely any further effort at methodical practice. As in worldly affairs, so in meditation, one's way of dealing with the "initial difficulties" will often be decisive for success or failure.

When faced by inner and outer disturbances, the inexperienced or uninstructed beginner will generally react in two ways. He will first try to shove them away lightly, and if he fails in that, he will try to suppress them by sheer force of will. But these disturbances are like insolent flies: by whisking—first lightly and then with increasing vigour and anger—one may perhaps succeed in driving them away for a while, but usually they will return with an exasperating constancy, and the effort and vexation of whisking will have produced only an additional disturbance of one's composure.

Satipaṭṭhāna, through its method of bare attention, offers a non-violent alternative to those futile and even harmful attempts at suppression by force. A successful non-violent procedure in mind-control has to start with the right attitude. There must be first the full cognizance and sober acceptance of the fact that those three disturbing factors are co-inhabitants of the world we live in, whether we like it or not. Our disapproval of them will not alter the fact. With some we shall have to come to terms, and concerning the others—the mental defilements—we shall have to learn how to deal with them effectively until they are finally conquered.

1. Since we are not the sole inhabitants of this densely populated world, there are bound to be *external disturbances* of various kinds, such as noise and interruptions by visitors. We cannot always live in "splendid isolation," "from noise of men and dogs untroubled," or in "ivory towers" high above the crowd. Right meditation is not escapism; it is not meant to provide hiding-places for temporary oblivion. Realistic meditation has the purpose of training the mind to face, to understand and to conquer this very world in which we live. And this world inevitably includes numerous obstacles to the life of meditation.

2. The Burmese meditation master, the Venerable Mahāsi Sayādaw, said: "In an unliberated worldling *mental defilements* are sure to arise again and again. He has to face that fact and know these defilements well in order to apply again and again the appropriate remedy of Satipaṭṭhāna. Then they will grow weaker, more short-lived and will finally disappear." To know the occurrence and nature of defilements is therefore as important for a meditator as to know the occurrence of his noble thoughts.

By facing one's own defilements one will be stirred to increase the effort to eliminate them. On the other hand, if out of a false shame or pride one tries to avert one's glance when they arise, one will never truly join issue with them, and will always evade the final and decisive encounter. By hitting blindly at them, one will only exhaust or even hurt oneself. But by observing carefully their nature and behaviour when they arise in one's own mind, one will be able to meet them well prepared, often to forestall them and finally to banish them fully. Therefore meet your defilements with a free and open glance! Be not ashamed, afraid or discouraged!

3. The third group of intruders disturbing the meditator's mind are *stray thoughts* and *daydreams*. These may consist of various memories and images of the past, recent or remote, including those emerging from subconscious depths; thoughts of the future—planning, imagining, fearing, hoping; and the casual sense-perceptions that may occur at the very time of meditation, often dragging after them a long trail of associated ideas. Whenever concentration and mindfulness slacken, stray thoughts or daydreams appear and fill the vacuum. Though they seem insignificant in themselves, through their frequent occurrence they form a most formidable obstacle, not only for the beginner, but in all cases when the mind is restless or distracted. However, when these invaders can be kept at bay, even long continuous periods of meditation can be achieved. As in the case of the mental defilements, stray thoughts will be entirely excluded only at the stage of Arahatship, when the perfect mindfulness thereby obtained keeps unfailing watch at the door of the mind.

If they are to shape our attitude, all these facts about the three kinds of disturbing factors must be given full weight and be fully absorbed by our minds. Then, in these three disturbing factors, the noble truth of suffering will manifest itself to the meditator very incisively through his own personal experience: "Not to obtain what one wants is suffering." The three other noble truths should also be exemplified by reference to the same situation. In such a way, even when dealing with impediments, the meditator will be within the domain of Satipaṭṭhāna. He will be engaged in the mindful awareness of the Four Noble Truths—part of the contemplation of mental objects (*dhammānupassanā*).[4] It is characteristic of right mindfulness, and one of its tasks, to relate the actual experiences of life to the truths of the Dhamma, and to use them as opportunities for its practical realization. Already at this preliminary stage devoted to the shaping of a correct and helpful attitude, we have the first successful test of our peaceful weapons: by understanding our adversaries better, we have consolidated our position, which was formerly weakened by an emotional approach; and by transforming these adversaries into teachers of the truths, we have won the first advantage over them.

4. Bhikkhu Soma, *The Way of Mindfulness* (Kandy: Buddhist Publication Society, 1975), p. 83.

Three Countermeasures

If we are mentally prepared by a realistic view of these three factors antagonistic to meditation, we shall be less inclined to react at once with irritation when they actually arise. We shall be emotionally in a better position to meet them with the non-violent weapons of which we shall now speak.

There are three devices for countering disturbances that arise in meditation. The three should be applied in succession whenever the preceding device has failed to dispose of the disturbance. All three are applications of bare attention; they differ in the degree and duration of attention given to the disturbance. The guiding rule here is: to give no more mental emphasis to the respective disturbance than is actually required by circumstances.

1. First, one should notice the disturbance clearly, but lightly: that is, without emphasis and without attention to details. After that brief act of noticing, one should try to return to the original subject of meditation. If the disturbance was weak or one's preceding concentration fairly strong, one may well succeed in resuming contemplation. At that stage, by being careful not to get involved in any "conversation" or argument with the intruder, we shall on our part not give it a reason to stay long; and in a good number of cases the disturbance will soon depart like a visitor who does not receive a very warm welcome. That curt dismissal may often enable us to return to our original meditation without any serious disturbance to the composure of mind.

The non-violent device here is: to apply bare attention to the disturbance, but with a minimum of response to it, and with a mind bent on withdrawal. This is the very way in which the Buddha himself dealt with inopportune visitors, as described in the *Mahāsuññata Sutta*: ... "with a mind bent on seclusion ... and withdrawn, his conversation aiming at dismissing (those visitors)." Similar is Śāntideva's advice on how to deal with fools: if one cannot avoid them, one should treat them "with the indifferent politeness of a gentleman."

2. If, however, the disturbance persists, one should repeat the application of bare attention again and again, patiently and calmly; and it may be that the disturbance will vanish when it has spent its force. Here the attitude is to meet the repeated occurrence of a disturbance by a reiterated "No," a determined refusal to be

deflected from one's course. This is the attitude of patience and firmness. The capacity for watchful observation has to be aided here by the capacity to wait and to hold one's ground.

These two devices will generally be successful with incidental stray thoughts and daydreams, which are feeble by nature, but the other two types of disturbances, the external ones and defilements, may also yield quite often.

3. But if, for some reason, they do *not* yield, one should deliberately turn one's full attention to the disturbance and make it an object of knowledge. Thus one transforms it from a *disturbance* to meditation into a legitimate *object* of meditation. One may continue with that new object until the external or internal cause for attending to it has ceased; or, if it proves satisfactory, one may even retain it for the rest of that session.

For instance, when disturbed by a persistent noise, we should give the noise our undivided attention, but we should take care to distinguish the object itself from our reaction to it. For example, if resentment arises, it should be clearly recognized in its own nature whenever it arises. In doing so, we shall be practising the contemplation of mind-objects (*dhammānupassanā*) according to the following passage of the Satipaṭṭhāna Sutta: "He knows the ear and sounds, and the fetter (e.g., resentment) arising through both." If the noise is intermittent or of varying intensity, one will easily be able to discern the rise and fall (*udayabbaya*) in its occurrence. In that way one will add to one's direct insight into impermanency (*aniccatā*).

The attitude towards recurrent mental defilements, such as thoughts of lust and restlessness, should be similar. One should face them squarely, but distinguish them from one's reaction to them, e.g., connivance, fear, resentment, irritation. In doing so, one is making use of the device of "naming," and one will reap the benefits mentioned above. In the recurrent waves of passion or restlessness, gradually one will likewise learn to distinguish phases of "high" and "low," their "ups" and "downs," and may also gain other helpful knowledge about their behaviour. By that procedure, one again remains entirely within the range of Satipaṭṭhāna by practising the contemplation of the state of mind (*cittānupassanā*) and of mind-objects (*dhammānupassanā*: attention to the hindrances).

This method of transforming disturbances to meditation into objects of meditation, as simple as it is ingenious, may be regarded as the culmination of non-violent procedure. It is a device very characteristic of the spirit of Satipaṭṭhāna, to make use of all experiences as aids on the path. In that way enemies are turned into friends; for all these disturbances and antagonistic forces become our teachers, and teachers, whoever they may be, should be regarded as friends.

We cannot forego quoting here a passage from a noteworthy little book, *The Little Locksmith* by Katherine Butler Hathaway, a moving human document of fortitude and practical wisdom acquired by suffering:

> I am shocked by the ignorance and wastefulness with which persons who should know better throw away the things they do not like. They throw away experiences, people, marriages, situations, all sorts of things because they do not like them. If you throw away a thing, it is gone. Where you had something, you have nothing. Your hands are empty; they have nothing to work on. Whereas, almost all those things which get thrown away are capable of being worked over by a little magic into just the opposite of what they were.... But most human beings never remember at all that in almost every bad situation there is the possibility of a transformation by which the undesirable may be changed into the desirable.

We said before that the occurrence of the three disturbing elements cannot always be prevented. They are parts of our world, and their coming and going follow their own laws irrespective of our approval or disapproval. But by applying bare attention we can avoid being swept away or dislodged by them. By taking a firm and calm stand on the secure ground of mindfulness, we shall repeat in a modest degree, but in an essentially identical way, the historic situation under the Bodhi Tree. When Māra the Evil One, at the head of his army, claimed the soil on which the future Buddha sat, the latter refused to budge. Trusting in the power of mindfulness, we may confidently repeat the Bodhisatta's aspiration on that occasion: *Mā maṃ ṭhānā acavi*! "May he (*Māra*) not dislodge me from this place" (Padhāna Sutta, Sutta Nipāta).

Let the intruders come and go. Like all the other members of that vast unceasing procession of mental and physical events that passes before our observant eyes in the practice of bare attention, they arise, and having arisen, they pass away.

Our advantage here is the obvious fact that two thought moments cannot be present at the same time. Attention refers, strictly speaking, not to the present but to the moment that has just passed away. Thus, as long as mindfulness holds sway, there will be no "disturbance" or "defiled thought." This gives us the chance to hold on to that secure ground of an "observer's post," our own potential "throne of enlightenment."

By the quietening and neutralizing influence of detached observation as applied in our three devices, the interruptions of meditation will increasingly lose the sting of irritation, and thereby their disturbing effect. This will prove to be an act of true *virāga* (dispassion), which literally means "decolouring." When these experiences are stripped of the emotional tinge that excites towards lust, aversion, irritation and other defilements of the mind, they will appear in their true nature as bare phenomena (*suddha-dhammā*).

The non-violent procedure of bare attention endows the meditator with the light but sure touch so essential for handling the sensitive, evasive and refractory nature of the mind. It also enables him to deal smoothly with the various difficult situations and obstacles met with in daily life. To illustrate the even quality of energy required for attaining to the meditative absorptions, *The Path of Purification* (*Visuddhimagga*) describes a test which students of surgery in ancient days had to undergo as a proof of their skill. A lotus leaf was placed in a bowl of water, and the pupil had to make an incision through the length of the leaf, without cutting it entirely or submerging it. He who applied an excess of force either cut the leaf into two or pressed it into the water, while the timid one did not even dare to scratch it. In fact, something like the gentle but firm hand of the surgeon is required in mental training, and this skilful, well-balanced touch will be the natural outcome of the non-violent procedure in the practice of bare attention.

3. Stopping and Slowing Down

Keeping Still

For a full and unobstructed unfoldment of the mind's capacities, the influence of two complementary forces is needed: *activating* and *restraining*. That twofold need was recognized by the Buddha, the great knower of mind. He advised that the faculties of energy (*viriy'indriya*) and of concentration (*samādh'indriya*) should be kept equally strong and well balanced.[5] Furthermore, he recommended three of the seven factors of enlightenment (*bojjhaṅga*) as suitable for rousing the mind, and another three for calming it.[6] In both cases, among the spiritual faculties and the enlightenment factors, it is mindfulness that not only watches over their equilibrium, but also activates those that are sluggish and restrains those that are too intense.

Mindfulness, though seemingly of a passive nature, is in fact an activating force. It makes the mind alert, and alertness is indispensable for all purposeful activity. In the present inquiry, however, we shall be mainly concerned with the *restraining* power of mindfulness. We shall examine how it makes for disentanglement and detachment and how it positively helps in the development of the mental qualities required for the work of deliverance.

In practising bare attention, we *keep still* at the mental and spatial place of observation, amidst the loud demands of the inner and outer world. Mindfulness possesses the strength of tranquillity, the capacity for deferring action and applying the brake, for *stopping* rash interference and for suspending judgement while pausing to observe facts and to reflect upon them wisely. It also brings a wholesome *slowing down* in the impetuosity of thought, speech and action. Keeping still and stopping, pausing and slowing down—these will be our key words when speaking now of the restraining effect of bare attention.

An ancient Chinese book states:

> In making things end, and in making things start, there is nothing more glorious than keeping still.

5. See Vism IV.47.

6. Ibid., IV.51, 57. The three rousing factors are investigation, energy and rapture; the three calming ones, tranquillity, concentration and equanimity.

In the light of the Buddha's teaching, the true "end of things" is Nibbāna, which is called the "*stilling* of formations" (*saṅkhārānaṃ vūpasamo*), that is, their final end or cessation. It is also called "the stopping" (*nirodha*). The "things" or "formations" meant here are the conditioned and impersonal phenomena rooted in craving and ignorance. The end of formations comes to be by the end of "forming," that is, by the end of world-creating kammic activities. It is the "end of the world" and of suffering, which the Buddha proclaimed cannot be reached by walking, migrating or transmigrating, but can be found within ourselves. That end of the world is heralded by each deliberate act of *keeping still, stopping or pausing*. "Keeping still," in that highest sense, means stopping the accumulation of *kamma*, abstaining from our unceasing concern with evanescent things, abstaining from perpetually adding to our entanglements in saṃsāra—the round of repeated birth and death. By following the way of mindfulness, by training ourselves to keep still and pause in the attitude of bare attention, we refuse to take up the world's persistent challenge to our dispositions for greed or hatred. We protect ourselves against rash and delusive judgements; we refrain from blindly plunging into the whirlpool of interfering action with all its inherent dangers.

> He who abstains from interfering is everywhere secure.
>
> (Sn v. 953)

> He who keeps still and knows where to stop will not meet danger.
>
> (Tao-Te-Ching, Chapter 44)

The Chinese saying quoted earlier states in its second part that there is nothing more glorious in *making things start* than in keeping still. Explained in the Buddhist sense, these things effectively started by keeping still are "the things (or qualities) making for decrease of kammic accumulation." In dealing with them, we may follow the traditional division of mental training into morality (or conduct), concentration (or tranquillity) and wisdom (or insight). All three are decisively helped by the attitude of *keeping still* cultivated by bare attention.

1. *Conduct.* How can we improve our conduct, its moral quality and its skill in making right decisions? If we earnestly desire such an improvement, it will generally be wisest to choose the line of least resistance. If we turn too quickly against those shortcomings deeply rooted in old habits or in powerful impulses, we might suffer discouraging defeat. We should pay attention first to our blemishes of action and speech and our errors of judgement caused by thoughtlessness and rashness. Of these there are many. In our lives there are numerous instances where one short moment of reflection might have prevented a false step, and thereby warded off a long chain of misery or moral guilt that started with a single moment of thoughtlessness. But how can we curb our rash reactions, and replace them with moments of mindfulness and reflection? To do so will depend on our capacity to *stop and pause,* to apply the brakes at the right time, and this we can learn by practising bare attention. In that practice we shall train ourselves "to look and wait," to suspend reactions or slow them down. We shall learn it first the easy way, in situations of our own choice, within the limited field of experiences met with during the periods of meditative practice. When facing again and again the incidental sense impressions, feelings or stray thoughts which interrupt our concentration; when curbing again and again our desire to respond to them in some way; when succeeding again and again in keeping still in face of them—we shall be preparing ourselves to preserve that inner stillness in the wider and unprotected field of everyday life. We shall have acquired a presence of mind that will enable us to pause and stop, even if we are taken by surprise or are suddenly provoked or tempted.

Our present remarks refer to those blemishes of conduct liable to arise through thoughtlessness and rashness, but which may be more or less easily checked through mindfulness. Dexterity in dealing with these will also affect those more obstinate deviations from moral conduct rooted in strong passionate impulses or in deeply ingrained bad habits. The increased tranquillity of mind achieved in keeping still for bare attention will restrain the impetuosity of passions. The acquired habit of pausing and stopping will act as a brake to the ingrained habits of indulging in unwholesome deeds.

By being able to keep still for bare attention, or to pause for wise reflection, very often the first temptation to lust, the first wave of anger, the first mist of delusion, will disappear without causing serious entanglement. At which point the current of unwholesome thought processes is stopped will depend on the quality of mindfulness. If mindfulness is keen, it will succeed at a very early point in calling a stop to a series of defiled thoughts or actions before we are carried along by them too far. Then the respective defilements will not grow beyond their initial strength, less effort will be required to check them and fewer kammic entanglements, or none, will follow.

Let us take the example of a pleasant visual object that has aroused our liking. At first that liking might not be very active and insistent. If at this point the mind is already able to keep still for detached observation or reflection, the visual perception can easily be divested of its still very slight admixture of lust. The object becomes registered as "just something seen that has caused a pleasant feeling," or the attraction felt is sublimated into a quiet aesthetic pleasure. But if that earliest chance has been missed, the liking will grow into attachment and into the desire to possess. If now a stop is called, the thought of desire may gradually lose its strength; it will not easily turn into an insistent craving, and no actual attempts to get possession of the desired object will follow. But if the current of lust is still unchecked, then the thought of desire may express itself by speech in asking for the object or even demanding it with impetuous words. That is, unwholesome mental *kamma* is followed by unwholesome verbal *kamma*. A refusal will cause the original current of lust to branch out into additional streams of mental defilements, either sadness or anger. But if even at that late stage one can stop for quiet reflection or bare attention, accept the refusal and renounce wish-fulfilment, further complications will be avoided. However, if clamouring words are followed by unwholesome bodily *kamma*, and if, driven by craving, one tries to get possession of the desired object by stealth or force, then the kammic entanglement is complete and its consequences must be experienced in their full impact. But still, if even after the completion of the evil act, one stops for reflection, it will not be in vain. For the mindfulness that arises in the form of remorseful retrospection will preclude a hardening of character and may prevent a repetition of the same action. The Exalted One once said to his son, Rāhula:

> Whatever action you *intend* to perform, by body, speech or mind, you should consider that action.... If, in considering it, you realize: "This action which I intend to perform will be harmful to myself, or harmful to others, or harmful to both; it will be an unwholesome action, producing suffering, resulting in suffering"—then you should certainly not perform that action.
>
> Also *while* you are performing an action, by body, speech or mind, you should consider that action.... If, in considering it, you realize: "This action which I am performing is harmful to myself, or harmful to others, or harmful to both; it is an unwholesome action, producing suffering, resulting in suffering"—then you should desist from such an action.
>
> Also *after* you have performed an action, by body, speech or mind, you should consider that action.... If, in considering it, you realize: "This action which I have performed has been harmful to myself, to others, or harmful to both; it was an unwholesome action producing suffering, resulting in suffering"—then you should in future refrain from it. (MN 61)

2. *Tranquillity*. We shall now consider how stopping for bare attention also helps one to attain and strengthen tranquillity (*samatha*) in its double sense: general peace of mind and meditative concentration.

By developing the habit of pausing for bare attention, it becomes increasingly easier to withdraw into one's own inner stillness when unable to escape bodily from the loud, insistent noises of the outer world. It will be easier to forego useless reactions to the foolish speech or deeds of others. When the blows of fate are particularly hard and incessant, a mind trained in bare attention will find a refuge in the haven of apparent passivity or watchful non-action, from which position it will be able to wait patiently until the storms have passed. There are situations in life when it is best to allow things to come to their natural end. He who is able to keep still and wait will often succeed where aggressiveness or busy activity would fail. Not only in critical situations, but also in the normal course of life, the experience won by observant keeping still will convince us that we need not actively respond to every impression we receive, or regard every encounter with people or things as a challenge to our interfering activity.

By refraining from busying ourselves unnecessarily, external frictions will be reduced and the internal tensions they bring will loosen up. Greater harmony and peace will pervade the life of every day, bridging the gap between normal life and the tranquillity of meditation. Then there will be fewer of those disturbing inner reverberations of everyday restlessness which, in a coarse or subtle form, invade the hours of meditation, producing bodily and mental unrest. Consequently, the hindrance of agitation, a chief obstacle to concentration, will appear less often and will be easier to overcome when it arises.

By cultivating the attitude of bare attention as often as opportunity offers, the centrifugal forces of mind, making for mental distraction, will peter out; the centripetal tendency, turning the mind inward and making for concentration, will gather strength. Craving will no longer run in pursuit of a variety of changing objects.

Regular practice of sustained attention to a continuous series of events prepares the mind for sustained concentration on a *single* object, or a limited number of objects, in the strict practice of meditation. Firmness or steadiness of mind, another important factor in concentration, will likewise be cultivated.

Thus, the practice of keeping still, pausing and stopping for bare attention, fosters several salient components of meditative tranquillity: calmness, concentration, firmness and reduction of the multiplicity of objects. It raises the average level of normal consciousness and brings it closer to the level of the meditative mind. This is an important point because often too wide a gap between these two mental levels repeatedly frustrates attempts at mental concentration and hinders the achievement of smooth continuity in meditative practice.

In the sequence of the seven factors of enlightenment, we find that the enlightenment factor of tranquillity (*passaddhi-sambojjhaṅga*) precedes that of concentration (*samādhi-sambojjhaṅga*). Expressing the same fact, the Buddha says: "If tranquillized within, the mind will become concentrated." Now in the light of our previous remarks, we shall better understand these statements.

3. *Insight.* It has been said by the Exalted One: "He whose mind is concentrated sees things as they really are." Therefore, all those ways by which bare attention strengthens concentration

also provide a supporting condition for the development of insight. But there is also a more direct and specific help which insight receives from keeping still in bare attention.

Generally, we are more concerned with handling and using things than with knowing them in their true nature. Thus we usually grasp in haste the very first few signals conveyed to us by a perception. Then, through deeply ingrained habit, those signals evoke a standard response by way of judgements such as good-bad, pleasant-unpleasant, useful-harmful, right-wrong. These judgements, by which we define the objects in relation to ourselves, lead to corresponding reactions by word or deed. Only rarely does attention dwell upon a common or familiar object for any longer time than is needed to receive the first few signals. So, for the most part, we perceive things in a fragmentary manner and thus misconceive them. Further, only the very first phase of the object's life-span, or a little more, comes into the focus of our attention. One may not even be consciously aware that the object is a process with an extension in time—a beginning and an end; that it has many aspects and relations beyond those casually perceived in a limited situation; that, in brief, it has a kind of evanescent individuality of its own.

A world perceived in this superficial way will consist of shapeless little lumps of experiences marked by a few subjectively selected signs or symbols. The symbols chosen are determined mainly by the individual's self-interest; sometimes they are even misapplied. The shadow-like world that results includes not only the outer environment and other persons, but also a good part of one's own bodily and mental processes. These, too, become subjected to the same superficial manner of conceptualization.

The Buddha points out four basic misconceptions that result from distorted perceptions and unmethodical attention: taking the impure for pure, the impermanent for lasting, the painful and pain-bringing for pleasant and the impersonal for a self or something belonging to the self. When the seal of self-reference is thus stamped again and again upon the world of everyday experience, the basic misconception, "This belongs to me" (*attaniya*) will steadily put forth roots into all the bodily and mental factors of our being. Like the hair-roots of a plant, these will be fine, but firm and widespread—to such an extent, in fact, that the notions of "I" and "mine" will hardly be shaken by merely intellectual convictions about the non-existence of a self (*anattā*).

These grave consequences issue from the fundamental perceptual situation: our rush into hasty or habitual reactions after receiving the first few signals from our perceptions. But if we muster the restraining forces of mindfulness and pause for bare attention, the material and mental processes that form the objects of mind at the given moment will reveal themselves to us more fully and more truly. No longer dragged at once into the whirlpool of self-reference, allowed to unfold themselves before the watchful eye of mindfulness, they will disclose the diversity of their aspects and the wide net of their correlations and interconnections. The connection with self-interest, so narrow and often falsifying, will recede into the background, dwarfed by the wider view now gained. The processes observed display in their serial occurrence and in their component parts a constant birth and death, a rise and a fall. Thereby the facts of change and impermanence impress themselves on the mind with growing intensity.

The same discernment of rise and fall dissolves the false conceptions of unity created under the influence of the egocentric attitude. Self-reference uncritically overrides diversity; it lumps things together under the preconceptions of *being* a self or *belonging* to a self. But bare attention reveals these sham unities as impersonal and conditioned phenomena. Facing thus again and again the evanescent, dependent and impersonal nature of life-processes within and without, we shall discover their monotony and unsatisfactory nature: in other words, the truth of suffering. Thus, by the simple device of slowing down, pausing and keeping still for bare attention, all three of the characteristics of existence—impermanence, suffering and non-self—will open themselves to penetrative insight (*vipassanā*).

Spontaneity

An acquired or strengthened habit of pausing mindfully before acting does not exclude a wholesome spontaneity of response. On the contrary, through training, the practice of pausing, stopping and keeping still for bare attention will itself become quite spontaneous. It will grow into a selective mechanism of the mind that, with an increasing reliability and swiftness of response, can prevent the upsurge of evil or unwise impulses. Without such a skill we may intellectually realize those impulses to be unwholesome, but still succumb to them owing to their own powerful spontaneity. The practice of pausing mindfully serves, therefore, to replace unwholesome spontaneity or habits with wholesome ones grounded in our better knowledge and nobler intentions.

Just as certain reflex movements automatically protect the body, similarly the mind needs spontaneous spiritual and moral self-protection. The practice of bare attention will provide this vital function. A person of average moral standards instinctively shrinks from thoughts of theft or murder. With the help of the method of bare attention, the range of such spontaneous moral brakes can be vastly extended and ethical sensitivity greatly heightened.

In an untrained mind, noble tendencies and right thoughts are often assailed by the sudden outbreak of passions and prejudices. They either succumb or assert themselves only with difficulty after an inner struggle. But if the spontaneity of the unwholesome is checked or greatly reduced, as described above, our good impulses and wise reflections will have greater scope to emerge and express themselves freely and spontaneously. Their natural flow will give us greater confidence in the power of the good within us; it will also carry more conviction for others. That spontaneity of the good will not be erratic, for it will have deep and firm roots in previous methodical training. Here appears a way by which a premeditated good thought (*sasaṅkhārika-kusala-citta*) may be transformed into a spontaneous good thought (*asaṅkhārika-kusala-citta*). According to the psychology of the Abhidhamma Piṭaka, such a thought, if combined with knowledge, takes the first place in the scale of ethical values. In this way we shall achieve a practical understanding of a saying in *The Secret of the Golden Flower*:[7] "If one attains intentionally to an unintentional state one has comprehension." This saying invites a paraphrase in Pali terms: *Sasaṅkhārena asaṅkhārikaṃ pattabbaṃ*, "By premeditated intentional effort spontaneity can be won."

If the numerous aids to mental growth and liberation found in the Buddha's teachings are wisely utilized, there is actually

7. A treatise of Chinese Taoism, strongly influenced by Mahāyāna Buddhism.

nothing that can finally withstand the Satipaṭṭhāna method; and this method starts with the simple practice of learning to pause and stop for bare attention.

Slowing Down

Against the impetuosity, rashness and heedlessness of the untrained mind, the practice of pausing and stopping sets up a deliberate slowing down. The demands of modern life, however, make it impracticable to introduce such a slowing-down of functions into the routine of the average working day. But as an antidote against the harmful consequences of the hectic speed of modern life, it is all the more important to cultivate that practice in one's leisure hours, especially in periods of strict Satipaṭṭhāna practice. Such practice will also bestow the worldly benefits of greater calm, efficiency and skill in one's daily round of work.

For the purposes of meditative development, slowing-down serves as an effective training in heedfulness, sense-control and concentration. But apart from that, it has a more specific significance for meditative practice. In the commentary to the *Satipaṭṭhāna Sutta*, it is said that the slowing down of movements may help in *regaining lost concentration* on a chosen object. A monk, so we read, had bent his arm quickly without remembering his subject of meditation as his rule of practice demanded. On becoming aware of that omission he took his arm back to its previous position and repeated the movement mindfully. The subject of meditation referred to was probably "clearly comprehending action," as mentioned in the *Satipaṭṭhāna Sutta*: "In bending and stretching he acts with clear comprehension."

The slowing-down of certain bodily movements during strict meditative training is particularly helpful in gaining *insight-knowledge* (*vipassanā-ñāṇa*), especially the direct awareness of change and non-self. To a great extent, it is the rapidity of movement that strengthens the illusion of unity, identity and substantiality in what is actually a complex evanescent process. Therefore, in the strict practice of Satipaṭṭhāna, the slowing down of such actions as walking, bending and stretching, so as to discern the several phases of each movement, provides a powerful aid for direct insight into the three characteristics of all phenomena. The meditator's contemplation will gain increasing force and significance if he notices clearly how each partial phase of the process observed arises and ceases by itself, and nothing of it goes over or "transmigrates" to the next phase.

Under the influence of pausing for bare attention, the average rhythm of our everyday actions, speech and thoughts will also become more quiet and peaceful. Slowing-down the hurried rhythm of life means that thoughts, feelings and perceptions will be able to complete the entire length of their natural lifetime. Full awareness will extend up to their end phase: to their last vibrations and reverberations. Too often that end phase is cut off by an impatient grasping at new impressions, or by hurrying on to the next stage of a line of thought before the earlier one has been clearly comprehended. This is one of the main reasons for the disorderly state of the average mind, which is burdened by a vast amount of indistinct or fragmentary perceptions, stunted emotions and undigested ideas. Slowing-down will prove an effective device for recovering the fullness and clarity of consciousness. A fitting simile, and at the same time an actual example, is the procedure called for in the practice of mindfulness of breathing (*ānāpānasati*): mindfulness has to cover the whole extent of the breath, its beginning, middle and end. This is what is meant by the passage in the sutta, "Experiencing the *whole* (breath) body, I shall breathe in and out." Similarly, the entire "breath" or rhythm of our lives will become deeper and fuller if, through slowing-down, we get used to sustained attention.

The habit of prematurely cutting off processes of thought, or slurring over them, has assumed serious proportions in the man of modern urban civilization. Restlessly he clamours for ever new stimuli in increasingly quicker succession, just as he demands increasing speed in his means of locomotion. This rapid bombardment of impressions has gradually blunted his sensitivity, and thus he always needs new stimuli, louder, coarser and more variegated. Such a process, if not checked, can end only in disaster. Already we see at large a decline of finer aesthetic susceptibility and a growing incapacity for genuine natural joy. The place of both is taken by a hectic, short-breathed excitement incapable of giving any true aesthetic or emotional satisfaction. "Shallow mental breath" is to a great extent responsible for the growing superficiality of "civilized man" and for the frightening spread of nervous disorders in the West. It may well become the start of a general deterioration of human consciousness in its qualitative level, range and strength. This danger threatens all those, in the East as well as in the West, who lack adequate spiritual protection from the impact of technical civilization. Satipaṭṭhāna can make an important contribution to remedying this situation, in the way we have briefly indicated here. Thus the method will prove beneficial from the worldly point of view as well.

Here, however, we are chiefly concerned with the psychological aspects of mindfulness and their significance for meditative development. Sustained attention, helped by slowing-down, will affect the quality of consciousness mainly in three ways: (a) in intensifying consciousness; (b) in clarifying the object's characteristic features; and (c) in revealing the object's relatedness.

(a) An object of sustained attention will exert a particularly *strong* and *long-lasting* impact on the mind. Its influence will be felt not only throughout the thought-series immediately following the particular perception, but may also extend far into the future. It is that causal efficacy which is the measure of the *intensity of consciousness.*

(b) Sustained attention leads to a *fuller picture* of the object in all its aspects. Generally, the first impression we gain of any new sense-object or idea will be its most striking feature; it is this aspect of the object which captures our attention up to the culminating point of the impact. But the object also displays other aspects or characteristics, and is capable of exercising functions other than those we initially notice. These may be less obvious to us or subjectively less interesting; but they may be even more important. There will also be cases where our first impression is entirely deceptive. Only if we sustain our attention beyond that first impact will the object reveal itself more fully. In the downward course of the first perceptual wave the prejudicing force of the first impact lessens; and it is only then, in that end phase, that the object will yield a wider range of detail, a more complete picture of itself. It is therefore only by sustained attention that we can obtain a *clearer understanding of an object's characteristic features.*

(c) Among the characteristic features of any object, physical or mental, there is one class we often overlook due to hasty or superficial attention, and which therefore needs to be treated separately. This is the *relatedness* of the object. The object's relatedness extends back to its past—to its origin, causes, reasons and logical precedents; it also extends outward to embrace the total context—its background, environment and presently active influences. We can never fully understand things if we view them in artificial isolation. We have to see them as part of a wider pattern, in their conditioned and conditioning nature; and this can be done only with the help of sustained attention.

Subliminal Influences

The three ways of heightening consciousness just discussed are clearly of prime importance for the development of insight. When consciousness is intensified, and its objective field clarified and discerned in its relational structure, the ground is prepared for "seeing things according to reality." But besides its obvious direct influence, this threefold process also has an indirect influence which is no less powerful and important: it strengthens and sharpens the mind's subliminal faculties of subconscious organization, memory and intuition. These again, on their part, nourish and consolidate the progress of liberating insight. The insight aided by them is like the mountain lake of the canonical simile: it is fed not only by the outside rains, but also by springs welling up from within its own depths. The insight nourished by these "underground" subliminal resources of the mind will have deep roots. The meditative results that it brings cannot be lost easily, even with unliberated worldlings who are still subject to relapse.

1. Perceptions or thoughts which have been objects of sustained attention make a stronger impact on the mind and reveal their characteristic features more distinctly than when attention is slack. Thus, when they sink into the subconscious, they occupy a special position there. This holds true for all three ways of enhancing the consciousness of an object. (a) In a process of consciousness, if attention is as strong in the end phase as in the earlier phases, then when the process is finished and the mind lapses back into subconsciousness, the latter will be more amenable to conscious control. (b) If an impression or idea has been marked by numerous distinct characteristics, then when it fades from immediate awareness, it will not be so easily lost in the vague contents of the subconscious or dragged by passionate biases into false subconscious associations. (c) Similarly, the

correct comprehension of the object's relatedness will protect the experience from being merged with indistinct subconscious material. Perceptions or thoughts of enhanced intensity and clarity, absorbed into the subconscious, remain more articulate and more accessible than contents originating from hazy or "stunned" impressions. It will be easier to convert them into full consciousness and they will be less unaccountable in their hidden effects upon the mind. If, through an improvement in the quality and range of mindfulness, the number of such matured impressions increases, the result might be a subtle change in the very structure of subconsciousness itself.

2. It will be evident from our earlier remarks that those impressions that we have called "matured" or "more accessible and convertible" lend themselves more easily and more correctly to recollection—more easily because of their greater intensity, more correctly because their clearly marked features protect them from being distorted by false associative images or ideas. Remembering them in their context and relatedness works both ways—it promotes both easier and more correct recollection. Thus *sati* in its meaning and function of mindfulness helps to strengthen *sati* in its meaning and function of *memory*.

3. The influence of sustained attention on the subconscious and on memory brings a deepening and strengthening of the faculty of intuition, particularly the intuitive insight which chiefly concerns us here. Intuition is not a gift from the unknown. Like any other mental faculty, it arises out of specific conditions. In this case the primary conditions are latent memories of perceptions and thoughts stored in the subconscious. Obviously, the memories providing the most fertile soil for the growth of intuition will be those marked by greater intensity, clarity and wealth of distinctive marks; for it is these that are most accessible. Here, too, the preserved relatedness of the impressions will contribute much. Recollections of that type will have a more organic character than memories of bare or vague isolated facts, and they will fall more easily into new patterns of meaning and significance. These more articulate memory images will be a strong stimulation and aid for the intuitive faculty. Silently, in the hidden depths of the subliminal mind, the work of collecting and organizing the subconscious material of experience and knowledge goes on until it is ripe to emerge as an *intuition*.

The breakthrough of that intuition is sometimes occasioned by quite ordinary happenings. However, though seemingly ordinary, these events may have a strong evocative power if previously they had been made objects of sustained attention. Slowing-down and pausing for bare attention will uncover the depth dimension of the simple things of everyday life, and thus provide potential stimuli for the intuitive faculty.

This applies also to the intuitive penetration of the Four Noble Truths that culminates in liberation (*arahatta*). The scriptures record many instances of monks and nuns who could not arrive at intuitive penetration when engaged in the actual practice of insight meditation. The flash of intuition struck them on quite different occasions: when stumbling against a rock or catching sight of a forest fire, a mirage or a lump of froth in a river. We meet here another confirmation of that seemingly paradoxical saying that "intentionally an unintentional state may be won." By deliberately turning the full light of mindfulness on the smallest events and actions of everyday life, eventually the liberating wisdom may arise.

Sustained attention not only provides the nourishing soil for the *growth* of intuition, it also makes possible the fuller utilization and even repetition of the intuitive moment. People of inspiration in various fields of creative activity have often deplored their common experience: the flash of intuition strikes so suddenly and vanishes so quickly that frequently the slow response of the mind hardly catches the last glimpse of it. But if the mind has been trained in observant pausing, in slowing-down and sustained attention, and if—as indicated above—the subconscious has been influenced, then the intuitive moment too might gain that fuller, slower and stronger rhythm. This being the case, its impact will be strong and clear enough to allow for full use of that flash of intuitive insight. It might even be possible to lead its fading vibrations upward again to a new culmination, similar to the rhythmic repetition of a melody rising again in harmonious development out of the last notes of its first appearance.

The full utilization of a single moment of intuitive insight could be of decisive importance for one's progress towards full realization. If one's mental grip is too weak and one lets those elusive moments of intuitive insight slip away without having utilized them fully for the work of liberation, then they might not recur until many years have passed, or perhaps not at all during the present life. Skill in sustained attention, however, will allow one to make full use of such opportunities, and slowing-down and pausing during meditative practice is an important aid in acquiring that skill.

Through our treatment of pausing, stopping and slowing-down, one of the traditional definitions of mindfulness found in the Pali scriptures will have become more intelligible in its far-reaching implications: that is, its function of *anapilāpanatā*, meaning literally, "not floating (or slipping) away." "Like pumpkin-pots on the surface of water," add the commentators, and they continue: "Mindfulness enters deeply into its object, instead of hurrying only over its surface." Therefore, "non-superficiality" will be an appropriate rendering of the above Pali term, and a fitting characterization of mindfulness.

4. Directness of Vision

> I wish I could disaccustom myself from everything, so that I might see anew, hear anew, feel anew. Habit spoils our philosophy.
>
> G.C. Lichtenberg (1742–1799)

In an earlier section we spoke about the impulsive spontaneity of the unwholesome. We have seen how stopping for bare and sustained attention is able to counter, or reduce, our rash impulsive reactions, thus allowing us to face any situation with a fresh mind, with a *directness of vision* unprejudiced by those first spontaneous responses.

By *directness of vision* we understand a direct view of reality, without any colouring or distorting lenses, without the intrusion of emotional or habitual prejudices and intellectual biases. It means: coming face to face with the bare facts of actuality, seeing them as vividly and freshly as if we were seeing them for the first time.

The Force of Habit

Those spontaneous reactions which so often stand in the way of direct vision do not derive only from our passionate impulses. Very frequently they are the product of *habit*. In that form, they generally have an even stronger and more tenacious hold on us—a hold which may work out either for our good or for our harm. The influence that habit exercises for the *good* is seen in the "power of repeated practice." This power protects our achievements and skills—whether manual or mental, worldly or spiritual—against loss or forgetfulness, and converts them from casual, short-lived imperfect acquisitions into the more secure possession of a quality thoroughly mastered. The *detrimental* effect of habitual spontaneous reactions is manifest in what is called in a derogative sense the "force of habit": its deadening, stultifying and narrowing influence productive of compulsive behaviour of various kinds. In our present context we shall be concerned only with that negative aspect of habit as impeding and obscuring the directness of vision.

As remarked earlier, habitual reactions generally have a stronger influence upon our behaviour than impulsive ones. Our passionate impulses may disappear as suddenly as they have arisen. Though their consequences may be very grave and extend far into the future, their influence is in no way as long-lasting and deep-reaching as that of habit. Habit spreads its vast and closely meshed net over wide areas of our life and thought, trying to drag in more and more. Our passionate impulses, too, might be caught in that net and thus be transformed from passing outbursts into lasting traits of character. A momentary impulse, an occasional indulgence, a passing whim may by repetition become a habit we find difficult to uproot, a desire hard to control and finally an automatic function we no longer question. Repeated gratification turns a desire into a habit, and a habit left unchecked grows into a compulsion.

It sometimes happens that, at first, we regard a particular activity or mental attitude as without any special personal importance. The activity or attitude may be morally indifferent and inconsequential. At the start we might find it easy to abandon it or even to exchange it for its opposite, since neither our emotions nor reason bias us towards either alternative. But by repetition, we come to regard the chosen course of action or thought as "pleasant, desirable and correct," even as "righteous"; and thus we finally identify it with our character or personality. Consequently, we feel any break in this routine to be unpleasant or wrong. Any outside interference with it we greatly resent, even regarding such interference as a threat to our "vital interests and principles."

In fact at all times primitive minds, whether "civilized" or not, have looked at a stranger with his "strange customs" as an enemy, and have felt his mere unaggressive presence as a challenge or threat.

At the beginning, when no great importance was ascribed to the specific habit, the attachment that gradually formed was directed not so much to the action proper as to the pleasure we derived from undisturbed routine. The strength of that attachment to routine derives partly from the force of physical and mental inertia, so powerful a motive in man; we shall presently refer to another cause for attachment to routine. By force of habit, the particular concern—whether a material object, an activity or a way of thinking—comes to be invested with such an increase of emotional emphasis, that the attachment to quite unimportant or banal things may become as tenacious as that to our more fundamental needs. Thus the lack of conscious control can turn the smallest habits into the uncontested masters of our lives. It bestows upon them the dangerous power to limit and rigidify our character and to narrow our freedom of movement—environmental, intellectual and spiritual. Through our subservience to habit, we forge new fetters for ourselves and make ourselves vulnerable to new attachments, aversions, prejudices and predilections; that is, to new suffering. The danger for spiritual development posed by the dominating influence of habit is perhaps more serious today than ever before; for the expansion of habit is particularly noticeable in our present age when specialization and standardization reach into so many varied spheres of life and thought.

Therefore, when considering the Satipaṭṭhāna Sutta's words on the formation of fetters, we should also think of the important part played by habit:

> ... and what fetter arises dependent on both (i.e., the sense organs and sense objects), that he knows well. In what manner the arising of the unarisen fetter comes to be, that he knows well.

In Buddhist terms, it is pre-eminently the hindrance of sloth and torpor (*thīna-middha-nīvaraṇa*) that is strengthened by the force of habit, and it is the mental faculties such as agility and pliancy of mind (*kāya-* and *citta-lahutā*, etc.)[8] that are weakened.

This tendency of habits to extend their range is anchored in the very nature of consciousness. It stems not only from the aforementioned passive force of inertia, but in many cases from an active will to dominate and conquer. Certain active types of consciousness, possessing a fair degree of intensity, tend to repeat themselves. Each one struggles to gain ascendancy, to become a centre around which other weaker mental and physical states revolve, adapting themselves to and serving that central disposition. This tendency is never quite undisputed, but still it prevails, and even peripheral or subordinate types of consciousness exhibit the same urge for ascendancy. This is a striking parallel to the self-assertion and domineering tendency of an egocentric individual in his contact with society. Among biological analogies, we may mention the tendency towards expansion shown by cancer and other pathological growths; the tendency towards repetition we meet in the freak mutations which loom as a grave danger at the horizon of our atomic age.

Because of that will to dominate inherent in many types of consciousness, a passing whim may grow into a relatively constant trait of character. If still not satisfied with its position, it may break away entirely from the present combination of life forces until finally, in the process of rebirths, it becomes the very centre of a new personality. There are within us countless seeds for new lives, for innumerable potential "beings," all of whom we should vow to liberate from the wheel of saṃsāra, as the Sixth Zen Patriarch expressed it.[9]

Detrimental physical or mental habits may grow strong, not only if fostered deliberately, but also if left unnoticed or unopposed. Much of what has now strong roots in our nature

8. About these important qualitative constituents of good, wholesome (*kusala*) consciousness, see the author's *Abhidhamma Studies* (Kandy: Buddhist Publication Society, 1965), pp. 51 ff.

9. This may be a somewhat ironical reference by that great sage to the fact that the well-known Mahāyānic Bodhisattva vow of liberating all beings of the universe is often taken much too light-heartedly by many of his fellow Mahāyānists.

has grown from minute seeds planted in a long-forgotten past (see the Simile of the Creeper, MN 45). This growth of morally bad or otherwise detrimental habits can be effectively checked by gradually developing another habit: that of attending to them mindfully. If we now do deliberately what had become a mechanical performance, and if prior to doing it we pause a while for bare attention and reflection—this will give us a chance to scrutinize the habit and clearly comprehend its purpose and suitability (*sātthaka-* and *sappāya-sampajañña*). It will allow us to make a fresh assessment of the situation, to see it directly, unobscured by the mental haze that surrounds a habitual activity with the false assurance: "It is right because it was done before." Even if a detrimental habit cannot be broken quickly, the reflective pause will counter its unquestioned spontaneity of occurrence. It will stamp it with the seal of repeated scrutiny and resistance, so that on its recurrence it will be weaker and will prove more amenable to our attempts to change or abolish it.

It need hardly be mentioned that habit, which has been rightly called "the wet-nurse of man," cannot and should not disappear from our lives. Let us only remember what a relief it is, particularly in the crowded day and complex life of a city-dweller, to be able to do a great number of things fairly mechanically with, as it were, only "half-powered attention." Habit brings considerable simplification to our lives. It would be an unbearable strain if all our little humdrum activities had to be done with deliberate effort and close attention. In fact, many operations of manual labour, much of the *technique* in art, and even standard procedures in complex intellectual work, generally bring better and more even results through skilled routine performance. Yet that evenness of habitual performance will also reach its end point. Unless enlivened by the creation of new interest, it will show symptoms of fatigue and start to decline.

Of course it would be absurd to advocate that all our little habits be abolished, for many are innocuous and even useful. But we should regularly ask ourselves whether we still have control over them; whether we can give them up or alter them at will. We can answer this question for ourselves in two ways: first, by attending to our habitual actions mindfully for a certain period of time, and second, by actually giving them up temporarily in cases where this will not have any harmful or disturbing effects upon ourselves or others. If we turn on them the light of *direct vision*, looking at them or performing them as if for the first time, these little routine activities, and the habitual sights around us, will assume a new glow of interest and stimulation. This also holds good for our professional occupations and their environment, and for our close human relationships if they should have become stale by habit. The relationship to one's marriage partner, to friends and to colleagues may thus receive a great rejuvenation. A fresh and direct vision will also reveal that one can relate to people or do things in a different and more beneficial way than one did before by force of habit.

An acquired capacity to give up minor habits will prove its worth in the fight against more dangerous proclivities. It will also come to our aid at times when we are faced with serious changes in our lives which forcefully deprive us of fundamental habits. Loosening the hardened soil of our routine behaviour and thoughts will have an enlivening effect on our vital energy, our mental vigour and our power of imagination. But what is most important, into that loosened soil we shall be able to plant the seeds of vigorous spiritual progress.

Associative Thought

Mental habituation to standard reactions, to sequences of activity and to judgements of people or things proceeds by way of associative thinking. From the objects, ideas, situations and people that we encounter, we select certain distinctive marks, and associate these marks with our own response to them. If these encounters recur, they are associated first with those marks selected earlier, and then with our original, or strongest response. Thus these marks become a signal for releasing a standard reaction, which may consist of a long sequence of connected acts or thoughts familiar through repeated practice or experience. This way of functioning makes it unnecessary for us to apply new effort and painstaking scrutiny to each single step in such a sequence. The result is a great simplification of life, permitting us to release energy for other tasks. In fact, in the evolution of the human mind, associative thinking was a progressive step of decisive importance. It enabled us to learn from experience, and thus led up to the discovery and application of causal laws.

Yet along with these benefits, associative thinking can also bring many grave dangers if it is applied faultily or thoughtlessly and not carefully controlled. Let us draw up a partial list of these danger points:

1. Associative thinking, recurring again and again in similar situations, may easily perpetuate and strengthen faulty or incomplete initial observations, errors of judgement and emotional prejudices such as love, hate and pride.

2. Incomplete observations and restricted viewpoints in judgement, sufficient to deal with one particular situation, may prove quite inadequate and entail grave consequences if mechanically applied to changed circumstances.

3. Due to misdirected associative thinking, a strong instinctive dislike may be felt for things, places or people which in some way are merely reminiscent of unpleasant experiences, but actually have no connection with them.

These briefly stated instances show how vital it is for us to scrutinize from time to time the mental grooves of our associative thoughts, and to review the various habits and stereotype reactions deriving from them. In other words, we must step out of our ruts, regain a direct vision of things and make a fresh appraisal of our habits in the light of that vision.

If we look once again over the list of potential dangers deriving from uncontrolled associative thinking, we shall better understand the Buddha's insistence upon getting to the bedrock of experience. In the profound and terse stanzas called "The Cave," included in the Suttanipāta, the Buddha says that the "full penetration of *sense impression* (*phassa*) will make one free from greed" and that "by understanding *perception* (*saññā*), one will be able to cross the flood of saṃsāra" (vv. 778ff.).[10] By placing mindfulness as a guard at the very first gate through which thoughts enter the mind, we shall be able to control the incomers much more easily, and shut out unwanted intruders. Thus the purity of "luminous consciousness" can be maintained against "adventitious defilements" (AN 1:51).

The *Satipaṭṭhāna Sutta* provides a systematic training for inducing direct, fresh and undistorted vision. The training

---

10. Compare also the passage on the significance of sense impression (or contact) in the concluding sections of the *Brahmajāla Sutta* (DN 1).

covers the entire personality in its physical and mental aspects, and includes the whole world of experience. The methodical application of the several exercises to oneself (*ajjhatta*), to others (*bahiddhā*) and alternatingly to both will help uncover erroneous conceptions due to misdirected associative thinking and misapplied analogies.

The principal types of false associative thinking are covered, in the terminology of the Dhamma, by the four kinds of *misapprehension or perverted views* (*vipallāsa*), i.e., wrongly taking (1) what is impermanent for permanent, (2) what is painful, or conducive to pain, for happiness, (3) what has no self and is unsubstantial for a self or an abiding substance, and (4) what is impure for beautiful. These perverted views arise through a false apprehension of the characteristic marks of things. Under the influence of our passions and false theories, we perceive things selectively in a one-sided or erroneous way, and then associate them wrongly with other ideas. By applying bare attention to our perceptions and impressions, gradually we can free them from these misapprehensions, progressing steadily towards the *direct vision* of things as they really are.

The Sense of Urgency

One who has clear and direct vision, stirred to a sense of urgency (*saṃvega*) by things that are deeply moving, will experience a release of energy and courage enabling him to break through his timid hesitations and his rigid routine of life and thought. If that sense of urgency is kept alive, it will bestow the earnestness and persistence required for the work of liberation. Thus said the teachers of old:

> This very world here is our field of action.
> It harbours the unfoldment of the holy path,
> And many things to break complacency.
> Be stirred by things which may well move the heart,
> And being stirred, strive wisely and fight on!

Our closest surroundings are full of stirring things. If we generally do not perceive them as such, that is because habit has made our vision dull and our heart insensitive.

The same thing happens to us even with the Buddha's teaching. When we first encounter the teaching, we receive a powerful intellectual and emotional stimulation; but gradually the impetus tends to lose its original freshness and impelling force. The remedy is to constantly renew it by turning to the fullness of life around us, which illustrates the Four Noble Truths in ever new variations. A direct vision will impart new lifeblood even to the most common experiences of every day, so that their true nature appears through the dim haze of habit and speaks to us with a fresh voice. It may well be just the long accustomed sight of the beggar at the street corner, of a weeping child or the illness of a friend which startles us afresh, makes us think and stirs our sense of urgency in treading resolutely the path that leads to the cessation of suffering.

We know the beautiful account of how Prince Siddhattha first came face to face with old age, illness and death while driving his chariot through the royal city after a long period of isolation in a make-believe world. This ancient story may well be historical fact, for we know that in the lives of many great men common events often gain a symbolic significance and lead to major consequences far beyond their ordinary appearance. Great minds find significance in the seemingly commonplace and invest the fleeting moment with far-reaching efficacy. But, without contesting the inner truth of that old story, we may reasonably believe that the young prince had actually seen before, with his fleshy eyes, old people, sick people and those who had succumbed to death. However, on all these earlier occasions, he would not have been touched very deeply by these sights—as is the case with most of us most of the time. That earlier lack of sensitivity may have been due to the carefully protected, artificial seclusion of his petty, though princely, happiness—the hereditary routine of his life into which his father had placed him. Only when he broke through that golden cage of easy-going habits could the facts of suffering strike him as forcibly as if he had seen them for the first time. Then only was he stirred by them to a sense of urgency that led him out of the home life and set his feet firmly on the road to enlightenment.

The more *clearly* and *deeply* our minds and hearts respond to the truth of suffering manifest in the very common facts of our existence, the less often shall we need a repetition of the lesson and the shorter will be our migration through saṃsāra. The *clarity* of perception evoking our response will come from an undeflected directness of vision, bestowed by bare attention (*sati*); and the *depth* of experience will come from wise reflection or clear comprehension (*sampajañña*).

The Road to Insight

Directness of vision is also a chief characteristic of the methodical practice of insight meditation. There it is identified with the direct or experiential knowledge bestowed by meditation, as distinguished from the inferential knowledge obtained by study and reflection. In the meditative development of insight, one's own physical and mental processes are directly viewed, without the interference of abstract concepts or the filtering screens of emotional evaluation. For in this context these only obscure or camouflage the naked facts, detracting from the strong immediate impact of reality. Conceptual generalizations from experience are very useful in their place; but if they interrupt the meditative practice of bare attention, they tend to "shove aside" or dispose of the particular fact, by saying, as it were: "It is nothing else but this." Generalizing thought inclines to become impatient with a recurrent type, and after having it classified, soon finds it boring.

Bare attention, however, being the key instrument of methodical insight, keeps to the particular. It follows keenly the rise and fall of successive physical and mental processes. Though all phenomena of a given series may be true to type (e.g., inhalations and exhalations), bare attention regards each of them as distinct, and conscientiously registers its separate birth and death. If mindfulness remains alert, these repetitions of type will, by their multiplication, exert not a reduced but an intensified impact on the mind. The three characteristics—impermanence, suffering and voidness of self—inherent in the process observed, will stand out more and more clearly. They will appear in the light shed by the phenomena themselves, not in a *borrowed* light; not even a light borrowed from the Buddha, the peerless and indispensable guide to these experiences. These physical and mental phenomena, in their "self-luminosity," will then convey a growing sense of urgency to the meditator: revulsion, dissatisfaction and awareness of danger, followed by detachment—though certainly, joy, happiness and calm, too, will not be absent throughout the practice. Then, if all other conditions of inner maturity are fulfilled, the first direct vision of final liberation will dawn with the stream-winner's (*sotāpanna*) indubitable knowledge: "Whatever has the nature of arising, has the nature of vanishing."

Thus, in the unfoldment of the power of mindfulness, Satipaṭṭhāna will prove itself as the true embodiment of the Dhamma, of which it was said:

"Well-proclaimed is the Dhamma by the Blessed One, visible here and now, not delayed, inviting inspection, onward-leading, to be directly experienced by the wise."

The Significance of the Four Noble Truths

by

V. F. Gunaratna

WHEEL PUBLICATION NO. 123

Introduction

I am happy to be able to speak to you this evening on a subject which forms the very heart and core of Buddhism. It is the realization of the eternal verities of life which the Buddha had gained by attainment to Enlightenment beneath the spreading branches of the Bodhi tree in Gayā, that he proclaimed over 2,500 years ago to a suffering world, in just four formulae or enunciations, which he himself called the "Four Noble Truths." These Truths were made known by him in his very first sermon[1] delivered seven weeks after his Enlightenment, and they constitute the essence of the Dhamma pervading every aspect and every part of it.

There is first the Noble Truth of Dukkha (suffering). Secondly, there is the Noble Truth of the Cause of Dukkha. Thirdly, there is the Noble Truth of the Cessation of Dukkha, and fourthly there is the Noble Truth of the Path leading to the Cessation of Dukkha.

In this lecture I propose first to dwell on the general nature of these Four Noble Truths as distinguished from their specific contents, and, thereafter, to proceed to consider their contents and their significance.

---

1. *Dhammacakkapavattana Sutta, Kindred Sayings*. V. p. 356.

General Nature of the Truths

At the outset, one may be tempted to ask why these Truths are called Noble (the Pali word is *ariya*), and why they are only four in number, not less, not more. The well-known commentator Venerable Buddhaghosa in his *Visuddhimagga* has answered both these questions. They are called "Noble" Truths for three reasons—because they have been discovered by the Noble One—the Buddha—because they can be fully realized only by the Noble Ones such as the Buddhas, the *Pacceka Buddhas* and the *Arahants*, and also because they are real and not unreal; they deal with Reality.

As regards the reason why there are only Four Truths, not less, not more, the explanation is that no other Truth can harmoniously exist side by side with these Four Truths, and not one of these Truths can be eliminated without loss of meaning. If one of these Truths is eliminated, the sequence suffers, the chain of reasoning breaks and the meaning in its fullness is lost. If one more Truth is added, that Truth is bound to be of a different significance and different type covering a different field, and will not fit in with the existing Truths. Hence it is not possible to conceive of either supplementing them or reducing their number. *Dukkha*, *dukkha*'s cause, *dukkha*'s cessation and the path leading to this cessation—so constitute a certain totality, a definite unity of logical considerations, that they must remain at four, not less, not more.

Not only do these Four Truths form the heart and core of Buddhism, these Truths are also so far-reaching, touching life at every point, so encompassing, taking in every aspect of life, that no amount of thinking on them can ever be deemed sufficient or complete until such thinking reaches the level of a definite spiritual experience, as distinguished from a mere theoretical understanding of them. One has only to glance through the pages of the 12th part of the Saṃyutta Nikāya known as the Sacca Saṃyutta or Kindred Sayings about the Truths, to realize the importance of repeatedly pondering on these Truths. Here, these Four Noble Truths are regarded as the topic of all topics, the one topic which appertains to Reality and leads to the awakening of the highest wisdom, the one topic for the complete realization of which "householders in the past have rightly gone forth from home to the homeless life."[2] This is the one line of thought worth cultivating, worth meditating on. "All other thoughts," says the Buddha, "are not concerned with real profit; they are not the rudiments of the Holy Life; they conduce not to revulsion, to cessation, to tranquility, to full understanding, to perfect wisdom. They conduce not to Nibbāna."[3]

How very vital these Four Truths are to man's spiritual development can be gauged from this significant remark of the Buddha appearing in the Sacca Saṃyutta.

"O monks, if there are any for whom you have any fellow feeling, if there are any who may deem you worth listening to, your friends and colleagues, your kinsmen and blood-relations, it is your duty to rouse them, admonish them and establish them in the comprehension of the Four Noble Truths."[4] Hence, every occasion for hearing these Truths should be regarded as an additional aid, a further approach to the process of realizing the wisdom of these inestimable Truths.

Those who have intently contemplated these Truths will tell you that a wonderful feature about these Truths is that each time you ponder deeply on them some new aspect of these Truths, some new feature, some new point of view will present itself before you. In short, you will know that you have learnt something new. This is so because it takes time to comprehend fully these Truths; they are so vast, so wide, so full and so profound, while man's ability to comprehend them and realize them is so weak and so poor.

It is said that nothing is more interesting to man than the study of man. Viewed in this light a study of the Four Noble Truths should be of the deepest interest to us since they are all about us, they concern us and are dependent on us. These Truths involve a consideration, of not so much the external world as the internal world of mind. Actually, the external is a reflection of the internal. There is no external world to be viewed, if there is no internal world which can view it. The physical is always a manifestation of the mental. Hence it is that the Buddha in the Rohitassa Sutta said, "In this one fathom long body along with its

2. *Kindred Sayings* V. p. 352.
3. Ibid., p. 354, p. 355, p. 378.
4. *Kindred Sayings* V. p. 368.

perceptions and thoughts do I proclaim the world, the origin of the world, the cessation of the world and the path leading to the cessation of the world."[5] The word "world" here means the world of *dukkha* (suffering) and *dukkha* is an experience of the internal world of self. It should therefore be our aim, meditating on these Truths, to be able to see in ourselves, in the everyday affairs of our lives, in every event and circumstance connected with ourselves, an exemplification of these Four Noble Truths until they become a definite living experience—a spiritual experience which is quite different from a theoretical understanding of these Truths.

Another feature about these Truths, which those who contemplate them intently will tell you, is that when the First Noble Truth is comprehended by anyone, the Second Noble Truth suggests itself to him; and when the Second Noble Truth is comprehended, the Third Noble Truth suggests itself; and similarly the Fourth. The Buddha is reported to have mentioned this, as stated by the Monk Gavampati in the Sacca Saṃyutta.[6] These Truths thus constitute a progressive series, each Truth leading up to the next and each throwing light on the next.

It is the failure to understand these Truths that is responsible for the distressing position in which man finds himself, tossed about as he is in a state of conflicting emotions, passions and desires. In the Koṭigāma Vagga of the Saṃyutta Nikāya the Buddha has said: "O Monks, it is through not understanding, not penetrating these Four Noble Truths that we have run on, wandered on, this long, long road, both you and I."[7]

One feature about these Truths, which needs special mention and which for practical purposes is perhaps the most important, is the urgency of understanding and realizing them. Many are the illustrations employed by the Buddha to emphasize this urgency. I shall content myself with mentioning just one. It is recorded in the Sacca Saṃyutta that the Buddha on one occasion asked this question: "O Monks, when one's turban is ablaze or one's head is ablaze what should be done?" The monks answered: "Lord, when one's turban is ablaze or head is ablaze, for the extinguishing

5. *Kindred Sayings* I. p. 86.
6. *Kindred Sayings* V. p. 369.
7. *Kindred Sayings* V. p. 565.

thereof, one must put forth extra desire, extra effort, extra endeavour, extra impulse, extra attention." "Monks," rejoined the Buddha, "it is just such an extra desire, effort, endeavour, impulse, mindfulness and attention that one should put forth for the comprehension of the Four Noble Truths."[8] Can the urgency of realizing these Truths be brought home more forcefully and more vividly?

The First Noble Truth

Now that we have considered from several angles the nature of the Four Noble Truths, let us proceed to consider the contents of these Truths and their significance.

The First Noble Truth deals with the indisputable fact of *dukkha*, that ever-present feature of existence, and rightly therefore, the starting point of the Dhamma. I say it is rightly the starting point, because the one aim of the Dhamma of the Buddha is to show a way of escape from *dukkha*. Hence he has said:

"*Dukkhañ c'eva paññapemi*
Dukkhassa ca nirodham."[9]

"One thing only do I teach
Sorrow and its end to reach."

Let us understand this Truth in the way enunciated by the Buddha. "This, O Monks," said the Buddha, "is the Noble Truth of Dukkha: Birth is *dukkha*, decay is *dukkha*, death is *dukkha*. sorrow, lamentation, pain, grief and despair are *dukkha*. Association with the unloved, separation from the loved—that is also *dukkha*. Not to get what one desires—that is also *dukkha*. In a word, this five-fold mass which is based on grasping—that is *dukkha*."[10] Except the last example just mentioned, to which reference will be made later, the others are examples of the obvious manifestations of *dukkha*.

Now what exactly is *dukkha*? The word *dukkha* is made up of two words, *du* and *kha*. *Du* is a prefix meaning bad, low, mean, base or vulgar. *Kha* means empty or hollow. The two words

8. *Kindred Sayings* V. p. 372
9. M I 180.
10. *Kindred Sayings* V. p. 357.

taken together therefore refer to that which is bad because it is empty, unsubstantial, unsatisfactory or illusory. It refers to a state of unsatisfactoriness if one may use the expression. The popular rendering of *dukkha* as "suffering" is not quite satisfactory since the word "suffering" is likely to convey the idea of pain only and does not introduce the idea of insubstantiality or illusoriness. The word *dukkha* must awaken in our minds not only thoughts of pain and distress, but also all those thoughts about the unsatisfactory and illusory nature of the things of this world, their insubstantiality, their failure to satisfy completely and their inevitable ending in disappointment, sorrow and disharmony. *Dukkha* consists of that state of unbalance, that continued agitation and disturbance to which all beings are subject by reason of the absence of stability and permanence in this world, by reason of the never-ending rise and fall of things leading to a universal "unsatisfactoriness" or disharmony. Perhaps the word "disharmony" can be regarded as the closest equivalent of *dukkha.* If however we prefer to use the word "suffering," we still may do so giving it however a wider connotation, so as to include the other shades of meaning to which I have just referred.

However obvious the fact of universal *dukkha* may be, there are many among us who refuse to believe that this world is a world of disharmony and suffering, and are quick to condemn Buddhism as a doctrine of pessimism. Nor is this to be wondered at. The Buddha himself hesitated to preach these Truths to an ignorant and doubting world, for he knew that they cannot be easily grasped. There is present in the human mind a tendency to resent the intrusion of a thought or idea which is likely to upset its own comforting view of things to which it has been long accustomed. It is for a similar reason that one might refuse to test one's temperature with a thermometer, or refuse to be medically checked up, for there is an aversion to the discovery that something is wrong within oneself. One likes to continue in the fond thought that all is well. Thus it so happens that many refuse to accept the Truth of Dukkha, because they resent the idea that they are suffering from the universal malady of *dukkha.* They close their eyes to these views which are disturbing and distressing, and are quick to placate themselves with the seemingly comforting thought that all is well, or else that all will somehow end well. Where ignorance is bliss, they prefer not to be wise. When, however, subsequent events and circumstances compel them to realize, with what ease friends can turn into enemies, with what ease health can turn into sickness, with what ease secure possessions can turn insecure, with what ease youth inclines in one direction only—the direction of old age, with what ease old age inclines in one direction only—the direction of decay and death, are they not then thoroughly disillusioned? Can they then be heard to say "This earth-life really satisfies us"? Then and then only, through sheer bitterness of experience do they develop a sane approach to the understanding of the Truth of Dukkha, and if they steadily persist in this line of thinking and pursue it, they will find little difficulty in some day appreciating the fact that all things of this earth-life are involved in *dukkha*, wedded to *dukkha* and are productive of *dukkha*, and that this earth-life itself, in the last resort, is empty, illusory and unsubstantial.

We have only to look around us with observant eyes and thoughtful mind to be convinced of the Truth of Dukkha. Who is the man whose course of life from birth to death has run undisturbed, like the unruffled waters of a placid stream, without even a single upheaval of worry, fear or grief to disturb that gentle drift? Which is the home that has not mourned the loss of a near and dear relative? Where in this world are the lips from which the cry of pain has never been heard? Where is the heart that has not heaved a sigh, and has not felt within itself the agony of sorrow at some time or other? Just at this moment, even as I am speaking and you are listening, can you visualize how many hundred thousands, nay, how many millions of sick men in this wide world are tossing about on beds of pain, in homes and in hospitals? How many millions of patients are, even at this precise moment, lying stretched on tables in operating theatres of hospitals, hovering perilously between life and death? How many millions, having arrived at the end of life's fitful journey, are this very moment gasping for the breath that is deserting them, gasping their last gasp? And how many millions of bereaved parents and bereaved children are weeping, pining for them that will not, and cannot, ever return? Not to see is not to know, except for the thoughtful. Then, consider the extent of poverty and unemployment in this world, and the terrible suffering they cause. Are not these unmistakable indications of universal *dukkha*? As Jacob Boehme once remarked, "If all the mountains were books and if all the lakes were ink and if all the trees were pens, still they would not suffice to depict all the misery in this world."

But the critic will now interpose a question: "What *dukkha* is there to the man blessed with health and wealth and the other good things of life?" Yes, he too is a victim of *dukkha*. He is no favoured exception to the rule of *dukkha*. The man blessed with health and wealth and the other good things of life, so long as he lives in this world, is part of this world, and as such, he will have to live and move with the rest of the world, for man is a gregarious animal. This means that he will have to associate with those who do not possess these good things of life. This invariably leads to situations of unpleasantness, to situations of jealousy and enmity, to situations of conflict between the haves and the have-nots, to the innumerable conflicts between the interests of labour and capital. Are not all these *dukkha* to the man who is said to be enjoying the good things of life?

Then what of the endless care and anxiety necessary to maintain oneself in health, to preserve unimpaired one's wealth and the other good things of life? Is not this an agony—the agony of maintenance? And is not this agony another form of *dukkha*? Then what of the agony of apprehension—the apprehension that all his good things of life may not stay long? What safeguards shall I adopt to protect my properties from the onslaughts of robbers and enemies, and also to protect them from the inroads of decay? "How long shall I be fortunate enough to enjoy my possessions?" These are the headaches, not of the "have-nots" but of the "haves." Are not all these indicative of *dukkha*? And when the protective methods adopted fail to answer their purpose, what of the agony of disappointment and the agony of loss? Where does not *dukkha* reign supreme?

I am now gradually leading you, from cases of obvious *dukkha* known as *dukkha-dukkhatā*, to cases of *dukkha* not so obvious, which occur as a result of the operation of the law of change. These latter are called *vipariṇāma-dukkhatā*. *Vipariṇāma* means change. The Buddha once used an expression of just three words which meant very much: "*Yadaniccaṃ taṃ dukkhaṃ*"! "Where there is change, there is *dukkha*...." Just consider, when everything is changing and nothing is stable, what is the logical outcome but disharmony? The very incidence of change bespeaks *dukkha* or heralds the approach of *dukkha*. Therefore change itself is *dukkha* because there is the potentiality of disharmony and suffering. Is there anyone who has given us a guarantee that fortune will not turn into misfortune, that satisfactory conditions will continue to be satisfactory? There will always remain the possibility and potentiality of change. As long as this bare possibility exists, so long will there be fear and anxiety about the continuance of satisfactory conditions. This is one aspect of *vipariṇāma-dukkhatā*. The very insecurity of the good things of life has from the earliest dawn of human history bespoken *dukkha*. The monarch fears for the security of his kingdom. Despite all his royal splendour he has his painful problems. We have heard it said "Uneasy lies the head that wears a crown." The subject fears for the security of his life. The capitalist fears for the security of his wealth. The labourer fears for the security of his employment. If everything is changing and nothing is at rest, there can be no peace, no security in this world. If there is no peace, no security in this world, what will there be in their stead? There will be fear and insecurity. This again is *dukkha*. The fear of economic upheavals, the fear of unemployment, the fear of epidemics, the fear of wars, the fear of revolutions and the fear of many a world crisis bespeak *dukkha*. Most of them result from world conditions of insecurity. Is not *dukkha* then a necessary evil in this world—a cosmological necessity? In this sense, *dukkha* may be said to have an existence apart from man's awareness of it. Can we forget that two of the three great characteristics of all world-phenomena as declared by the Buddha are *anicca* (impermanence) and *dukkha*?

We can now appreciate the extent to which this element of change or *vipariṇāma* can undermine all worldly happiness. When conditions change, as change they must, the very sweetness of the pleasure of sense-gratification turns into the bitterness of *dukkha*. It is the same with every other form of worldly happiness. The joys of family life may be comforting, the joys of friendship may be exhilarating, but conditions changing, the break up of the ties of family life, the tearing asunder of the bonds of friendship, through so many possible causes as misunderstanding, ill-feeling, acts of third parties and lastly through death, are bound to produce as great a sorrow as was the original joy. In short, great as was the joy of attachment, so great will be the sorrow of detachment, or even greater. The greater the height from which you fall, the greater is the pain you will experience. The axe of impermanence is always there to fell the tree of joy. It hangs over all worldly joys like Damocles' sword. Mark you—it is not for nothing that the all-knowing Buddha has proclaimed: "*Nandi pi dukkha*," "Joy itself is sorrow."

Not only are the things enjoyed constantly changing, but—what is more—the person enjoying them is also constantly changing. He too is subject to the inexorable law of change. We thus witness the amusing spectacle of a changing being pursuing a changing object. This brings us to the third aspect of *dukkha* known as *saṅkhāra-dukkhatā*.[11] We have already dealt with *dukkha-dukkhatā*, the obvious aspect of *dukkha*. Then we dealt with *vipariṇāma-dukkha*, that aspect of *dukkha* which results from change or the possibility of change. Now we shall deal with the *saṅkhāra* aspect of change. *Saṅkhāra*, a word which has many secondary meanings, in its original sense refers to that which is formed by many things joining together, a composition, a group or aggregate or mass. In the present context it refers to the human being regarded not as an entity but as a mass or collection of five groups or aggregates. These constitute the being called man. Of these five groups or aggregates (*pañcakkhandha* is the Pali word), which constitute the composite man, one is the physical factor of *rūpa*, the body, and the other four are the mental factors of *vedanā*, the sensations, *saññā*, the perceptions, *saṅkhāra*, the volitions and *viññāṇa*, the states of consciousness. They are called groups or aggregates because each is again a combination of several other factors. None of these aggregates or component factors is self-existing. They arise out of a cause. They are conditioned. That is to say, their existence depends on certain conditions and when these conditions and causes cease to exist, they too cease to exist. Thus the human body is constantly undergoing a kind of metabolic change. Old cells are continually breaking down and new cells are continually taking their place. Physiology concedes this. Often owing to the imperceptibly slow pace of this change, it is not perceived as

11. For this threefold classification of *dukkha* see D III 210.

change but nevertheless there is change: Hence the human body is not an entity but a process. Infancy, childhood, youth, old age, are but stages in this process. The human mind, *nāma*, is also not an entity. It is also constantly changing. It is just a flow or succession of never-ending sensations, perceptions, volitions and states of consciousness, all of which mental factors are collectively called *nāma* or mind. In this flow of mental factors, each follows the other with such a rapidity of succession, that what is in reality a plurality assumes the semblance of an entity or unity, even as the fire in a lighted stick, made to turn round and round, assumes the semblance of a circle or ring of fire, whereas in reality there is only a succession of positions taken up by the fire of the lighted stick. So there only seems to be a static thing called mind, whereas what exists is just a process or flow of mental factors. The mind is correctly said to be *nadi soto viya*, i.e., like the flow of a river, and is never the same for two consecutive moments. The river one crosses in the morning is not the river he re-crosses in the evening. Each time, each moment, it is a different set of waters that flow. Similarly where the mind is concerned, each time it is a different sensation or perception or volition or consciousness that exists, only to pass away giving rise to another. Psychology concedes this. So we arrive at the all-important conception that the *nāma-rūpa* or mind-body combination which constitutes the composite being called man is not a permanent self-existing unity but a process. It is a conditioned process, i.e., it comes into existence on account of certain causes and conditions. When these causes and conditions cease to exist, the process also ceases to exist. As has been aptly said in the Saṃyutta Nikāya,[12] *hetuṃ paṭicca sambhūta*, by reason of a cause they came to be; *hetubhaṅgā nirujjhati*, by rupture of a cause they die away. Being a process, it is something that is changing and is not permanent. For that very reason, it is *dukkha*. So we see that *dukkha* is inherent in the very formation of the human being. This is *saṅkhāra-dukkhatā*. This is that last example of *dukkha* that was referred to by the Buddha when in his enunciation of the First Noble Truth he said, "This five-fold mass which is based on grasping—that is *dukkha*." It is in the very nature of this mass of groups or aggregates to suffer *dukkha*. The being itself is *dukkha*.

12. *Kindred Sayings* I. p. 169.

In its very formation it is *dukkha*. In this sense, one may say that *dukkha* is a biological and psychological necessity.

The Second Noble Truth

Now that we have understood the First Noble Truth and its significance, let us proceed to the Second Noble Truth, which points out the cause of *dukkha*. The First Noble Truth is like the diagnosis of a disease by a physician. The Second Noble Truth is like the physician's discovery of the cause of the disease. The Third Noble Truth is like the assurance of the physician that there does exist a cure for the disease, and the Fourth Noble Truth is like the physician's prescription for the cure of the disease.

Let us understand this Second Truth in the way it has been enunciated by the Buddha: "What now, O Monks, is the Noble Truth of the cause of suffering? It is this *taṇhā* or craving which leads from birth to birth, which is accompanied by pleasure and greed, finds ever fresh delight now here, now there."[13] Craving is here shown as the great motivating factor back and behind all actions of deluded man, driving him now in one direction, now in another.

All *dukkha* is rooted in this selfish craving for the things of the world, in this inordinate attachment, this passionate clinging, which is known as *taṇhā*. The word *taṇhā* is often inadequately rendered as "desire," but the word "desire" hardly conveys all that is connoted by the Pali word *taṇhā*. The word "desire" can sometimes refer to some very laudable human inclination such as the yearning to be good or to serve mankind. But in the Pali word *taṇhā* (Sanskrit *tṝṣnā*) there is always present the element of selfishness. The word "craving," therefore, is the best rendering of *taṇhā*.

It is this element of selfishness in *taṇhā* that creates all the havoc for man. Craving can never be completely satisfied. Craving gratified begets further craving, even as the attempt to quench one's thirst with salt water only redoubles the thirst. Craving is a powerful urge. It is a dangerous urge. It is responsible for nearly all the ills of this world. The political upheavals of the various countries of this world, their social and economic problems can,

13. *Kindred Sayings* V. p. 357.

almost all, be traced to the nefarious influence of this powerful *taṇhā*. This selfish craving is the mainspring of almost all human activity, the prime causative factor of nearly all the struggles and efforts of deluded man. What is it that makes the murderer raise his hands against his victim? What is it that makes the thief remove another's goods? What is it that makes one man jealous of another's success? Clearly it is selfish craving, one's love of self, manifesting itself in some form or other, and looking at things only from the point of view of self and not from the point of view of others. Sometimes the manifestation of selfishness is obvious, sometimes it is subtle.

Now, the love of a lover to his beloved is often a good example of selfishness manifesting itself in a subtle form. A lover's love is seldom a selfless love. It is a love which craves for recognition and claims a return. In short, it emanates from a love of self. In the generality of cases, a man loves another because he loves himself better, and craves to give himself the pleasure of loving and being loved. Intrinsically therefore, he is out to please himself, and his love for another is but self-love disguised. Otherwise, love cannot so easily and suddenly turn into hatred as it sometimes does when the love offered is rejected. Have we not heard of instances where the lover is the murderer of his beloved? These incidents can happen only when love springs from selfishness. When it was reported to the Buddha that Queen Mallikā, wife of King Pasenadī of Kosala, had said in answer to the king that she loves herself more than anyone else in the world and that King Pasenadī also being similarly questioned by the queen had said that he loves himself more than anyone else in the world, the Buddha was not surprised. He replied as follows: "You may traverse the whole wide world in all directions with your thought but you will nowhere find any one dearer to man than his own self."[14] So man's craving or *taṇhā* in whatever way you may look at it, and in whatever form it appears, is man's attempt to gratify himself.

Now, one may be tempted to ask, "Why does this *taṇhā* or craving bring *dukkha* in its wake?" It is because *taṇhā* is a hankering after that which is itself changing, a hankering after the unreal. When man pursues a goal which is elusive, a goal which

14. *Kindred Sayings* I. p.102.

continually recedes and retreats as often as he attempts to approach it, what else can he expect but the disharmony of *dukkha*?

It may now be asked, "Why do we hanker after the unreal?" Our ignorance (*avijjā*) makes us mistake the unreal for the real, the shadow for the substance, and makes us pursue the shadow. The Dhammapada says:

> "In the unreal they see the real. In the real they see the unreal. Those who abide in the pasture ground of wrong thoughts never arrive at the real."[15]

As long as we fail to develop that intuitive highest wisdom (*paññā*) which is latent in us and which, if developed, would enable us to see things as they really are and in their correct perspective, so long shall we continue to mistake the unreal for the real. Thus do we pursue the gratification of the senses, little knowing that we are pursuing a phantom and hoping that this will give a lasting satisfaction. Our eyes crave for pleasant sights. Our ears crave for pleasant sounds. Our tongues crave for pleasant tastes. Our noses crave for pleasant smells. Our bodies crave for pleasant contacts. Our minds crave for pleasant thought-impressions. But these various objects of sense are constantly changing, and to cling to that which is changing is as foolish and painful as to cling to a perpetually moving wheel. Thus craving misleads us. Craving confuses. Craving misrepresents. Craving also consumes us as if it were a fire. "*Natthi rāga samo aggi,*"[16] said the Buddha once. This means: "There is no fire like lust." It is so consuming.

Self-evident facts are often apt to be overlooked. Hence the Buddha employed so many different similes to portray the transitoriness, the illusiveness, the unworthiness and the dangers of craving. It is not only to a consuming fire that craving has been compared by the Buddha. He has compared it to a net that ensnares and clings to one,[17] to the onrushing current of a river which carries away everything that comes before it[18] and to a

15. Dhp 11.
16. Dhp 251.
17. *Gradual Sayings* I. p. 225.
18. *Itivuttaka*, Woodward's translation, p. 194.

seamstress who brings two ends together and binds them.[19] Each one of these similes reveals some particular aspect of *taṇhā*.

So far we have considered the reaction of man's craving on himself. Let us now consider the reaction of craving on others, on the outside world. Nowhere has this been so vividly described by the Buddha as in the Majjhima Nikāya: "Verily, O Monks," said the Buddha, "due to sensuous craving kings fight with kings, princes with princes, priests with priests, citizens with citizens, the mother quarrels with the son, the son quarrels with the mother, the father quarrels with the son, the son quarrels with the father, brother with brother, brother with sister, sister with brother, friend with friend."[20] Craving thus is a malignant growth. It spreads its roots far and deep. Its career is "to have and to hold" as the notarial expression goes. Hear then the voice of the Buddha who cried halt to this mad careering when he exclaimed, "*taṇhā*ya *mūlaṃ khaṇatha*."[21] Dig up the very roots of *taṇhā*; not otherwise are we safe. One may venture to say that it was the Buddha, who, for the first time in the history of religious thought, expounded the cause of *dukkha* without reference to any external or supernatural agency. My sufferings are due to my actions, and my actions are due to my craving or *taṇhā*. In the Second Truth are therefore involved two doctrines—the doctrine of kamma and the doctrine of Rebirth. The former deals with the law of action and reaction. The latter deals with the law of reproductive thought.

The Third Noble Truth

We will now proceed to dwell on the Third Noble Truth, which declares that with the cessation of *taṇhā* or craving, *dukkha* ceases to exist. You can see for yourself that the Third Noble Truth is a corollary to the Second Noble Truth. If craving is the cause of *dukkha*, then surely the cessation of craving must mean the cessation of *dukkha*. Kill the germ and the disease is killed. Remove the cause and the effect is removed. This is the import of the Third Noble Truth. If there was no Third Noble Truth, well

19. *Gradual Sayings* II. p. 286.
20. *Middle Length Sayings* I. p. 144.
21. Dhp V. 337

might Buddhism have been called a doctrine of pessimism and gloom but with the Third Noble Truth followed by the Fourth, it is a doctrine radiating with hope and joy.

Let us understand the Third Noble Truth in the way it has been enunciated by the Buddha. "What now, O Bhikkhus, is the Noble Truth of the Cessation of Suffering?" "*Yo tassa yeva taṇhāya asesa-virāga-nirodho*"—It is the Cessation of craving without a trace of it left behind, *cāgo*—the abandonment of it, *paṭinissaggo*—the renunciation of it, *mutti*—the liberation from it, *anālayo*—the detachment from it. "*Idaṃ vuccati, bhikkhave, dukkhanirodhaṃ ariyasaccaṃ.*" "This, O Monks, is the Noble Truth of the Cessation of Suffering."[22]

As a result of this string of words employed in this description to emphasize more or less the same idea from different aspects, a few conclusions emerge. The first is that the renunciation of craving can be complete. The next is that, judging from the words used—cessation, abandonment, renunciation, liberation, detachment—what is contemplated is not a forcible control or suppression of craving but a voluntary abandonment, a letting go. The thought also emerges that craving is a dangerous burden to carry with us in the journey of life, a hurtful appendage which must be abandoned and dropped without the slightest delay in order to ensure a comfortable journey. It is this Third Truth which affirms that craving is not an inseparable appendage but that it can be abandoned and dropped. The very expression "*dukkha nirodha*"—cessation of suffering—implies this.

Let us consider the effects on the mind of this complete abandonment of craving, this complete renunciation. A person who has completely ceased to crave is none other than an *arahant* and therefore in considering the effects on the mind of the cessation of craving, we are considering the nature of the *arahant*-mind. It is a psychological marvel.

The *arahant* cannot create kamma, i.e., moral or immoral actions which produce a reaction, in as much as with the complete cessation of craving there is no *cetanā* or worldly intention which could motivate his actions. The mind is completely freed from all that is temporal, earthly or gross. Of him it is said:

22. *Kindred Sayings* V. p. 357.

"*pāpañca puññañca ubho saṅgaṃ upaccagā.*"[23] That is to say, he has transcended the attachments of both good and evil. It is not only evil that has to be transcended but even good. Further reference to this view will be made later.

Another result of the complete cessation of craving is the beautiful and perfect tranquility of mind that the *arahant* enjoys. Says the Dhammapada:[24]

> "Calm is the mind, calm is the speech, calm is the deed of him who, rightly understanding and perfectly placid, has gained liberation."

Complete freedom from grief and fear is another result of the cessation of craving. Grief and fear are states of mind which can arise only when there is craving. Says the Dhammapada:[25]

> "From craving springs grief. From craving springs fear. For him who is freed from craving, there is no grief. Whence fear?"

The *arahant* is also supremely happy. An expression used to describe them is "*pītibhakkā,*" i.e., feeders on joy. How the *arahants* refer to their own happiness is expressed in the Dhammapada:[26]

> "Ah! Happily do we live without craving among those who crave. Among the men who crave we live without craving."

The *arahant*'s freedom from craving and his consequent domination of his senses is so complete, that he can look at all beings, all things, all conditions, unaffected and unmoved. He is not attached to anything. He is not repelled by anything. Perfect equanimity reigns supreme in his mind.

Not only is he unmoved by all contacts and sensations, he has also within him—paradoxical though it may seem—the ability to consider pleasant sensations as unpleasant, and unpleasant sensations as pleasant, or to view them all with complete indifference. This is because he has transcended the sense-level. In the Dīgha Nikāya the

23. Dhp V 41.
24. Ibid., V 96.
25. Ibid., V 216.
26. Ibid., V 199.

Buddha makes pointed reference to this twofold ability by using the following two expressions: "*appaṭikkule paṭikkūlasaññī*," seeing the pleasant in the unpleasant, and "*paṭikkule appaṭikkūlasaññī*," seeing the unpleasant in the pleasant.[27] This ability to control the sense data comes only to those who have completely renounced craving.

When the Buddha, meditating under the Bodhi tree at Gayā in the last watch of that memorable night reached this glorious and blessed state of the cessation of all craving, and realized that it was craving that motivated Life, in triumphant joy he uttered a beautiful stanza containing a very exquisite and vivid allegory. It is one of the best allegories in all the world's literature. It is in the form of an imaginary address to craving, whom he regards as a house-builder, the builder of the House of Existence:

"*Anekajāti saṃsaraṃ, sandhāvisaṃ anibbisaṃ*
Through many a birth in *Saṃsāra* have I, without success, wandered,

Gahakārakaṃ gavesanto
Searching for the builder of this house.

Dukkhā jāti punappunaṃ
Painful indeed is repeated birth.

Gahakāraka diṭṭhosi
Now, O house-builder, thou art discovered.

Puna gehaṃ nakāhasī
Never shalt thou build again for me.

Sabbā te phāsukā bhaggā
Broken are all thy rafters.

Gahakūṭaṃ visaṅkhitaṃ
Thy ridge pole is shattered.

Visaṅkhāragataṃ cittaṃ
My mind has attained to the unconditioned.

Taṇhānaṃ khayamajjhagā
Achieved is the cessation of craving."[28]

---

27. D II 107. See also *Kindred Sayings* V. p. 100.
28. Dhp 153, 154.

How exactly the cessation of craving brings about the cessation of *dukkha*, and how exactly existence can come to an end, can only be understood by a close study of the doctrine of Dependent Origination, known as the *paṭicca samuppāda*. Suffice it for the present to follow a simile used by the Buddha in the Majjhima Nikāya:[29] "Suppose, monks, the light of an oil lamp is burning, generated by oil and wick, but no one from time to time pours oil or attends to the wick. Then, monks, according as the fuel is used up and no new fuel is added, the lamp for want of nourishment will become extinct. Even so, monks, in him who contemplates the transitoriness of existence, craving ceases. Through the cessation of craving, grasping ceases. Through the cessation of grasping, becoming ceases. Through the cessation of becoming, rebirth ceases. Through the cessation of rebirth, old age, sickness, death, pain, lamentation, suffering, sorrow and despair cease. Such is the cessation of the whole chain of *dukkha*."

We can appreciate this phenomenon if we picture the sight of a creeper that is entwined round a tree, a creeper that is just uprooted. The creeper has been spreading from branch to branch. The tender tendrils of this creeper will no more reach out to contact any further branch so as to cling to it and grasp it and help it to continue its existence. The process of clinging and grasping having ceased, the creeper will just cease to grow, will gradually wither away and perish never to regain life anymore. The roots of the creeper have dried up, because they now lack the nutriment of the soil, which is necessary to sustain the creeper.

So it is with human life, which is also a process of living by clinging and grasping and willing to live. A thought tends to reproduce itself. It is by reason of this reproductive power of thought, that the will to live makes man re-live, or as Dahlke put it, "We live eternally through our lust to live." Clinging to life makes life cling to us. The Pali word to express this clinging and grasping is *upādāna*. Like the physical creeper, the creeper of human life needs nutriment to sustain it. Craving is this nutriment. Craving is that which causes *upādāna* or grasping and thus helps to maintain the onward movement of the creeper of human life. By grasping is meant not grasping by the hand only. The Pali

29. M II 292.

word *upādāna* refers to six kinds of grasping, which correspond to the six senses. Thus there is grasping by the eye of sights; there is grasping by the ear of sounds; there is grasping by the nose of smells; there is grasping by the tongue of tastes; there is grasping by the body of tangible things. In Buddhist psychology there are six senses, not five. Therefore, sixthly, there is grasping by the mind of thought-impressions and ideas. These acts of grasping are mental energies or forces set in motion. Energy is indestructible. No energy therefore is ever lost. So the mental energies released by these graspings, combined with the residual karmic energy at the moment of death, make for the continuity of life in any appropriate sphere or plane, when it ends here. Along with the parental sperm and ovum they condition the foundations for the arising of another life. Contact of seed with soil is not sufficient to engender plant life. There must be a third element—the outside element of light and air.

Similarly, the outside elements, where the engendering of human life is concerned, are these energies released by craving, and distance is no bar to the operation of these energies. In the degree therefore in which you reduce craving, fewer and fewer things will be grasped by you, fewer and fewer sense objects will attract you. As craving continues to decrease, grasping becomes weaker and weaker and, like the tendrils of the uprooted creeper, will gradually lose their strength and power to grasp, until finally the whole creeper fades away. When craving completely ceases, the power to grasp also completely ceases; the creeper of human existence then will lie dried up at its root. Indeed, at the moment of death, it is only such a one as an *arahant*, who has completely shed every trace of craving and grasping, who can triumphantly exclaim:

"Oh Life! to thee I no more cling
Oh Death! where is thy sting?"

The question is always asked: "What happens after death to the *arahant* who has destroyed all craving? Does he exist or does he not exist? If he does exist, where does he exist? If he does not exist, how can you speak of the bliss of Nibbāna which he is said to be enjoying after death?" All these questions appertain to the nature and condition of Nibbāna. In the questioner's question lies an assumption that he is capable of understanding Nibbāna.

But Nibbāna is said to be *atakkāvacara*, which means "cannot be reached by logic and reason." Reason is not the highest faculty of man. Reason has its limitations. Nibbāna and like matters are realized not through reason, but through a higher faculty called *paññā*, lying dormant in us, but which we all can arouse and develop by means of meditation. With the arising of this intuitive or supernormal or supra-mundane knowledge, this highest wisdom, one is able to sense the Truth as naturally and easily as one would sense cold or heat. It is so different from that arduous process of reasoning at the end of which also one is still in doubt whether one has realized the whole Truth or not. Where this higher faculty is concerned there is no effort to comprehend. The understanding just dawns on one. Some prefer to call it revelation, others call it intuition, yet others call it a latent sixth sense, but whatever name is given to it, whatever label is appended to it, it is a source of understanding that works independently of the senses and the reasoning faculty. It is a transcendental faculty lying dormant in us. The finite can never grasp the Infinite, but by meditation we can transcend the finite. Nibbāna is Reality itself. It is the Infinite. It is the Absolute, and the Absolute cannot be explained in terms of the relative. As someone has aptly remarked, reason cannot be more reasonable than ceasing to reason on things beyond reason.

This very question as to what happens to an *arahant* after his death was put to the Buddha by one Upasiva as mentioned in the Sutta Nipāta[30] and the Buddha's answer was as follows:

> "Of one who's passed away there is no measure,
> Of him, there is naught, whereby one may say aught.
> When once all things have wholly been removed,
> All ways of saying too have removed."

And elsewhere he has said, "*Ākāse'va sakuntānaṃ padaṃ tassa dūrannayaṃ*."[31] "The path of the *arahant* after death cannot be traced, it is like the path of birds in air."

All that which the limited faculty of reason can suggest is that the existence of Nibbāna appears to be logically sound and that it appears to be a cosmic necessity. Everything is seen to exist in

30. Sn 1076.
31. Dhp 93.

pairs of opposites. If there is hot, there is cold. If there is small, there is large. Hence if there is the finite, there must be the infinite. If there is the relative, there must be the absolute. If there is that which is born, that which is become, that which is made, that which is compounded, there must also be the opposite of it. And it is to this opposite that the Buddha referred when he was speaking of Nibbāna. In the Udāna he has said: "There is, O Monks, a not-born, a not-become, a not-made, a not-compounded."[32] Beyond such considerations, logic and reason cannot carry us any further in our attempt to understand Nibbāna, precisely because it is something beyond the scope of logic and reason. It must be left to the intuitive or supra-mundane faculty of *paññā* to help us to understand Nibbāna. This faculty is latent in us but it has to be aroused and developed by meditation. We can then understand Nibbāna not as a theoretical exposition but with the flavour of immediate experience. As Radhakrishnan has said:

"Then great truths of philosophy are not proved but seen.... In moving from intellect to intuition, we are not moving in the direction of unreason but are getting into the deepest rationality of which human nature is capable. In it ... we see more truly and not simply measure things by the fragmentary standards of intellect."[33]

The Fourth Noble Truth

We now come to the Fourth and last Truth, the Noble Truth of the Path leading to the cessation of *dukkha*. This is the prescription of the All-Knowing Buddha for the ills of life. By this Truth the Buddha prescribes a way of life which is calculated to bring about a complete cessation of that powerful urge of *taṇhā* ever present in man. This way of life is the Noble Eightfold Path.

It is only if we are thoroughly convinced that all life is ill, that all life is *dukkha*, that we will welcome any suggestion of a way of escape from *dukkha*, not otherwise. Hence it is, that to some the Noble Eightfold Path has no attraction at all, to some the attraction is mild, often only of an academic nature, while to just a handful it is something absorbingly vital, something wonderfully

32. *Verses of Uplift* p. 98 (Woodward's translation).
33. *An Idealist View of Life,* p.120.

energizing and uplifting, something very dear and personal. To this handful, the treading of the Path even in its initial stages brings with it inspiration and joy which later lead to a profound spiritual experience.

At the outset of this aspect of the subject, it is important to appreciate why this remedy for *dukkha* is referred to as a Path (in Pali, *magga*). It might have been called the Eightfold Remedy or the Eightfold Cure, but why Eightfold Path? A remedy or a cure may or may not have been used by anyone before it is offered to us. There is nothing in the word "remedy" or in the word "cure" to suggest that it has been tried and tested earlier, but not so when the word "Path" is used. A Path must have been treaded by someone before it can be called a Path. There is inherent in the connotation of the word "Path" (*magga*) the idea that someone had treaded it before. A Path cannot come into existence all of a sudden. Someone must have first cut through a jungle, cleared a way and walked along it. Similarly the Noble Eightfold Path has been treaded before by many a Buddha in the past. It has also been treaded before by many a Pacceka Buddha and many an *arahant*. The Buddha only discovered the Path but did not create it, since it existed from the ancient past. Indeed it is an Ancient Path (*pūraṇa magga*) as was described by the Buddha himself in the Saṃyutta Nikāya. Here he has said, "Just as if, O Monks, a man faring through the forest sees an ancient path, an ancient road, traversed by men of former days and he were to go along it and going along it should see an ancient city ... even so I, O Monks, have seen an ancient Path, an ancient road, traversed by the rightly Enlightened Ones of former times. And what, O Monks, is that ancient Path, that ancient road, traversed by the rightly Enlightened Ones of former times? It is just this Noble Eightfold Path ... I have gone along that Path, and going along that Path, I fully came to know Suffering, the Arising of Suffering, the Cessation of Suffering and the Way leading to the Cessation of Suffering."[34] You will thus appreciate the psychological importance of using the word "Path," which is calculated to inspire the highest confidence (*saddhā*) in the remedy that has been prescribed.

34. *Kindred Sayings* I. p. 74.

This Path is also called the Middle Path (*majjhima-paṭipadā*) because it steers clear of two extremes. It avoids, on the one hand, the debasing indulgence of the sensualist and the laxity of the pleasure-seeking Epicurean, and on the other hand, it avoids the absurd austerities and meaningless self-mortification of religious fanatics. The Middle Path proclaimed by the Buddha, however, is a Path of reason and prudence.

This Fourth Noble Truth is not a mere enunciation of a fact. It is a Path and so it must be trodden. It is something essentially practical. To know this Truth properly one must tread the Path. This Truth contains a careful and wise collection of all the important ingredients necessary for the spiritual development of man. These ingredients are well known to every Buddhist, viz., *Sammā Diṭṭhi*—Right Understanding, *Sammā Saṅkappa*—Right Thought, *Sammā Vācā*—Right Speech, *Sammā Kammanta*—Right Action, *Sammā Ājīva*—Right Livelihood, *Sammā Vāyāma*—Right Effort, *Sammā Sati*—Right Mindfulness and *Sammā Samādhi*—Right Concentration.

These eight factors constitute the very essence of the ideal Buddhist life. It is a carefully considered programme of purification of thought, word and deed, ultimately resulting in the complete cessation of craving and the consequent dawning of the highest wisdom.

An important feature to be noted in regard to this Path is that these eight factors are interrelated and interdependent. Hence they are not to be cultivated one by one in the order in which they are listed, as if they were a series of successive steps that have to be taken one after another. They are not mutually exclusive. They are mutually supporting factors. Development of one factor therefore helps in the development of other factors and, what is more, the perfection of one factor coincides with the perfection of all the other factors. Thus, ultimately, at the highest level all these factors will be seen to function simultaneously. Hence one is free to develop these factors in whatever degree he likes. It is useful to keep in mind the Venerable Bhikkhu Sīlācāra's most instructive comparison[35] of these eight factors to eight different strands that are closely intertwined in one rope which a man is attempting to climb. Each time the climber grasps the rope, his

35. *The Noble Eightfold Path*, Bhikkhu Sīlācāra, p. 21.

fingers will come into closer contact with one particular strand than with any other. At the next moment the contact will be with another strand. Yet all the while he is climbing. Similarly in the treading of the Eightfold Path, sometimes one may concentrate on one factor, at other times on another, with however no loss of progress at any time.

Another feature in regard to these eight factors is that they fall into three different groups or categories of *sīla*, *samādhi* and *paññā*, i.e., virtue, concentration and wisdom. This is known as the threefold division of the Eightfold Path. This threefold division is very important for practical purposes. It represents the three stages of spiritual progress. In the Majjhima Nikāya[36] it is said that the three divisions are not arranged in accordance with the Eightfold Path but that the Eightfold Path is arranged according to the three divisions.

Sīla (virtue) refers to moral discipline or purity of conduct and under this category appear three of the eight factors, viz., Right Speech, Right Action and Right Livelihood. *Sīla* is the sine qua non for spiritual development. It is the first step. It is the foundation for further progress along the Path. Right Speech is essential for *sīla*. Man possesses the power of speech, unlike animals. This is man's channel of expression of thought and he should not abuse it but use it in a manner so as to cause good thoughts to arise in others and not bad thoughts. He should speak in a manner so as not to cause harm or hurt or loss to others. The factor of Right Speech thus conduces to *sīla* or purity of conduct by ensuring abstention from falsehood, tale-bearing, harsh speech and idle gossip.

Similarly man's ability to act should not be abused. He can act in so many more and more effective ways than animals could. He should not make use of this ability to cause harm or hurt or loss to others. So the factor of Right Action conduces to purity of conduct by ensuring abstention from killing, from stealing and from wrongful sexual indulgence.

The factor of Right Livelihood is also important. Man's struggle for existence, his pressing necessity to procure the material needs of life to maintain himself and his family, compel

36. M I 363.

him to regard the business of earning a livelihood as his most important task in life and therefore there is the great urge to go to any length in order to achieve this end. Considerations of fair play and justice are all thrown to the winds, and considerations of resultant loss or harm to others are apt to be lightly overlooked. This is a temptation to be guarded against if purity of conduct is to be maintained at all costs. Hence the factor of Right Livelihood conduces to purity of conduct by ensuring abstention from trading in arms, from trading in animals for slaughter, from trading in human beings, from trading in intoxicating drinks and from trading in poisons. There is a popular belief that these are the only forms of wrong livelihood. It is not so. In the Majjhima Nikāya,[37] practising "trickery, cajolery, insinuation, dissemblance, rapacity for gain upon gain" are considered wrong livelihood. In general terms, as mentioned in the Dīgha Nikāya,[38] Right Livelihood means the avoidance of a wrong way of living and the obtaining of a livelihood by a right way of living. *Micchājīvena pahāya sammā jīvitaṃ kappenti.* Thus by the development of these three factors of Right Speech, Right Action and Right Livelihood, purity of conduct (*sīla*) is ensured. One knows of no other religion where there is a code of ethical conduct so comprehensive in its details, and so exacting in its requirements. All this is necessary in order to ensure perfect purity of conduct.

But in Buddhism purity of conduct is not an end in itself. It is a means to an end. Perfect conduct divorced from a purpose, not directed to a desirable end, has but little meaning from the Buddhist point of view—a very lofty point of view, not easy to comprehend. Not only evil but also good must be transcended. They are both of this world (*lokiya*) and do not appertain to things that transcend this world (*lokuttara*). Even the Dhamma has to be transcended. The Buddha has compared Dhamma to a raft to be used by us, *nissaraṇatthāya*, i.e., for the purpose of crossing over in safety, and *na gahaṇatthāya*, i.e., not for the purpose of retention. Once we have reached the other shore; we do not have to carry the raft with us. It has to be put aside.[39] So, the next

37. M II 118.
38. D I 344.
39. *Middle Length Sayings* I p. 174.

two categories after *sīla*, namely, *samādhi* and *paññā*, show the direction in which lies the purpose of *sīla*. The purpose of *sīla* then is to help in the development of mental concentration and the realization of the highest wisdom. The purer one's conduct is, the purer is one's mind, and the purer one's mind is, the greater is his ability to concentrate. Then purity of conduct and purity of mind help in the realization of Wisdom. An impure mind can never be a fitting receptacle for the highest Truths of life.

Into the second category of *samādhi* fall three factors, namely, Right Effort (*Sammā Vāyāma*), Right Mindfulness (*Sammā Sati*) and Right Concentration (*Sammā Samādhi*).

Right Effort here has a very special meaning, since it is concerned with the development of the mind. Right Effort then is the effort to prevent the arising of evil states of mind that have not arisen, the effort to overcome evil states of mind that have already arisen, the effort to produce good states of mind that have not arisen and the effort to develop further the good states of mind that have already arisen. This classification will show you how vast, how penetrating and how stupendous is the mental effort that is needed for progress in *samādhi*. Can there be any doubt then that this will some day lead to mind-mastery and wisdom?

The next factor in this category of *samādhi* is *Sammā Sati* or Right Mindfulness. Right Mindfulness is the quality of awareness. It ensures complete awareness of all the activities of the body as they occur (*kāyānupassanā*), complete awareness of all sensations and feelings as they occur (*vedanānupassanā*), complete awareness of all activities of the mind as they occur (*cittānupassanā*) and complete awareness of all mental objects when the appropriate situations arise (*dhammānupassanā*). This attitude of complete awareness brings about powerful results. It sharpens to the finest degree man's powers of observation, induces the deepest calm and ensures that nothing is said or done or thought unguardedly or hastily, mechanically or without deliberation. He who develops this factor is able to take count of every single and minute activity of the mind, even such activities as are generally considered to occur when the mind is passive and receptive; so penetrating and powerful is his sense of awareness.

The last factor in this category of *samādhi* is Right Concentration, which ensures one-pointedness of mind (*ekaggatā*).

It is the ability to focus steadily one's mind on any one object and one only, to the exclusion of all others. There are many exercises in mind-concentration which space does not permit me to mention, much less to describe. Long continued practice of mental concentration makes the mind highly penetrative. It becomes like a high-powered light which can thoroughly illuminate any object on which it is focussed. Hence any object of thought which presents itself to such a mind is thoroughly penetrated and comprehended through and through. Now this concentration of the mind, like *sīla*, is not an end in itself. The purpose of developing this *samādhi* or concentration is to make use of its penetrative power to understand existence and thereby to realize the highest wisdom (*paññā*).

We now come to the third category, namely, *paññā* or wisdom. When this highly concentrated mind abiding in *samādhi* is made to focus its attention on the three great characteristics of existence, namely, *anicca* (impermanence), *dukkha* (disharmony) and *anattā* (egolessness or soullessness), the mind is able to see things as they actually are (*yathābhūtañāṇa*). The result is the dawning of that highest understanding—*Sammā Diṭṭhi*. One sees reality. This coincides with the cessation of craving and the attainment of Nibbāna. So *Sammā Diṭṭhi* is one of the factors in the category of *paññā*. This is *Sammā Diṭṭhi* at its highest level. *Sammā Diṭṭhi* at its lower levels is a general understanding of the nature of existence and the understanding of right and wrong. This modicum of *Sammā Diṭṭhi* is helpful at the start to begin the practice of *sīla*. Without this modicum of *Sammā Diṭṭhi* there will be no proper incentive to the practice of *sīla*. It will thus be seen that Right Understanding becomes the beginning as well as the end of the Eightfold Path.

The other factor that falls within the category of *paññā* is sammā saṅkappā or Right Thought. Thoughts are all important. Words and deeds are nothing but expressions of thought. Thought rules the world. The power to think is greatest in man—not so in the lower animals. It should therefore be man's endeavour to make the best use of this power of thought which he is privileged to possess and to think none but the best of thoughts. From the point of view of Buddhism the best of thoughts are threefold—thoughts of renunciation (i.e., thoughts free from craving), thoughts of benevolence, and thoughts of compassion. The practice of *Sammā Saṅkappa* therefore ensures freedom from lust, freedom from hatred and freedom from cruelty or harm. Even this factor is developed for a purpose: to make it possible for the mind when purified to see Reality, to gain the highest wisdom.

The description of the Eightfold Path is now over. It will be seen that this is a Path of progressive self-culture leading from purity of conduct to concentration of mind and from concentration of mind to wisdom. But it does not mean that complete *sīla* must first be achieved before *samādhi* is begun or that *samādhi* must be completed before *paññā* is begun. There are different levels of these qualities and the practice of one helps the other and the level of each rises. This is what was meant when it was earlier stated that these factors are interdependent and mutually supporting. This view is of great practical importance and cannot be overemphasized. The Buddha has expressed this view forcefully and vividly in regard to the interdependence of *sīla* and *paññā*. In the Sonadaṇḍa Sutta of the Dīgha Nikāya.[40] He has said, "As one might wash hand with hand and foot with foot, even so, wisdom is purified by virtuous conduct and virtuous conduct is purified by wisdom" (*Sīlaṃ paridhoto paññā, paññā paridhoto sīlaṃ*). Further, the Buddha continues:

"*Yattha sīlaṃ tattha paññā,*
Yattha paññā tattha sīlaṃ."[40]

"Where virtue is, there wisdom lies,
Where wisdom is, there virtue lies."

40. D I 156.

Conclusion

I have reached the end of my discourse. I have endeavoured to give some understanding of the Four Noble Truths, not to satisfy any intellectual curiosity, not to provoke argument but with the sole purpose of giving an incentive to the treading of the Path. Once you do so, you can then see for yourselves the result, as you proceed. Idle speculation and hair-splitting arguments are to no purpose. The Buddha has strongly condemned the study of the Dhamma for the sake of criticism or vain talk.[41] What is needed is not talking about the Path, but walking it. "*Ehi-passiko*" is an epithet of the Dhamma. It means, "Come and see for yourselves." The proof of the pudding is in the eating of it, not in any learned chemical analysis of its component parts. Some may fear that the mental training involved in the treading of the Path is too severe and is doomed to failure. But it must be remembered that the more the mind is exercised the more it gains in strength and the more it becomes controllable. The Buddha has said in the Aṅguttara Nikāya,[42] "Monks, I know not of any other single thing so tractable as the cultivated mind." Hence it is that the number of brain cells that can arise in a man is unlimited. Finally, I would wish to say that if all the wisdom of the Four Noble Truths can for practical purposes boil down to one single instruction, to one single admonition, to one single dictate, that instruction, admonition and dictate is contained in the words once uttered by the Buddha, viz., "*taṇhāya mūlaṃ khanatha*"— "dig up the very roots of *taṇhā*."[43] Without the elimination of this pernicious element of craving no true happiness can ever come to man. It has been amply shown how potently this law of change is operating at all times, in all places, in all ways, in this world and how everything in this world without a single exception is subject to its inexorable rule. It is this phenomenon of change that strikes at the root of all worldly happiness. Viewed against this background of shifting situations and shifting scenes, worldly

41. M I 171.
42. A I 4.
43. Dhp 337.

happiness is just a passing show: The entire world is in a state of perpetual change and unrest, and so is its inhabitant, man. There is tension everywhere. Hence man's search for worldly happiness is nothing but an empty race, a futile rush, a maddening thirst that is never quenched.

Man's search for happiness has gone on from age to age but it can never be found in the way it is sought—in merely adjusting the conditions of the external world and ignoring the internal world of mind. The history of the world proves this. Social reforms, economic reforms, legal reforms and political reforms, however well-intentioned and well-calculated they may have been, never brought complete and genuine happiness to man. Why? When one set of unsatisfactory conditions that have appeared has been eliminated, another rears its head, and when that is eliminated yet another appears. This appearance and reappearance, this rise and fall is the essence of all mundane things and conditions. There can never be any mass production of true happiness. It is something personal and individual. It comes from within and not without. It is not so much the external world that one has to explore in the search for happiness as the internal world of mind.

The modern scientific age, with its brilliant scientists and its wonderful inventions, has no doubt economized labour, shattered distance and captured time. But I ask you, has science invented one single machine, one single instrument or other contrivance to shatter *dukkha*? The modern scientific age is transplanting hearts and transporting or attempting to transport men to the moon. But I ask you, is not the moon but another earth subject to the same infirmities, the same limitations and the same lamentations as are prevailing on earth? What is the great gain to man, I ask you, by adding one or more of these revolving planets to man's possession of this *dukkha*-laden earth? Why should he saddle himself with the problems of the moon, when he has not as yet solved the problems of this earth? What is needed is not an extension or furtherance of the sphere of human existence but a deliverance from existence itself. And as for the change of heart, I ask you, is not the best change of heart the change that results, not from the surgical removal of the physical heart, but the psychic removal of *taṇhā* or craving? The change of heart that thereby results is a glorious achievement. We are our own surgeons to effect that change of heart. In those surgical removals, the operation will succeed but the patient may succumb. In these psychic removals, if the operation succeeds there is greater success and glory to the patient.

Sisters and brothers, I thank you for the attention you have given me. May you—one and all—some happy day in your lives get the urge to contemplate seriously these Four Noble Truths and may that contemplation bring you pure joy ending finally in the attainment to that Reality, that Highest Wisdom, that Everlasting Peace and Security and Happiness which is called Nibbāna.

That Nibbāna may you all attain.

Buddhism in South India

by

Pandit
Hisselle Dhammaratana Mahāthera

With an Appendix with Extracts from the Manimekhalai

WHEEL PUBLICATION NO. 124/125

The Introduction of Buddhism to South India

It is not generally known that Buddhism flourished in South India in ancient times. The ancient chronicles of Sri Lanka such as the *Dīpavaṃsa* and *Mahāvaṃsa* are silent on the subject.

While studying Tamil literature, I became interested in this subject, which is one of which we should not be ignorant. Therefore, in order to acquaint myself with it, I had to peruse books on the history of South India and Sri Lanka, the Pāli texts and commentaries, in addition to studies in Tamil literature. The Tamil book entitled *Bauddhamum Tamil Ilakkiamum* (*Buddhism and Tamil Literature*) by Seeni Vengadasamy of Madras was particularly helpful to me.

In this work I propose to deal with the arrival of Buddhism in South India, its spread and its decay. I shall also touch on famous Buddhist cities, the impact of Buddhism on the local Hindu religion, and on Buddhist teachers and their literary work. There is a division of opinion regarding the period in which Buddhism was introduced to South India. However, on perusal of Tamil literary works, a solution to this problem can be found.

The earliest literary work in which Buddhism is traceable is a book called *Puraṇānūru*. No trace of Buddhist influence can be found in books written prior to this. In the *Puraṇānūru* there is reference to the *Sivi Jātaka*. The full impact of Buddhism in South India is unmistakably shown in *Sīlappadhikāram* and *Maṇimekhalai*, which are two epic works of the 3rd Sangam period[1] in Tamil literature (2nd century CE). Of these, *Maṇimekhalai* is a purely Buddhist work, which in addition to the narrative, contains also expositions of the Buddhist doctrine.[2] Extracts from other poems written by the author of *Maṇimekhalai*, Sīthalai Sāttanār, are found in other Tamil literary works. Quotations from Ilambodhiyar, the Buddhist poet, are found in the *Natrinai* (p. 72). Thus we are able to arrive at the conclusion that Buddhism came to South India before the 3rd Sangam period of Tamil literature (2nd century CE).

---

1. The *Sangam* was a convocation of Tamil poets and literary critics to whom poetic works were submitted for their approval or otherwise.
2. See Appendix.

Tamil literary works provide a clue to finding the time of the advent of Buddhism. Apart from this, the inscriptions of King Asoka also shed much light on the subject. Two inscriptions of King Asoka found at Girnar in Surashtra are particularly helpful.

> "The merciful Emperor, endowed with favours from the gods, has arranged for medical facilities to be provided to men and beasts, in Coḷa, Cera, Pāṇḍya, Tāmrapārṇi (Sri Lanka), and in the kingdom of the Greek king Antiochus."

From this it is clear that the Emperor Asoka provided medical facilities in the kingdoms of South India. Nothing is mentioned here of the spread of Buddhism. Yet in edict number XIII found near Peshawar, there is reference to the Buddhist missions of Asoka. Among the countries referred to are Coḷa, Pāṇḍya, and Sri Lanka. This inscription was written in 258 BCE and is direct evidence of the Buddhist missions of Asoka to South India and Sri Lanka. As Buddhist missions to Sri Lanka had to come by way of South India, the spread of Buddhism in Sri Lanka and South India should be considered contemporary events.

At the third Buddhist Council convened under the patronage of King Asoka, missionaries were selected to be sent to various countries round about India. The Emperor Asoka's son Mahinda Mahā Thera was selected to propagate Buddhism in Sri Lanka. In the 3rd century BCE the Venerable Mahinda arrived in Sri Lanka with his Buddhist mission. He ordained many disciples and started missionary activities on a big scale. His chief disciple was the Venerable Ariṭṭha, who assisted his teacher in his missionary endeavours.

It is unfortunate that Sri Lanka's ancient chronicles, which have taken pains to give details of the life and missionary activities of King Asoka, should have omitted to record the introduction of Buddhism to South India. The historian Vincent Smith has advanced the view that as South Indian Tamils constantly harassed the Sinhalese with invasions the Buddhist monks who wrote the chronicles were prejudiced against them and did not wish to give them a place in their books.

Despite this omission, it is now accepted by all scholars that Buddhism was introduced to South India by the Venerable Mahinda himself. The aforementioned facts alone are sufficient to establish this assumption. Although our chronicles say that the Venerable

Mahinda arrived in Sri Lanka through his supernormal powers, scholars are of the opinion that he travelled by sea and called at Kāveripaṭṭanam in South India. He sojourned here in a monastery called Indra Vihāra, which was one of the several monasteries constructed in this part of the country by the Emperor Asoka.

The celebrated Chinese pilgrim Hiuen Tsang arrived at Kāñchipura in South India in 640 CE during the course of his travels. He mentions a stūpa 100 feet in height which existed there. With regard to the Buddhist monuments in the Pāṇḍya country Hiuen Tsang writes as follows:

"Near the city of Madura there is a monastery built by Mahinda Thera, the brother of King Asoka. To the east of this there is a stūpa built by King Asoka."

The monastery and stūpa were in a dilapidated condition at the time. Tamil literature does not mention anything about these two shrines.

The commentator Dhammapāla Thera mentions in his works that he resided in a monastery which was built by King Asoka in a place called Bhadaratīrtha.

Several Sinhalese princes, including Mahā Ariṭṭha, were ordained by Venerable Mahinda in Sri Lanka. All of them assisted the Mahā Thera in his missionary activities. Further, there is evidence that they assisted the Mahā Thera in propagating the Dhamma in South India.

Early in the history of Buddhism in Sri Lanka, rock caves were made habitable and offered to the Saṅgha. Such caves are still to be seen at Vessagiri, Chetiyagiri, and Topigala. Similar caves are to be seen in the Madura district of the Pāṇḍya country. Beds cut in the rocks for monks to rest upon are seen in these caves. Inscriptions are also found indicating the names of the donors. The Brāhmī script used by King Asoka in his inscriptions has been utilised in some writings. One such cave in the Pāṇḍya country is situated in a place called Arittapattī. This name is derived from Venerable Ariṭṭha, who resided in this particular cave conducting his missionary activities.

From the aforementioned facts it may be concluded that Buddhism was introduced to South India by King Asoka and his son, the Venerable Mahinda, about the same time as the introduction of Buddhism to Sri Lanka.

The Rise, Spread, and Decay of Buddhism in South India

It is well known that the three Buddhist Councils held in India contributed much to the spread of Buddhism throughout India and in other countries. In particular the third council convened by King Asoka delegated various Arahants with the task of leading missions to selected lands. Both in the time of the Buddha and in subsequent times Buddhist monks went about from village to village spreading the word of the Master. Those who went to South India had to take up the challenge from Jain and Hindu opponents and engage themselves in debate with them, apart from struggling against other difficulties and obstacles. The monks thus endeavouring to spread the Dhamma met with encouragement and support from kings, wealthy merchants and noblemen. As a result of this they went out to each and every village and city of South India and propagated the Buddha Dhamma, building monasteries and erecting centres of Buddhist learning. Some of the monks residing in the monasteries, became skilled medical practitioners. They provided free medical services and free education in the monastic school thus rendering invaluable service. They got the people to assemble at the monastery premises, and preached Jātaka tales, the life of the Buddha, read Suttas from the Buddhist scriptures, and thus increased the knowledge of the Dhamma by explaining and clarifying what the people could not understand. With the help of kings and rich men they maintained alms-halls for the benefit of the blind, deaf, and maimed. Thus on account of their social services and devoted work in the propagation of the Dhamma, Buddhism spread rapidly in South India.

Another point in their favour was that these monks ignored caste differences, and this was a great relief to the masses of depressed classes who suffered acutely on account of caste-discrimination. The oppressed classes found their emancipation in Buddhism. Opposition to the rigid and inhuman caste system was one of the major reasons for the popularity of Buddhism.

One can gain a good idea of the popularity of Buddhism in South India by reading the *Sīlappadhikāram* (*The Book of the Anklet*)[3] by the Jain poet Ilango Aḍigal, the *Maṇimekhalai* by the Buddhist poet Sāttanār,

3. Translated by Rāmachandra Dikshitar. Oxford Union Press, 1939.

the *Thevāram* hymns of the Hindu saints such as Appar, Sundarar, and Tirujñāṇasambandhar. All these poets lived in the 2nd to 7th century CE. Further the works of the Vaishnavaite saints of the 8th and 9th century, extolling the virtues of their god, and the *Periyapurāṇam* by the 12th century poet Sekillār, and the *Nīlakesī* written by the Jains against Buddhism, give a clear picture of the popular place Buddhism held for several centuries in South India.

Buddhism, which flourished in South India from the 3rd century CE, began to decline gradually from about the 7th century for several reasons.

The Vedic religion of North India, Jainism, and the Ājīvaka faith had preceded Buddhism in South India. These religions had turned South India into a debating ground. It is not clear what the indigenous religion was before the arrival of these faiths from the North. The religions contending for popularity vied with one another to win over kings and influential men. At the start it was Buddhism that emerged triumphant from this struggle for popularity.

The Ājīvaka religion was left behind in this struggle. Only the Buddhist, Jain, and the Vedic religions were left to contend. Now Buddhism had to contest with two rival faiths which were envious of its popularity and planned to destroy it. The Buddhist position was undermined by the combined efforts of these two rival faiths. Buddhism itself split into several sects. The *Nīlakesī* mentions three rival Buddhist sects, Mahāyāna, Śrāvakayāna, and Mantrayāna. The Hindu saint Tirujñāṇasambandhar mentions in his *Thevāram* that during his time Buddhism was divided into six sects. This disunity itself contributed to the decline of Buddhism.

Further, the Buddhist monks gave up the social and welfare work which had brought them popularity. They became self-centred and deteriorated from their high principles. Hence they lost the support of the kings and influential men. Thus a weakened Saṅgha found itself unable to withstand the combined onslaught of the two rival faiths. With the decline of Buddhism in the 5th and 6th centuries Jainism gained ascendancy. At this time the Vedic religion was not influential in South India. With the upsurge of Jainism, the Jains concentrated their attack on Buddhism. The Buddhist monks found themselves not equal to the task of defending Buddhism. It is mentioned in a Jain work that the Jain teacher Akalankar defeated Buddhist monks in controversy and chased them off to Sri Lanka. But in spite of these setbacks Buddhism was by no means eradicated. For several centuries Buddhism still survived, though in a state of decline.

The Vedic religion of the Brahmins, which had hitherto been in a weak position, began to make headway and gain the support of the kings and men in high positions. Thereupon Brahmanism got the upper hand over Jainism. It was at this stage that Buddhism disappeared from South India. This Brahmanism had been unpopular for several centuries on account of its animal sacrifices and observance of the caste system. The depressed classes detested this religion as it forbade them to study the Vedas. After the 5th century, Brahmanism began to change its emphasis on these unpopular doctrines. It also incorporated popular South Indian gods such as Kālī, Skanda, Gaṇapati, and Vishnu into its pantheon. This new phase of the Hindu religion adopted hymns overflowing with faith as a means of gaining popularity. Just as the Jains when they gained power directed their attacks on Buddhism, Hinduism with its new orientation directed its onslaught on Buddhism as well as Jainism.

Hindu saints such as Tirujñāṇasambandhar, Appar, Sundarar, Tirumangai-ālvār, Peri-ālvār, and other such, appeared in the 7th and 8th century CE and were responsible for the renaissance of Hinduism. They successfully engaged Buddhist and Jain teachers in controversy. Hinduism at that time was not broken up into sects such as the Shaivaites and Vaishnavaites. Hence Buddhists, themselves divided, were unequal to the attack of the united Hindus.

The *Thevāram* psalms of Tirujñāṇasambandhar mention that he engaged Buddhists in controversy and converted them to his faith. *Tiruvāsagam*, written by Manikkavāsagar of Sidambaram, mentions that he defeated Buddhist teachers in controversy and made them flee to Sri Lanka.

Tirumangai-ālvār mentions in his works that he stole a golden image of the Buddha from a monastery in Nāgapaṭṭanam and offered it to build up the Tiruvarangam Hindu temple. Though Buddhism suffered such hazards and became weakened it was not until the 14th century that it disappeared from South India.

The continuation of the *Mahāvaṃsa* mentions that in the 13th century King Parākramabāhu of Dambadeniya brought down Buddhist monks and scriptures from Coḷa to revive Buddhism in Sri Lanka. During this period there was a great deal of cultural intercourse between South India and Sri Lanka. The chief of the monks who were brought from South India was Venerable Dhammakitti. He wrote the continuation of the *Mahāvaṃsa* from the time of King Sirimevan up to his time. He is also considered to be the author of the Pali poem *Dāṭhāvamsa*, though there is division of the opinion about this. The Venerable Dīpaṅkara of Coḷa, known as Buddhappiya, also came to Sri Lanka for his studies in Buddhism. The Pāli poem *Pajjamadhu* (*Nectar of Verses*) was written in adoration of the Buddha by him. He is also the author of *Rūpasiddhi*, a Pāli grammar. The Venerable Buddhamitta and Mahā Kassapa were also two Coḷian Bhikkhus who came to Sri Lanka. They studied the Dhamma here and rendered great service in the cause of the religion. From these facts it will be seen that up to the 13th century Buddhism was still strong in South India. Up to the 14th century there were Buddhists, monasteries, and centres of Buddhist learning in some parts of South India. After that Buddhism disappeared, leaving only traces of its heyday in the many ruins and the influence it brought to bear on Hinduism.

Buddhist Monuments in South India

In order to find out where Buddhism flourished, and in what condition it existed prior to the 14th century it is necessary to study the ruins of Buddhist buildings in the chief kingdom of South India, namely, the Coḷa country.

The capital of Coḷa was Kāveripaṭṭanam. It was so called because it was situated on the mouth of the river Kāveri. From the very start this city was a centre of Buddhist activities. The Jātaka book mentions this city as the home of the sage Akitti, who gave away his wealth to the poor, became a hermit, and lived in a wood close to the city. As large numbers of people flocked to pay him homage he found no leisure there. Therefore he left the place and went to Karaitivu island off the north coast of Sri Lanka.

The Venerable Mahā Mahinda, while leading the Buddhist mission to Sri Lanka, sojourned in this city. I have previously mentioned a monastery here. The Tamil poems *Sīlappadhikāram* and *Maṇimekhalai* refer to this monastery as the Indra Vihāra. It is derived from the elder's name Mahā Indra (Mahendra) in its Sanskritised form. In the 2nd century a Bhikkhu called Aravaṇa Aḍigal occupied this monastery. It is mentioned in the poem *Maṇimekhalai* that there was a small Buddhist shrine in a park called Upavana and a replica of the Buddha's footprint was worshipped there. In the same poem it is said that King Killivalavan, who reigned in the 2nd century, became a Buddhist and converted the prison to a preaching hall at the request of the nun Maṇimekhalai. Later he built a Buddhist monastery there.

The *Rasavāhinī*, a Pāli book of Buddhist stories written in the 13th century in Sri Lanka, mentions that a king of the Coḷa country erected a temple to the god Shiva, but being converted by Buddhist monks, he made the temple a Buddhist *vihāra*. The Venerable Buddhadatta, commentator of great fame, mentions in his books that he resided in a monastery at Kāveripaṭṭanam. He was supported by the king of the time. Among the Tamil commentators and Buddhist teachers he stands out pre-eminent.

In the introduction to the Pāli *Abhidhammāvatāra*, the Venerable Buddhadatta says that he lived in a monastery at Kāveripaṭṭanam constructed by a minister named Krishnadāsa. He describes in verse this flourishing city with its wide streets filled with busy people. Again in the *Madhurattha Vilāsini*, his commentary to the *Buddhavaṃsa*, he mentions that he wrote this book while residing in the same monastery.

Among the famous Buddhist centres of ancient Coḷa was the city of Bhūtamangala. Here too the Venerable Buddhadatta resided in a monastery built by one Vishnudāsa. The Pāli work *Vinaya Vinicchaya* was written by him there. He describes the city of Bhūtamangala in the same strain as he wrote of the Coḷian capital, Kāveripaṭṭanam. Bodhimangai was another city where Buddhism found a foothold. It was here that the Buddhist teachers Buddhanandi and Sāriputra lived. The *Periyapurāṇam* mentions a debate between Tirujñāṇasambandhar and these two teachers. The very name Bodhimangai is suggestive of its Buddhist associations.

Ponpaṭṭri of the Tañjai district was another Buddhist stronghold. Here the Buddhist teacher Buddhamitra lived in the 11th century. The Tamil grammar *Vīrasolium* was written by him. The book was so named in honour of the Coḷian King Vīrājendra.

Nāgapaṭṭanam

This city, situated near a port of the Coḷa country, was an important Buddhist centre from ancient times. Here a monastery called Badaratīrtha Vihāra was built by King Asoka. In the 8th century BCE, Venerable Dhammapāla resided here and wrote the *Nettippakaraṇa* commentary. In the year 720 CE a *vihāra* was constructed with the assistance of King

Narasinhapothavarman for the use of Chinese mariners who called over here for purposes of trade. This was known as the Chinese monastery. Marco Polo, travelling from China to Venice, mentions this monastery.

In the 8th century the Vaishnavaite teacher Tirumangai-yālvār stole a golden Buddha image from a Buddhist *vihāra* in Nāgapaṭṭanam and used the gold for renovating a Hindu temple. This fact is mentioned in the *Guruparamparai Parbhāram*, a Tamil work of the period. During the reign of the powerful Coḷa King Rājarāja (985–1014 CE), a monastery called Siri Sailendra Cūḍāmaṇi Vihāra was built here. The king of Srī Vijaya in Sumatra had helped the Coḷian king to put up this shrine. A copper plate with an engraving of the lands endowed by this king to the monastery was removed to Leiden museum, where it is preserved.

In the 14th century, too, Chinese merchants called at this port for merchandise. They engraved an inscription at the *vihāra*. Chinese records also make reference to this inscription.

In the 15th century eleven Burmese Bhikkhus and one envoy despatched to Sri Lanka by the Burmese King Rāmpatirāja were shipwrecked while returning to their native land. Fortunately they reached Nāgapaṭṭanam and resided in the Chinese *vihāra*. This is confirmed by the Kalyāṇi Sīmā rock inscription in Burma.

Sir Walter Elliot mentions that to the north of Nāgapaṭṭanam a large *gopuram* (temple tower) existed by the sea in 1836. It served as a lighthouse for mariners. In 1867 the government of India permitted Christian missionaries to demolish this Buddhist structure and erect one of their buildings. While the large tree by the *gopuram* was being uprooted, five Buddha statues were found. Four of them were of metal and one was of porcelain. One depicted the Buddha in the posture of expounding the Dhamma. When Lord Napier, the British governor, visited the place, the missionaries presented him with these antiquities. In the pedestal of the *Buddharūpa* an inscription in 12th century Tamil was found. It read, "May it be auspicious! The Teacher to whom Agama Paṇḍitar went for refuge for the emancipation from Saṃsāra."

There is at present a Brahmin village in Nāgapaṭṭanam called Putaṃkoṭṭam. Mr. S. Krishnaswāmy Iyengar mentions that this village was constructed after demolishing a Buddhist monastery there. In Madras museum are to be found several types of Buddha images and Buddhist carvings. From these facts one can conclude that Nāgapaṭṭanam was a stronghold of Buddhism. It was the pride of Indian Buddhists for several centuries. The great commentator Buddhaghosa embarked for Sri Lanka from this port. The village Buddhakuḍi, as the name implies, was the abode of Buddhists. After the 15th century, particularly with the arrival of the Europeans, Buddhist remains are lost.

Uragapura and Other Minor Towns

Of the ancient Coḷian cities, Uraiyūr, called Uragapura in Sanskrit, was the home of the celebrated commentator Buddhadatta. This city too was a Buddhist centre from the time of the arrival of Buddhism in the South.

So far we have discussed only the celebrated centres of Buddhist learning in the Coḷa country. Apart from these there were also a large number of minor towns where Buddhism was active. Of these, Buddhamangalam, Saṅghamangalam, Kumbakonam, Mayūrapaṭṭanam, Alamkuḍipaṭṭi, and so on are also important centres of Buddhist culture. Towns having names including the words *Buddha*, *Saṅgha*, *Ālam* (i.e., Bodhi tree), unmistakably reveal their Buddhist past. In some of the Hindu temples of these cities Buddha statues are seen with Hindu variations.

The Thoṇḍaimaṇḍala region of South India was also an area inhabited by Buddhists but unlike the Coḷa country it had no great centres of Buddhist activity. Only a few Buddhist cities such as Kūvam, Saṅghamangai, Tiruppādirippuliyūr, and Kāñchipuram existed there. Of these, Kūvam was a Buddhist stronghold from the early days. A large Buddha statue, which was found here, is to be seen at the Madras museum. Even today Saṅghamangai is considered a Buddhist village. The very name reveals its connection with the Buddhist Saṅgha. This is the birthplace of Sākiya Nāyakar, a Buddhist teacher who is said to have embraced Shaivaism at a later stage. Tiruppādirippuliyūr was a centre of Buddhist learning. A Buddhist university is said to have existed there.

Kāñchipuram

The chief city of the Tondaimaṇḍala region, Kāñchipuram, occupies an important place in South Indian Buddhist history. From early times it was a meeting place for the four chief religions which contended for supremacy in this region. By far most of its population was Buddhist. Hiuen Tsang, who visited it in the 7th century, mentions that King Asoka had erected a stūpa there. In the Tamil classic *Maṇimekhalai* it is mentioned that King Killivalavan built a stūpa in the city in honour of the Buddha. It is further mentioned in the same work that the king offered a park named Tarumadavana to the Buddhist order. A shrine containing an imprint of the Buddha's feet was erected in the park. The Buddhist teacher Aravaṇa Aḍigal is reported to have migrated from Kāveripaṭṭanam to the city.

Maṇimekhalai, having become a Buddhist nun, lived in this city to the end of her days. Even today there is a Hindu temple called Maṇimekhalāi Amman Kovil in this city. This is a Buddhist temple converted into a Hindu shrine. Ācariya Dharmapāla, rector of the Nālandā University, and Anuruddha Thera, author of *Abhidhammatthasaṅgaha*, were natives of this city. The well known commentator of the early 5th century Ācariya Buddhaghosa mentions in the concluding stanzas to his commentary on the Aṅguttara Nikāya (*Manorathapurāṇī*) that at the time of compiling the work he lived at Kāñchipura, with his friend Bhikkhu Jotipāla. Again in the *Papañcasūdani*, the commentary on the Majjhima Nikāya, he mentions that the book was written when he was residing at Mayūrapaṭṭanam with a Bhikkhu named Buddhamitta. In the *Samantapāsādikā*, the Elder states that when residing at Kāñchipura, he saw the Telugu commentary known as the *Andhaṭṭhakathā*.

Hiuen Tsang, who arrived at Kāñchi in 640 CE, mentions that about 100 Buddhist monasteries were there at the time with about a thousand monks in them. He also mentions that the Buddhist teacher Ācariya Dīgnāga was a native of Sinhavaktra (modern Siyamangala) near Kāñchi. Mahendravarman, the Pallava king, wrote his Sanskrit work, *Mattavilāsa-Prahāsana*, in the 8th century. In this he refers to the existence of many Buddhist *vihāras* at Kāñchi, the chief of which was Rāja Vihāra.

Of the Pallava kings who reigned at Kāñchipuraṃ, Buddhavarma was a Buddhist. He erected Buddhist monasteries and supported them. It is mentioned that King Himasītala of the 8th century was a supporter of the Buddhists. The Jain named Akalanka defeated the Buddhist monks in a debate in the presence of the king. He converted the king and made the Buddhist monks flee to Sri Lanka.

At present there is a shrine called Kāmākriyamman Kovil in Kāñchi. This was originally a shrine of the Mahāyāna Buddhists dedicated to the goddess Tārā. Indian archaeologists are of the opinion that it was later converted to a Hindu place of worship. In fact even today there are Buddha statues in the Kovil. There is a standing image there called "Sāttan," a word derived from the Pāli word "*satthā*," teacher, namely, the Buddha. According to the Hindu story, this Sāttan was the son of their goddess Kāmākriyamman. The present Kacchīsvara Kovil, Ekāmbaresvara Kovil, and Kurukāṇil Amarandāl Kovil are converted Buddhist shrines. In these are found Buddha images done up as Hindu gods. The Buddhist temple at Kaccikkunāyanār Kovil has been so demolished that nothing of it remains. There are inscriptions which mention land endowments to this Buddhist *vihāra*.

An eminent poet of Java writing in the 14th century mentions the existence of thirteen Buddhist monasteries in Kāñchi. He mentions that at this time Buddhism and Vaishnavism had got so mixed up that it was difficult to distinguish one from the other.

The conversion of Buddhist *vihāras* to Hindu Kovils, parading Buddha statues in the guise of Hindu gods and transferring the Buddhist history of these shrines to Hindu ones are a source of grief to the Buddhist who sees them. Apart from the many statues found broken up, the use of numerous Buddhist images for building walls, foundations, and other building work is also a source of grief to the Buddhist. Apart from the loss sustained by Buddhism, Buddhist art in Asia has been deprived of valuable treasures.

From these facts it is seen that Kāñchipuram was a great centre of Buddhism even as Anurādhapura was in Sri Lanka. Renowned Buddhist teachers such as Aravaṇa Aḍigal, Maṇimekhalai, Dinnāga, Bodhidharma, the commentator Ācariya Dhammapāla, Anuruddha, and Buddhāditiya lived in this city. The present Tirumāli Vaishnavaite shrine was formerly a Buddhist centre. Here too are found a large number of rock caves. Asoka characters (of the Brāhmī script) are found in them. Mr. V. R. Rāmachandra is of the opinion that these were occupied by Buddhist and Jain monks.

Similarly, Buddhist towns and villages existed in the Pāṇḍya country. This region was the birthplace of Ācariya Dhammapāla, Vajirabodhi, and other Buddhist scholars. There are many rock caves here which were once inhabited by Buddhist monks.

Finally, we have to consider the Cera kingdom and its Buddhist centres. This region is also called Kerala, or the Malayālam country. King Elāra, who conquered and ruled Sri Lanka (220 BCE), was a native of Kerala.

Vañchi

This was the capital of the Cera country. *Sīllappadhikāram*, the Tamil poem, describes the capitals of the chief kingdoms of South India, Coḷa, Cera, and Pāṇḍya. It is mentioned in the *Maṇimekhalai* that the great grandfather of Kovalan, hero of the *Sīllappadhikāram*, built a Buddhist shrine (*stūpa*) at Vañchi. He was won over to Buddhism by a Bhikkhu living in a place called Pādapanka Jamalaya. He spent all his wealth on Buddhist causes. In the 2nd century this cetiya and several others existed at Vañchi. It is mentioned in the poem *Maṇimekhalai* that Kovalan's father, Maṇimekhalai, and the Bhikkhu Aravaṇa Aḍigal went to Vañchi and worshipped its many Buddhist shrines.

Several Hindu temples bearing such names as Sāttan Kāvu and Aiyappan Kovil exist today in the Malayālam country. All these were former Buddhist shrines. *Sāttan*, as mentioned before, is a name for Buddha. *Kāvu* is a garden or monastery. Hence Sāttankāvu means "Monastery of the Buddha."

Madhurā

Another region where Buddhist cities and villages existed is found in the Pāṇḍya country. Its capital, Madhurā, was a centre of Buddhist activity. *Madhuraikkāñchi*, a work written in the last Sangam period of Tamil literature, mentions the existence of Buddhist monasteries and Buddhists in this city. In the poem *Maṇimekhalai* the existence of a shrine dedicated to Cintādevī is referred to. Historians are of the view that this is a shrine dedicated to the Mahāyāna goddess Tārā. This view is confirmed by the fact that Tārā was also known by the name Cintādevī.

Hieun Tsang, who arrived here in the 7th century, mentions that he saw the ruins of a monastery built by King Asoka. He also saw the ruins of a *vihāra* constructed by Mahinda Thera close to this. No reference to these monasteries is found in Tamil literature. Whoever built these *vihāras*, the fact that Buddhist monasteries existed in Madhurā is established. Reference has already been made to Ariṭṭapaṭṭi, which derived its name from the rock cave used by the Buddhist teacher Ariṭṭha from Sri Lanka. Inscriptions in Brāhmī characters have been found in the rock caves that were occupied by Buddhist monks.

Podiyakanda, mentioned in Tamil literature, also became a centre of Buddhist activity. The Mahāyānist teacher Vajrabodhi (661–730) was born here. He went out to China and Japan to propagate Dhyāna (Zen) Buddhism. The present Tanjore district was known in ancient times as Tanchai. Ācariya Dhammapāla, who wrote commentaries to thirteen books of the Khuddaka Nikāya (Sutta Piṭaka), was a native of this province. There is evidence of this region being inhabited by Buddhists.

It was the custom from the Buddha's time to erect monasteries in parks and gardens. This practice prevailed both in India and Sri Lanka. Further, Manavūr and Tuḍitapura were Buddhist cities with numerous shrines. In a paraphrase written to the Tamil poem *Yakka Yāgapparani* there is reference to a city called Buddha-pura (Buddhist city). This has so far not been identified.

From the foregoing one can get a glimpse into the flourishing state of Buddhism in Coḷa, Pāṇḍya, Cera (Kerala), and the Thondaimaṇdala regions which comprise South India. From the available literature and the ruins, we get the impression that Buddhism was prevalent all over South India. Sekkilār, the author of the *Periyapurāṇam*, a Hindu religious work, mentions that in the 7th century the Shaivaite religion was moribund, Buddhism was triumphant and victorious. He says that the Shaivaites prayed to Shiva to destroy Buddhism and build up Hinduism. By Shiva's divine providence Tirugnānasabandhar was born to redeem Shiva's faith. Sekkilār cannot be incorrect with regard to the flourishing state of Buddhism that he refers to.

The Impact of Buddhism on Hinduism

When Buddhism made its exit, it left behind indelible impressions of its impact on the life and religious thought of South India. Buddhist ideas were incorporated into the Hindu religion. Modern Hinduism is imbued with Buddhist as well as Jain ideas. Not only this, the Hindus made an attempt to absorb the Islamic faith. During the time of King Akbar, a new Upanishad named *Allah-Upanishad* was composed.

Let us now consider the Buddhist ideas that have been introduced into Hinduism. Many South Indian Hindus do not even know that some of their ideas have come to them from the impact of Buddhism when it flourished in their land. Although Buddhism was wiped out, the fact remains that the Hindus worship the Buddha as the ninth

Avatar or incarnation of their God Vishnu. That became necessary because the worship of the Buddha was popular among the masses and hence the necessity to incorporate him into the Hindu pantheon. One cannot say with precision during which period this occurred. In Amarasiṃha's Sanskrit dictionary of the 8th century it is mentioned that the Buddha was the son of King Suddhodana and Queen Māyā. In the book on Vishnu's nine incarnations (*Dasāvatāralarita*), written in the 11th century, it is mentioned that the Buddha is the ninth incarnation of Vishnu. Therefore we may conclude that this incorporation of the Buddha into the Hindu pantheon occurred between the compilation of these two works.

While one branch of Hinduism, the Vaishnavaites, made the Buddha an incarnation of their god, the other branch, the Shaivaites, not to be outdone by them, also made the Buddha one of their gods, calling him Sāstā Aiyanār and Dharmarājan. Again the Buddha was called Vināyaka and was equated to the elephant-faced god Ganesh. Vināyaka was a name used by the Buddhists for the Buddha. The Hindus call Ganesh, "Vināyaka." The Dharmarāja Vihāra and Vināyaka Vihāra were converted into Dharmarāja Kovil and Vināyaka Kovil.

The Buddha categorically denounced animal sacrifices which the Vedic Brahmins taught were highly meritorious. On account of the Buddhist influence some Hindus renounced the slaughter of animals and adopted the first Buddhist precept. Thus with the help of Buddhist teachings the Hindus managed to reform their religion, which was losing ground and became moribund.

The Bodhi tree is a sacred object to Buddhists because the Buddha attained Enlightenment under one such tree. Tamil Buddhist poets writing in adoration of the Master referred to him in such terms as, "the Noble One who attained Enlightenment under the Bodhi tree," and "the mine of mercy who sat under the Bodhi tree." The Shaivaite teachers Apper, Sundarār, Tirujñāṇasambandhar, in their *Thevāram* hymns, refer to Buddhists as *"bodhiyār"* or worshippers of Bodhi trees. One of the Buddhist poets of the Sangam period was called Ilambodhiyār. In the anti-Buddhist poem *Nīlakesī*, written by the Jains, reference is made to the worship of Bodhi trees by Buddhists. This Buddhist practice is retained by the Hindus of South India. They do not even know that this practice of theirs is a legacy from their Buddhist ancestors.

Buddhist monks erected monasteries in villages, resided there, and taught the Dhamma. This practice was adopted by the Hindus who opened "*maḍams*" (resting places) for similar purposes. It is also a well-known fact that the *Advaitavāda* of Saṃkarāchāriya, which also goes by the name of *Māyāvāda*, *Ekātmavāda* and *Smārtavāda*, was influenced by Mahāyāna philosophy. Having studied the Buddhist philosophies of Sunyavāda and Vijnānavāda he adopted these systems to his teachings. The Hindu teacher Rāmānuja called Saṃkara's *Advaitavāda* "hidden Buddhism." Mādhavāchārya, an exponent of Dvaitavāda, refuted Saṃkara's philosophy, saying it was Buddhism in a different garb. The *Padmapurāṇa* too calls this teaching "hidden Buddhism." Thus from the very mouth of Hindu teachers we have evidence of the strong influence exercised by Buddhism on Saṃkara.

Further, popular gods and goddesses of the Mahāyāna Buddhists were given Hindu names such as Kālī, Pidārī, and Draupadī and were worshipped in the original shrines. The shrine of the Buddhist goddess Maṇimekhalai at Kāñchi became Kāmākriyamman Ālayam. The shrine of the Mahāyāna goddess Tārā became Draupadiyamman Kovil. These are two more of the many Hindu kovils in South India which were originally Buddhist shrines.

These are some of the legacies which Hinduism derived from Buddhism. The erection of "*maḍams*," Saṃkara's *Advaitavāda*, the conversion of Buddhist deities to Hindu gods, Buddha being made an incarnation of Vishnu, the reduction of animal sacrifices, are the six items where the influence of Buddhism is seen to advantage. These practices and teachings are carefully adhered to even today. Though Buddhism was expelled from South India, yet many vestiges of it have remained. Buddhism lost in South India. Yet the Buddha's teachings and philosophy did not fail to win over the minds of men.

Tamil Literary Works by South Indian Buddhist Authors

South India produced many Buddhist teachers who made valuable contributions to Tamil, Pāli, and Sanskrit literature. They composed numerous works on a variety of subjects such as religion, philosophy, history, grammar, etymology, astronomy, and medicine. Reference to their works is found in Tamil literature and other historical records.

It is most unfortunate that of the large number of books written from the 3rd to the 14th century only very few are available today. One literary work and a book on grammar are all that remain to us. The names of some other books are available. The large number of books that were destroyed is lost to posterity.

The Jains and Buddhists propagated their faith in the local languages. The Buddhist monks who came to South India studied the local language, preached, and wrote books for the edification of the native population. Though their literary works were destroyed by enemies they have left enduring marks of their influence.

In the 4th century the celebrated commentator Āchariya Buddhadatta lived in Buddhist cities such as Uragapura (Uraiyūr), Kāveripaṭṭanam, and Bhūtamaṅgalam and wrote several commentaries in Pāli. Rhys Davids mentions that he took material for his commentaries from the Buddhist literature available to him in Tamil. In the paraphrase of the *Nīlakesī* and *Vīrasoliyam* there are extracts from Tamil Buddhist poems which existed at the time. Today it is not possible to say from which books the extracts were taken. There is no doubt that many Buddhist works in Tamil existed during the heyday of Buddhism.

It is possible that books were destroyed during religious controversies. This happened several times in Sri Lanka, too. The Jains and Shaivaites opposed Buddhism tooth and nail. It is likely that these adversaries destroyed Buddhist books. After the decline of Buddhism the tussle for supremacy was between the Jains and Hindus. In this the Hindus came out triumphant while Jainism began to decline. The Jains, who were scattered all over, took sufficient precautions to preserve their Tamil literature. The Buddhists were not able to do even this, and all Buddhist books except two were lost. Although the Tamil books were destroyed, the Pāli books written by Tamil Buddhist scholars are preserved in Sri Lanka, Burma (Myanmar), and Siam (Thailand), even today. As Tamil Buddhist books were not used outside India these books perished with Buddhism in South India. In the 14th century Venerable Toṭagamuvē Rāhula, Buddhist scholar in Sri Lanka, made use of a Tamil glossary to the Jātaka when he wrote the *Pañcikāpradīpa*. Even this book has been lost. The loss of Tamil Buddhist literature was a death blow to Buddhism in South India.

The Poem *Maṇimekhalai*

The five epics in Tamil literature are *Sīlappadhikāram*, *Maṇimekhalai*, *Valaiyāpathy*, *Kuṇḍalakesī*, and *Jīvaka Cintāmani.* It is a strange fact that not one of these was written by Hindu Tamils. *Maṇimekhalai, Valaiyāpathy,* and *Kuṇḍalakesī* are the works of Tamil Buddhist poets. The remaining two are Jain works. Although the epics of the Jains are preserved intact, of the Buddhist works only *Maṇimekhalai* remains to tell the grandeur and glory of Buddhism in a land where it is no more. The story of *Maṇimekhalai* is unknown in Pāli, Sanskrit, and Sinhala literature. It is a treasure house of Buddhist doctrinal expositions and a narrative of unusual charm. It is a monument of the glorious days of Buddhism in South India.

The beautiful Hindu maiden, Maṇimekhalai, studied the six systems of philosophy in Hinduism, and other prevalent religions of the time. She compared them to the teachings of the Buddha and became impressed with the latter. Later, on hearing doctrinal expositions from the Buddhist teacher Bhikkhu Aravaṇa Aḍigal, she became a Buddhist nun and devoted her time to the propagation of Buddhism in South India. These are the highlights of the story. There is doctrinal exposition in the poem dealing with the Four Noble Truths, Dependent Origination (*paṭicca-samuppāda*), mind (*citta*) and mental states (*cetasikas*), and Buddhist practices like *sīla* and non-violence (*ahiṃsā*) are well explained.

The aim of the author was to compare Buddhism favourably with the other prevailing religions. He takes the occasion to criticise Jainism, the chief opponent of Buddhism at the time. While exposing the weaknesses of the contemporary religions he enthrones the Buddha Dhamma as the perfect religion. His intention was thereby to propagate Buddhism. The poem contains 30 cantos and its story is a continuation of the *Sīlappadhikāram*. This poem is invaluable to the student of South India's Buddhist history. *Maṇimekhalai* is a mine of information on the history of South India, Buddhism, and its place during that period, contemporary arts and culture, and the customs of the times. Its author was Sīthalai Sāttanār, bard of the Buddha in Tamil literature.

Kuṇḍalakesī

This is one of the five great classic epics in the Tamil language. It is now lost, but quotations from it are found in books by authors who had access to this classic. The poem was written for the purpose of showing to advantage Buddhist philosophy by comparative evaluation with Vedic and Jain philosophies. The Jains wrote *Nīlakesī* as a reply to this book, and this is still preserved intact. That *Kuṇḍalakesī* is a Buddhist work needs no further proof. The biography of the Bhikkhunī Kuṇḍalakesī is found in the commentary to the Therigātha, Dhammapada Commentary, and in the Aṅguttara Nikāya. The story of Kuṇḍalakesī in the Tamil work is the identical biography with a few differences. The commentary to the work *Nīlakesī* also touches on the story of Kuṇḍalakesī. The story was taken from the *Kuṇḍalakesī* in order to present the Jain reply to Buddhist criticism. Bhikkhunī Kuṇḍalakesī was originally a Jain nun who went about India expounding Jainism and challenging anybody to refute her views. Venerable Sāriputta, a disciple of the Buddha, took up the challenge one day and in the ensuing debate Kuṇḍalakesī was defeated. She renounced Jainism and became a Buddhist nun. The author of the poem depicts the Buddhist nun Kuṇḍalakesī championing the Buddhist doctrines and refuting Jainism. This drew the Jain reply, *Nīlakesī,* which alone is now available. *Kuṇḍalakesī* was written prior to the 5th century. It is said the author was a Buddhist named Nāgaguttanār. The Vinaya sub-commentary named *Vimativinodanī* refers to the *Kuṇḍalakesī* as a work by a Tamil Buddhist teacher written to refute heretical views. The Pāli text is as follows:

> *"Pubbe kira imasmiṃ damiḷa-raṭṭhe koci bhinnaladdhiko Nāgaseno nāma Thero Kuṇḍalakesīvatthuṃ paravāda-mathanañāya dassana-tthaṃ damiḷa-kabbarūpena karonto...."*

> "Formerly, in this Tamil country an elder named Nāgasena compiled a work in Tamil containing the story of Kuṇḍalakesī, for refuting heretical doctrines, adducing arguments for demolishing the views advanced by non-Buddhists."

The Pāli name Nāgasena may have been Tamilised to Nāgaguttanār. The destruction of *Kuṇḍalakesī* was a severe blow to Buddhism. A splendid source of Buddhist history, the record of the culture and other details of the times lost with that work.

Valaiyāpathy

This work too is now lost and no details can be given. It is not even certain whether this is a Buddhist or Jain work. Some scholars are of the opinion that it was a Buddhist book. They base their evidence on quotations from the *Valaiyāpathy* found in other literary works. As the author of *Valaiyāpathy* has quoted the *Tirukural,* it is possible that the author drew his inspiration from the latter.

Vīrasoliyam

This is a Tamil grammatical work written on the lines of the Sanskrit works on the subject. The author was Buddhamitra, a Mahāyānist Bhikkhu. A commentary to this was written by his pupil, Perum Devanār. The work was so called in honour of the king of the time who was a patron of the author. This book is now in disuse. Being the work of a Buddhist author who used examples from lines describing the virtues of the Buddha, it became distasteful to Hindu scholars. It was compiled in the 11th century. With the help of *Vīrasoliyam* and its glossary one can get a glimpse into Buddhism in South India at the time. Some of the historical facts mentioned in this work about Coḷian kings are confirmed by inscriptions engraved on rocks. Moreover, in the glossary one comes across the names of several works in Tamil literature. Even in examples given for the purpose of elucidating rhetorical devices there is always mention of the Buddha and his virtues. This work enables us to get a general knowledge of Tamil literature and its history. Like all other Buddhist works it was on the verge of extinction when it was rescued by a Sri Lankan Tamil scholar, C. Y. Thāmotharam Pillai. Even now this book is not available in South India.

Siddhāntattokai

This too is a Buddhist work which has now been lost. From the name it appears to have been a work on the Abhidhamma. It is not certain whether it is the work of one author or several authors. In a paraphrase to the Shaivaite religious book named *Sivajñāna Siddhiyār*, its author Jñānaprakāsar, a Shaivaite scholar, makes reference to some quotations from this poem. In a paraphrase of the Jain work *Nīlakesī* there is reference to *Siḍḍhāntattokai*. From these facts it can be concluded that it was a Buddhist work. Apart from this there is no other source of information about it.

Tiruppadigam

From the title it can be inferred that this was a panegyric on the Buddha. Jñānaprakāsar, who wrote a paraphrase to the Hindu work *Sivajñāna Siddhiyār* quotes a verse and says, "this is taken from the *Tiruppadigam*." The author of the paraphrase to the *Nīlakesī* quotes two verses from this work, but does not mention from where he got the quotation. But, as he has quoted one of the verses which Jñānaprakāsar has acknowledged while quoting, it can be assumed that he was quoting the Buddhist work mentioned above. These two verses are hymns in praise of the Buddha, referring to his *dāna* and *sīla pāramitā*. Hence this was probably a Tamil book of Buddha-hymns, which is now lost. No details of its author, its length, or when it was written are available.

Bimbisāra Kadai

That such a book existed can be seen from a reference to it in the paraphrase to the *Nīlakesī*. There, four verses are quoted and the remark is made, "this quotation is from the *Bimbisāra Kadai*, a Buddhist work."

The Hindu scholar Jñānaprakāsar too quotes verses from this Buddhist work and acknowledges the source. Details regarding this book too are not available, as it has been lost and is now forgotten. The theme of the book must have been the life of King Bimbisāra, who was a devoted follower of the Buddha. From the available quotations one gets the impression that like the *Maṇimekhalai* this was written in the Āsiriyappā metre in Tamil poetry.

Eminent Buddhist Teachers Who Lived in South India

The fact that Buddhism flourished in South India is amply proved by Buddhist ruins, the present day customs, manners and ideas of

Buddhist origin, and the books written by Buddhist authors of South India. In addition, there is evidence of many South Indian Buddhist teachers, both lay and monastic, who graced the land of their birth. We shall here include brief references to them.

1. Ilambodhiyār

The last Sangam of Tamil literature was held in the 1st or 2nd century CE. Ilambodhiyār, the Buddhist poet, lived during this period. Several of his verses are found in the 72nd verse of a work called *Naṭṭrinai,* composed during the last Sangam period. His very name indicates that he was a Buddhist.

2. Aravaṇa Aḍigal

Information about this Buddhist teacher is found in the *Maṇimekhalai.* He lived for a long time at Kāveripaṭṭanam. During his youth he travelled north up to the river Ganges and south to Srī Pāda (Adam's Peak) in Sri Lanka. The author of *Maṇimekhalai* portrays him as a versatile exponent of the Dhamma who engaged himself in Buddhist missionary work. He was the head of the Buddhist monastery at Kāveripaṭṭanam. It was to him the bereaved Mādhavī, mother of Maṇimekhalai, went for consolation after the murder of her husband, Kovalan. There, both mother and daughter were instructed in the Dhamma and they undertook to observe the Buddhist precepts. Later when Maṇimekhalai was imprisoned by the queen of the Coḷa country, it was the intervention of this Buddhist teacher at the palace which obtained her release. From the story it is evident that even the royal family held him in reverence. When Kāveripaṭṭanam was ravaged by a tidal wave, he left for Vañchi. After living there for a short time, he finally settled down at Kāñchipura. He lived during the latter part of the 1st century or in the early part of the 2nd century.

3. Bhikkhunī Maṇimekhalai

She is the heroine of the Tamil classical poem *Maṇimekhalai* by Sīthalai Sāttanār. In Kāveripaṭṭanam there lived a wealthy man named Kovalan. He had a mistress named Mādhavī, who was a dancer by profession. Their daughter was Maṇimekhalai. She grew up amidst riches and became a skilful musician and dancer. Attracted by her beauty and talents, the son of the king of Coḷa, Prince Udaya, fell in love with her. In order to get rid of her father, he had him charged on a false accusation when he went to Madhurā. On this charge Kovalan was executed. When his wife came to hear of this horrible crime, she was deeply moved and became disgusted with the world. She went with her daughter, Maṇimekhalai, to the Bhikkhu Aravaṇa Aḍigal, who consoled her in her grief by preaching the Dhamma, and both mother and daughter became Buddhists. Maṇimekhalai's grandmother tried to persuade both of them to continue their profession as dancers, and Prince Udaya too made advances to Maṇimekhalai. But this was of no avail. Sensual pleasures had no appeal for her, and her mind being firmly set upon the religious life she became a Buddhist nun. The prince visited her several times and tried to persuade her to revert to the lay life. On a pilgrimage to Sri Lanka, Maṇimekhalai worshipped at the Nāgadīpa shrine on an island off the northern coast of Sri Lanka. There she worshipped the Buddha's footprint, and while at the shrine saw a vision of her previous birth wherein the prince had been her husband. A deity at the shrine gave her a miraculous bowl from which she could feed any number of people without the supply of food becoming exhausted. When she returned to Kāveripaṭṭanam she gave alms daily to the poor in a public hall. The king of Coḷa was pleased with her good work and gave her permission to ask for a boon. She asked that the royal prison be converted to an alms-hall, and this was done.

A woman named Kāyacaṇḍikā left her husband and came to Kāveripaṭṭanam, where she lived on alms along with other beggars fed by Maṇimekhalai. She was beautiful and resembled Maṇimekhalai in some ways. Her husband too arrived at Kāveripaṭṭaṇam in search of her. He saw the Prince Udaya speaking to Maṇimekhalai in the alms-hall. During this conversation Maṇimekhalai spoke of the transient and worthless nature of the human body, and urged the prince to renounce his passion for her.

Kāyacaṇḍikā's husband mistook Maṇimekhalai for his wife. He thought a young man was paying amorous attention to his wife. He hid in the alms-hall and when a suitable occasion came he attacked the prince and struck him with a sword, killing him on the spot, not knowing his true identity. This incident became known to the public and religious men residing at the alms-hall reported it to the king. The king ascertained the facts and saw to it that Maṇimekhalai was given protection from men who might try to avenge the death of the prince on her. The queen managed to get Maṇimekhalai imprisoned on a false charge. Later, when the facts of the case were known, the queen relented; she freed Maṇimekhalai and begged her pardon.

Maṇimekhalai, finding that she was not safe in the city, went on a pilgrimage to Java. Returning from there, she arrived at Kāñchi, where she studied various religions under several teachers. Finally, she returned to Kāñchi, where the Buddhist teacher Aravaṇa Aḍigal lived. She pursued further studies in Buddhism and lived the holy life of a Buddhist nun to the end of her days. She lived in the 2nd century CE.

4. Sīthalai Sāttanār

He was the author of the Tamil epic *Maṇimekhalai*. A Buddhist poet of the Sangam period, he was a master in the exposition of the Dhamma. The three Sangams were convocations held under royal patronage of the Tamil kings of Coḷa, Cera, and Pāṇḍya. These convocations were organised on the lines of the Buddhist Councils. Sāttanār is called a Sangam poet because he took part in one of those convocations. The full name of the author of *Maṇimekhalai* was Madhurai Kūlavāṇikan Sīthalai Sāttanār. Madhurai refers to his native city, Madhurā. Kūlavāṇikan indicates his profession as that of a grain merchant. *Sīthalai* means "from whose (fore-) head pus flowed." It is told that when he found mistakes in the works of contemporary poets scrutinised by him, he used to strike his forehead with his iron style and this caused frequent wounds which suppurated. *Sāttanār* was his personal name, often abbreviated to Sāttan. He was not only a first-class poet and an eminent literary critic, but also an able exponent of the Buddhist doctrine.

Well versed in religion, logic, and philosophy, he showed the superiority of Buddhism, evaluating it against the background of contemporary religious thought. He was held in honour by Ilango Aḍigal, the distinguished author of the Tamil classic *Sīlappadhikāram*. His classic *Maṇimekhalai* is a lasting monument to his scholarship, encyclopaedic knowledge, and excellence as a Tamil poet. From chapter 27 of the *Maṇimekhalai* one can see his proficiency in the six systems of Hindu philosophy. There were several other poems by him, verses from which are found in poems such as *Nattriṇai, Kurunthokai Puranāṇūru,* and *Ahanāṇūru.* The aim of writing the *Maṇimekhalai* was the propagation of the Buddha Dhamma. It is seen that *Maṇimekhalai* was written after the *Tirukkural* was composed, because there are two verses from the *Tirukkural* quoted in *Maṇimekhalai.* Therefore it can be assumed that Sāttanār lived in the latter half of the 2nd century.

5. The Coḷian Bhikkhu Saṅghamitta

Well known to all students of Sri Lankan history, he was a Mahāyānist Bhikkhu who caused a great upheaval there in the 3rd century. He was a Tamil who hailed from Coḷa. King Gotābhaya (253–266 CE.) expelled 60 Bhikkhus from Sri Lanka for being incorrigible heretics. They went to South India and lived in the Coḷa country. Saṅghamitta met them and made up his mind to avenge his brethren of the Mahāyāna sect. He came to Sri Lanka and started to propagate the Mahāyāna faith. The Bhikkhus of the Mahāvihāra, the sect of orthodox Theravāda, reported him to the king. The king asked them to debate with Saṅghamitta in his presence and promised to support the victorious party. The Mahāvihāra Bhikkhus were led by the Elder Saṅghapāla, an uncle of the king. Saṅghamitta triumphed in this debate and the king kept his promise. The king entrusted the teaching of his two sons to this teacher, who found the younger and more able prince receptive to his influence. The elder prince disliked his teacher.

When the elder prince Jeṭṭhatissa became king, Saṅghamitta left the island as he felt that he was not safe. Ten years later, when the king died and his younger brother ascended the throne, Saṅghamitta returned and he himself crowned Mahāsena as king of Sri Lanka.

Now Saṅghamitta planned to destroy the Mahāvihāra, the seat of Theravāda Buddhism. He told the king that the Mahāvihāra monks were not following the true teachings of the Buddha, and got the king to forbid his subjects to support them. The monks of the Mahāvihāra, finding that the people did not support them with their daily necessities of life, left the capital, Anurādhapura, and went to the southern part of Sri Lanka. Saṅghamitta now pointed out that property without an owner belonged to the state and the king handed over the monastery to Saṅghamitta. He had the great monastery demolished, and made use of all the articles that were in it to build up the Abhayagiri Vihāra, the centre of the Mahāyānist teachings.

The queen was grieved to see the ancient religion of Sri Lanka, the pristine doctrines of the Buddha, ruined by this monk from South India. She had him and his collaborator, the minister Sona, assassinated. Thus ended Saṅghamitta's scheme to convert Sri Lanka to the Mahāyāna doctrine. There is no report that he had written any book.

6. Nāgaguttanār

He was the author of the Buddhist poem *Kuṇḍalakesī*. We know him as its author, because in the commentary to *Nīlakesī* a verse is quoted from the *Kuṇḍalakesī*, and it is followed with the remark, "this is a verse from Nāgaguttanār." Yet according to the Pāli commentary called *Vimativinodanī*, the author of *Kuṇḍalakesī* is called Nāgasena. It is possible that this name was converted into Nāgaguttanār by Tamil writers. No further details about this poet are available. As the *Nīlakesī* was written early in the 10th century, we have to conclude that *Kuṇḍalakesī* was written prior to this.

7. Commentator Ācariya Buddhadatta

Ācariya Buddhadatta, held in profound veneration by Buddhists as a commentator of the Buddha-word, was a Tamil from South India. He lived in the famous South Indian Buddhist cities, Kāveripaṭṭanam, Uragapura, Bhūtamaṅgalam, Kāñchi, and also at the Mahāvihāra monastery, Anurādhapura, Sri Lanka. The commentary called *Madhuratthavilāsinī* was written when he resided in a monastery built by a Buddhist minister named Krishnadāsa, at Kāveripaṭṭanam. *Madhuratthavilāsinī* is a Pāli commentary to the Buddhavamsa of the Sutta Piṭaka. He wrote the renowned treatise on Abhidhamma, *Abhidhammāvatāra*, at the invitation of a Bhikkhu named Sumati. He is also the author of the Pāli work on the Vinaya called *Vinayavinicchaya*. It is mentioned in the book that this was written in the reign of the Coḷian King Acyutavikrama. While residing in Anurādhapura, Sri Lanka, he wrote the *Uttara-vinicchaya*. The Pāli poem of adoration to the Buddha, *Jinālaṅkāra Kāvya*, is another of his excellent literary works.

In this work he describes his native Coḷa country and its cities such as Kāveripaṭṭanam and Bhūtamaṅgalam in mellifluous verses. He was a senior contemporary of the great commentator Buddhaghosa, who has paid a glowing tribute to him in one of his works. "After his (Buddhadatta's) demise even men like me are considered scholars," says Ācariya Buddhaghosa. Ācariya Buddhadatta is second only to the great Buddhaghosa in erudition, scholarship, and ability as a commentator to the Buddha-word. He lived in the 5th century.

8. The Mahā Thera Buddhamitra

He lived in South India in the 5th century. He should not be confused with the Bhikkhu Buddhamitra, the author of *Vīrasoliyam*, the Tamil grammar. This Mahā Thera resided at Mayūrapaṭṭanam (the present Māyāvaram). At that time the celebrated commentator Buddhaghosa was his guest. *Papañcasūdani*, the commentary to the Majjhima Nikāya, was written at his invitation. In the conclusion to the *Papañcasūdani*, Ācariya Buddhaghosa says:

> "*Āyācito sumantinā therena bhadanta buddhamittena*
> *pubbe mayūrarūpapaṭṭanamhi saddhiṃ vasante.*"
>
> "When I was formerly living at Mayūrapaṭṭaṇam,
> with the Thera Buddhamitta, I was invited to write this."

9. Bodhidharma

He was formerly a prince hailing from a royal South Indian family. A Mahāyānist Buddhist teacher named Prajñottara won him over to the Mahāyāna faith and ordained him as a monk. During his youth he worked for the propagation of his faith in South India. Towards the latter part of his life he left for China as a Buddhist missionary. At Canton he met the Emperor Wu-ti, but failed to impress him. Thereupon he went to the north of China and founded the Dhyāna school of Buddhism (Chinese: Chṃan; Japanese: Zen). He lived there till he passed away. He deprecated the making of offerings to the Buddha; it was purity of the mind and enlightenment that he stressed.

10. Ācariya Dignāga

Hiuen Tsang in his *Records of the Western World* gives an account of this teacher. He was a native of Sīyamangalam, which is situated to the south of Kāñchi. He studied comparative religion and philosophy and became a monk of Vātsīputrīya Nikāya. Later he went to North India and became a Mahāyānist under the influence of Vasubandhu. At Nālandā he defeated non-Buddhists in a debate, and won the admiration of the monks of the university. A philosopher and a debater of great repute, he toured India, lecturing and debating. Finally he settled down at Kāñchi. He is the founder of the Viññāṇavāda school of Buddhist philosophy. Among his pupils was the vice-chancellor of the Nālandā University, Dharmapāla Mahā Thera. His numerous works include the *Nyāyapravesa* (*Introduction to Logic*) and *Nyāyasamucchaya* (*Compendium of Logic*), two Sanskrit books. There is no mention of any books in Tamil by him. He lived between 345–425 CE.

11. Vice-Chancellor Dharmapāla of Nālandā

He should be differentiated from the commentator Dhammapāla, who lived at Badaratīrtha and was a master of the Theravāda. The Thera Dharmapāla of Nālandā on the other hand was a distinguished exponent of the Mahāyāna doctrines. He was the third son of a Tamil king who ruled at Kāñchi. Although his father arranged to have him married, he secretly went to a Buddhist teacher and entered the Order. He travelled in India and abroad and acquired a great store of knowledge. He excelled in all arts and sciences.

Whilst on a lecture tour he arrived at Kosambī. There Buddhists were locked in a great controversy with their opponents and were faring badly. Coming to the rescue of the Buddhists he displayed his brilliant oratory and encyclopaedic knowledge, tearing to shreds the arguments of his Hindu opponents. By this victory he won over the king, who was on the spot with a large number of distinguished visitors. The Elder's fame spread far and wide and he was offered the vice-chancellorship of Nālandā University, a position reserved for India's foremost Buddhist scholar.

His pupil was Sīlabhadra, himself a versatile scholar under whom Hiuen Tsang studied Sanskrit when he was at Nālandā. Sīlabhadra succeeded his teacher.

The vice-chancellor died young, at the age of 32. It is a great mistake that some scholars have made trying to identify Aravaṇa Aḍigal, mentioned in *Maṇimekhalai*, with the Vice-Chancellor Dharmapāla.

12. Badaratīrtha Dhammapāla

He is the Ācariya Dhammapāla mentioned in Pāli literature as a great commentator. A native of South India, he lived in the city of Tañjā, where the river Tāmraparṇi flows. This is identified with Tanjore of the Coḷa country. Other scholars are of the opinion that Ācariya Dhammapāla was a native of a town by the name of Tanjavur in the Pāṇḍyan country. It is also evident from the *Nettippakaraṇa* commentary compiled by him that he also lived at Badaratīrtha Vihāra at Nāgapaṭṭanam. He went to Sri Lanka and resided at the Mahāvihāra, Anurādhapura. During this time the commentaries on the Thera- and Therīgāthā, Udāna, Itivuttaka, Peta Vatthu, Vimānavatthu, Cariyā Piṭaka, and the *Nettippakaraṇa* were written. All these commentaries are named *Paramattha Dīpanī*. He also wrote a voluminous sub-commentary to the *Visuddhimagga*, called *Paramatthamañjūsā*. He lived somewhere about 796 CE. In the *Nettippakaraṇa* commentary he says:

> "*Saddhammotaraṇaṭhāne*
> *Paṭṭane nāga savhaya*
> *Dhammāsoka Mahārāja*
> *Vihāre vasatā mayā.*"

> "(I wrote this commentary) while I was residing at the monastery built by King Asoka at Nāgapaṭṭanam, which is like unto a port for embarking on the ocean of the Dhamma."

The *Sāsanavaṃsa* refers to him as follows:

According to the *Sāsanavaṃsa*, a 19th century bibliography of Pali works, Ācariya Dhammapāla compiled the commentaries to

Itivuttaka, Udāna, Cariyāpiṭaka, Thera & Therī-gāthā, Vimānavatthu, Petavatthu and the Netti and resided at Badaratittha in the Tamil country, near the Island of Sri Lanka. Further he is said to be the author of the sub-commentaries on the *Visuddhimagga*, Dīgha Nikāya, Majjhima Nikāya, and Saṃyutta Nikāya.

13. The Theras Buddhanandi and Sāriputra

These two Elders are reported to have lived at Bodhimangai in the Coḷa country. We have an account of them in the *Periyapurāṇam*, a Shaivaite work which records a debate between Buddhists and Shaivaites. During this time the Shaivaite teacher Tirujñāṇasambandhar went round the city, which was a stronghold of Buddhism. He rode in procession raising triumphal cries, blowing conch shells and trumpets. The Buddhists of Bodhimangai told him, "You cannot thus go in triumphal procession through our city! Come let us debate on religion." Tirujñāṇasambandhar accepted the challenge. The Buddhists retained the Elder Buddhanandi as their spokesman. Tirujñāṇasambandhar's assistant, by exercising his magical powers through a mantram, caused a thunderbolt from heaven to strike the Elder down. The Buddhists persisted, saying "Do not come to display magical powers, come to debate on doctrinal matters." Tirujñāṇasambandhar is said to have defeated Buddhanandi Thera. No further details of these two Elders are available. Tirujñāṇasambandhar lived in the 7th century CE.

14. Vajrabodhi

He was a native of Podiyakanda in the Pāṇḍya country. His father was a royal chaplain. He went to Nālandā in North India for his studies and returned when he was 26 years old. At that time his country was in the grip of a severe drought and King Narasinhapothavarman appealed to Vajrabodhi for help. He was able to cause rain to fall by the exercise of his occult powers. Vajrabodhi was a Mahāyānist Bhikkhu adhering to the Vajrayāna faction. He visited Sri Lanka and resided there for six months at the Abhayagiri Vihāra. During this time he attempted to spread Mahāyānism in Sri Lanka, but returned soon to his native land.

From there he went to China with his pupil, Amoghavajra, and did missionary work there. He passed away in the year 730 CE. In accordance with his wishes his pupil returned to Sri Lanka and India to propagate the Vajrayāna doctrines. He is said to have been received with honour by Sīlamegha, king of Sri Lanka.

15. Buddhamitra

Apart from his name the concluding verses to his Tamil grammar *Vīrasoliyam* reveal his deep faith in Buddhism. He was the local ruler in a province of South India. His book was named after Vīracola, also known as Vīrarajendra, the Coḷa king, who invited him to write his work. This king ruled from 1063 to 1070. The inscriptions of the time eulogise him very highly. So does Buddhamitra, who calls him "the ruler who subdued the whole earth." Both Buddhamitra and his royal patron lived in the 11th century. Buddhamitra was a Mahāyānist Bhikkhu. He should not be confused with another Theravāda Bhikkhu of the same name, with whom Ācariya Buddhaghosa resided when he wrote the *Papañcasūdanī*. The paraphrase to Buddhamitra's *Vīrasoliyam* was written by his pupil Perumdevanār. He too was a devoted Buddhist.

16. Dīpaṅkara Buddhappiya Thera

In Sri Lanka he is known as the Coḷian Buddhappiya Thera, or Coḷian Dīpaṅkara. He is the author of the Pāli grammar, *Rūpasiddhi*, used in monastic colleges even today. This is a very popular book written on the lines of Kaccāyana's grammar. His book of the Pāli verses in praise of the Buddha is called *Pajjamadhu* (*Nectar of Verses*). It is a standing monument to his excellence as a poet and his deep love for the Buddha. In Sri Lanka he studied Buddhist scriptures under the Venerable Ānanda Vanaratana. He returned to Coḷa and lived as the abbot of the Baladitya monastery.

In the concluding stanzas to his *Rūpasiddhi* he mentions that he was born in Coḷa and resided for some time in Sri Lanka. He was a master of Pāli literature and grammar. While he sojourned in the island, "he was like unto a banner hoisted over Sri Lanka." He lived in the 12th century.

17. Coḷa Kassapa Thera

He was a master of the Tipiṭaka and the Pāli language. Among his works are the commentary on the Abhidhamma, works called *Mohavicchedanī*, the commentary to the Vinaya Piṭaka, *Vimativinodanī*, and the *Anāgatavaṃsa*. In the *Sāsanavaṃsa* (*History of Buddhism*), and a Burmese Pāli work called the *Ganthavamsa*, it is mentioned that he was a Tamil from Coḷa. In the concluding stanzas to *Mohavicchedanī* he mentions that he was a resident of a monastery called Nāgana in Nāgapaṭṭanam of the Coḷa country.

18. Anuruddha Thera

He lived in the 10th or 11th century and his birthplace is said to have been Kāveripaṭṭanam. His most famous work is a manual of Abhidhamma, the *Abhidhammatthasaṅgaha,* which has served as an introduction to the Abhidhamma philosophy for over eight centuries. It is still very popular, e.g., in Burma (Myanmar) and Sri Lanka. Throughout the centuries, many commentaries have been written on it and in our times it has been translated into Western languages. Another two treatises on the Abhidhamma, written in verse, have been attributed to Anuruddha Thera, *Paramatthavinicchaya* and *Nāmarūpapariccheda;* but his authorship of these two is doubted by some scholars, as also that of the *Anuruddhaśataka.*

19. Dhammakitti Thera

He was a Coḷian Bhikkhu of the 13th century who came from South India to Sri Lanka. He wrote the first part of the *Cullavaṃsa*, which is a continuation of the *Mahāvaṃsa*, the famous chronicle of Sri Lanka. His addition to it extended from King Sirimevan up to his own time. Also a *Chronicle of the Tooth Relic* (*Dāṭhāvamsa*) has been ascribed to him.

Further, we could infer from historical information that a large number of learned Buddhist monks and laymen lived in the various cities and villages of South India. Most of the books they wrote, except two, have perished. From the list of names of the Buddhist villages and hamlets, from the names of Buddhist monks and laymen still available, from the large number of Buddhist ruins still surviving, we can draw the inference that Buddhism once flourished in South India from the 3rd to the 13th century of the common era.

From the history of Sri Lanka we can get further information about the state of Buddhism in South India in the 14th and 15th centuries. King Pandit Parākramabāhu early in the 14th century got a learned Bhikkhu who was a linguist, to help in the translation of the Jātaka book to Sinhala. A minister of King Bhuvanekabāhu IV of Gampola, named Senādhilaṅkāra, caused a Buddhist monastery to be built at Kāñchipura. This is evidence of Buddhism in South India even at this late stage. From these facts we can conclude that right up to the coming of the Europeans Buddhism existed in South India.

Though Buddhism in India had to yield to Hinduism, yet the period when Buddhism flourished was one of which the Tamil nation can rightly be proud in view of its outstanding contribution to Buddhist literature in Tamil, Pāli and Sanskrit. Now, after the time of religious rivalries is passed, this period may well be remembered as a strong bond between the Tamil nation and the Buddhist countries.

Appendix
Extracts from the Maṇimekhalai

translated by
Rao Bahadur Krishnaswāmi Aiyangar

Reproduced with the kind permission of the publishers, Messrs. Luzac & Co. Ltd., London, from *Maṇimekhalai in Its Historical Setting* (1928).

Extracts from the Maṇimekhalai

Modern inter-religious conferences seem to have had a precursor at the time when the Maṇimekhalai was composed. Book I contains the royal announcement of the annual Indra Festival, celebrated at Puhār (Kāveripaṭṭanam), in which we read:

> "Let those well-versed in the holy teachings take their place under awnings or in canopied halls. Let those well versed in various religions assemble in the halls of learning set apart for discussion. Give up feeling of enmity even to those who are inimical to you."
>
> (Book I. Transl. p. 115)

From Book V

The hermit Saṅghadharma taught her (i.e., Maṇimekhalai's friend, Sutamatī) the teaching of the Buddha:

> "My king possessed of all good qualities by nature, the embodiment of all good qualities without diminution, having learned by experience various kinds of life in this world, took it upon himself to use his life not for the attainment of his own salvation, but for the exercise of kindness to living beings, in order that the whole mass of living beings might attain to that salvation. Thus turning the wheel of the law he conquered desire." (p. 123)

... Just then appeared, in the guise of a lady of the city, the goddess Maṇimekhalai, with a view to witnessing the celebration of the great festival just then taking place in the city. She went round the pavilion containing the seat of the Buddha, reciting the following laudation:

"Shall I describe you as the knowing One, the pure One of good deeds, the ancient One, the exalted One, who knew how to lead life in this world? Shall I describe you as the One who got beyond the reach of love, who was the sure guardian of all, as the One who destroyed the enemy, evil conduct? How shall I describe the feet of him who set the wheel of a thousand spokes in motion, without a thousand tongues to describe with"[4] (p. 124).

Book VI relates that for protecting young Maṇimekhalai from Prince Udyakumāra, who was in search of her, the goddess Maṇimekhalai put her to sleep by a charm and "carried her through the air thirty yojanas south, to an island called Maṇipallavam, which has been identified with the island Nāgadipa, off the coast of Sri Lanka. The story continues: ... Maṇimekhalai woke up from her sleep on the sandy beach of Maṇipallavam. Looking round she found nothing that was familiar to her and felt herself as strangely placed as a soul in a new birth.... She wandered about till she came to what seemed to be a seat of the Buddha. The seat had been placed there by Indra and had the miraculous power to let those who worshipped it know their previous life, as Buddha himself had delivered a sermon sitting on it. This happened on the occasion when two neighbouring Nāga chiefs, related to each

4. An alternative rendering of this passage:

"O Lord! You are the Wise, the Pure, Pious and the Ancient, above all others in austerity.

O Lord! You destroyed the evils and discarded anger: you are the Omniscient.

O Lord! You conquered Māra; you are the blissful and you condemned the unholy and false ways.

O Lord! Your feet are marked with thousand-spoked wheels.

You do not have thousand tongues

How shall I praise thee?"

From *The Story of Buddhism with Special Reference to South India*, published by the Department of Information and Publicity, Government of Madras, 1960.

other, fought for possession of it. As the war proved destructive, Buddha appeared before them and pacified the combatants by preaching a sermon (Book VIII, pp. 131–132).

At sight of this, Maṇimekhalai forgot herself in wonder. Her hands automatically folded over her head, from her eyes flowed tears of joy; she "circumambulated" the divine seat three times and prostrated before it. Getting up, she looked at the seat again, and began to recollect all that had taken place in her previous existence (Book IX, p. 132).

Maṇimekhalai walked about admiring the beauty of the sand dunes, flower gardens and cool tanks. In a short while there appeared before her a lady who addressed her: "Who are you that have arrived here alone like a woman who had suffered shipwreck?" (After replying to her), Maṇimekhalai wished to know who the other lady was. The lady said that in the neighbourhood of that island was another called Ratnadvīpa (The Island of Jewels). "There on a high peak of the hill Samantakūṭa[5] there are the footprints of the Buddha. Having offered worship at the footprints, I came to this island long ago. Since then I have remained here keeping guard over this 'Dharma-seat' under the orders of Indra. My name is Tiva-Tilakai (Dvīpa Tilakā). People following the Dharma of the Buddha strictly, offering worship to this 'Buddha seat,' will gain knowledge of their previous birth, knowing their past as a result of this worship. It is only those few who are fit to acquire Dharmapada forsooth. Since by such worship you have acquired knowledge of your previous birth, you must be such a great one. In front of this seat there is a little pond full of cool water overgrown with all varieties of water-lily. From that will appear a never-failing begging bowl by name Amuda-Surabi (Amṝta Surabhi). The bowl appears every year on the day (of full moon) in the season of the early sun, in the month of Rshabha, in the fourteenth asterism, the day on which the Buddha himself was born. That day this year is today and the hour is just now. That bowl, I ween, will come into your hand. Food put into it will be inexhaustible. You will learn about it from Aravaṇa Aḍigal who lives in your own native city."

Maṇimekhalai, on hearing this, making her obeisance to the "Buddha seat," went along with Tiva-Tilakai, circumambulating

5. This refers to the Sri Pāda peak ("Adam's Peak") in Sri Lanka.

the pond and stood in front of it. The bowl emerged from the water, and turning round to the right reached the hands of Maṇimekhalai. She felt delighted beyond measure and uttered the following chant in praise of the Buddha:

> "Hail! holy feet of the Hero who subdued Māra!
> Hail! holy feet of Him, who destroyed the evil path!
> Hail! holy feet of the Great One! Labouring to set others in the path of Dhamma!
> Hail! holy feet of the Perfectly Wise, who gives to others the eye of wisdom!
> Hail! holy feet of Him, whose ears are deaf to evil words!
> Hail! holy feet of Him, whose tongue never uttered other than truth!
> Hail! holy feet of Him, who visited hell itself to destroy suffering there!
> Hail! holy feet of Him, destroyed the sorrows of those of the Nāga world!

To praise you is beyond the power of my tongue; to bow at your feet is alone possible for my body."

To Maṇimekhalai in this attitude of prayer, Tiva-Tilakai expounded the sufferings of hunger and the merit accruing to those that enable creatures to appease hunger. "Hunger," she told Maṇimekhalai, "will destroy good birth, will kill nobility, will cut off the hold that learning has upon the learned people as the great support of life will deprive people of all feeling of shame, will spoil qualities that are beautiful, will make people stand at the door of others with their wives. Such indeed is the nature of the sinful craving hunger.

> "Food provided to allay the hunger of those that cannot otherwise satisfy it, is true charity, and all right kind of life in this world comes to such people. Among those that live in this world, those that give food are those that give life. Therefore to those that are hungry give that which will destroy hunger." (Book XI, p. 137)

Book XXX

Maṇimekhalai, who had already learned all that had happened in her previous birth, after having taken upon herself the duty of giving gifts (*dāna*) and walking the path of right conduct (*sīla*), worshipped three times the triple jewel of Buddha, Dharma and Saṅgha, placing herself entirely under its protection, and then saluted the Bhikkhu Aravaṇa Aḍigal. The Bhikkhu, in expounding to her the righteous path of the Dharma, said:

> "At that time when the world was full of beings poor in understanding, the Buddha, at the earnest entreaty of all the celestial beings of Tusitaloka, appeared on earth leaving that heaven of joy empty. Then, seated at the foot of the Bodhi tree, he conquered the enemy Māra and became the victor (*jina*). The good teaching of the Four Truths which the beautiful victor imparted after having pulled out by the roots the three faults,[6] were taught with ineffable beneficence in the pact by innumerable other Buddhas. These Truths provide the means of crossing the ocean of existence by destroying the twelve primal causes (*nidānas*).[7] These latter appear one from the other in order as cause and effect, and being capable of reappearance, (each link) as consequent upon that which is before it, assume the form of a never-ending circle. When in this order of cause and consequence the first ceases to exist, the next follows in cessation; when it comes into existence, that which follows it does so inevitably. So these are properly described as a chain of causes and conditions. Thus arranged these twelve primal causes fall into four divisions,[8] showing three links.[9] Appearance in birth or rebirth is of three kinds (human, heavenly or of the nether world), and is of three divisions, past, present and future.[10] These also produce the

---

6. The three roots of evil (*akusala-mala*): greed, hate, and delusion.
7. The twelve primal causes which make up the links of Dependent Origination (*paṭiccasamuppāda*).
8. The four sections (*cattāro saṅghā*), see *Visuddhimagga* (tr. by Ñāṇamoli), Ch X VII, § 290.
9. The three links (*ti-sandhi*). See *Visuddhimagga* XVII, § 289.
10. See *Visuddhimagga* XVII, § 287.

faults, deeds and their consequences,[11] and are impermanent and cause only sorrow. He who gets to understand this character of these primal causes, he knows what will assure him the permanence of release (Nirvāna)."

Further it becomes the means for the cultivation of the Four Truths[12] and is constituted of the five *skandhas*. It is capable of being argued in the six forms beginning with the 'assertion of truth."[13] It results in the four forms of excellence. It is open to question in four ways and being capable of respective answers in four ways similarly. It is without origin and without end. It is a series of continuous becoming without ever reaching final destruction. It neither does nor can it be described as being done. It is neither self nor is it possessed by another self. It is nothing that is gone, nothing that is to come. It cannot be brought to an end nor is it to end itself. It is itself the result of the deed, birth and cessation. Such is the nature of the twelve causes and conditions beginning with ignorance and called the primal causes. These twelve are:

1. Ignorance (*pedamai*, Sanskrit: *avidyā*),
2. Action (*seykai*, Sanskrit: *karma*),
3. Consciousness (*uṇarvu*, Sanskrit: *vijñāṇa*),
4. Name and form (*aru-uru*, Sanskrit: *nāmarūpa*),
5. Six organs of sense (*vāyil*, Sanskrit: *saḍāyatana*),
6. Contact (*uru*, Sanskrit: *sparṣa*),
7. Sensation (*nuharvu*, Sanskrit: *vedanā*),
8. Thirst or craving (*vetkai*, Sanskrit: *tṛṣṇā*),
9. Attachment (*parru*, Sanskrit: *upādāna*),
10. Becoming or existence (*pavam*, Sanskrit: *bhava*),
11. Birth (*torram*, Sanskrit: *jāti*),
12. The result of action, old age and death (*vinayppayan*, Sanskrit: *jarā-maraṇa*).

If people understand the twelvefold nature of the chain of cause and effect, they then understand the supreme truth and will enjoy permanent bliss. If they do not, they are bound to suffer in the depths of hell.

11. See in *Visuddhimagga* XVII, § 298, the threefold round (*ti-vatta*) of defilements (*kilesa*), kammic action (*kamma*) and kamma-result (*vipāka*).

12. See *Visuddhimagga* XVII, § 300.

13. "Six forms," see ib. § 299.

(1) Ignorance consists in not understanding what was explained above, in being liable to delusion and in believing in what one hears to the neglect of that which one is able to see for oneself, as believing in the existence of the horns of a rabbit because someone else says that they do exist.

(2) In the three worlds, life is illimitable, and living beings in them are of six classes. They are men, gods, Brahmas, the inhabitants of hell, the crowd of animals and spirits. According to good deeds and bad, birth will take place in one or other of these. Ever since it assumes the form of embryo, the results of these deeds will show themselves either in the happiness of mind or in anxiety of suffering. Of these evil deeds, killing, theft and illicit sexual behaviour show themselves as evils springing up in the body. Lying, speaking ill of others, harsh words and useless talk, these four show themselves as evils of speech. Desire, anger and illusion are three evils that arise in the mind.[14] These ten the wise would avoid. If they should fail to do so, they would be born as animals or spirits or beings of the nether world, and make themselves liable to extreme anxiety of suffering. Good men, on the contrary, would avoid these ten, and assuming the good discipline (*sīla*) and taking upon themselves to do deeds of charity (*dāna*), will be born in the three higher classes of beings, such as devās (gods), men or brahmas, and live a life of enjoyment and happiness as a result of good deeds.

(3) Consciousness (*uṇarvu*) consists in feeling like one asleep, without the feeling leading to any action, or to any satisfaction.[15]

(4) Name and form consist in that which has the feeling described above, and constituting mind and body.

(5) Organs of sense are, on examination, those that carry consciousness to the mind (*vijnāña* or *ullam*).

(6) Contact consists in *vijnāña* and the organs of sense experiencing touch with other things (*veru pulangal*).

(7) Sensation (*nuharvu*) consists in the mind or *vijnāña* enjoying that of which it has become conscious.

---

14. These are the "ten unwholesome courses of action" (*dasa akusala kamma-patha*).

15. This might be a reference to the definition of consciousness, in this context, as rebirth consciousness (*paṭisandhi-citta*) which is a kind of subliminal consciousness (*bhavaṅga-citta*).

(8) Thirst or craving consists in not feeling satisfied with that which is thus enjoyed.

(9) Attachment consists in the desire for enjoyment impelling one into action.

(10) Becoming consists in the accumulation of deeds indicating the consequence to which each leads.[16]

(11) Birth (*tonral*) consists in the result of deeds leading to the conscious taking of birth in one or other of the six forms of birth in the inevitable chain of cause and effect.

(12) Disease (*piṇi*) consists in the suffering of the body by a change from its natural condition in consequence of the result of deeds. Old age (*mūppu*) consists in the loosening of the body as one draws nearer and nearer to the end. Death (*sākkāḍu*) ultimately consists in the human body, composed of life and body, disappearing as the setting sun.

From ignorance arises action; from action springs consciousness; from consciousness come name and form;[17] from name and form spring the organs of sense; through organs of sense contact becomes possible; contact results in sensation or experience; experience produces desire; from desire springs attachment; from attachment comes into existence collection of deeds; as the result of this collective deed arise various other forms of birth; birth inevitably brings along with it age, disease and death, and the consequent anxiety and the feeling of incapacity to get rid of it. This never-ending suffering is the ultimate result.

In such a never-ending circle of experience, when ignorance ceases, action will cease; with action ceasing consciousness will cease; with consciousness ceasing name and form (mind and body) will cease; with the cessation of name and form, organs of sense will cease; with the cessation of the organs of sense, contact will cease; contact ceasing, sensation or experience will cease; with sensation or experience ceasing, desire will cease; desire ceasing to exist, there will be no attachment; without attachment, there is no accumulation of deeds; without the accumulated mass of deeds, there will be no becoming; with the cessation of becoming, there will be no

16. This refers to a twofold division of becoming (*bhava*), the kamma-process (*kamma-bhava*) and the rebirth-process (*upapattibhava*).

17. I.e., mind and body.

birth, no disease, no age, no death, and in consequence, no anxiety and no helplessness. Thus this never-ending series of suffering will be destroyed.

Of these twelve primal causes, the first two, ignorance and action, are regarded as belonging to the first section. All those that follow, spring from these two. The following five, namely, name and form, organs of sense, contact, sensation, these five, as springing from the former two, are regarded as constituting the second division. Thirst, attachment and the collection of deeds constitute the third division as the result, as evil in the enjoyment of the previous five, and in consequence, as action resulting therefrom. It is from the folly of desire and consequent attachment that becoming arises. The fourth division includes birth, disease, age and death, since these four are experienced as a result of birth.[18]

Action is the cause of birth and consciousness springs out of it; where these two meet they mark the first conjunction. Where sensation and craving meet, it marks the second conjunction. The third junction comes in where the accumulation of deeds results in birth. Thus are marked the three points of junction in this chain of twelve causes and conditions.

The three forms of birth are those of men, gods and animals. These result from the consciousness in previous births as a result of the conformations springing out of ignorance. This happens either from the delusion that this kind of birth is actually cessation of birth or the taking of birth in a new form without the consciousness, or the new birth coming with consciousness and the new form existing together. The three times are the past, present and future. Of these, the past includes ignorance and action. To the present refer consciousness, name and form, the organs of sense, contact, sensation, thirst (or craving), the becoming and birth. To the future belong birth, disease, age and death. The resulting anxiety and helplessness are evils that spring out of the previous series of present action.

Desire, attachment and ignorance, and the birth resulting therefrom, constitute action in the present and cause future birth. Consciousness, name and form, organs of sense, contact, sensation (or experience), birth, age, disease and death, are the consequential

18. See Vism XII, § 290.

experience in life, both present and future. These are full of evil, of deeds and of consequences resulting from these deeds, and thus constitute suffering. Being such, they are all impermanent. While the nature of release (*vīḍu*), consists in the understanding that there is nothing like a soul in anything existing.

Consciousness, name and form, the organs of sense, contact, sensation, birth, disease, age, death, with the resulting anxiety and helplessness, these constitute disease. For this disease, the causes are ignorance, action, desire, attachment and the collection of deeds. For suffering and birth, attachment is the cause; for bliss and cessation of birth, non-attachment is the cause. Words that embody this idea constitute the Four Truths, namely, suffering, the cause of suffering, the removal of suffering and the way to the removal of suffering.

There are four kinds of questions and answers:

(1) To give a definite reply; (2) to separate the component parts of an issue and answer these separately; (3) to answer by a counter question; and (4) to keep silence in answer to a question.[19]

To a question whether a thing that comes into existence will also go out of existence, if the answer is "it will," this is to give a definite reply.

To a question whether a dead man will be born again or not, the inquiry whether in life he was without attachment or not is to answer by separating the issues involved and to give separate answers to it.

To a question whether it is the seed that is first or the palm-tree, the enquiry which seed and which particular tree is to answer by a counter question.

To a question whether "the sky flower" is new or old, silence is the best answer; this is one way of getting round an inconvenient question.

Bondage and release result from the *skandhas* (the aggregates of experience). There is no agent outside entitled to bring them into contact. For the *skandhas* and their manifestations as described above, the cause is the group of three evils: desire, anger and illusion.

Examine separately and understand that everything is

19. See *Aṅguttara-Nikāya*, Threes, No. 68; Fours, No. 42.

impermanent, full of suffering, without a soul and unclean; thus treating it, give up desire! Realizing that friendliness, compassion and joy (at the well-being of others) constitute the best attitude of mind, give up anger! By the practice of hearing, (*sruti*), contemplation (*cintana*), experiencing in mind (*bhāvanā*) and realizing in vision (*darsana*), reflect, realize and give up all illusion! In these four ways get rid of the darkness of mind!

In these auspicious words, free from inconsistency, (Aravaṇa Aḍigal) exhibited the illuminating lamp of the knowledge. Maṇimekhalai, having assumed the habit of an ascetic (*tāpasī*) and having heard the excellent exposition of the Dharma, devoted herself to penance[20] that she may get rid of the bondage of birth.

20. *Noṭṭā.* Better to be translated as "religious life."

The Way of the Noble

by

T. H. Perera

WHEEL PUBLICATION NO. 126

Homage to that Blessed One, the Perfect One, the Buddha Supreme!

The Way of the Noble

"Yea, by my troth this have I seen, no hearsay this,
In one communion bound of holy life
A thousand (saints who had) abandoned death;
Disciples of these too, five hundred yea,
And more, ten hundred, yea, and ten times that
Who all had reached the Stream, the Holy Way."[1]

The title of this essay is the English rendering of the Pāli term *Ariya Magga*—the Noble Way or Path. The *Ariya-Aṭṭhaṅgika-Magga* is the Noble Eightfold Path of Buddhism, which leads to the state of an *ariya* or Noble One. The Buddha-Dhamma claims no affinity to the word *āryan* which is used to distinguish a stock of the human species from other stocks of the same species on the basis of colour and race. The Buddha-Dhamma views with disfavour adventitious distinctions, such as the colour or caste of a man, for the satisfying reason that, born of the knowledge of the real nature of phenomenal existence, it embraces in a compassionate oneness all living things in the entire universe with an all-pervading loving-kindness.

The word *aryan* comes from the Pāli word *ariya* (*Sanskrit: ārya*), which means pure or noble. The Buddha-Dhamma recognizes one who has cleaned himself of the impurities of mind as noble or pure. In this respect, Lord Buddha is acclaimed as the Greatest *Ariya*. Hence, the Four Eternal Verities which he discovered are called the Four Noble Truths (*ariya sacca*). The disciples of the Buddha who had understood and realized the

1. This quotation is from the Brahmā Suttas of the Saṃyutta Nikāya VI 2, 3. Brahmā Sahampati visits the Buddha, who was living with the Magadhese at Andhakavinda. He notices a large assemblage of monks seated in front and on either side of the Buddha. Among them are a large number of *arahants* (saints), and also a numerically larger number of those who have reached "the Stream, the Holy Way," the subject of this essay.

Four Noble Truths are called the Noble Ones (*ariya-puggala*). The word *ariya* also means one who sees things as they truly are.[2] It is only when one sees this psycho-physical (*nāma-rūpa*) combination called a being, as it really is, that he gets an aversion for existence, and is urged to take the "ascent" leading to the Ariyan Way, the exclusive *via sacra* of the Noble Ones.

In this essay I shall confine myself to the first stage of the Ariyan Way—the first stage of the Way that leads to full sanctity—Arahantship. A person who steps on the first stage of the Ariyan Way is also called a Stream-Winner. The Pāli word *sota* means a stream. He wins or attains the stream (*sotāpatti*), and is, then, a Stream-Winner (*sotāpanna*). He is taken up the Stream that leads to Nibbāna. He is rewarded with a glimpse of Nibbāna, for the first time, in the ups and downs of his *saṃsāric* existence (the process of repeated births).

This supreme achievement, the initial step to cross over the turbulent waters of the cosmic ocean of births and deaths, demands of the aspirant to the Way a systematic, sustained and steadfast preparation anterior to its consummation—a consummation which is possible only by putting forth "human strength, human energy and human striving."[3]

What is it that prompts us to embark on this great spiritual adventure on "the sea of the six senses with its waves and whirlpools, its sharks and demons (symbolizing its dangers and temptations)."[4] It is suffering (*dukkha*) inherent in life. The Buddha-Dhamma alone, of all religions, positively affirms that life is suffering—life wherever it exists from the highest *Brahma* world to the uttermost hell is suffering. Life in the immeasurable past was suffering and life yet to come will also entail suffering. This is *saṃsāric* suffering (*bhava-dukkha*). The present suffering is visible in so many ways, as physical and mental suffering, as man's conflict with his environment and as the result of man's insatiate

2. It is Insight Wisdom (*vipassanañāṇa*) that helps to reveal phenomenal existence as it really is: its impermanency (*anicca*), its imperfectness (*dukkha*) and its impersonality (*anattā*).

3. Saṃyutta Nikāya II 28, 29.

4. *The Basic Position of Sīla* by Miss I. B. Horner, published by the Bauddha Sahitya Sabha.

desire to pamper his "I," his Ego. We have plenty of evidence in the Buddhist Canon[5] to establish the suffering inherent in the process of Becoming (*bhava*). Based on this knowledge and on the suffering now being felt, and with implicit confidence (*saddhā*) in the Buddha, the Dhamma and the Saṅgha, Buddhists genuinely interested in overcoming suffering embark on this great adventure.

Now, let us discuss the prior preparations that he, we shall call him the pilgrim on the Way, has to make for the purpose of stepping on the Ariyan Way. The Saṅgīti Sutta of the Dīgha Nikāya (No. 33) mentions four necessary conditions for Stream entry (*sotāpattiyaṅgaṃ*).

They are:

1. Association with the good (*sappurisa saṃseva*).
2. Hearing the good Teaching (*saddhamma savanaṃ*).
3. Wise reflection (*yoniso manasikāra*).
4. Practice in those things that lead up to the Teaching and its corollaries (*dhammānudhamma paṭipatti*).

1. *Association with the Good*

It will be admitted on all hands that through association with the good, the pilgrim on the Way enriches his mind with all that is wholesome and noble. In the galaxy of the good Lord Buddha shines without a peer. He has passed away, but his Teaching is with us, in its pristine purity, as a living symbol to speak to us of the exceeding rare goodness which permeated his entire vigorous, radiant personality. Here are his own words in support: "Therefore, O Bhikkhus, you to whom the truths I have perceived have been made known by me, having thoroughly made yourselves masters of them, practise them, meditate upon them, and spread them abroad, in order that the pure religion may last long and be perpetuated, in order that it may *continue to be for the good and happiness of the great multitudes, out of pity for the world, to the good and the gain and the weal of gods and men.*"[6]

The Noble Ones who have gained the four stages of Holiness and their respective Fruition (*phala*) are also among the good. Those

5. Majjhima Nikāya I 173. Also Saṃyutta Nikāya 15:1; 15:3; 15:13.
6. Mahā parinibbāna Sutta, Dīgha Nikāya Sutta 16.

worldlings who are treading the mundane Noble Eightfold Path with a view to gaining Deliverance come next. Those individuals who have dedicated their lives to ameliorating human suffering such as philanthropists and social service workers are also among the good. The Dhammapada[7] advises us not to associate with friends who are evil-doers, or friends whose lives are blameworthy; on the other hand, to associate with friends who are good, the best of men. There are two conspicuous characteristics visible in the good, namely, gratitude (*kataññutā*) in its manifestation by word and deed. Lord Buddha gazed steadfastly for seven days at the Bodhi Tree beneath whose shade he gained Supreme Enlightenment.

2. *Hearing the Teaching*

The benefits gained by hearing the Good Law are so obvious that their recapitulation here seems to me rather superfluous. In the days long gone, the mode of receiving the Dhamma was by hearing. The word *sāvaka,* meaning a disciple of the Buddha, has its origin in the word *savanaṃ*. The Mahā Maṅgala Sutta hails the hearing of the Dhamma as a Blessing (*kālena dhamma-savanaṃ etaṃ maṅgalamuttamaṃ*), and immediately after in the next verse the Sutta proceeds to hail religious discussions (*dhamma-sākacchā*) as a blessing. These twin tasks invariably reinforce and strengthen confidence, already referred to, which our pilgrim carries as his staff till the goal of the holy life is reached. In modern times there are many books on various aspects of the Buddha-Dhamma. In Buddhist countries the radio is also a very useful medium in the dissemination of the Dhamma. Despite these modern facilities the time honoured custom of hearing the Dhamma, seated cross-legged at the feet of venerable monks, awakens a deep sense of piety and a spiritual exhilaration. The Dhammapada pays this excellent tribute to those who hear the Dhamma: "He who imbibes the Law lives happily; his mind is serene. The wise always rejoice in the Law, well-proclaimed by the Buddha."[8]

Knowledge of the Dhamma (*pariyatti*) leads to its practice (*paṭipatti*) and practice leads to the realization (*paṭivedha*) of

7. Dhammapada v. 78.
8. Ibid., Verse 79.

Nibbāna, the end of suffering. Wherefore, "the Dhamma is well-expounded by the Buddha, to be self realized, with immediate fruit, inviting investigation, leading to Nibbāna, to be comprehended by the wise, each for himself" (*The Mirror of the Dhamma*, Nārada Thera, Wheel Publication 54).

3. *Wise Reflection*

The Dhamma that has been either heard or read has to be wisely reflected upon, and then acted upon. It is, indeed, a matter for much concern and of much regret that most Buddhists listen to or read the Dhamma as a matter of course and then resign it to oblivion. Thereafter they turn once again to chase after pleasure. Let them wisely reflect on this quotation from the Sutta Nipāta, Verse 62 (transl. by Lord Chalmers):

> "... Be sure
> pleasure's a chain, brief bliss,
> short rapture, long drawn woe,
> a baited hook for fish."

Wise Reflection has to be clearly distinguished from Unwise Reflection (*ayoniso-manasikāra*). Wise Reflection functions as a wholesome agent. Says the Buddha, "thus employed, O monks, it leads to the Highest"—the Highest which is the very opposite of the recurrent process of births and deaths. On the other hand, Unwise Reflection does nobody any good. It is the womb which gives birth to unwholesome things. Says the Buddha, "Monks, I have not seen (with the Buddha eye) any single thing which conduces more to the arising of wholesome things that have not yet arisen, and to the expulsion of unwholesome things that have already arisen, than Wise Reflection." In this context, Wise Reflection shortens the process of Becoming, while Unwise Reflection lengthens this sorrow-fraught process.

Wise Reflection, with mindfulness keeping guard, brought to perfection by sustained and indefatigable endeavour, leads to mental synthesis, to mental equipoise and "one-pointedness" of mind, the prelude to Insight, which then illumines the pilgrim's vision to see things as they truly are. More of this later. The Dhammapada encourages the pilgrim thus:

> "He who dwells in the Law, delights in the Law, meditates on the Law, reflects on the Law, that Bhikkhu will never fall away from the true Law."[9]

4. *Practice in Those things that Lead Up to the Teaching and Its Corollaries*

The Buddha-Dhamma, it should be noted here, is not meant for the purpose of exhibiting one's intellectual legerdemain, nor is it for the purpose of displaying one's dialectical skill; nor does it encourage salvation by proxy through prayerful appeals by a sinner to a supernatural being; nor does it preach a vicarious salvation. The Buddha-Dhamma is a practice (*paṭipadā*), a gradual practice upon a well-mapped and tested Path, based on the ethical potential of man, for the one and only purpose of crossing over and going beyond the confines of the space-time cosmos. And for the purpose of crossing over, the pilgrim has to walk the Path himself by his own efforts and energy, and without taking a wrong turning. The Buddhas merely show the Way. The Dhammapada, at verse 276, is quite emphatic on this point:

> "Striving should be done by yourselves, the Tathagatas (Buddhas) are only teachers. The meditative ones who enter the Way are delivered from the bonds of Māra."

The Buddha-Dhamma is a discovery. The Buddha Gotama rediscovered the Ancient Path which the Buddhas of the past trod to gain deliverance. The Ancient Path is the Noble Eightfold Path. "This is the Middle Path, which the Perfect One has discovered, which makes one both to see and to know, and which leads to peace, to discernment, to enlightenment and to Nibbāna."[10]

The Blessed One, on the occasion of sending forth his first mission of sixty Arahants, spoke about the Ancient Path in this manner: "Preach, O Bhikkhus, the Dhamma, excellent in the beginning, excellent in the middle, and excellent in the end."[11] The Dhamma is excellent in the beginning (*ādi-kalyāṇa*), which is

9. Ibid., Verse 364.
10. Saṃyutta Nikāya 46:2.
11. Vinaya Mahāvagga p. 10.

morality (*sīla*), exhorting to avoid all evil (*sabba-pāpassa akaraṇaṃ*). It is excellent in the middle (*majjhima-kalyatā*), which is concentration (*samādhi*), exhorting to do good (*kusalassa upasampadā*). It is excellent in the end (*pariyosāna-kalyāṇa*), which is wisdom (*paññā*) exhorting to cleanse one's mind (*sacitta-pariyodapanaṃ*). And this is the Ancient Path.

This is the triple division of the Noble Eightfold Path, in which the pilgrim has to train himself anterior to his stepping on the Ariyan Way or winning the Stream. The training is gradual, step by step, "for the attainment of Wisdom does not come at once, but by a gradual training, a gradual working out of cause, a gradual practice (*anupubba-sikkhā, anupubba-kriyā, anupubba-paṭipadā*).[12]

It would be relevant, at this point, to set side by side the factors of the Noble Path and the triple training in Morality, Concentration and Wisdom:

3. Right Speech (*sammā vācā*)	*Morality* (*sīla*)
4. Right Action (*sammā kammantā*)	
5. Right Livelihood (*sammā ājīva*)	
6. Right Effort (*sammā vāyāma*)	*Concentration* (*samādhi*)
7. Right Mindfulness (*sammā sati*)	
8. Right Concentration (*sammā samādhi*)	
1. Right Understanding (*sammā diṭṭhi*)	*Wisdom* (*paññā*)
2. Right Thought (*sammā saṇkappa*)	

The sequence of the Path Factors has been here transposed for indicating that this is the order in which the perfecting of the Noble Eightfold Path has to proceed. Nevertheless, a degree of Right Understanding is indispensable at the very start, for giving the right and cogent motivation for one's endeavour.

I make bold to say that the Tipiṭaka, or the Three Baskets containing the entirety of the Teaching of the Buddha, is devoted to this triple training. I am fortified in my view in that the Blessed One says, "Just as, O Bhikkhus, the mighty ocean is of one taste, the taste of salt, even so, O Bhikkhus, this Dhamma is of one taste,

12. Majjhima Nikāya I 479.

the taste of Deliverance (*vimutti*)."[13] And in the Dhammapada he says, "Following upon this Path you will put an end to suffering."[14]

The Dhamma has to be lived in and practised according to the above triple training. There is absolutely no deviation from this training. The mastery of Morality (*sīla*) makes possible the mastery of Concentration (*samādhi*) and this of Wisdom (*paññā*). No skipping of any of the factors is allowed. We are advised not to follow the technique of the jumping frog. There is no shortcut to Nibbāna.

There are no special occasions on which to practise the Dhamma, nor is it confined to the four *poya*[15] days only. The Dhamma is part and parcel of one's life, and is closely associated with oneself. Wherefore, the Buddha says, "Abide with oneself as an island, with oneself as a refuge, abide with the Dhamma as an island, with the Dhamma as a refuge. Seek not for external refuge."[16]

The pilgrim is warned not to seek external refuge. Why? The Buddha, in conversation with his last convert, Subhadda, told him that it was only in his dispensation that the Noble Eightfold Path existed, and hence, the four true *samaṇas*. He further added that other schools of thought did not contain the Noble Eightfold Path and therefore they were devoid of the four true *samaṇas*.[17]

The four *samaṇas* are: (i) The Stream-Winner (*sotāpanna*), (ii) the Once-Returner (*sakadāgāmi*), (iii) the Never-Returner (*anāgāmi*) and (iv) the Perfect One (*arahant*). These four stages and their respective Fruitions (*phala*) together with Nibbāna are the Nine Transcendental Dhammas (*nava lokuttara dhamma*) which every genuine Buddhist ardently endeavours to consummate ere long.

The pilgrim should always bear in mind the fact that he has taken Refuge in the Buddha, the Dhamma and the Saṅgha in order to gain a clear understanding and perception of the Four Noble Truths: This is Misery. This is the Origin of Misery. This is the Cessation of Misery. This is the Path leading to the cessation of

13. Udāna p. 67.
14. Dhammapada v. 275.
15. The four phases of a lunar month. The Sinhala term for Uposatha days.
16. Mahā Parinibbāna Sutta, Dīgha Nikāya 16, D II 108.
17. Another term for Noble disciples.

Misery—the Noble Eightfold Path. It is only by the realization of the Four Noble Truths by the pilgrim that he can cry a halt to this incessant turning of the Wheel of Life, and attain the end of suffering.[18]

The pilgrim, therefore, is advised not to go off the Path by seeking refuge elsewhere, for in the words of the Buddha, "Men, driven by fear, go to many a refuge—to mountains and forests, to groves, to fanes and trees."[19] The Buddha in no uncertain terms assures the pilgrim that in none of them is found a refuge, and that none of them can ever deliver him from the woes of recurrent existence.[20]

There is one other aspect in the practice of the Dhamma which to my mind is of paramount importance. I mean the practice of the Dhamma in its spirit and in its letter is of far greater importance than the mere external manifestations of devotion (*bhakti*). I certainly do not frown at the traditional modes of worshipping the Buddha, the Dhamma and the Saṅgha by visiting temples. The thought processes that run across the mind during these moments of devotion are undoubtedly wholesome (*kusala*). They provide the pilgrim with spiritual nutriment to support him on the Way.

However, these acts of devotion and piety by themselves will not tend to purify his inner being. They are powerless to crush the might of *Māra* (Death). And the successful conquest of *Māra* is the conquest of one's self through internal purification. "Though one should conquer a million men in the battlefield, yet he, indeed, is the noblest victor who has conquered himself."[21] The same idea is again amplified: "One's own self conquered is better than all other people conquered; not even a god, *Brahmā* or *Māra* can change into defeat the victory of a man who has conquered himself."[22] And this conquest of one's self is one's own business. It is achieved by wisdom. The Buddha-Dhamma teaches deliverance of mind

18. The *raison d'etre* of the Buddha-Dhamma is the Four Noble Truths. It is only by a clear understanding and perception of the Four Noble Truths that one can call a halt to the process of Becoming.
19. Dhammapada Verse 188.
20. Ibid., Verse 189.
21. Ibid., Verse 103.
22. Ibid., Verse 105.

by Wisdom, and definitely not by following mere tradition, purposeless rites and unreasoning dogma.

Turn wherever you will, the Buddhist texts insist on the inner purification of the being. And this inner purification is only possible through external ethical behaviour or moral conduct (*sīla*). The Dhamma provides a number of precepts[23] or moral observances or pledges which a lay person takes upon himself to promote his moral well-being. These precepts are not commands. Their observance is left to the individual with himself as tribunal, on the assumption that their observance is good for himself, as well as to the society of which he is a member, and in regard to our pilgrim the observance of the precepts is the initial step of his training.

The pilgrim, having established himself well and truly on Morality, now proceeds to train his mind—the fickle and restless mind. As he has already controlled the sense-doors which provide nutriment to the mind, he will find his task not so difficult. His task is to purge the mind of all impure states by employing the four great efforts,[24] so that the mind can be tranquillized[25] and stabilized to hold on to one object, and exclude all other objects that enter his mental periphery.

23. While admitting that the monastic rules (*pātimokkha*) are more exacting and demanding so far as monks are concerned, however, the fact remains that the precepts laid down by the Buddha for monk or layman have one underlying motive behind them, namely, the successful walk on the Way resulting in the purification of vision. The initial step to gain this all too important vision is morality (*sīla*) consisting in purity of body's actions, in purity of speech and in purity of living.

24. The Four Great Efforts are (i) the Effort to avoid the arising of evil, unwholesome things that have not yet arisen, (ii) the Effort to overcome the evil, unwholesome things that have already arisen, (iii) the Effort to arouse wholesome things that have not yet arisen, (iv) the Effort to maintain the wholesome things that have already arisen, and to bring them to growth, to maturity and to perfection.

25. It is by employing the technique called Mental Development (*bhāvanā*) that mental tranquillity is produced. Mental tranquillity is the precursor to the development of Wisdom (*paññabhāvana*) or clear Insight (*vipassanabhāvana*). For further information please read Chapter 4 of *Fundamentals of Buddhism* by the late Venerable Ñāṇatiloka Mahā Thera.

This done, the pilgrim enters upon the third stage of his training to gain Insight-Wisdom (*vipassanā-ñāṇa*), which is the sole monopoly of the Buddha-Dhamma. This helps him to penetrate phenomenal existence, which then presents him with Reality, or the true nature of all existence—its impermanency (*anicca*), its imperfectness (*dukkha*) and its impersonality (*anattā*). He has thus completed the triple training, which could be summed up as the training of his body's actions, the training of his mind and the acquisition of Insight-Wisdom.

This triple training has yet another important aspect which deserves to be mentioned here. It is an aspect which is a natural growth and it synchronizes with the training. I have in mind the Seven Stages of Purity[26] contained in the Rathavinīta Sutta (Majjhima Nikāya),[27] which is illustrated by the simile of a grand state drive laid out in seven stages. I do not propose to dwell on this Sutta here, but I shall draw from it relevant matter in the course of developing this essay.

There is one more significant matter which I should touch upon before I close this fourth condition preparatory to the pilgrim's "Ascent." I am referring to the Nine Great Insight Knowledges (*nava mahā vipassanā ñāṇa*), each of which is a fundamental asset in the development of the pilgrim's mind leading up to Maturity Knowledge (*gotrabhū ñāṇa*), at which point he gains Purity of Insight into the four Paths of Holiness (*ñāṇa-dassana-visuddhi*).

Let us now follow the pilgrim on the Way. He has arrived at Right Concentration on the mundane Path. With mind tranquillized and stabilized and with one-pointedness of mind, known as "attainment concentration" (*appanā-samādhi*),

26. The Seven Stages of Purity are (i) Purity of Morality (*sīlavisuddhi*), (ii) Purity of Mind (*cittavisuddhi*), (iii) Purity of Views (*diṭṭhivisuddhi*), (iv) Purity consisting in overcoming all doubts (*kaṅkhavitaraṇavisuddhi*), (v) Purity of Insight regarding the Right and Wrong Path (*maggāmagga-ñāṇadassanavisuddhi*), (vi) Purity of Insight regarding the Path of Progress (*paṭipadañāṇadassanavisuddhi*) and (vii) Purity of Insight into the Four Paths of Holiness (*ñāṇadassanavisuddhi*).

27. Cankerless. It is by totally destroying the Cankers (*āsavā*), also called the floods (*ogha*), that the *anāgāmin* attains the state of an arahant. Vide: *The Four Cankers*, Bodhi Leaf No. 34, by the present writer.

he penetrates this fathom-long body and perceives the three characteristics already mentioned above, characteristics common to all compounds (*saṅkhāras*). Furthermore, wherever he turns, he sees these three characteristics everywhere, throughout the entire universe.

Engaged in this deep contemplation on the evanescent nature of all phenomena, a day arrives when the pilgrim notices an aura (*obhāsa*) radiating from his body. His whole personality is permeated with a joy and happiness never before felt by him. While in this ecstatic state, he may believe that he has attained enlightenment. However, a little while later, his mind clears itself and he realizes through Purity of Insight regarding the right and wrong path (*maggāmagga-ñāṇa-dassana-visuddhi*) the distinction between the mundane Noble Eightfold Path of the worldling and the supramundane Noble Eightfold Path of the Noble One.

Perceiving the Right Path, the pilgrim pursues his contemplation on the three characteristics, with added zeal and vigour. This confers upon him Purity of Insight into the Path of Progress (*paṭipadā-ñāṇa-dassana-visuddhi*). At this point the pilgrim obtains, step by step, a clearer and more comprehensive knowledge of his progress on the Path heading for the ariyan Way. This knowledge is ninefold, as I have already mentioned. I shall give here a bare summary, without which the reader will fail to understand the gradual evolution of the pilgrim's mind to the supramundane.

The pilgrim, who has perceived the arising and passing away of all conditioned things, takes hold of the passing away of things, which is more conspicuous than their arising. He directs his mind to the dissolution (*bhaṅga*) of things and perceives that both mind and matter, which make up the so-called being, are a constant flux, not remaining the same for two consecutive seconds. This knowledge of the dissolution of things creates in his mind a fear, a terror (*bhaya*) for the five aggregates of existence. This knowledge that views existence with fear leads him to grasp the misery and vanity (*ādinavā-ñāṇa*) of existence. This knowledge leads to aversion, to disgust (*nibbidā-ñāṇa*), which, in turn, leads to the will for deliverance from existence (*muñcitukamyatā-ñāṇa*). Thus willed, he proceeds to develop the three characteristics of the impermanency, the imperfectness and the impersonality of all things (*paṭisankhā-ñāṇa*). This knowledge results in an attitude of neither attachment nor aversion to the things of the world—he looks at everything with complete equanimity (*saṅkhār-ūpekkhā-ñāṇa*).

Arriving at this point of his spiritual culture, the pilgrim takes one of the three characteristics of existence, whichever appeals to him most, and begins to develop it to the utmost degree. He is gradually drawn towards the stream (*sota*), and prepares to take the plunge, for he knows that at any moment the Path will reveal itself. He tightens his grip on the particular characteristic he has chosen, and awaits the event. Behold! His mind-door alerts and a *javana* (impulsion) thought process runs thus:

1	2	3	4	5	6 & 7
parikamma (preliminary)	*upacāra* (access)	*anuloma* (adaptation)	*gotrabhu* (maturity)	*magga* (path)	*phala* (fruit) (knowledge)

The pilgrim has now arrived on the Ariyan Way, having taken the "Ascent" with the knowledge associated with Purity into the Four Paths of Holiness (*ñāṇa-dassana-visuddhi*). He is now no more a worldling (*puthujjana*). He has transcended the mundane consciousness (*lokiya citta*) and has gained the supramundane consciousness (*lokuttara citta*). He has entered the Stream. He is a Stream-Winner (*sotāpanna*) and is taken up the Stream to Nibbāna. He is a Noble One (*ariya puggala*). He gets a glimpse of Nibbāna for the first time in the ups and downs of his *saṃsāric* existence. The Stream-Winner becomes conscious of Fruition (*phala*) immediately after, with no interval between (*samādhim-ānantarikaññam-āhu*), the Path and the Fruition of Stream-entry.

Our pilgrim, if he fails to attain Nibbāna in this life itself, will be born seven times at the most, and never an eighth time. He will not be born in the four states of woe. He will not commit the five weighty (*garuka*) crimes, namely: (i) parricide, (ii) matricide, (iii) killing an *arahant*, (iv) shedding blood from the Buddha's body and (v) causing a schism in the Saṅgha.

Our pilgrim, on entering the Stream, breaks the first three fetters (*saṃyojana*) that bind him to the Wheel of Life.

They are:

i. Self-Illusion (*sakkāya-diṭṭhi*). This is the belief that there exists in the individual a permanent, stable and an abiding entity called a soul.[28] The Buddha dismissed the soul-theory as untenable in the light of his minute analysis of the five aggregates which make up the so-called individual.

ii. Doubts (*vicikicchā*). They are doubts in regard to (a) the Buddha, (b) the Dhamma, (c) the Sangha, (d) the monastic rules of conduct, (e) the past, (f) the future, (g) both the past and future (leading to *kamma* and *vipāka*) and (h) Dependent Origination (*paṭiccasamuppāda*).

iii. The belief in the efficacy of ceremonies and rites (*sīlabbata-parāmāsa*). This is the view held by ascetics and *brahmins* that purification can be gained by rules of moral conduct or by rites or by both rules of moral conduct and rites.

Although it was my intention to follow the pilgrim up to the moment he stepped upon the Ariyan Way, I now feel that I should follow him as he graduates through the remaining three stages of the Path of Holiness. Accordingly I shall briefly provide the reader with the basic information regarding his further progress on the Path.

The noble pilgrim, encouraged by a glimpse of Nibbāna, renews his contemplation on the three characteristics again and again. He also reviews the Seven Stages of Purity. In the fifth thought-moment of the supramundane (*javana*) thought-process he attains the state of a Once-Returner (*sakadāgāmi*). Thereby he neutralizes the force of seven births assigned to a Stream-Winner and limits it to one birth only, i.e., within the sense sphere. He gets a vision of Nibbāna in its Fruition consciousness (*magga-phala*). He attenuates or weakens the fourth and fifth fetters, namely, sense-desires (*kāma-rāga*) and ill will (*patigha*), two powerful fetters that had bound him to existence from a beginningless past.

Thereafter, the noble pilgrim, now a Once-Returner, develops as before the contemplation on the three characteristics and reviews the Seven Stages of Purity. In the supramundane thought-process at the fifth thought-moment, he gains the state of a Never-Returner (*anāgāmi*). He destroys the force present in a Once-Returner of being born once. As a Never-Returner he destroys

28. The Dhammasaṇgaṅī lists twenty soul theories. Also see: *The Truth of Anattā* by Dr. Malalasekera (The Wheel No. 94).

completely the fetters of sense-desires and ill will. Hence, he does not return to this planet nor does he seek a celestial abode. If he fails to attain Nibbāna in this life, he is reborn in the Pure Abodes (*suddhāvāsa*), a special reserve for *Anāgāmis*. There he attains full sanctity (*arahanthood*), and on passing from there is reborn no more.

Our noble pilgrim, as before, pursues his contemplation and reviews the Seven Purities. At the fifth moment of the supramundane thought-process, cankerless[29] he attains the supreme goal of the Holy Life, that of a Perfect One (Arahant). A Perfect One totally eradicates the five higher Fetters of (i) the desire for the Form World (*rūpa-rāga*), (ii) the desire for the Formless World (*arūpa-rāga*), (iii) conceit (*māna*), (iv) restlessness (*uddhacca*) and (v) ignorance (*avijjā*). Our noble pilgrim now comprehends, "Destroyed is birth, done is what was to be done and there is no more of being such or such."

I have now to make a few observations regarding the Stream-Winner, who is, in fact, the theme of this essay. As I indicated earlier, the fifth supramundane (*javana*) thought-moment is the Path-consciousness (*magga-citta*), and the two succeeding thought-moments, the sixth and the seventh, are the Stream-entry Fruition-consciousness (*sotāpatti-phala-citta*). It is during this infinitesimally short period of time that a Stream-Winner gets a glimpse of Nibbāna.

At the moment when the pilgrim wins the Stream he comprehends the Four Noble Truths: This is Suffering. This is the Origin of Suffering. This is the Cessation of Suffering. This is the Path leading to the Cessation of Suffering. This knowledge concerning the Four Noble Truths helps him to steer clear of the rocks and shoals—that is, the numerous views (*diṭṭhi*) which he comes across on the Stream.

1. The knowledge of Suffering (*dukkha-ñāṇa*) steers him clear of (i) the view of an abiding self or soul and (ii) the view that the aggregates are lasting, beautiful, pleasurable and self.

2. The knowledge of the Origin of Suffering (*dukkha-samudaya-*

29. It is by totally destroying the cankers (*āsava*), also called the floods (*ogha*), that the Anāgāmi attains the state of an Arahant. See *The Four Cankers* (Bodhi Leaves No. B. 34) by the present writer.

ñāṇa) steers him clear of (i) the view that there is no birth after death (*uccheda-diṭṭhi*), (ii) the view that there is a Creator God and (iii) the view that everything comes into being spontaneously without a cause (*ahetuka-vāda*).

3. The knowledge of the Cessation of Suffering (*dukkha-nirodha-ñāṇa*) steers him clear of (i) the view of Eternalism (*sassata-diṭṭhi*), (ii) the view that the Realm of Neither Perception nor Non-Perception is Nibbāna and (iii) the view that the sphere of beings devoid of consciousness (*asañña-satta*) is Nibbāna.

4. The knowledge of the Path leading to the Cessation of Suffering (*dukkha-nirodha-gāmini-patipadā-ñāṇa*) steers him clear of (i) the view that there is no effect (*vipāka*) in giving (alms), nor reward for good deeds nor punishment for evil deeds (*akiriya-diṭṭhi*), (ii) the view that there is neither this world nor a world beyond, there is no moral obligation towards father and mother, and that in this world there are no recluses or *Brahmins* of virtuous conduct, who with wisdom revealed proclaimed the true nature of things (*natthika-vāda*), and (iii) the view that eternal happiness can be had by following either self-indulgence or self-mortification.

The knowledge of winning the Stream (*sotāpatti-ñāṇa*) is spoken in terms of "all that is bound to arise is bound to cease," or, in other words, whatever is born must die (*uppāda-vaya dhammino*). This realistic view of the transience of all compound things is best illustrated in the tragic story of the young mother Kisā Gotamī which is found in the commentary to the Aṅguttara Nikāya. Almost demented at the loss of her first-born baby boy, she ran along the streets of Sāvatthi crying, "Give me medicine for my son." A kindly person directed her to the Buddha, who sensing the spiritual maturity in her, sent her on a mission to fetch a few grains of mustard from any house where no one had ever died. She failed to obtain the grains of mustard in the manner instructed by the Buddha. While returning to the Buddha, it suddenly dawned upon her that her son was not the only one that death has overcome, and that that was a law common to all mankind. She then took her dead child to the charnel ground.

When she stood before the Buddha, he gently asked her, "Gotamī, did you get the tiny grains of mustard seed?" "Done, Reverend Sir, is the business of the mustard seed." She had gained the knowledge of Stream-entry.

The Saṅgīti Sutta (mentioned earlier) speaks of four qualities or accomplishments found in a Stream-Winner (*sotāpannassa-aṅgāni*). They are born of an unshakable confidence (*aveccapasāda*) in the Buddha, the Dhamma and the Saṅgha. He has realized (i) that the Buddha is indeed that Blessed One, Worthy, Fully Enlightened, endowed with knowledge and virtue, Well gone, Knower of the three worlds, Incomparable Charioteer of Beings to be tamed, Guide of gods and men, the Enlightened Lord.

He has realized (ii) that the Dhamma is well-expounded by the Lord, is visible, immediate, inviting to come and behold, leading to deliverance and to be understood through experience by the wise.

He has realized (iii) that the Saṅgha is on the Path to final happiness, on the straight Path, on the Path of wisdom, on the Path of correct living, has attained the four Paths (of holiness) and their fruitions, is worthy of offerings brought from afar, is worthy of hospitality, of gifts, is worthy of reverence, is an incomparable field of merit to the world.

He is also conscious of the fact that (iv) the Stream-Winner is possessed of the purest virtue (*ariyakantehi sīlehi samannāgato hoti*), leading to supramundane concentration.

What, then, is this purest virtue? It is virtue that is unbroken and continuous at the beginning, the middle and the end, and wherein the precepts are not broken at any point, but are observed throughout in their natural order; it is a virtue where the precepts are not broken here and there; it is a virtue free from craving; it is a virtue praised highly by the wise; it is a virtue unadulterated by desire and false views; it is a virtue that induces neighbourhood (*upacāra*) and attainment (*appanā*) concentration.

As I conclude this essay, I must repeat, with all the emphasis at my command, that inner purification is productive of greater good than evanescent material possessions or temporary celestial comforts. For, as the Blessed One says,

> "Better than absolute sovereignty over the earth,
> better than going to heaven,
> better than lordship over all the worlds is the
> Fruit of a Stream-Winner."[30]

30. Dhammapada v 178.

Everyone should ask oneself the question: What is the meaning of life? To the materialist who worships at the altar of hedonism, the meaning of life is, "Eat, drink and enjoy, for tomorrow we die." To the Buddhist, who understands the Law of Causality, "He who sees uprising by way of cause sees Dhamma; he who sees Dhamma sees uprising by way of cause" (*yo paṭiccasamuppādaṃ passati, so dhammaṃ passati, yo dhammaṃ passati so paṭiccasamuppādaṃ passati*).[31] To him the meaning of life is to gain Insight and see himself as he really is. To this end he treads the Noble Eightfold Path as taught by the Shower of the Way. Insight rewards him with entry into the Stream. May you with stirred up energy, with human strength and with determined zeal, strive to gain the Stream here and now.

With this fervent and sincere appeal we dedicate this essay to our readers. If in the perusal of it they obtain the inspiration and earnestness to embark on this greatest spiritual adventure possible to man, we can then have the satisfaction of knowing that our labours have been worthwhile, and by that they are fully compensated.

> "Great is the goal that the man of
> stirred up energy, remote from evil,
> unfavourable things, can make perfect."
>
> (*Saṃyutta Nikāya* II 29)

31. Majjhima Nikāya I 190-191.

Aspects of Reality

as Taught by Theravada Buddhism

by

Dr. G. P. Malalasekera

Editor-in-Chief, *Encyclopedia of Buddhism*,
Chairman, National Council for Higher Education,
Sri Lanka

WHEEL PUBLICATION NO. 127

Aspects of Reality as Taught by Theravada Buddhism

In regard to the question "What is ultimate reality?" the different schools of philosophy or systems of thought seem to fall into two main divisions. Some of them say that the ultimate reality is one: they believe in a permanent unity behind all the variety and change of the world. They are the monists, theists, animists, eternalists, traditionalists, fideists, dogmatists, ontologists, realists, idealists, and energists. All these schools, though distinct among themselves and even opposed to each other on many points, nevertheless have this in common: they accept an ultimate reality as an entity in the metaphysical sense, whether that entity be called substance, or soul, or God, or force, or categorical necessity, or whatever other name may yet be invented. They may be said to follow a subjective method, molding reality on concepts. Hence theirs is mostly a method of conjecture. The other schools say, some of them not very explicitly but still implicitly in their doctrines, that the ultimate reality is plural. They follow an objective method, molding their conceptions on observations. They generally deny a unity behind or within nature's plurality. These are the dualists, pluralists, atheists, nominalists, relativists, rationalists, positivists, phenomenalists, annihilationists, occasionalists, transformists, progressivists, materialists, and so on. Here again, all these schools, though differing among themselves on many points, have this in common: they reject a metaphysical entity.

Now, what is the place of Buddhism among these different "isms"? The answer is that it does not belong to either group. The ultimate reality of the phenomena in the universe (the chief phenomenon around which all others centre) being the "I," the self, is, according to Buddhism, neither plural, nor one, but *none.* In religion and philosophy, as well as in metaphysics, the words "real" and "reality" express more than one aspect of things: the actual as opposed to the fictitious; the essential as opposed to the accidental; the absolute or unconditioned as opposed to the relative or conditioned; the objectively valid as opposed to the ideal or the imagined; that which ultimately and irreducibly is opposed to that which by means of various names signifies the mind's stock of knowledge. It must be admitted that in the suttas, or discourses, attributed to the Buddha we do not find any terms exactly corresponding to "real" and "reality," but all the above antitheses do occur and find expression in a variety of ways. The Buddha's teachings are more deeply and directly concerned with truth and the pragmatic importance of things, more with what might be called "spiritual health" than with theories. There are certain facts regarding spiritual health, however, about which it is necessary to have right views in order that action may be taken accordingly. These are the actualities; other things are of very much less value. The true is, therefore, the actual, that which is. It is expressed by the Pali word *sacca* (Sanskrit, *satya*), which means "the fact" or "the existent."

It must always be borne in mind that Buddhism is primarily a way of life and, therefore, that it is with the human personality that it is almost wholly concerned. Various metaphors are used to describe the essential nature of the personality.[1] They are meant not so much to indicate the ontological unreality of objects and sense impressions (like the *māya*, or illusion, which we come across in the Vedānta) as to express a repudiation of permanence, a sense of happy security, a superphenomenal substance or soul underlying them. They are also meant as a deprecation of any genuine, satisfying value in spiritual life to be found either in "the pride of life" or in the lust of the world.

At the time of the Buddha there were in India views similar both to those of the Parmenidean school of Greater Greece (that the universe is a plenum of fixed, permanent existents) and to that other extreme field by Gorgias and the Sophists (that nothing is). In all things the Buddha's teachings represent what he terms the Middle Way (*majjhima paṭipadā*), the doctrine of the golden mean, the theory of conditioned or causal becoming, the most succinct statement of which is to be found in the *Saṃyutta-Nikāya*: "'Everything is': this, Oh Kaccāyana, [is the first] extreme.

1. E.g., "To regard the body as something of worth would be like taking frescoes to be real persons." Or again, "As one would view a bubble, as one would view a mirage, so should the world be looked at" (Dhammapada verse 170). "The world is like a dream" (*Saṃyutta Nikāya*, III 141).

'Everything is not': this is the second extreme."[2] The Tathāgata (that being the term which the Buddha used when speaking of himself), not accepting these two extremes, preaches his doctrine of the Middle Way.

The followers of the first extreme were known to the Buddha as eternalists (*sassatavādino*). Some of them stuck to the old sacrificial religion which promised blissful existence in heaven after death. Others favoured a monistic view of the universe and believed in the attainment of a supreme bliss which consisted in the dissolution of personality in an impersonal, all-embracing Absolute. There were others who held the idea of an eternal, individual soul, which, after many existences, would return to its genuine condition of free spirit as a result of accumulated merit. These various views are described in the *Brahmajāla Sutta* of the *Dīgha-Nikāya*.[3] It is interesting to note from these descriptions that the various schools of idealism, which later appeared in the West, had their counterparts in the India of the Buddha, e. g., subjective idealism (which holds that it is the "I" alone which exists, all the rest being a modification of my mind), objective idealism (which holds that all, including the "I," are mere manifestations of the Absolute), or the absolute idealism of Hegel (which informs us that only the relation between the subject and object is real). All these varieties of idealism the Buddha held to be "painful, ignoble, and leading to no good, because of their being intent upon self-mortification."[4] Idealism, according to the Buddha, has but one reality, that of thought, and strives for but one end, the liberation of the thinking self. Addiction to self-mortification is merely the practical side of the speculations of idealism, in which the "self" is sublimated, with the natural consequence that the "self" must be liberated from matter, the "soul" must be freed from the bonds of the body. The passions of the body must be subdued even

---

2. *Saṃyutta Nikāya*, S II 17. See Mrs. Rhys Davids, trans., in F. L. Woodward, *Kindred Sayings* (London: Oxford University Press, 1926), Vol. IV, p. 13.
3. The first discourse of the *Dīgha Nikāya*. See T. W. Rhys Davids, trans., *Dialogues of the Buddha* (London: Oxford University Press, 1901), Vol. I.
4. *Saṃyutta Nikāya*, S IV 330f. *Dhammacakkapavattana Sutta*. See Lord Chalmers, trans., *Further Dialogues of the Buddha* (London: Oxford University Press, 1926).

by force. Body becomes the eternal enemy of the spirit, to be overcome by prayer, fasting, and other austerities.

The followers of the second extreme, who denied any survival of the individual after death or any retribution for moral and immoral deeds, the Buddha called annihilationists (*ucchedavādin*). The annihilationists, too (or, as they came to be called later, the materialists), had many varieties of belief in ancient India. Some, like the Epicureans, denied any external agency as the cause of matter and maintained that the highest good was pleasure. Others, very much in the manner of Hobbes, Comte, or John Stuart Mill, held that only the sensuous could be an object of knowledge. But all of them saw only one origin, matter, and strove only for one end, material well-being. Increase of comfort, said the Buddha, only leads to desire for still more, and the desire for more leads, and will always lead, to conflict and conquest. He, therefore, condemned materialism as "despicable, vulgar, ordinary, base, and leading to no good."[5]

In the Buddha's view, both idealism and materialism, though theoretically opposed, converge both in their starting-point and in their goal, for "self is their beginning and satisfaction their end." Between these two extremes, therefore, of materialistic self-indulgence and idealistic self-denial (not as a compromise, but, "avoiding both"), the Buddha formulated the Middle Way, "the way of knowledge and wisdom," not in the wavering of speculation, or in the excitement of discussion, but "in tranquillity of mind and penetrative insight, leading to enlightenment and deliverance, enlightenment with regard to the real nature of things and deliverance from suffering and its cause."[6]

In following the middle course the Buddha borrowed from the eternalists their doctrine of the gradual accumulation of spiritual merit in a series of existences, but rejected their doctrine of an eternal spiritual principle. He saw contradiction in assuming an eternal, pure, spiritual principle which for incomprehensible reasons became polluted with the filth of mundane existence only to revert later to original purity. With the annihilationists he denied every permanent principle. The Buddha's originality

5. Ibid.
6. Ibid.

consisted in denying substantiality altogether and converting the world process into a progression of discrete, evanescent elements. His position was not an easy one because he had also to find a theoretical basis to establish morality. He was faced with the contradiction of a moral law without a personality on whom the law was binding, salvation with nobody to reach the goal. How he solved the problem will appear in the sequel. The shortest statement of the Buddha's doctrine is contained in a formula which has come to be regarded as the Buddhist credo: "Whatsoever things proceed from a cause, the Tathāgata [i.e., the Buddha] has declared the cause thereof; he has explained their cessation also." This is the doctrine of the recluse. It declares, in other words, that the Buddha has discovered the elements and their causal connection, and a method to suppress forever their active efficiency and secure their quiescence.

The Buddha claimed that his was a practical teaching: its object was to show a way of escape from the ever-revolving round of birth-and-death, which constitutes *saṃsāra* and which is considered a condition of degradation and suffering (*dukkha*). This way of escape was meant primarily for human beings. True to this central conception, therefore, as stated above, the Buddha started with a minute analysis (using "analysis" in its strictest sense of "dissolution") of the human being into the elements of which his being is composed. Analysis has always played a very important part in Buddhist teaching; in fact, one of its names is the doctrine of analysis (*vibhajjavāda*).

In this analysis, the human being was found to consist of two parts, *nāma* and *rūpa* (loosely translated as mind and matter), *rūpa* representing the physical elements and *nāma* the mental ones. Matter is composed of the four elementary qualities of extension, cohesion, caloricity (*tejo*), and vibration. The relative qualities of hardness and softness and the occupation of space are due to the elementary quality of extension (*paṭhavī*). It is the element of cohesion (*āpo*) which makes the many parts adhere intrinsically and to one another, and this prevents an aimless scattering about or disintegration, thus giving rise to the idea of a "body." Caloricity depends on vibration (*vayo*), for by increased vibration the temperature rises and when the temperature is lowered the speed of vibration is reduced. Thus do gases liquify and solids solidify.[7] The mental elements are similarly divided into four groups: feelings or "receptions" (*vedanā*), ideas or "perceptions" (*saññā*), what is variously translated as "mental activities" or "complexes" (*saṅkhāra*),[8] and cognition or "conception" (*viññāṇa*). *Rūpa* (matter), and these four mental groups are called *khandha* (aggregates or groups). The whole, in brief, is an analysis of the "I" or "personality" (*sakkāya*). The apparently unitary "I" is broken up into a number of layers, as in a burning flame a number of layers of colour can be distinguished. But the layers of colour in a flame are not parts laid out after the fashion of pieces in mosaic, alongside one another. So also is it with the five *khandha* or groups. They are a continuous, unbroken process of action, of which it is expressly said that they are "burning."

In all of them an arising and a passing away are to be cognized. They are not parts of a whole but forms of action, a process of mental-corporeal "nutrition" or "sustenance," in which the corporeal as well as the mental forms of grasping (*upādāna*)[9] fall together into one conceptual unity. They are different modes in which the "I" enters into relation with the external world, lays hold of it, "seizes" it. The relationship is not an immediate relation with the external world in which a metaphysical "I" is endowed *a priori* with the power of cognizing, nor is it the mediate relation of a purely physical process in which the "I" only builds itself up *a posteriori* on the basis of continued experiences.

The external world with which the human being comes into relationship is also analyzed into its component elements. This relationship is one of cognition, and in discussing how this cognition is established mention is made of cognitive faculties (*indriya*) and their objects (*visaya*). There are thus six cognitive

7. For a very good exposition of this and what follows, see Th. Stcherbatsky, *The Central Conception of Buddhism* (London: Royal Asiatic Society, 1923).

8. *Saṅkhāra* is a very difficult term to translate, since it means various things in various contexts. Etymologically, it means "what is put together as a composite thing." See T. W. Rhys Davids and W. Stede, *Pali-English Dictionary* (Pali Text Society), s. v.

9. "Form, O monks, is burning" (*rūpaṃ bhikkhave ādittaṃ*) and so on with the other *khandha*." *Saṃyutta Nikāya*, S IV 21. See F. L. Woodward, *Kindred Sayings* (London: Oxford University Press, 1927), Vol. IV.

faculties or senses: the senses of vision, audition, smell, taste, touch, and the faculty of intellect or consciousness.[10]

Corresponding to these as objects of cognition are, respectively, colour and shape, sound, odour, savours, tangibles, and non-sensuous objects. These twelve factors (the cognitive faculties and their objects) are called *āyatanāni*, or bases of cognition. The term *āyatana* means place, sphere, entrance, or point of support, and is used to cover both organ of sense (internal or *ajjhattāni āyatanāni*) and sense object (external or *bāhirāni āyatanāni*), the meeting of which constitutes cognition (*viññāṇa*). This cognition, which results from the meeting, can be divided into six classes, according to the cognitive faculty concerned and the sense object, such as eye-cognition (*cakkhuviññāṇa*), and so on.

In the case of the sixth cognitive faculty (*manas*), consciousness itself (i.e., its preceding moment) acts as a faculty for apprehending non-sensuous objects. The three constituents that comprise a cognition, sense faculty, sense object, and resultant consciousness, are classified under the name *dhātu* (element). We thus get eighteen *dhātu*: the six sense faculties, their six sense objects, and the six varieties of resultant consciousness. This consciousness is the experience of the unity between concept and object; it is not something that is, but something that *becomes.* It is not an object of knowing, but knowing itself, an ever-repeated new becoming, new up-springing out of its antecedent conditions. As such it resembles what the physicist calls living-force, vital energy. It is formed, enfleshed, in *nāma-rūpa* (mind-form, i.e., mind and body). Mind-form is the antecedent condition of consciousness, on the basis of which the next new up-springing of consciousness will assume new individual value.

Consciousness is actuality as action, which means something that is not but which, in order to be present, first must ever spring up anew. Between mind-form and consciousness exists the same ceaseless, quivering, leaping play which exists among the ever-repeated, new moments of combustion of a flame and its external shape. Without sufficient cause (*aññatra paccaya*) no consciousness

10. For an excellent exposition of this point, see Paul Dahlke's *Buddhism* (London: The Macmillan Company, 1927), pp. 129 ff.

can arise.[11] Just as for consciousness to be present, it must ever and again spring up anew, similarly the antecedent conditions upon the basis of which it springs up must also be present. It is from the friction of the living contact of senses with things that consciousness is born. It is thus a process of nutrition, of grasping, which embraces itself in its grasping, a process of growth, in which one moment is neither the same as the next, nor yet another, but in which every moment becomes another, passes into that other, just as one moment of a flame is neither the same as the next, nor yet another, but becomes the next.

The human personality, and the external world with which it enters into relationship, are thus divided into *khandha, āyatana,* and *dhātu.* The generic name for all three of them is *dhamma* (plural *dhammā*), which is translated as "element of existence." In Buddhism these *dhammā* are the only ultimate reality. Broadly speaking, the *dhammā* are divided into two classes, *saṅkhata* (conditioned, i.e., subject to various conditions) and *asaṅkhata* (unconditioned). According to Theravada, Nibbāna is the only *asaṅkhata-dhamma*: all other *dhammā* are *saṅkhata* (conditioned). The *saṅkhata* (conditioned *dhamma*) have four salient characteristics: they are non-substantial (*anattā*), evanescent (*anicca*), in a beginningless state of commotion (*dukkha*), and have quiescence only in a final cessation (*nirodha*).

It must always be recalled that the basic idea of this analysis is a moral one. Buddhism is defined as a religion which teaches defilement and its purification (*saṅkilesa* and *vodāna*). Purification or salvation lies in *Nibbāna* or *nirodha*, which is cessation from *saṃsāra.* Thus, when the elements of being are analyzed, they are divided into purifying and defiling elements, good and bad (*sāsava* and *anāsava*), propitious to salvation and averse to it (*kusala* and *akusala*). Purifying, good, and propitious factors are those elements, those moral factors, that lead to *Nibbāna;* their opposites lead to or encourage *saṃsāra.*

This analysis was part of the Buddha's attempt to find answers to the great, primary questions which lie at the bottom of every religious system, which form the seed of religious development. Upon these answers depends the nature of any religious philosophy, viz.

11. See the *Majjhima Nikāya, Sutta* No. 38, *Mahātaṇhāsaṅkhaya Sutta.*

Whence am I? Whither do I go? What happens to me after death? How do I know myself? How does this world enter into me, into my consciousness? To the Buddha's way of thinking, all these questions have one great fallacy, that of begging the question, *petitio principii.* His view was that there should be another question prior to all these inquiries, upon which depends the very possibility of further questioning, namely: Is there anything at all which deserves the designation "I"? Here was a problem which the Buddha felt could not be solved by argument or mere logic (*atakkāvacara*), for in logic one has to presuppose the reality of the thinking subject as standing outside the process of thinking, as a witness or, rather, as a judge. Only one kind of logic, he said, could help here: the logic of events, because it is beyond sophistry. Actuality can be understood not by argument but by analysis (*yoniso manasikāra*).[12]

As a result of such analysis, the Buddha discovered that the individual, conventionally called "I" or the "self," is a mass of physical and psychical elements without any permanent entity behind them to keep them together, without any "soul" inhering in them, the elements themselves being a mere flux (*santāna*), a continuity of changes. In postulating a mythical, unchanging entity as the possessor of changing qualities, one merely assumes, he said, the existence of that which has to be proved. The conviction that men hold that, though thought and actions change, the thinker and the doer remain the same, was a delusion, for it is exactly by thought that we change our minds, by actions that we change our lives. Actions cannot exist apart from the doer, cannot exist freely as such. If the action changes, the so called actor must change at the same instant. Thus, the "I" must be identified with action. It is only the "I" which can walk and sit and think and eat and sleep. But that "I" is not a permanent, unchanging entity; it is identified with the action and is the action itself, and thus changes with the action. "I" cannot stay at home while "I" go out for a walk. It is the conventional language (*sammuti*) which has spoiled the purity of conception (*paramattha*—ultimate sense, the supreme-thing-meant), though, in some cases, language does remain pure enough, as when we say, "It rains." Who rains? Simply, it rains, meaning,

12. For an explanation of this very significant word, see *Pali-English Dictionary*, s.v.

there is rain. Likewise, the concept should not be: "I think," but "There is thinking." This is the teaching which came to be known as the doctrine of *anattā.* In this doctrine, the Buddha went counter to the three main systems of philosophy that were current in India in his day: the teaching of the Upaniṣads, of the *sāṅkhya*. Briefly stated, the Upaniṣadic teaching is a kind of monism, where a real being, Brahman, is assumed to be something eternal, without beginning, change, or end, and man's soul (*ātman*) is assumed to be an integral part of that Being, Atman and Brahman being one. The Jains had a highly developed theory of moral defilement and purification, and a theory of spiritual existence extending even to plants and inanimate, non-organic things, which are also supposed to possess souls. The saṅkhya taught the existence of a plurality of souls, on the one hand, and of a unique, eternal, pervasive, substantial matter, on the other. Buddhism is opposed to all three systems. Forsaking the monism of the Upaniṣads, it declares that there is no real unity at all in the world. Everything is discrete, separate, split up into an infinity of minute, impermanent elements, without any abiding stuff. It agrees with Jainism in opposing the monism of the Upaniṣads and in maintaining that being is joined to production, continuation, and destruction, but disagrees with the Jain doctrine which ascribed to a *kamma* a physical nature. To the dualism of saṅkhaya the Buddha opposes the most radical pluralism, converting the world process into an appearance of evanescent elements, and calls the eternal pervasive matter, which is imagined as their support or substratum, a mere fiction.

The term *anattā* (Sanskrit, *anātman*) is usually translated as "no soul," but, strictly speaking, *atta* is here synonymous only with a permanent, enduring entity, ego, self, conscious agent, etc. It is the permanence that is denied in *anattā.* The underlying idea is that, whatever may be designated by these names, it is not a real, ultimate fact; it is a mere name for a multitude of interconnected facts which Buddhist philosophy attempts to analyze by reducing them to real elements (*dhammā*). Buddhism does not deny the existence of a personality or a "soul" in the empirical sense. What it does deny is that such a "soul" is an ultimate reality, a *dhamma.* The Buddhist teaching of *anattā* does not proclaim the absence of an individuality or self; it says only that there is no permanent individuality, no unchanging self.

Personality or individuality is, according to Buddhism, not an entity but a process of arising and passing away, a process of nutrition, of combustion, of grasping. Man's personality is conceded as being something real, a fact (*sacca*) to him at any given moment, though the word "personality" is only a popular label and does not correspond to any fixed entity in man. In the ultimate constituents of conditioned things, physical and mental, Buddhism has never held that the real is necessarily the permanent. Unaware of this anticipation, modern philosophers like Bertrand Russell are asking modern philosophy to concede no less.

The Buddhist term for an individual, a term which is intended to suggest the Buddhist view as opposed to other theories, is *santāna* (stream), viz., the stream of interconnected facts. It includes the mental elements as well as the physical, the elements (*dhamm*) of one's own body and external objects, as far as they constitute the experience of a given personality.

The representatives of the eighteen classes of *dhātu* mentioned earlier combine to produce the interconnected stream. Every combination of these elements represents a nominal, not an ultimate, reality. The number of psychical elements at any given moment is variable. It may be very considerable, because undeveloped, dormant faculties are also reckoned as actually present. Some *dhammā* are constant, present at every moment, others only under certain conditions. Elements which combine at any moment vary both in number and in intensity. In any individual, at a given moment, a certain element may predominate. All mind at every moment is an assemblage of mental faculties (*saṅkhāra*) or elements. Two elements, which are constantly present, are most precious: *samādhi* (power of concentration) and *paññā* (insight). If they become predominant they change the character of the individual and his moral value. The predominant element in ordinary men is ignorance (*avijjā*), which is the reverse of *paññā* and not merely its absence. It is a separate element, present at the same time with dormant *paññā*. But it is not constant, and can be cast out of the mental stream.

There is a special force of *kamma*, sometimes called *prapti*, that holds these elements in combination. It operates only within the limits of a single stream and not beyond. The stream of elements kept together is not limited to the present life but has its source in past existences and its continuation in future ones. This is the

Buddhist counterpart of the soul or self in other systems. From the denial of substance follows the denial of every difference between the categories of substance and quality. There is no "inherence" of qualities in substance; in this respect all real elements (*dhammā*) are equally independent. As separate entities they then become "substances" *sui generis.* All sense data are also substances in the sense that there is no stuff they belong to. We cannot say that matter *has* extension, cohesion, temperature, and vibration, but that matter *is* extension, etc., and that without these qualities there is nothing called matter. Matter is thus reduced to mere qualities and forces which are in a constant state of flux, in which there is no entity to support the qualities or to be the possessor of attributes or, as substance, to stand under them all, to uphold them all, and to unite all the phenomena associated with it. Independent of attributes, there is no substance, no substratum, not even the idea, because the idea is dependent on certain conditions.

When science bends more and more to the view that all matter is merely a form of energy, a grouping and re-grouping of forces, as advocated by scientific materialism (or, as some would prefer to call it, energism), it is only admitting in different words the unsubstantiality of matter, which the Buddha declared more than two thousand years ago.

The same principle applies to the mental sphere. Mind is not an entity but a function. Consciousness is thought, and it arises when certain conditions are present. Thought does not arise as the action of a "thinking subject," but is conditioned by, originates from, is dependent on, other states. As such, it will again be the condition, the origin, the *raison d'etre,* of further states. When it ceases to be it passes on its momentum, thus giving the impulse to new arising. Yet the individuality of consciousness is not a mere physical process either. It is a process of grasping and will last only as long as grasping lasts. Just as a fire can burn only as long as it lays hold of new fuel, so the process of individuality is a constant arising, an ever-renewed laying hold of the objects of its craving. It is craving that causes the friction between sense objects and sense organs, and from that friction leaps forth the flame of new *kamma* which, because of *avijjā* (ignorance), will not be extinguished, but in grasping lays hold of fresh material (thus keeping alive the process of burning).

Thus the universe, with all that is in it, represents an infinite number of discrete, evanescent elements, in a state of ceaseless activity or commotion. They are only momentary flashes of efficient energy, without anything perdurable or stable, not in a condition of static being, but in a state of perpetual becoming. Not only are entities such as God, soul, and matter denied reality, but even the simple stability of empirical objects is regarded as something constituted by our imagination. The empirical thing becomes a thing constructed by a process of synthesis on the basis of sensations. Reality does not consist of extended, perdurable bodies, but of point-instants (*khaṇa*) picked up in momentary sensations and constituting a string of events. Our intellect, then, by a process of synthesis, so to speak, puts them together and produces an integral image, which has nothing but an imagined mental computation. A single moment of existence is thus something unique, unrepresentable, and unutterable. In itself, set loose from all imagination, it is qualityless, timeless, and spaceless (indivisible); timeless not in the sense of an eternal being, spaceless not in the sense of being ubiquitous, motionless not in the sense of an all-embracing whole, but all these in the sense, respectively, of having no duration, no extension, and no movement. It is a mathematical instant, the moment of an action's efficiency. A representation and a name always correspond to a synthetic unity, embracing a variety of time, place, and quality, but this unity is a constructed unity, constituted by an operation of the mind, a chain of moments cognized as a construction on the basis of some sensation. Actions take place in time and space, as the expression of the pure simultaneousness of things, and time as the pure successiveness of the process, but there is no space or time apart from their being correlatives of the concept.[13] There are thus two kinds of reality: the one, ultimate or pure reality (*paramattha-sacca*), consisting of bare point-instants (*khaṇa*), without definite position in time or space and with no sensible qualities. And the other, empirical reality (*sammuti-sacca*), consisting of objectivized images, endowed by us with a position in time and space and with all the variety of sensible and abstract qualities.

13. The Buddhist conception of time and space is given in *Saṃyutta Nikāya*. See Woodward, *Kindred Sayings*, Vol. I.

How, then, is the illusion of a stable, material world, and of perdurable personalities living in it, produced? It is in order to explain this that the Buddha put forward the doctrine of Dependent Origination (*paṭicca-samuppāda*). Just as the Four Noble Truths (of suffering, its cause, its cessation, and the Way thereto) form the heart of the Buddha's teaching, so does the doctrine of *paṭicca-samuppāda* constitute its backbone. According to this doctrine, although the separate elements (*dhammā*) are not connected with each other either by a pervading stuff in space or by duration in time, there is nevertheless a connection among them. It is this: their manifestations are subject to definite laws, the laws of causation (*hetu-paccaya*). The flow of evanescent elements is not a haphazard process (*adhicca-samuppanna*). Every element, though appearing only for a single moment, is a "dependently-orginating-element," i.e., it depends for its origin on some other preceding element or elements. Thus, existence becomes dependent existence (*paṭicca-samuppāda*), and this is expressed by the formula, "If there is this, there comes to be that" (*asmiṃ sati idaṃ hoti*). Every momentary entity springs into existence or flashes up in coordination with other moments. Strictly speaking, there is no causality at all, but only functional independence, no question of one thing producing another, since one momentary entity, disappearing as it does at once, cannot produce any other entity. The relation is one of "consecution," in which there is no destruction of one thing and no creation of another, no influx of one substance into another, but only a constant, uninterrupted, infinitely graduated change.

Thus, the formula, "If there is this, there comes to be that" came to be supplemented by another formula: "Not from itself, not from something else, nor from a combination of both, nor by chance, does an entity spring up." It is coordinated, not actually produced. There is neither *causa materials* (continuing substance) nor *causa efficiens*. This view of causality, that the law of causality is rather the law of coordination between point-instants (*khaṇa*), is not strange to modern science and philosophy. The world of Buddhism is like the world of the mathematician: the world dies and is born afresh at every instant. It is evidently the world that Descartes was thinking of when he spoke of "continuous creation."

The fact that the Buddha declared the *khandha* to be completely free from any unchanging, undying essence does not mean that

Buddhism taught annihilation of body and mind at death. For, besides the doctrine of transience (*anicca*) and soullessness (*anattā*), there is also the doctrine of *kamma*, or the transmitted force of the act, bodily and mental. A living being is a *khandha*, complex, ever changing, but ever determined by its antecedent character, and ruled by *kamma.* The long-drawn-out line of life is but a fluctuating curve of evolving experience. Man, even in this life, is never the same, yet ever the result of his pre-existing self. Action, which is another word for *kamma*, will be present as long as there is existence, because existence is not something static but a process. A process must proceed and this is done by activity, the activity of the senses. Just as a flame cannot exist without consuming, its very nature being combustion, so also the senses cannot exist without activity. But this is not the same as the psychological determinism of Leibniz and Herbart, for *kamma* is not fatalism. "If anyone says," declares the Buddha, "that a man must necessarily reap according to all his deeds, in that case no religious striving is possible, nor is there an opportunity to end sorrow."[14]

How is the doctrine of rebirth to be reconciled with that *anattā*? The question, "What is reborn?" is based on ignorance of the selfless process of *kamma*. *Kamma* is not an entity that goes from life to life, like a visitor going from house to house. It is life itself, in so far as life is the product (*vipāka*) of *kamma*. In each step we take now in full-grown age lie also the feeble attempts of our babyhood. The present actuality, which expressed itself as the result of all the preceding processes, carries in its very action all the efforts which went into the making of the previous actions. When a seed becomes a sprout this is done by the last moment in the seed, not by those moments when it lay placidly in the granary. Yet, it is also true in a sense that all the preceding moments of the seed are the indirect causes of the sprout. Every moment in the phenomenal world has its own totality of causes and conditions owing to which it exists. What we regard as a break in the continuity is nothing but the appearance of an outstanding or dissimilar moment. Death is but one such moment.

14. *Aṅguttara Nikāya*, A I 237. See F. L. Woodward, *Gradual Sayings* (London: Oxford University Press, 1923), Vol. I.

When a man dies, the component elements of his new life are present from its very inception, though in an undeveloped condition. The first moment of the (apparently) new life is called conventionally *viññāṇa*, "conception." Its antecedent is *kamma*, which in the formula of the doctrine of dependent origination (*paṭicca-samuppāda*) is designated *saṅkhāra* (pre-natal forces). These *saṅkhāra*, which through conception (*viññāṇa*) find continuity in the new life, contain latent in them the *anusaya,* which is the name for the resultant of all the impressions made on the particular flux (*santāna*) of elements in the whole course of its faring (*saṃsāra*). It is these latent factors that the psychoanalyst, for instance, finds as so much refuse and slag in a man's mind when he penetrates into it. They are his heritage of action (*kamma-dāyāda*), brought down through countless lives and not inherited by him, as is sometimes stated, as the heritage solely from the past of his race. Life is kinetic; rebirth in Buddhism is nothing but a continuity of impulse, *kamma-santati.*

It is sometimes said that the doctrine of *anattā* takes away moral responsibility and that with it goes overboard the whole fabric of social morality. But it will be seen from what has already been stated that there is no contradiction at all between the denial of an unchanging entity and the fact that former deeds engender a capacity for having a consequence. In fact, the doctrine of *anattā* enhances the idea of responsibility, for there is here no saviour or redeemer to intercept the unfailing consequence of one's action. Likewise, the statement that the doctrine of *anattā* is inconsistent with free will is also due to a misconception. If nothing arises without a cause, if everything is of "dependent origination," can there be free will? That is the question. There is a tradition that the doctrine of dependent origination (*paṭicca-samuppāda*) itself was established by the Buddha in defence of free will and against a theory of wholesale determinism. The Buddha singled out for special animadversion the doctrine of his contemporary, Makkhali Gosāla, who maintained that all things are unalterably fixed and that nothing can be changed. The Buddha called this the "most pernicious" of doctrines.[15] On the other hand, the Buddha declared himself to be an upholder of "free action" (*kiriyavādī*).

15. Ibid., I 33.

The law according to which a moral or immoral deed must have its fruition is the law of *kamma*, but in order to have a consequence the action must be produced by an effort of the will. The Buddha declared, "Will alone is *kamma*" (*cetanāhaṃ bhikkhave kammaṃ vadāmi*).[16] It must also be remembered that free will really means "strong will," for the possibility of choosing shows the presence of two or more opposites. If there were no attraction or motive, equilibrium would have been established already and no choice would be necessary. When inducement or coercion is not absent, it is a contradiction to speak of free will. Will is thus only a milder term for craving, and craving exists only in dependence upon feeling. Our real freedom lies, therefore, not in the will but in being without will. How is the cessation of this round of birth-and-death, which is "transient, sorrow-fraught, and soulless," brought about? By following the path laid down by the Buddha. There are two factors that help a man to get started on the path: the one is right reflection (*yoniso manasikāra*) and the other is friendship with the good (*kalyāṇamitta*). The Buddha is man's best friend. That is why the appearance of a Buddha in the world is an event of such significance. The cessation of suffering is called *nirodha* or *Nibbāna*. *Nibbāna* has so often been discussed that there is no need to say much here. Only when the grossly wrong views regarding personality are disposed of is the path entered upon which leads to final deliverance. *Nibbāna* consists of two stages. When, by treading the Noble Eightfold Path, the process of the arising of craving has come to a stop, the grasping of the "aggregates" (*khandha*) which form the individual will cease also. When the lust for life has ceased, no further rebirth will take place, and the highest state, that of a saint (*arahant*) is attained. But when the lust for life has ceased, life itself will not disappear simultaneously. Just as the heat in an oven, produced by fire, will remain for some time even after the fire is extinct, so the result of the craving which produced rebirth may remain a while even though the fire of the passions be extinct. In this state of sainthood or *arahantship* which is called *Nibbāna* with residue (*saupādisesa-nibbāna*), neither act nor thought can be regarded as moral or immoral. The *arahant's* apperception is ineffective. His actions are

16. *Aṅguttara Nikāya*, A III 415.

not influenced by craving and do not, therefore, produce *kamma*. They are free from tendencies, from likes and dislikes. Where no new *kamma* is produced no results follow. But, when the result of previous *kamma* is exhausted and the *arahant's* life comes to an end, this state is called *Nibbāna* without residue (*anupadisesa-nibbāna*). In this final emancipation, all suffering (*dukkha*) ceases. *Nibbāna* is where lust, ill will, and delusion are not. In Buddhism, life is a process which has its sufficient cause neither in something metaphysical, like God, nor in something physical, like parents. It is a process which is destined to come to an end and awaits the moment of coming to an end. Ignorance (*avijjā*), i.e., ignorance about life itself, is the beginningless starting point from which life ever and again springs forth, as from some hidden source that never dries up as long as it remains undiscovered. Life is begotten of ignorance; what keeps it going is grasping or clinging, which is prompted by craving (*taṇhā*). In life, grasping is the only activity, and there is only one actual object of this grasping, that which is conventionally called personality. Personality is the object in dependence upon which grasping exists, and, at the same time, is that which exists in dependence upon grasping. It is grasping that gives life its nutrition (*āhāra*). Through this nutrition, through the power of maintaining itself, life proves itself to be life. But to say this is not to say that grasping is the cause of life; that would be like saying that the cause of a flame is the fuel there present. Fuel creates no flame; it only maintains the flame. To understand this, to realize this, to live it out is, in the deepest sense, Buddhism. Ignorance is destroyed by knowledge, by insight. The first step is insight into the real nature of conditioned things (*sammasana-ñāṇa*), as having the three characteristics of impermanence, suffering, and soullessness. He who perceives suffering only, but not the transiency thereof, has only sorrow, but when the unreality of life is understood, the unreality of suffering will also be perceived. From this understanding will ensue insight into the nature of all things as processes (*udayabbaya-ñāṇa*), the knowledge that there is nothing but a process of becoming. The next step is insight that becoming is ceasing (*bhaṅga-ñāṇa*).

Becoming and ceasing will be seen as two aspects of one process. This is followed by knowledge of the dangers that have to be feared (*bhaya-ñaṇa*) and the understanding of the perils inherent in clinging (*ādīnava-ñāṇa*), together with the reasons for being disgusted with such an empty show (*nibbidā-ñāṇa*). Thereupon arise the desire to be set free and the knowledge thereof (*muñcitukamyata-ñāṇa*), which will grow into recontemplation (*paṭisaṅkhāna-ñāṇa*), that is, contemplation of the characteristics of transiency, sorrow, and soullessness, but with increased insight as seen from a higher plane. This will be followed by even-mindedness regarding the activities of life, which is due not to lack of interest but lack of self-interest. The climax of discernment is reached with the insight of adaptation (*anuloma-ñaṇa*), which is the gateway to emancipation (*vimokkha-mukha*), where the mind is qualified for final deliverance.

The basis of all this is renunciation. Renunciation cannot be learned; it must grow, like the dawn. When it is night we can admire the millions of stars, but all their beauty (and the glory of the moon too) fade with the first rays of the sun. Renunciation begins when one learns to distinguish between the value a thing has because one wants it and the value it has apart from one's desire. The value of a thing is regulated by one's desire for it; if one wants to know its real value one must give up one's desire for it, but then it will be seen at once that it has lost all value. To be carefree is the secret of happiness, but not to be careless. This freedom from care is the result of forgetting the self, the result of self-renunciation. When pleasures vanish of their own accord, they end in keen anguish of the mind; when relinquished by one's own will, they produce infinite happiness, proceeding from tranquillity. Just as darkness can be experienced only when all light is extinguished, so also *Nibbāna* can be realized only when all attachment has been destroyed.

The realization of this truth is attained by the threefold practice of *sīla, samādhi*, and *paññā*. *Sīla* is discipline of both body and mind, whereby the defilements that cloud wisdom are removed. But mere morality is not enough; it must be accompanied by mental development. All morality which strives to perpetuate the self is a subtle kind of selfishness. The more subtle and sublimated it is, the more rationalized and idealized, the more dangerous. *Samādhi* is the stilling of thought, the perfect equilibrium of mind, which is attained by the *jhāna* (Sanskrit: *dhyāna*), the so-called "trances." They constitute the first taste of the happiness of *Nibbāna*. It is the joy of having found a possibility of escape from the round of birth, suffering, and death. The increase of this joy becomes sheer delight, which then gives place to serene tranquillity, and then to a sense of security and equilibrium, the bliss of well being (*susukha*), which is the very opposite of insecurity and unbalanced striving. In that state of tranquillity, not disturbed by likes and dislikes, not made turbid by passions, not hazed by ignorance, like sunlight that penetrates a placid lake of clear water, there arises the supreme insight (*paññā*) that "All birth and death have ceased; the noble life has been lived; what had to be done has been accomplished, and beyond this there is no more." This is the supreme moment of illumination when the saint (*arahant*) sees the whole universe with the vividness of a living reality. It is described as a double moment, a moment of feeling as well as a moment of knowledge. In sixteen consecutive thought-instants, the *arahant* has been through the whole universe and has seen it in the four stages of its evolution toward quiescence. This supreme moment of illumination is the central point of the teaching regarding the path to deliverance.

Such is *Nibbāna*, where the insight of non-self has taken the place of delusion and ignorance; where being will be seen as a mere process of becoming, and becoming as ceasing; where the spell that has kept us in bondage will be broken; where the dream-state will vanish into reality, and reality will be realized. This reality is not the eternalization of a self but the escape therefrom, not the deliverance or the salvation of the self but the deliverance and salvation from the self, from the misconceived "I." And with this, the last word has been said. Where craving has ceased, the process of becoming, which is grasping, has ceased also. Where there is no more becoming, there is no more birth, with all its concomitants of sorrow, decay, and death.

Is *Nibbāna* annihilation? Yes and no. Yes, because it is the annihilation of the lust for life, of the passions, of craving and grasping, and all the things that result therefrom. But on the other hand, where there is nothing to be annihilated, there can be no annihilation. That which constantly arises and is arising is nothing but a process of change and in changing also constantly ceases. That cannot be said to be destroyed; it merely does not arise again. *Nibbāna* is thus best described as deliverance, surpassing all understanding, above all emotion, beyond all striving, the non-created, the non-conditioned, the non-destructible, which all may attain through insight and realization. It is the culmination of the Buddha's teaching: "Just as, O monks, the ocean has but one taste, the taste of salt, so the doctrine and the discipline have but one taste, the taste of deliverance."[17]

"Hard is the infinite to see; truth is not easy to see; craving is pierced by him who knows; for him who sees, naught remains."[18]

17. Ibid., IV 201.

18. *Udāna,* 8.2. See F. L. Woodward, trans., *The Minor Anthologies of the Pali Canon,* Pt. II (London: Humphrey Milford, Oxford University Press, 1935).

Aspects of Buddhist Social Philosophy

Two Essays

by

K. N. Jayatilleke

M.A. (Cantab.), Ph.D. (London)

Professor of Philosophy

University of Ceylon

WHEEL PUBLICATION NO. 128/129

A Recent Criticism of Buddhism

Professor Toynbee, in his recent work, *An Historian's Approach to Religion,* makes certain criticisms of Buddhism on the basis of what he believes to be the account given of the life and teaching of the Buddha in the Hīnayāna[1] scriptures. It is proposed in this article to examine these criticisms in the light of the relevant material in the Pali Canon, which the Hīnayāna School holds in high regard as its main source of knowledge and inspiration with regard to the Buddha and his doctrine.

Toynbee's criticisms may be listed briefly as follows. He asserts that (a) there is a basic inconsistency between the life and teaching of the Buddha and that (b) it would seem that his life has at least more value than his teaching since (i) the account given of human nature in his teaching is wanting, (ii) the goal it sets forth would appear to be intrinsically unattainable and that (iii) even if it were attainable it would not seem desirable.

I

Let us examine the grounds on which these criticisms are made and see whether they are justified in the light of the account given of the life and teaching of the Buddha in the Pali Canon.

Toynbee says that "the Buddha was an illogical evangelist" (p. 77) and speaks of his "sublime inconsistency" (p. 64) or "sublimely illogical practice" (p. 73). Now, what is the nature of his inconsistency? There seem to be three respects in which a religious teacher may be held to be inconsistent. His life may be inconsistent in the sense that his response or pattern of behaviour in some situations may be radically different from that of other situations which are essentially like them. His teaching may be inconsistent in that there are at least two propositions in it, one of

1. "Hīnayāna" is not a very happy term to denote the Theravāda School of the Southeast Asian countries, partly because it is a term of contempt, but mainly because it tends to presuppose the Mahāyāna metaphysics. I am using it, as no doubt Toynbee does, merely to denote by it the Southern School of Buddhism.

which or what it entails contradicts the other or what the other entails. Lastly, while his life may be perfectly consistent and his teaching a coherent whole when taken independently of each other, his life may not be compatible with his teaching and vice versa. When Toynbee speaks of the inconsistency of the Buddha he seems to have this last sense in mind.

Strictly speaking there is nothing "illogical" in this kind of inconsistency since such a state of affairs is quite conceivable and perhaps not uncommon, since it is not everyone who for better or for worse practises what he preaches. Consider, for instance, the case of a person who says quite sincerely that it is bad to smoke but continues to smoke or says that it is good to have a regular medical check-up but does not himself do so. In both cases we find a person asserting that a certain proposition *p* is true and behaving as if he does not believe *p* or finds it difficult to live up to the demands that *p* makes on him. In such situations, however valid the grounds for asserting the truth of *p* may be, his behaviour seems to undermine or impugn it, since not only do his actions not seem to follow on the track of his beliefs but appear to go contrary to them. I suppose this is part of what Toynbee intends to convey by calling this relationship between teaching and practice "illogical." But perhaps he means more. Consider the case of the person who says that he has given up smoking but continues to smoke. Such a state of affairs is also quite conceivable and therefore cannot strictly be called "illogical," but his behaviour shows that his statement is false. In the previous case the statement "it is bad to smoke" could still be true even if he smoked, but the statement "I have given up smoking" cannot possibly be true in the light of his behaviour since his behaviour is directly relevant to the truth or falsity of his statement.

Consider Toynbee's own statement of the case he makes: "The Hīnayāna scriptures purport to be recording the Buddha's practice as well as his preaching; and if their record is true, we are bound to conclude from it that the Buddha was not preaching what he was practising. In preaching, if he did preach this, that man's paramount aim ought to be self-extinction, he was recommending to others a course of action which he had rejected for himself when the Tempter, after his attainment of Enlightenment, had suggested to him that he should make his exit into Nirvāna without delay. In choosing, instead, deliberately to postpone his own release from Suffering in order to work for the release of his fellow sentient beings, the Buddha was declaring, in a positive act, that for himself, he believed that 'to suffer in the cause of Love was a better course than to release himself from Suffering through Self-extinction'." (p. 292) In other words, if Buddha taught the proposition that "man's paramount aim ought to be self-extinction", (*p*), then in not extinguishing himself when he gained this knowledge he was acting as if he did not believe in *p* as far as he was concerned. Toynbee puts this argument in a slightly different form elsewhere. He says that if the attainment of Nirvāna involves the suppression of both good and bad desires, then after attainment there should be no motive or desire on his part to preach. If he does preach out of love or compassion, this would be incompatible with his teaching about Nirvāna since there would be at least some desires (love, compassion) which have not been suppressed and continue to influence his behaviour. Either his claim about the nature of Nirvāna as a state in which all desires (good and bad) are suppressed is false or his behaviour is not compatible with his teaching. So "if this impartial suppression of all desires, good and bad alike, was thus a logical consequence of the Hīnayāna Buddhist doctrine, the Buddha himself was guilty of a sublime inconsistency" (p. 64). In short, if the Buddha's teaching about the nature of Nirvāna and the means of achieving it is true, then his practice is not only quite incompatible with it but seems to show that this teaching was false.

It is worth pointing out that, although Toynbee sees an incompatibility between the teaching and practice of the Buddha, one of the points often stressed in the Pali Canon is that the Buddha "preached what he practised and practised what he preached" (*yathāvādī tathākārī yathākārī tathāvādī*; It 122). Let us start at a point where Toynbee and the Pali Canon seem to agree, namely, that what the Buddha suffered during the forty-five years of his ministry was inspired by his love for mankind. As Toynbee puts it, "Even if he did recommend in his teaching a self-centred pursuit of self-extinction, he was tacitly countermanding his words by his acts of self-devoting love" (p. 292). The Pali Canon makes frequent reference to the love and compassion of the Buddha. One of his lay disciples, Jīvaka, says on one occasion,

"I have heard it said that God is loving (*Brahmā mettāvihārī*), but I have seen with my own eyes how full of love the Blessed One is" (*Bhagavā mettāvihārī*; M I 369). Where the Buddha converts the robber Aṅgulimāla at the risk of his life, his kindness is referred to (*Buddho ca kāruṇiko;* M II 100), and it is often mentioned that the Buddha preaches not through desire for gain or glory but out of compassion and benevolence (*anukampako Bhagavā hitesī anukampaṃ upādāya dhammaṃ desesi*; M II 238).

If the Buddha practised love, did he also not preach it? The injunctions to practise love and compassion towards our fellow beings are much more numerous in the Pali Canon than the references to his own example. The Buddha tells his followers, "Just as a mother loves her only child even more than her life, extend a boundless love towards all creatures" (Sn 149). The importance that he attaches to the cultivation of love for our fellow beings above all else is seen from the following statement that he makes: "None of the good works employed to acquire religious merit, O monks, is worth a fraction of the value of loving-kindness" (*mettā;* It 19–21). Then there is the well-known saying to his disciples, "Even if ruffians were to seize you and cut you limb from limb with a double-handled saw, you would not have carried out my bidding if you felt the slightest anger towards them" (M I 129, 186).

It would appear therefore that not only did the Buddha practise love but he preached it, and viewed in this manner, there does not seem to be any inconsistency between what he practised and what he taught. But Toynbee is now likely to raise the question as to how his teaching about self-sacrificing love would be compatible with the proposition, "If he did preach this, that man's paramount aim ought to be self-extinction" (p. 292). If love and compassion along with selfish desires were to be extinguished in Nirvāna, how can they continue to influence a person after his attainment of Nirvāna? If the latter is true, the teaching about Nirvāna would be false.

In spite of Toynbee's use of the epithet "self-extinction" to denote the ideal set-up in Buddhism, it seems to be fairly clear from his references to the concept of Nirvāna (pp. 62, 63) that he quite rightly does not subscribe to the annihilationist view of Nirvāna, which has been discarded by scholars on the ground that it does not take account of the positive description of Nirvāna in the Pali Canon as also Buddha's own categorical denial that Nirvāna was annihilation. But Toynbee does not seem to take account of all the implications of this view. Just as much as it is man's duty to attain "self-extinction" it is equally a duty of his to attain ultimate reality, for "self-extinction" and "ultimate Reality" are paradoxically synonymous. The Buddha's view seems to have been that the categories of logic do not apply to Nirvāna (*atakkāvacara*). As such Nirvāna cannot strictly be described by positive or negative epithets. Positive epithets suggest empirical reality and negative ones annihilation, both of which are misleading. Nirvāna is a transcendent reality beyond space (*na katthaci kuhiñci*), beyond time since "the distinctions of past, present and future do not apply to it," and beyond causation (*na paṭiccasamuppannaṃ*). The passage from our finite self-centred existence to Nirvāna is pictured as one from bondage to freedom (*vimutti*) and power (*vasī*), from imperfection to perfection (*parisuddhi, parama-kusala*), from unhappiness to perfect happiness (*parama-sukha*), from ignorance to knowledge (*vijjā, aññā*), from finite consciousness to transcendent infinite consciousness (*ananta-viññāṇa*), from the impermanent to the permanent (*nicca*), from the unstable to the stable (*dhuva*), from fear and anxiety to perfect security (*abhaya*), from the evanescent to the ineffable (*amosadhamma*), from a state of mental illness to a state of perfect mental health[2], from darkness to light (*āloka*) etc.

In Mahāyāna we are familiar with the conception of the Buddha as embodying infinite wisdom (*mahāprajñā*) and infinite love (*mahākaruṇā*) but this conception seems to have its roots in the Pali Canon where Nirvāna is depicted not only as a state of perfect knowledge (*vijjā, aññā, jñāna*) but as a state in which the "boundless states" (*appamaññā*) of love (*mettā*), compassion (*karuṇā*), sympathetic joy (*muditā*) and equanimity (*upekkhā*) find their fulfilment (M I 297). Nirvāna is frequently defined as a state in which craving (*lobha*), hatred (*dosa*) and delusion (*moha*)

2. A II 143. Here diseases are classified as bodily (*kāyika-roga*) or mental (*cetasika-roga*) and it is said that while we have bodily diseases from time to time, mental illness is almost continual until Arahantship is attained so that only the saint can be said to have a perfectly healthy mind.

are completely extinguished, but with the elimination of hatred, for instance, perfect love (*mettā*) takes its place. One who has attained Nirvāna is therefore endowed with the finest qualities of compassion, utterly refined and removed from the slightest tinge of selfishness. With the total elimination of the finite self-centred qualities of craving, hate and delusion, the transcendent mind, shining with its natural lustre (*pabhassaraṃ cittaṃ*), is wholly filled with perfect renunciation and charity (*alobha, arāga, cāga*), loving-kindness (*mettā*) and perfect wisdom (*amoha, paññā*). So with the eradication of the selfish desires, love and compassion find their perfect expression.

In other words, far from it being inconsistent for one who has attained Nirvāna to minister and preach unto others out of pity and compassion, it would be quite natural for him to do so. He does this not out of earthly considerations of gain or glory or out of a sense of duty, for, as one who has attained the highest, he is described as one who is "free from debt" (*anaṇa*) and as one who has "discharged one's obligations" (*katakaraṇīya*) but because it would be just what such a person would quite naturally do by virtue of his attainment.

The role of love and compassion before and after the attainment of the ideal is not infrequently referred to in the texts. A person, for instance, who attains final salvation after the cultivation of these qualities of love, compassion and meditation is described as "one who is cleansed with an internal bathing" (*ayaṃ vuccati bhikkhave bhikkhu sināto antarena sinānena*; M I 39), and it is urged that this bathing is to be done not in the river but "in the waters of love and compassion for one's fellow beings" (*idheva sināhi brāhmaṇa sabbabhūtesu karohi khemataṃ*; M I 39). Consider again the following passage:

> In whatever monk who was covetous, covetousness is got rid of, who was malevolent, malevolence of mind is got rid of, ... wrath ... grudging ... hypocrisy ... spite ... jealousy ... stinginess ... treachery ... craftiness ..., who was of evil desires, evil desire is got rid of, who was of wrong view, wrong view is got rid of. He beholds himself purified of all these evil unskilled states, he beholds himself freed (*vimuttaṃ attānaṃ samanupassati*). When he beholds himself freed, delight is born; rapture is born from delight; when he is in rapture, the body is tranquil;

> when the body is tranquil, he experiences joy; being joyful the mind is concentrated. He dwells, suffusing one direction with a mind of loving-kindness (*mettāsahagatena cetasā*), likewise the second, likewise the third, likewise the fourth; just so above, below, across; he dwells having suffused the whole world everywhere, in every way with a mind of friendliness that is far-reaching, wide-spread, immeasurable, without enmity, without malevolence. He abides ... with a mind of compassion (*karuṇā*) ... with a mind of sympathetic joy (*muditā*) ... with a mind of equanimity (*upekkhā*) ... without enmity, without malevolence. It is as if there were a lovely lotus-pond with clear water, sweet water, cool water, limpid, with beautiful banks; and a man were to come along from the east, west, north or south, overcome and overpowered by the heat, exhausted, parched and thirsty and on coming to that lotus-pond might quench his thirst with water and quench his feverish heat. Even so ... one who has come into this *Dhamma* and discipline taught by the Buddha, having thus developed loving-kindness, compassion, sympathetic joy and equanimity attains inward calm. (M I 283)

That love and compassion cease or ought to cease with the attainment of Nirvāna is a basic misconception due to misunderstanding the nature of this ideal. It is quite expressly stated that the saint, who has attained perfection (*sampannakusalaṃ paramakusalaṃ uttamapattipattaṃ samaṇaṃ ayojjhaṃ*; M II 29), is endowed among other things with "right thoughts (*sammā-saṅkappa*) which do not require to be further disciplined" and these right thoughts include *ahiṃsā* (*avihiṃsā-saṅkappa*), which is a positive concept in Jainism and Buddhism.

That a person on attaining perfection, whether he be the Buddha or one of his disciples, ought to pass away immediately into Nirvāna without being a light unto the world by his example and teaching is an idea which is quite alien even to Hīnayāna ways of thinking. The Buddha exhorted his disciples who were Arahants to go and preach unto the world for the good and happiness of mankind (Vin I 21). Perhaps Toynbee was misled by the significance to be attached to the first "temptation" of the Buddha. According to the explanation in the Pali scriptures themselves, the Buddha's compassion is in no way compromised by his attainment of Nirvāna. He hesitates for a moment wondering as to whether he should preach, not because of any lessening or lack of love on his part for his fellow beings nor because he thought that Nirvāna "was a prize to be clutched" (p. 293) but because he wonders whether the world, immersed in and getting satisfaction from its petty self-centred desires, hates and its cherished erroneous beliefs, would hearken unto a teaching which involves a total abnegation of all this. His thoughts on this occasion as recorded in the scriptures are as follows: "Should I teach what I have found with difficulty? This Dhamma is not readily comprehensible to those given to craving and hate. It goes against the current, is subtle, profound and difficult of comprehension and as such those who are slaves to their desires and are enveloped in darkness, would fail to see its truths" (M I 168). It is only after he looks into the hearts and minds of men and sees that there are among them those who would understand that he decides to preach.

Love and compassion as ideals exemplified in the lives of Buddha and his disciples, far from being incompatible with the teaching of the Buddha, have a central place in Buddhism both as a means to the attainment of Nirvāna and in a refined and transcendent form comprising the goal itself. Nirvāna was only the extinction of the fires of greed, hate and delusion in the infinite waters of transcendent and unconditioned love and wisdom. When the Buddha or one of his disciples attained this transcendent state, he came back to make use of his psycho-physical personality to serve others until it passed away. The theory that it would be an act of selfishness to seek to share one's spiritual gains with another is unequivocally condemned by the Buddha in a sermon on the ethics of teaching. The Brahmin, Lohicca, holds the view, "If a religious person acquired some spiritual state, then he should tell no one else about it. For what can one man do for another? To tell others would be like the man who, having broken through an old bond, should entangle himself in a new one. Like that is this desire to preach to others; it is a form of selfishness. For what can man do for another?" (D I 224 ff). The Buddha dismisses this as a false and evil view (*pāpakaṃ diṭṭhigataṃ*) and among the reasons given for doing so is that such a person would be one who is lacking in love and sympathy for the welfare of others.

II

If the Buddha's life has value, as Toynbee grants, it would be difficult to see how his teaching, of which his life was an expression, lacks value. Here again Toynbee seems to entertain this view owing to a misunderstanding of Buddhist teaching. Let us consider his criticisms in detail. Toynbee says that the Hīnayāna account of human nature is defective: "If a twentieth-century inquirer, brought up in the Christian tradition, found oneself called upon to answer these questions as best as he could, no doubt he would be likely to declare in favour of Christianity and the Mahāyāna as against the Hīnayāna. On the question of fact, he would find the Hīnayāna's diagnosis superficial in its failure to distinguish between self-devoting and self-centred desires. He would find that a superficial diagnosis had led to a wrong valuation and a wrong prescription" (p. 291). Earlier in his work Toynbee seems to concede the distinction between good and bad desires, but both are to be suppressed for the attainment of Nirvāna: "If the Buddha was right, as surely he was, in holding that absolute detachment can be achieved only through the extinction of all desire whatsoever, then the Hīnayāna must require not only the suppression of desires that are ordinarily regarded as being selfish, such as those of personal pleasure, prosperity, and power for oneself, but also the suppression of desires that are ordinarily regarded as being altruistic, such as love and compassion for one's fellow sentient beings" (p. 64).

Although the analysis, classification and valuation of desires in Buddhism would not be the same as what Toynbee adopts, it would be quite incorrect to say that Buddhism fails to distinguish between self-devoting and self-centred desires. According to Buddhism, the springs of action are six-fold, comprising the three immoral bases of action (*akusala-mūla*), namely, craving (*lobha, rāga*), hate (*dosa*), and erroneous beliefs (*moha*), and the three moral bases of action (*kusala-mūla*) consisting of their opposites, selflessness (*alobha, cāga*), love (*adosa, mettā*) and wisdom (*amoha, paññā*). One of the terms generally translated as desire (*taṇhā*) literally means "thirst" (Skr. *tṛṣṇā*) and there are said to be three thirsts: the thirst for sensuous pleasures (*kāmataṇhā*), the thirst for selfish pursuits (*bhavataṇhā*) and the thirst for destruction (*vibhavataṇhā*). Of these the thirst for sensuous gratification (*kāmataṇhā, kāmarāga*) and the thirst for selfish pursuits (*bhavataṇhā*), such as the desire for self-preservation, self-continuity (personal immortality), self-assertion (power), self-display, self-respect, etc., arise from the basis (lit. root, *mūla*) of craving (*rāga*, i.e., *kāmarāga*, *bhavarāga*). The thirst for destruction (*vibhavataṇhā*) springs from (the root of) hate. These are the three forms of thirsts or desires, which continually seek and find temporary satisfaction (*tatratatrābhinandinī*) though ever remaining unsatisfied and provide the fuel for the process called the individual. The distinction made between these unwholesome desires (*taṇhā*) based on craving and hate, and righteous aspirations (*sammā-saṅkappa*) based on selflessness and love is so marked that the term "thirst" is not used to denote the latter. What springs from selflessness and love are not "thirsts" unlike the products of craving and hate. Love (*mettā*) is as such not termed a desire since a desire in the above sense of a "thirst" (*taṇhā*) is basically self-centred and its role would be to build the house that is the individual from birth to birth. Selflessness (*alobha, cāga*) and love (*mettā*) as the opposites of craving and hate, when they occur in their purest form, do not have these characteristics and are hence not considered desires in the sense of "thirsts." In fact, by not doing so, Buddhism recognises the wide gulf that exists between the two. Desires are narrow and selfish (*pamāṇakataṃ*), while selflessness and love are boundless (*appamāṇā*; M I 297). And what the Buddha recommends is the complete elimination and eradication of the former until the mind is entirely suffused by the latter in their most refined state. The distinction and opposition between the two as motives of action is often mentioned. For instance, it is said that "one's speech may be opportune or inopportune, true or false, gentle or harsh, useful or futile and inspired by love (*mettacitta*) or influenced by hate (*dosantarā*; M I 26)." The narrow desires are in fact to be eliminated by the development of the latter, their opposites. It is said that "by cultivating love (*mettaṃ bhāvayato*), ill-will (*byāpāda*) subsides." (M I 424)

The criticism is sometimes made that, although the cultivation of selflessness and love may be recommended as a means to an end, namely, in order to expel craving and hatred, they too have to be given up in order to attain the state of perfect detachment which is

Nirvāna. There are passages in the canon which *prima facie* appear to favour such a theory. It is said, for instance, that the mind's emancipation through love (*mettācetovimutti*) is conditioned (*abhisaṅkhata*) and as such, impermanent and liable to cease, and realising this, he attains the supreme secure state of Nirvāna (M I 351). To cite another instance, it is recommended that one should work for the cessation of evil habits (*akusalānaṃ sīlānaṃ nirodhāya paṭipanno*) as also for the cessation of good habits (*kusalānaṃ sīlānaṃ nirodhāya paṭipanno*) or for the cessation of good aspirations (*kusalānaṃ saṅkappānaṃ nirodhāya paṭipanno*; M II 26)." It is perhaps passages of this sort, which, if not carefully examined in their respective contexts, are likely to lead one to the conclusion that the Buddha recommends the suppression of both good and evil and that both are almost valued alike.

But if these very same passages are carefully studied in their contexts and on the general background of canonical thought, they would acquire quite a different meaning and significance. Let us take the passage that we have just referred to. Here the question is asked: "How should one conduct oneself in order to eliminate evil habits?" (M II 26). The answer given is that we should exercise our will (*chandaṃ janeti*) or master-desire as Toynbee would have it (see below) and, by a process of self-analysis and effort on our part, strive (a) to eliminate evil states that have arisen, (b) to be on our guard against the arising of evil states not arisen, (c) to make arise good states not arisen, and (d) to preserve (*thitiyā*), to not allow to fall into desuetude (*asammosāya*), to further develop (*bhiyyobhāvāya*), to bring to maturity (*vepullāya*), to cultivate (*bhāvanāya*) and to perfect (*pāripūriyā*) good states that have arisen. Evil, in other words, is to be eradicated and prevented from influencing us and part of the means for doing so is to cultivate the good. Now, in this same passage when we come to the question, "How is one to conduct oneself in order to eliminate good habits?" the answer given is precisely the same as the above, comprising (a), (b), (c) and (d). Indeed it would look paradoxical as to how one can eliminate good habits (*kusalānaṃ sīlānaṃ nirodhāya paṭipanno*) were not the crucial distinction drawn in this passage between "conditioned virtue" (*sīlamayo*) and perfected "natural virtue" (*silavā*). It is said that the perfect saint, who has attained final salvation (*cetovimuttiṃ paññāvimuttiṃ yathābhūtaṃ pajānāti*), is "naturally virtuous and not virtuous through conditioning" (*sīlavā hoti no ca sīlamayo*).

With regard to the elimination of the good aspirations, we find the same paradoxical statement that this is to be done by eliminating evil states of mind and cultivating the good states of mind to perfection and here again the saint "who has attained the highest perfection (*sampanna-kusalo*), the highest good (*parama-kusalo*) and the highest attainment (*uttama-pattipatto*)," is said to be, among other things, "endowed with righteous aspirations which do not need further refinement or disciplining (*asekhena sammā-saṅkappena samannāgato*)." This conception of the Arahant is surely far removed from that of a person who has attained a state of cold quietist indifferentism prior to extinction.

The distinction made in the Pali Canon is that of the conditioned (*saṅkhata*) goodness of those whose self-centred desires (i.e., the three-fold thirsts) are not completely eradicated and the pure goodness of the perfect ones or the Arahants in whom these thirsts or desires have been completely extinguished. The conditioned goodness requires further disciplining (Pali *sekha*; Sk. *śaikṣya* from the root *śikṣ*, to discipline, train) while the perfect goodness (*parama-kusala*) of the saint does not require such disciplining or further refinement (*asekha*). The latter is naturally virtuous (*sīlavā*) while the virtue of those who have not as yet attained perfection is artificial and conditioned (*sīlamayo*). This is no denial of the importance of selflessness and love, the cultivation of which is necessary though not sufficient for the extinction of the self-centred desires but a recognition of the extent to which these same self-centred desires may condition and dominate much of our so-called acts of selflessness and love, so that it is only on attaining the detachment (*virāga*) of Nirvāna that our love and compassion could be entirely disinterested. What passes for love and compassion is influenced consciously or unconsciously by our desire for gain or glory in earth or heaven and other such self-centred considerations such as fear of man or God. Disinterested love and compassion can arise only when the mind at all its levels is totally purged of all such self-centred desires and considerations.

III

Now, this goal, says Toynbee, "looks intrinsically unattainable." "Absolute detachment looks as if it might be intrinsically unattainable, because it is hard to see how the intensely arduous spiritual effort to detach oneself from all other desires can be achieved without attaching oneself to the single master-desire of extinguishing every desire save this. Is the extinction of the desire to desire nothing but the extinction of desire a psychological possibility?" (p. 64). To say that absolute detachment is "intrinsically unattainable" would of course imply that the claims made by the Buddha and some of his disciples to have attained such a state are in fact mistaken or false, but it is not primarily by an examination of these claims that Toynbee makes this assertion. Instead, he (a) asserts that the giving up of desires entails the presence of a single master-desire intent on eliminating all desires save this and (b) questions the psychological possibility of extinguishing this master-desire.

That the giving up of desires is to be accomplished by attaching oneself to a master-desire is precisely what Buddhism states: "Desires are to be given up depending on desire" (*taṇhaṃ nissāya taṇhaṃ pahātabbaṃ*; A II 146). This master-desire is more usually designated by the term "will" (*chanda*, sometimes translated as "desire," see *Kindred Sayings* V 239; also p. 243 fn.) and is defined as "the will to prevent the arising of evil states of mind not arisen, the will to keep out evil states of mind which have arisen, the will to make arise good states of mind which have not arisen and the will to preserve, develop, refine and perfect good states of mind which have arisen" (S V 268). In short, it is the will or desire to do away with the unwholesome desires ("thirsts," *taṇhā*) and to refine the wholesome states of mind to perfection by completely eliminating the impact of the former on the latter until these good states of mind (selflessness, love, wisdom) cease to be in the least affected by erroneous beliefs. This is the role of the master-desire which in a wider sense comprises the acts of will (*chanda*), the physical and mental energy (*viriya*), the thoughts (*citta*) and the mental investigations and analyses (*vīmaṃsā*) directed towards the above end. So, on this count, the Buddhism of the Pali Canon would have no quarrel with Toynbee's assertion that a master-desire would be necessary to give up every desire save this.

The disagreement would be with the next step of Toynbee, namely, his statement that it would be psychologically impossible to extinguish this master-desire. If by "the desire to desire nothing but the extinction of desire" Toynbee means "the master-desire," the objection would be "Is the extinction of the master-desire a psychological possibility?" But why is this psychologically impossible? Apart from the mere suggestion, Toynbee does not seem to make it at all clear as to why this is so. He does not provide any empirical grounds or logical reasons for holding that this would be psychologically impossible. Would he say that from what we know of the psychology of man it would by no means be likely for one to have a desire to do away with desires or to extinguish a desire to do away with desires? Now, Buddhism would grant that in desiring to do away with desires one would be going against the natural current (*paṭisotagāmī*) of the mind which continually seeks the gratification of its self-centred desires without ever finding satisfaction. But Buddhism would not grant that this is psychologically impossible and would point at least to the example of the Buddha and some of his disciples. It would be psychologically difficult particularly for those whose self-centred desires are strong but by no means psychologically impossible even for them.

On the other hand, is Toynbee's objection to the possibility of desiring the extinction of the master-desire primarily a logical one? Is he saying that just as much as we need have a master-desire to extinguish desire, it would seem necessary to have a super-master-desire to extinguish the master-desire and that this would lead to an infinite regress? And is he also suggesting that the master-desire like the first-order desires cannot achieve permanent satisfaction? If the objection is in this form, it has already been raised and met in the Pali Canon itself. A Brahmin asks Ānanda how desire can be fully extinguished since the extinction of desire by desire would be an unending process.

> "What is it, Master Ānanda, for which the holy life is lived under Gotama, the recluse"?
>
> "For the sake of abandoning desire (*chanda*), Brahmin, the holy life is lived under the Exalted One."
>
> "But is there any way, is there any practice, Master Ānanda, for the abandoning of desire?"

"There is a way, Brahmin, there is a practice for abandoning desire."

"Pray, Master Ānanda, what is that way and that practice?"

"Herein, Brahmin, a monk cultivates the basis of psychic power of which the features are desire (*chanda*) ... energy (*viriya*) ... thought (*citta*) ... investigation (*vīmaṃsā*) together with the co-factors of concentration and struggle. This, Brahmin, is the way, this is the practice for the abandoning of desire."

"If that be so, Master Ānanda, it were a task without end not one with an end. That he should get rid of desire by means of desire is an impossible thing."

"Then, Brahmin, I will just question you on this matter. Do you answer as you think fit.

"Now, what do you think, Brahmin? Was there not previously a desire in you (urging you) thus: 'I will go to the park?' When you got to the park was not that particular desire abated?"

"Yes, indeed it was, Master."

"Was there not previous energy (*viriya*) in you (urging you) thus: 'I will go to the park' ... thought (*citta*) in you ... deliberations (*vīmaṃsā*) in you ... When you got there did not energy ... thought ... deliberations subside?"

"Yes, indeed, Master."

"Very well, then, Brahmin. That monk who is an Arahant ... who is released by perfect insight—that desire which he had previously to attain Arahantship, now that Arahantship is won, that desire is abated ..." (*Kindred Sayings* V 243–45)

The argument is that logically the master-desire is not on the same footing as the first-order desires, for, unlike these self-centred desires which continually seek gratification without being permanently satisfied, the master-desire would achieve final satisfaction and be extinguished with the eradication of the self-centred desires.

IV

The next criticism is posed in the form of the question as to whether the pursuit of absolute detachment, if feasible, is also good: "They sought to detach themselves from every form of mundane society and beyond that from the lust of mundane life itself; and the very sincerity and resoluteness with which these Hīnayāna Buddhist philosophers pursued their spiritual quest raise two questions: Is absolute detachment an attainable objective? And supposing it to be attainable, is the pursuit of it a good activity?" (pp. 63, 64). Perhaps this criticism, which was based on the misconception that love and compassion were extinguished in Nirvāna along with the self-centred desires, is already met in so far as we have pointed out that these good states of mind, far from being effaced in Nirvāna, are refined and perfected so that they are no longer dependent on the egoistic base of the self-centred desires.

Yet the objection may be raised in another form. It may be asked how love and compassion can be cultivated in the abstract by cutting oneself away from the life of society for the sake of one's own salvation. Is this not a radically egoistic pursuit in itself? Is not the ethic of Hīnayāna Buddhism rooted in the idea of achieving one's own salvation with no concern for others and even one may say at the expense of others who have to provide with their toil and sweat the basic necessities of life without which even their selfish ascetic existence would not even be possible?

This picture does not do justice to the Buddhist conception of the religious life. The Buddha does not say that the contemplative life (*vita contemplativa*), lived apart from the active life of society, was essential even to seek the goal of Nirvāna in this life itself, although there is no doubt that the contemplative life was recommended in view of the better opportunities that it provides the individual. The life of the Buddhist contemplative, i.e., the monk, is not the same as that of the ascetic who retires from the world. He dwells aloof from society but nevertheless in society giving moral guidance and spiritual instruction to laymen. This work of his for society is considered as valuable as the production of mundane goods and services on the part of the other members of the society. Although he seeks to achieve the final goal by his own individual effort, yet the means of achieving it as well as the goal itself is stamped with selflessness. If he achieves his goal he continues to be of the greatest service to others because of his spiritual knowledge and attainments with no expectation whatsoever of earthly or heavenly reward.

Can such a life be called egoistic? Although the term "egoist" strictly refers to an individual who seeks his own welfare, we normally use the term to denote one who seeks primarily his personal material welfare even at the expense of others. But would a person who seeks primarily his own spiritual welfare at the expense of his material welfare or even his life, and seeks it partly by his selfless service in the present and in order to be of the greatest service to others in the future, rightly be called an egoist? In so far as he seeks primarily his own spiritual welfare until he reaches the goal he may be called an enlightened egoist. But in so far as he does this by cultivating a selfless love for his fellow beings, culminating in a state of perfect selfless love, which enables him to live the rest of his life solely in the service of others, it would at the same time be the life of an enlightened altruist. Buddhism holds to the principle that one cannot save another without first saving oneself. The Buddha tells Cunda, "It is not possible for one who is stuck in the mud to help another out but it is possible for one who is not stuck in the mud to help another who is stuck in the mud. It is not possible that a man who has not saved himself can save another but it is possible for a man who has saved himself to save another" (M I 46).

Toynbee says that "the Mahāyāna Buddhist's verdict on the Hīnayāna philosopher can be summed up in an inversion of the Scribes' and Pharisees' jibe at Christ on the Cross: "He saved himself; others he cannot save" (p. 65). The Hīnayāna philosopher's reply would be: "He saved himself so that others he can save." The Buddha first trained his disciples to be Arahants and then sent them into the world to work and preach for the good and happiness of mankind. It would seem odd to call egoists these Arahants (who like Puṇṇa went among unknown peoples ready to meet the worst persecution and even death with hearts of love). The ethical ideal recommended in the Pali Canon, as representative of the Hīnayāna viewpoint, is that of enlightened egoism-cum-altruism, the one being dependent on the other. The Buddha says, "Monks, there are these four persons in the world.

What four? He who is neither bent on his own welfare nor on the welfare of others; he who is bent on the welfare of others but not his own; he who is bent on his own welfare but not of others; and he who is bent on the welfare both of himself as well as of others. He who is bent on the welfare of oneself as well as of others is of these four persons the chief and best, topmost, highest and supreme" (A II 95). According to this valuation the best of all people is he who works for his own good as well as for the good of others, there being no conflict between the two ends when the good happen to be moral and spiritual.

Some Aspects of the Bhagavad-Gīta and Buddhist Ethics

Comparing the ethical teachings of the Bhagavad-Gīta (= Gīta) with Buddhism, Rādhakrishnan in his *Indian Philosophy* (pp. 526–27) makes the following observations: "Both protest against the absolute authority of the *Vedas* and attempt to relax the rigours of caste by basing it on a less untenable foundation. Both are manifestations of the same spiritual upheaval which shook the ritualistic religion though the Gīta was the more conservative, and therefore a less thorough-going protest.... In the descriptions of the ideal man the Gīta and Buddhism agree. As a philosophy and religion the Gīta is more complete than Buddhism which emphasises overmuch the negative side. The Gīta adopts the ethical principles of Buddhism while it, by implication, condemns the negative metaphysics of Buddhism as the root of all unbelief and error."

The impression that this passage leaves in the mind of the reader is that the Gīta, though less critical of the *Vedic* tradition than Buddhism, nevertheless adopts, on the whole, the ethical principles of Buddhism and gives them a less extremist interpretation on the background of a more satisfying positive metaphysics. Now, whatever the difference of opinions that scholars have about the origin of the Gīta, they seem generally to agree that the work in its present form is eclectic in character and contains in it many strands of Hindu thought somewhat loosely knit together. As such it is not surprising that the *jñānamārga* (way of intuitive knowledge) of the *Upaniṣads* should be well represented. Now, it is from these passages (i.e., II.55–72; IV.16–25; V.18–28; XII.13–16) that Rādhakrishnan quotes in support of his statement that "in the descriptions of the ideal man the Gīta and Buddhism agree." But this agreement in the content of these passages which idealise the *muni* or the "contemplative seer" (II.56; V.28; XII.19) is understandable for there is much in common between the way of salvation in Buddhism and the *jñānamārga* of the *Upaniṣads*, and to this extent, the ideal man and the ideal life pictured in each is very much similar. It may also be granted that the Gīta references to this life have a more Buddhist tone than the *Upaniṣads* in that phrases and concepts more typically Buddhist than Hindu such as *rāga-dveṣa* (II.64), *maitri* (XII.13), *kāruṇya* (XII.13) and *Nirvāṇa* (II.72) occur among them, betraying possible Buddhist influence on the Gīta.

But surely the Buddhist ideal is at variance with the *jñānamārga* of the *Upaniṣads*, if we go by the main trend of its thought and its special emphases, which show a persistent and distinct preference for the Personal conception of God as against the Impersonal, for devotion (*bhakti*) as against abstract meditation on the impersonal Absolute, and for the path of disinterested action based on moral imperatives (*karmayoga* and *svadharma*) as against the way of contemplative knowledge (*jñānamārga*). It is true that in this respect the Gīta contradicts itself or at least provides only a very loose synthesis of doctrines apparently mutually inconsistent. For instance, although it is essential and generally maintained that the worship of the Personal Lord is better than meditation on the Impersonal Being (XII.I,2) which is unmanifested (*avyaktaṃ*), yet it is expressly mentioned earlier that "men of no understanding think of Me, the Unmanifest (*avyaktaṃ*) as having manifestation (*vyaktiṃ āpannaṃ*) not knowing my higher nature" (VII.24).

These two conceptions of God show up the inconsistency of the Gīta teaching. On the one hand we are told that the highest intuition of God reveals his Being as Impersonal, and without this intuition salvation is not possible. On the other hand it is said that worship of God as Personal (which necessarily entails an erroneous conception of the divine being according to the former view) is the easier, the more proper and the natural path to salvation, thus implying that entertaining an erroneous conception is not only no bar to salvation but is in fact the better path to it.

The same inconsistency is manifest where the life of the *muni* or sage, who on attaining perfection, is in no need of work that needs to be done (III.17) is represented, on the one hand, to be the ideal while the life of disinterested action is more often held up as the superior (V.2; VI.2), though both guarantee salvation (V.5).

Yet notwithstanding this divergence of doctrines in the Gīta we should not overlook the fact that the ideal man as portrayed in the main teaching of the Gīta is far removed from the *Upaniṣadic* ideal of the contemplative seer even though an *Upaniṣad* like the *Īśā* is almost an epitome of the religious philosophy of the Gīta while the contemplative seer finds a place, though not an important place, in the total background of Gīta teaching. The Gīta ideal is the man of action, who performs his social duties purely out of a sense of obligation and devotion to God.

In the circumstances it would be unfair both by the Gīta as well as by Buddhism to say that "in the descriptions of the ideal man the Gīta and Buddhism agree" merely on the ground of the similarity between the Buddhist sage and the contemplative seer of the *Upaniṣads* for whom the Gīta finds a not too important place in the scheme of things. If therefore we study the Gīta ideal in relation to the Buddhist, it is at the level of social ethics that we have to make the comparison, no doubt on the general background of the metaphysics of each.

Now, it would seem from the statements of Rādhakrishnan (e.g., the passage quoted above) that even at the level of social ethics there is a similarity rather than a disparity in the ethical attitudes and outlook of the Gīta and Buddhism. I propose to show that this is by no means the case and that in this respect the ethics of the Gīta is to be contrasted rather than compared with the ethics of Buddhism. For this purpose I would like to show that there is a significant radical disparity between the attitude of the Gīta and that of Buddhism at least on the problem of war and the belief in caste.

But before we go into the details of these problems it is necessary to point out that the fundamental difference between the metaphysical background of the ethical doctrines of the Gīta and of Buddhism is not that the metaphysics of the Gīta is positive and that of Buddhism is negative as Rādhakrishnan has tried to point out, but that the Gīta metaphysics throughout maintains a deterministic view of the universe and of all events in it, while Buddhism on the contrary vehemently upholds free will though granting the causal relatedness of events. This seems to be the essential difference between the metaphysical standpoints of the Gīta and Buddhism touching ethics.

It would seem that one of the fundamental prerequisites of ethical action is that man should be free to choose between alternative courses of action open to him and should be solely responsible for the decisions he makes. If this is not granted moral injunctions would appear to lose their point. No one would deny that the Gīta contains moral advice, but this advice, it should be noted, is given in a context in which it seems on the whole to be taken for granted that the actions of men are strictly determined by Nature (*prakr̄ti*), which is controlled by the fiat of God. Nothing is more striking than the advice that Arjuna, who has been seeking an answer to the moral question as to whether he should fight or not, gets in the last chapter, where he is told that he has no choice in the matter for "if indulging in self-conceit you think, 'I will not fight,' vain is this your resolve. Nature will compel you" (*prakr̄tis tvāṃ niyokṣyati*; XVIII.59), notwithstanding the statement that "he may ponder over it fully and do as he chooses" (XVIII.63).

This deterministic role or compelling power of *prakr̄ti* or Nature over which the individual has no control is one of the basic themes of the Gīta and reference is often made to it. Thus in making a case for the necessity for action (*karma*) one of the arguments employed is that for individuals action is inevitable "for no one can remain even for a moment without doing work; everyone is made to act (*karma kāryate*) helplessly (*avaśāḥ*) by the impulses born of Nature" (*prakr̄tijaiḥ*; XVIII.5). It would appear that individuals cannot help but act and that their actions are the mere working out of impulses generated by Nature (*prakr̄ti*) over which they have no control whatsoever—a fact which is clearly indicated by the term "*avaśāḥ*," which implies that the individual "has no power of mind" to offset the force of the impulses which dominate his actions. Later in the same chapter it is argued that this dominant power of Nature, under whose yoke man can but only humbly submit, afflicts even the man of knowledge for "even the man of knowledge (*jñānavān*) acts in accordance with his own Nature (*prakr̄ti*). Beings follow their Nature (*prakr̄tiṃ yānti bhūtāni*). What can repression accomplish?" (III.33). Saṃkara here interprets *prakṛti* to mean "the sum total of the good and evil mental dispositions due to past actions manifest in this life." (*Prakṛti nāma pūrvakṛtadharmādisaṃskāro vartamānajanmādāvabhivyaktaḥ.*) Rādhakrishnan however explains that this verse seems to suggest the omnipotence of Nature over the soul and requires us to act according to our Nature, the law of our being, and adds that "it does not follow that we should indulge in every impulse. It is a call to find out our true being and give expression to it" (*The Bhagavadgita*, p. 146). Yet if we take this verse for what it states in the context of the traditional comment of Saṃkara it is clear that *prakṛti* here does not mean "our true being" as opposed to our false nature, but our being as composed of all the modes which have potencies for both good and evil; and what the verse implies is not that we should not indulge in every impulse but that we cannot help but give vent to our impulses which we are unable to suppress, in that we are under the domination of *prakṛti.*

The relation of this *prakṛti* with the Supreme Being appears to be differently conceived in different contexts. On the one hand the omnipotence of the Supreme Being requires that he should be the ultimate cause and ground for the operations of *prakṛti.* On the other hand since the Supreme Being is transcendent though immanent in every individual it was necessary that his being should be conceived apart from the operations of *prakṛti.* We thus find it stated in one place that the Supreme Being sends forth the multitude of beings fixing the *prakṛti* of each: "I send forth again and again this multitude of beings who are helpless (*avaśaṃ*) under the power of *prakṛti* (*prakṛter vaśāt*) having fixed the *prakṛti* of each (*prakṛtiṃ svāṃ avaṣṭabhya*)."[3] But in another context, *svabhāva* or inherent nature, which is the same as *prakṛti* in connotation (see below), is said to operate independently of the Supreme Being: "The Lord does not create for the world agency or acts; nor does he connect acts with their consequences. It is inherent nature which works these out" (V.14).

3. IX.8. Rādhakrishnan translates *prakṛtiṃ svāṃ avaṣṭabhya* as "taking hold of nature which is my own." Even this translation would grant the ultimate power over *prakṛti* to God, but to take *svāṃ* as "each one's own" is more consistent with the Sanskrit idiom.

Here the word *svabhāva* is used in a context in which *prakṛti* would have fitted equally well. *Svabhāva* or "intrinsic nature" is here regarded as the ultimate agent or cause of all action as well as what brings about the natural consequences of these, very much in the manner in which *prakṛti* was considered to perform this role in similar contexts (Cp. XVIII.59; III.33). But the use of the word *svabhāva* is much more significant in this context, where *svabhāva* is said to function independently of the Lord, since the word seems in its origin to have reference to a theory which gave a purely mechanistic or deterministic account of the universe without theistic assumptions.

The earliest reference we have is possibly the *Śvetāsvatara Upaniṣad* (I.2), where *svabhāva* along with time (*kāla*), fate (*niyati*), etc., are mentioned as possible alternatives to the theistic explanation of the universe. Again, Jñānavimala, commenting on the *Praśnavyākaraṇa Sūtra* (no. 7), says that "some believe that the universe was produced by *svabhāva* and that everything comes about by *svabhāva* alone." Then in the *Tarkarahasya-dīpikā*, a commentary on the *Ṣaḍdarśana-samuccaya* (ed. L. Suali, Calcutta, 1905, p. 13), we find Guṇaratna quoting from the upholders of the theory of *svabhāva* a stanza which says, "What makes the sharpness of thorns and the varied nature of beasts and birds? All this comes about by *svabhāva*. There is nothing which acts at will. What is the use of effort?" This shows that the term *svabhāva* had reference to a theory which maintained that the universe was strictly determined and that all the processes in it were fully explicable in terms of such determinism and as a result denied free will and the value of human effort to alter the course of events.

We cannot be certain whether the author of the Gīta was trying to synthesise *svabhāva-vāda* as well into its general metaphysic. It is also difficult to determine the exact relationship between the workings of *prakṛti* or *svabhāva* and the Supreme Being of the Gīta, since on a monistic or monotheistic interpretation the *prakṛti* or *svabhāva* would be ultimately dependent on Deity, while on a dualistic Sāṅkhya analysis they would be independent (*prakṛtiṃ puruṣaṃ caiva/ viddhyanādyubhāvapi*; XIII.19). And the Gīta does not seem to support wholeheartedly one interpretation, although the emphasis on a Personal God as the highest reality, lends support to the monotheistic rather than the dualistic analysis. But so much seems to be clear, that whatever interpretation we adopt and whatever the import of moral injunctions in the Gīta, the Gīta metaphysic is thoroughly deterministic and as such is opposed to the doctrine of free will and to the possible value of human effort since human beings are helpless (*avaśāḥ*) in the predicaments in which they are placed.

It is, therefore, to be expected that in the last chapter, after a long-winded argument, Arjuna should be told that Nature (*prakṝti*), over which he has no control, "will compel him" to fight. It is also not surprising that one of the arguments employed to urge Arjuna to fight should be that "his enemies are already slain by God before the event" (*mayi'vai' nihatāḥ pūrvam-eva;* XI.33) or that "he should kill them and not desist since they are already doomed by him" (*mayā hātans tvaṃ jahi mā vyatiṣṭhāḥ*; XI.34) and that he is not ultimately responsible morally for their death since "he is to be only an occasion (or an instrument) for God's action" (*nimittamātram bhava*; XI.33). The metaphysical import and ethical significance of this argument has been well expressed in the words of Rādhakrishnan himself where he says that "the writer seems to uphold the doctrine of divine predestination and indicate the utter helplessness and insignificance of the individual and the futility of his will and effort. The decision is made already and Arjuna can do nothing to change it. He is a powerless tool in God's hands.... Arjuna should feel, 'Nothing exists save your will. You alone are the doer and I am only the instrument'" (*The Bhagavadgita,* p. 280, 1).

Very much on the same lines is another argument as to why Arjuna should fight, namely, that since salvation is predestined and assured for all beings including Arjuna there is no cause for worry and he should carry out his allotted task whatever this may be. "Beings originate in the unmanifest (*avyakta*), in the middle they are manifest and they would be immersed in the unmanifest in the end. So why worry?" (II.28).

Attainment of the state of *avyakta* or the unmanifest, which is the highest state of the absolute (VII.24), is equivalent to salvation, so that what is implied in this verse is that all beings would finally attain salvation in spite of the many vicissitudes they would have to go through in the course of their evolution and this is predetermined or predestined by the fiat of God.

If we compare this deterministic or fatalistic ethic and metaphysics with that of Buddhism, we find that the latter is totally opposed to it. Not only do the Buddhist texts repeatedly uphold the doctrine of free will and the value of human effort in offsetting the burden of the past and altering the course of the future, but they strongly condemn all types of metaphysical theories which give a deterministic or fatalistic account of the universe.

One such metaphysical theory, which is often singled out for criticism in the Buddhist texts, is that of Makkhali Gosāla and this theory is condemned because of its unmitigated fatalism. Now, in this respect, it would appear that there is much in common between the metaphysics of the Gīta and the philosophy of Makkhali. Makkhali denies the value of personal effort or human endeavour (*natthi attakāre ... natthi purisākāre ... natthi ... purisaparakkamo*; D I 53); so does the Gīta when it says that "mental suppression (of the impulses) can accomplish nothing" (III.33). There is even verbal agreement in the description of the state of man and the processes of nature. "All beings" (*sabbe sattā, sabbe bhūtā*), according to Makkhali, "are devoid of the power of will" (*avasā*), an epithet frequently used in the Gīta to denote the same (e.g., *sarvaḥ ..., avaśaḥ,* everyone is devoid of the power of will [III.5], *bhūtagrāmam ... avaśaḥ prakṝter vaśāt,* the multitude of beings helpless without the power of will on account of the power of *prakṝti*). Man is thus impotent in the Gīta since he is subject to the power of *prakṝti* or *svabhāva*; in the philosophy of Makkhali all beings are impotent and helpless in that they are "subject to Destiny (*niyati*), Fate (*saṅgati*) and Nature" (*bhāva-pariṇatā*; D I 53). As A. L. Basham says, "*Bhava* seems in this context to be synonymous with *svabhāva*, i.e. inherent character or nature. It suggests, below the fundamental category of *niyati*, sets of conditions and characteristics in each entity which, acting as factors subordinate to the great principle, control growth, development and rebirth" (*History and Doctrines of the Ājīvikas*, London, 1950, p. 226). There is yet another significant feature in respect of which the two philosophies seem to agree. Salvation as taught by Makkhali is predestined for each individual "for, just as a ball of thread when thrown would unwind itself to the end, the wise and fools alike will attain salvation after journeying through *saṃsāric* states" (D I 54). This view has been called *saṃsāra-suddhi*

(D I 54; cf. M I 81) or salvation through transmigration and has been more explicitly referred to in a stanza in the *Jātakas* where the dependence of salvation on destiny is clearly brought out. "There is no open door to salvation, Bījaka. Await thy destiny (*niyati*). Joy or sorrow is obtained by destiny. All beings are purified through transmigration (*saṃsāra-suddhi*); so do not make haste (to attain) what is to come" (J-a VI 229).

It would be seen that these sentiments are very similar to what is found in a stanza of the Gīta (II.28) where it is said that "the beings who originate in the unmanifest reality and live in a manifest state in the middle will eventually attain the unmanifest reality. So why worry?" The context of this stanza of the Gīta reveals the import of the argument, namely, that Arjuna should not desist from fighting since his ultimate salvation as well as that of all beings including his enemies is assured. In fairness to the Gīta, however, it must be mentioned that this doctrine of the inevitability of salvation appears to go against the grain of the moral advice of the Gīta (XVIII.64–6), although it is implicit in its deterministic metaphysics.

How strongly these doctrines, which denied free will and the value of human effort and proclaimed the inevitability of salvation, have been condemned in Buddhism may be seen by the references which Buddha makes to Makkhali and his theories in the Pali texts. In one place the Buddha says that he knows of no other person (than Makkhali) born to the detriment and disadvantage of so many people, comparing him to a fisherman casting his net at the mouth of a river for the destruction of many fish (A I 33). In another passage his doctrines are said to be the worst of all the doctrines of the recluses (A I 286).

There is also the pointed reference to and a criticism of aspects of these doctrines when taken up separately. Very often the denial of free will (*akiriyavāda*) is denounced. It is said that "the view that there is no free will when as a matter of fact there is free will is a false view" (M I 405). The value of personal effort (*attakāro*), no doubt in making the future course of events different from what they would otherwise be, is often stressed and it is maintained that there is such a thing as initiative (*ārabbha-dhātu*), enterprise (*nikkama-dhātu*), endeavour (*parakkama-dhātu*), courage (*thāma-dhātu*), perseverance (*ṭhiti-dhātu*) and human instrumentality (*upakkama-dhātu*; A III

337 ff) against the determinists who denied such a factor in human undertakings. The doctrine that salvation would be attained in due course by faring on in *saṃsāra* or the empirical states of existence is also severely criticised; it is said that "the goal of existence (i.e. salvation), where there is neither birth nor decay, cannot be realised by merely faring on (*gamanena*; A II 48).

The main difference between the determinism of Makkhali and that of the Gīta is of course the fact that the latter is theistic. Though the Gīta would grant that all activity is directed by the operations of *prakṝti* over which we have no control, it would, as we have shown above, submit that *prakṝti* would find its ultimate sanction in the Divine Being, though there were passages betraying the dualistic Sāṅkhya analysis that the Divine Essence was quite separate from the workings of *prakṝti*. Saṃkara's comment that *prakṝti* was the sum total of good and evil mental dispositions of actions committed in the past (*pūrvakṝta*) is more in accord with the latter view and is an attempt to explain the present and the future in terms of the past activity of the individual. On the other view which appears to be the dominant one, the *prakṝti* of each individual is fixed at creation in accordance with the prescience and providence of the divine will. Now, it is worth noting that Buddhism distinguishes between these two types of determinism, though condemning both of them unequivocally. One is the theory that our present actions are fully determined by the actions of the past (*pubbe-kata-hetu*; A I 173–175) and that we are in no sense free to act. The other is that all our actions are fixed in their entirety by the fiat of God (*issaranimmāṇavāda*; A I 173–175); as Rādhakrishnan (op. cit. p. 229) would say, "there is nothing however small or insignificant that has not been ordained or permitted by God even to the fall of a sparrow." Now, it is significant that both these theories are condemned in the Pali canonical texts (A I 173–175) and with it the framework of Gīta metaphysics which appears to synthesise both these theories.

In spite of the deterministic background of the Gīta ethic there is no doubt that there is much in common between the moral injunctions of the Gīta and of Buddhism and this is not surprising considering the eclecticism of the Gīta. But it is equally important to stress the differences especially when these differences are fundamental to the philosophy of each and reveal mutually opposed ethical attitudes to the problems of life. I propose to illustrate these differences by taking up the divergent attitudes that Buddhism and the Gīta adopt in respect of the problem of war and caste.

I would hold that the attitude to war in the Gīta is totally opposed to that of Buddhism. Yet, before we could illustrate the differences in the attitudes of each, it would be necessary to clarify the Gīta attitude to the problem of war. I would hold that the Gīta maintains that it is the moral duty of the soldier to fight in the event of any war in which the state is engaged. Rādhakrishnan's interpretation of the Gīta appears to be fundamentally different in that he seems to believe that the Gīta speaks of war only in a metaphorical sense as referring to the moral struggle in man and nature and not to military action. Thus, commenting on the opening verse of the Gīta, Rādhakrishnan (op. cit., p. 79) takes *dharma-kṣetre* to refer to the world instead of taking it as an epithet of *kuru-kṣetre*, the classical home of Vedic dharma. He says, "The world is *dharmakṣetra*—the battle ground for a moral struggle." Then again, commenting on the phrase *māmānusmara yudhya ca* ("remember me and fight"; VIII.7) he says (op. cit., p. 229): "It is not a fight on the material plane that is intended here for it cannot be done at all times. It is the fight with the powers of darkness that we have to carry on perpetually." This metaphorical interpretation is often reinforced by frequent attempts to give the figurative meaning of otherwise literal statements. Thus Gīta I.14, which states that "Kṛṣṇa and Arjuna blew their celestial conches when stationed in their great chariot yoked to white horses," is to be taken metaphorically for, says Rādhakrishnan (p. 85), "throughout the Hindu and Buddhist literature the chariot stands for the psycho-physical vehicle. The steeds are the senses, the reins their controls, but the charioteer, the guide, is the spirit of real self, *ātman*. Kṛṣṇa, the charioteer, is the spirit in us."

However ingenious Rādhakrishnan's attempt may be to give a metaphorical account of the Gīta injunctions to fight, it does not appear to be successful, for the greater majority of the passages containing references to war, far from admitting of metaphorical interpretation, have sense only when taken literally. On the other hand, the few passages which may possibly be interpreted metaphorically are so interpreted only at the cost of obscuring their meaning, especially when we consider their contexts. Thus the fact that Kṛṣṇa and Arjuna are stationed in their chariots is mentioned in a general description of the battle field and the events taking place in it. If we interpret "chariot" here to mean the psycho-physical vehicle and Kṛṣṇa as representing the spirit in us, as Rādhakrishnan does, it would be difficult to explain in similar terms the other paraphernalia of war mentioned, as well as the significance of the numerous other personalities besides Kṛṣṇa who are mentioned by name. And again the only passage which Rādhakrishnan adduces as not admitting of a literal explanation (VIII.7) would be given a more natural interpretation if "*sarveṣu kāleṣu*" is taken as qualifying the nearest verb "*anusmara*" rather than "*yudhya*" and the stanza translated, "therefore remember me at all times but fight."

On the other hand an analysis of the positive injunctions to fight would show that it was at least incumbent on a soldier (*kṣatriya*) to fight in the event of a war in which the state is engaged, for fighting in such a war is always part of his dharma or social duty as being one of the demands made by the state on the soldier. It is said that "having regard to his own duty the *kṣatriya* should not falter, for there exists no greater good for a *kṣatriya* than a war enjoined by duty" (II.31). It is true that there are injunctions to the effect that the fight should be undertaken with selfless motives in a spirit of self-denial "free from desire and egoism" (III. 30; VIII. 7) and that fighting regardless of consequences, "treating alike pleasure and pain, gain and loss, victory and defeat," brings with it no sin (II.38). Even if we grant that it is psychologically possible to engage in war "free from desire and egoism," the effect of these passages is more or less nullified by the numerous appeals made to selfish reasons as grounds for fighting. Thus moral grounds appear to be set aside when it is said that the refusal to fight amounts to "unmanliness" (II.3). Failure to answer the call to fight is "ignoble and un-Aryan and causes disgrace on earth" (II.2). Warriors who desist from fighting "incur ill-fame, and ill-fame is worse than death" (II.34,5). Could anything be sadder, it is asked, than hearing the taunts of his enemies (II.36), e.g., "If you are victorious you enjoy the earth" (XI.33) and "if slain you go to heaven" (XI.37). Fighting in a war enjoined as duty by the state is an open door to heaven (II.32). The general impression these passages seem to leave in the mind of the reader is that the Gīta is recommending the soldier to fight at any cost in a war in which the state is engaged. If he fights with selfless motives (and the psychological possibility of this many people would be inclined to doubt), he incurs no sin, whereas if he fights with selfish motives he would still stand to profit either by the gain and honour on earth or by the glory in heaven.

This teaching, that the soldier should fight at any cost in such a war, is reinforced by the metaphysical arguments in support of war. It is implied that Arjuna should not feel for the death of his enemies among whom were his teachers and kinsmen, since "wise men do not grieve for the dead or the living" (II.11). Now, it is true that according to the best teaching of the *Upaniṣads* and Buddhism, those who have transcended and overcome the world do not entertain thoughts of grief. But to argue that the soldier should likewise "not grieve for the dead" is to commit the fallacy that, since the wise do not grieve for the dead, those who do not grieve for the dead are wise. Then there are those arguments which seem to imply that the soldier is in fact not morally responsible for the act of killing either because he is not a moral agent as he is devoid of free will and is not morally responsible for his actions (as discussed above) or that since God is finally and solely responsible for the death of Arjuna's enemies in that "his enemies are doomed," Arjuna is only an instrument in God's hands (I.33,4). Finally, it is argued on metaphysical grounds that physical killing is not in reality killing, for the souls of people are eternal (II.12) and indestructible (II 17–25) and "one is not slain when the body is slain" (II.O).

The contrast between the Gīta attitude to war and the Buddhist is brought out in the advice Buddha gave when he was placed in a similar situation to that of Kr̥ṣṇa on the eve of a battle between his own people, the Sākyas, and their blood brothers, the Koliyas. The immediate cause for going to battle was that the Sākya and Koliya tribes were both making claims and demands on the waters of the river Rohiṇī, which flowed between their territories. The soldiers or *kṣatriyas* on each side were assembled (as the Kurūs and Pāṇḍavas had assembled) when the Buddha intervenes and asks them what the war was about. The answer was that it was over water and the Buddha asks them what the water was worth, to which it was replied that it was worth little.

It turns out that both sides in their folly were prepared to sacrifice the invaluable lives of their soldiers for the sake of water which was of little worth. And the futility of their war becomes apparent when the Buddha advises them in the words, "Why on account of some water of little worth would you destroy the invaluable lives of these soldiers?" (J-a V 412–4). The merits and demerits of the war as a whole are judged here by its possible consequences, and the suggestion seems to be that the causes for which wars are fought and lost are trivial in comparison with the human sacrifices involved. While the Gīta held that victory brings in its train honour and the gain of a kingdom (XI.33) while annihilation secures the reward of heaven (X.32), the Buddha (commenting on the war between kings Ajātasattu and Pasenadi) is supposed to have said that "victory arouses enmity and the defeated live in sorrow" (S I 83). Wars result only in further wars, according to Buddhism, for "the victor obtains for himself a vanquisher" (S I 85). War, as such, is condemned as an evil since it involves the destruction of invaluable human lives, and such evils, we are told, should not be committed even though it be deemed that it is part of one's duties to one's king (*rañño rājakaraṇīyaṃ kātuṃ*; M II 188–191). It is therefore not surprising that the life of the soldier was looked down upon in Buddhism and even "trading in the weapons of war" (*sattha-vaṇijjā*) was considered a wrong mode of livelihood (A III 208).

This seems to be the antithesis of the Gīta attitude to war and the fact may be further illustrated if we go into the details. It seems to have been an epic tradition that "the warrior who falls in the battle ground while fighting attains heaven" (*Mahābhārata, Udyogaparva* 32,65). As such it finds expression in the Bhagavad-Gīta, where it is said that "if slain you shall go to heaven" (II.37) and "happy are the *kṣatriyas* for whom such a war comes of its own accord as an open door to heaven" (II.32). Now, this tradition finds mention in the Buddhist texts where a warrior chief (*yodhājīvo gāmaṇi*) tells the Buddha that he has heard from his ancestral teachers in the martial arts that the spirited soldier who fights with zeal and slays his opponents in battle is rewarded by being born in the company of gods in heaven. The warrior chief wants to know whether this is so and Buddha's reply is that on the contrary he is born in hell for his actions (S IV 308–309).

It is therefore not surprising that it is Arjuna's attitude, which is condemned in the Gīta, that would appear to be similar to the Buddhist. Although *ahiṃsā* or non-violence is mentioned in the Gīta (X. 5; XIII. 7; XVI. 2; XVII. 14) as one among a list of virtues, nowhere is the concept woven into the central themes of Gīta philosophy and it is difficult to see how a soldier, whose duty is to fight and kill as many of the enemies as possible, can exercise *ahiṃsā* in these acts. The injunction to fight is therefore a negation of the ideal of *ahiṃsā* and the only representative, if at all, of the philosophy of *ahiṃsā* in the Gīta seems to be Arjuna. Arjuna's indecision and anxiety are not due to any lack of courage on his part but arise out of a moral conflict. On the one hand the love of his enemies for whom he feels compassion (I. 28; II. 2), a typically Buddhist virtue, makes him desist from the fight but on the other hand he is not sure whether it is not his duty to fight. The Gīta resolves the conflict by dismissing the former and making a case for the latter alternative. As such it would not be fair when Arjuna calls his a "mood of sentimental self-pity" (*The Bhagavadgita* p. 98), for, in a Buddhist context, Arjuna would have resolved the conflict by being a "conscientious objector" or non-resister who considered it his moral duty not to fight, without blindly obeying the dictates of his king or state and believing them to be part of his moral duties.

Left to his own devices Arjuna seems to favour the Buddhist solution, for he weighs the consequences of the war as a whole and finds them disastrous (I.38–43). He is by no means impelled by cowardice or selfish motives, for "he does not long for victory, kingdom or pleasures or even his own life" (I.32). Rādhakrishnan (op. cit., p. 91) accuses Arjuna of "talking in terms of enlightened selfishness" but Arjuna, on the contrary, is prepared to offer non-resistance and sacrifice his life for the sake of what he considers at heart to be right without desiring the gains and glories of earth or heaven. "These I would not consent to kill though killed myself even for the kingdom of the three worlds; how much less for the sake of the earth?" (I.35). "Far better would it be for me if the sons of Dhṝtarāṣṭra, with weapons in hand, should slay me in the battle while I remain unresisting and unarmed" (I.46). To do justice to Arjuna, one must say that except for his indecision and failure to apprehend clearly that it was no moral duty of his to fight and kill fellow human beings, his general attitude is Buddhist to the core. The *Bhagavad-Gīta* in condemning this right along, therefore, takes up a position which is the antithesis of the Buddhist attitude to war.

Rādhakrishnan (*Indian Philosophy*, pp. 570–571) sums up the Buddhist and Gīta teachings on caste by saying that "both attempt to relax the rigours of caste by basing it on a less untenable foundation." He is of course much less explicit when he elaborates on this point for he says that "the Gīta recognises the caste divisions ... the Gīta broadly distinguishes four fundamental types of individuals answering to the four stages of the upward ascent. Basing caste on qualities the Gīta requires each individual to do duties imposed by his caste.... The confusion of birth and qualities has led to an undermining of the spiritual foundation of caste." Here again I would hold that the Gīta attitude on caste is the very opposite of that of Buddhism and that while the Gīta in keeping with the Vedic tradition gives religious sanction to caste and attempts to provide an intellectual justification for it, Buddhism denies the validity of such a religious sanction and holds that there is no basis whatsoever for holding to caste distinctions. This would be clear if the specific arguments or assumptions on which caste is upheld in the Gīta were placed side by side with the relevant arguments against caste as found in Buddhism. It may however be granted that the Gīta agrees with Buddhism in holding that people of all castes may obtain the highest spiritual attainments, but the important difference lies in the fact that while the Gīta upholds caste distinctions on religious and genetic grounds, Buddhism denies the reality and validity of these distinctions on these very grounds.

One of the arguments of Arjuna was that among the undesirable consequences of war was the possible danger of the "intermixture of castes" (*varṇa-saṃkara*). Since the prohibition of intermarriage as between castes was one of the principles of caste theory, it shows that according to the author of the Gīta the "intermixture of castes" was a disastrous consequence. In Buddhism, on the other hand, intermixture of castes, considered both as an historical fact and as a possibility, was adduced as an argument against the reality and validity of caste distinctions. It is said that even those who claim caste purity have had mixed ancestors, the implication being that the hereditary distinctions of caste are unreal (D I 92–97). If this is an argument to show the historicity of caste mixture, the biological possibility of the mixture of castes, it may be mentioned, is also brought forward as an argument against the reality of caste distinctions (D II 153–154). Arguing for the unity of mankind as against the distinctions of caste, the Buddha says that there are differences of species and genera among plants and animals, "although such distinctions are not found among humans" (*evaṃ n'atthi manussesu liṅgaṃ jātimayaṃ puthu*; Sn 118).

Now, the crucial passage in the Gīta, which according to Rādhakrishnan undermines the traditional Hindu basis of caste, is the one which says (to follow Rādhakrishnan's translation): "The fourfold order was created by Me according to the divisions of quality and work" (*cāturvarṇyaṃ mayā sṛṣṭaṃ guṇa-karma-vibhāgaśaḥ*). Commenting on it, Rādhakrishnan (op. cit., p. 160) says, "the emphasis is on guṇa (aptitude) and karma (function) and not *jāti* (birth). The *varṇa* or the order to which we belong is independent of sex, birth or breeding. A class determined by temperament and vocation is not a caste determined by birth and heredity." If this interpretation is intended for the two lines of the stanza quoted above its absurdity would be apparent if its full implications are worked out. For, if it is correct, what is meant by these two lines is that there are four and only four types of individuals, each with a special aptitude for performing a special type of social duty which is obligatory on his part. Now, the references to the four types (as is evident from the word *cāturvarṇyam*) is obviously a reference to the four castes, viz. the brahmins, kṣatriyas, vaiśyas and *sūdras*. But, if as Rādhakrishnan says "the *varṇa* or order to which we belong is independent of birth," then what is meant is that there may be Brahmins who have the aptitude of *śūdras* and *śūdras* who have the aptitude of Brahmins, so that it becomes the duty of these people who have been born in the wrong castes to do the work for which they have a special aptitude. This would cut the ground beneath the concept of *svadharma* in the Gīta.

Now, if the individual types were created in accordance with their *guṇas* or aptitudes and *karmas* or social functions, it is difficult to see why the number of types should be four and not less or more, for, if the types represented the *guṇas*, there would have been three types corresponding to the *guṇas* of *sattva, rajas* and *tamas,* while if they represented the *karmas* or social duties, surely many more.

But these two lines could be interpreted without absurdity in the general background of Gīta thought if they are construed as an attempt to give a religious sanction as well as a justification for the hereditary basis of caste. On such an interpretation it would appear that the fourfold caste structure of society (based on heredity) is fundamental, absolute and divinely ordained as being the creation of God himself, and is not a product of human conventions. The purpose of such a creation would be to ensure the stability and maximum efficiency of society since each caste had a special aptitude for performing the social duties they were expected to perform and it was the specific duty (*svadharma*) of the members of each caste to perform the duties for which they were so created.

This appears to be the more natural interpretation, but if so, it means that the Gīta not only holds that caste is a creation of God but attaches special sanctity to the four castes qua *four.* Now, both claims have been contested in Buddhism. The Brahmin claim was that the Brahmins were created from the mouth of God (*mukhato jātā ... brahmanimmitā*; M II 149), a theory which goes back to the *Puruṣa Sukta* of the Ṛgveda (X.90), which says that the Brahmin was the mouth of God (*brāhmaṇo'sya mukham āsīt*) and that all castes were created out of the Divine Person. This claim to a special association with Divinity was criticised by Buddhism on the grounds that the Brahmins like the people of all the other castes were evidently born of human parents (M II 149). But it is equally important to note that Buddhism held that there was nothing absolute even about the quarternity of castes. The Buddha argues that "among the Yonas and Kāmbojas and others living in the bordering territories there were only two castes (*dveva vaṇṇā*), namely the lords and serfs" (ibid.). In fact it is asserted that caste names have only an occupational significance (Sn 119) and that birth is no index to caste (S I 166), thus denying the hereditary basis of caste altogether, while the theory of caste as promulgated by the Vedic Brahmins is referred to as a false and immoral view (*pāpakaṃ diṭṭhigataṃ*; M II 154). It would thus appear that, while the Gīta tries to uphold, justify as well as give a religious sanction to the caste theory, Buddhism in countering these very arguments is presenting the opposite view so that it would be neither fair by the Gīta nor by Buddhism to say with Rādhakrishnan that "both attempt to relax the rigours of caste by basing it on less untenable foundations."

The Buddhist Monk's Discipline

Some Points Explained for Laypeople

by

Bhikkhu Khantipālo

WHEEL PUBLICATION NO. 130/131

Preface

In the small treatise which follows, the good of both Bhikkhus (Buddhist monks) and of the lay Buddhist householders has been aimed at and the information presented, the writer believes, is available in no other book. The standards of conduct described here are those of the Vinaya well-practiced and of the layman's discipline well-applied. What use indeed is there in presenting other than the high standards laid down by Lord Buddha himself in the Vinaya, since falling away from good conduct is all too easy and may all too easily be seen, not least in Buddhist lands? For those who follow the training in Buddhist Doctrine and Discipline (Dhamma-Vinaya) only the best, surely, is good enough.

As to terminology, the writer has used the Pali word *añjali* for what is often called "placing together the palms of the hands" (*añjali-kamma*), and the "five-point-rest" (*pañcaṅga-vandana*) for what is commonly called "prostration."

This book has greatly benefited from the corrections and additions suggested by my revered *upajjhāya*, Ven. Chao Khun Sāsana Sobhana, and others.

May this work be for the practical welfare of all who strive on the Path of Saddhamma!

Bhikkhu Khantipālo
Wat Bovoranives Vihara
Bangkok, Thailand
8th day of the Waning Moon of Citta, BE. 2510

Introduction

The teachings given by Lord Buddha, which are preserved and practiced to the present day, are known in the ancient texts as the *Dhamma-Vinaya.* Although there is a great loss of meaning when translating these two terms into English, they may be rendered as *Doctrine* and aspects of *Discipline.* Numerous books are given over to explaining aspects of Dhamma but perhaps because of its monastic meaning the Vinaya seems neglected and not given due prominence. It will be the task of this booklet to examine Vinaya from a particular point of view—that of the Buddhist layman and how a knowledge of some of its rules can be useful to him.

This term "Vinaya" has not only monastic connotations. It is true that the Vinaya-collection[1] contains at great length and in detail the training rules, prohibitions, allowances, and regulations governing a Bhikkhu's life, but there is at least one important instance of the term being applied to the conduct of lay people. The subtitle of the famous discourse called the "Exhortation to Sigāla" is "Gihi-vinaya" or the "Householder's Discipline," a worthy name for a masterly exposition.[2] In a more narrow sense, the layman's Vinaya is his Five Precepts,[3] since these have the same function of "removing the unskillful" as the much greater body of training rules in the Vinaya-collection has for a Bhikkhu. This is in fact what the word "Vinaya" means: driving out, abolishing, destruction, or removal—that is, of all the overt ways of behavior which obstruct progress along the Practice-path of Dhamma.

Why then were the Vinaya training rules laid down? Many times in the Vinaya-collection Lord Buddha says: "On account of (some event necessitating action), O Bhikkhus, I shall make known the training rule for Bhikkhus" (sometimes adding), "founded upon these ten reasons:

1. See Bibliography.
2. See "*Everyman's Ethics,*" *The Wheel* No. 14.
3. See "*The Five Precepts,*" *The Wheel* No. 55.

1. For the welfare of the Sangha (community of monks),
2. For the comfort of the Sangha,
3. For the control of unsteady men,
4. For the comfort of well-behaved Bhikkhus,
5. For the restraining of the pollutions (*āsavā*) in this present life,
6. For guarding against pollutions liable to arise in a future life,
7. For the pleasing of those not yet pleased (with Dhamma),
8. For the increase of those pleased,
9. For the establishment of true Dhamma, and
10. For the benefit of the Vinaya[4]"

The great Teacher and Commentator, Ven. Buddhaghosa, gives the following verse-definition of the Vinaya in the *Atthasālinī*:

"This Vinaya (Discipline) is called the Vinaya
By those knowing the meaning of Vinaya.
Because it disciplines (actions of) body and speech,
(Since consisting of) various and excellent principles."

This verse stresses the usefulness of Vinaya in disciplining the body and speech (as the Five or Eight Precepts do for lay people) and this again drives home the support given by Vinaya to Dhamma. To have one without the other is actually inconceivable from a Buddhist point of view. For instance, a Dhamma taught without Vinaya would be a teaching in which no opening or beginning was shown of a path to be practiced. A Vinaya without Dhamma on the other hand would be an empty formalism, a discipline bearing little fruit or advantage. Both parts of the Buddhist Dispensation (*sāsana*) go hand-in-hand whether one considers the Bhikkhu's or the layman's training.

A good Buddhist layman is one who makes every effort to keep pure the Five Precepts and to practice at least the Dhamma taught in the "Exhortation to Sigāla." In the same way a good Bhikkhu strives to train himself, without falling into offenses,

4. In the Anguttara Nikāya (Book of Twos), two further reasons are found: "for sympathy with householders" (a very important consideration) and "for breaking up factions of evil-minded Bhikkhus" (stressing how the Vinaya has protected the Sangha).

in the two hundred and twenty-seven training rules of the Pātimokkha which, at the time of his acceptance as a Bhikkhu, he has undertaken to observe. It is often said that the laymen keep five, while the Bhikkhu's load is 227 precepts, but for the latter this is only part of the truth since he has, besides the fundamental rules in the Pātimokkha,[5] numerous others to train in, these being found scattered throughout the Vinaya-collection.

Here we may remark upon one difference between the precepts of a layman and those of a Bhikkhu. The former are all of a moral nature, such as are esteemed in all religions (with the possible exception of the fifth, since in some faiths abstinence from alcohol is not taught). For this reason, they fall into the class of "natural" precepts (*pakati-sīla*). But the Bhikkhu, besides having precepts of this nature, has many more which are special to his mode of life. These precepts are called "formulated" (*paññatti-sīla*). Although they have little or no application in the life of a layman, they are very important for the Bhikkhu, including all sorts of ways of restraint and good conduct proper for him. It should not be thought this latter sort of precept is less important to him than those in the group of natural morality, for this would be to apply worldly standards of judgment to a code of discipline designed to promote an unworldly way of life.

The concern among both Bhikkhus and laity, for keeping the precepts pure and for not falling into any offense, may be called scrupulousness. Many times in the Vinaya it is mentioned that "scrupulous Bhikkhus" (*kukkuccāyantā Bhikkhu*) would not accept some article until Lord Buddha had made it allowable. Again, we find constant references to "Bhikkhus of few wishes" (*appiccha Bhikkhu*) who were ashamed of the unbecoming and unscrupulous behavior of other monks. Light is thrown here upon an important connection between precepts generally and the Dhamma. In being "scrupulous" or "of few wishes" a number of skillful mental factors valuable to one's training are present. Among these, the pair known as shame and fear of blame (*hiri-ottappa*) are actually called by Lord Buddha "the guardians of the world." Shame is seen when one reproaches oneself for an evil done or about to be done and when one has an inward fear derived from thinking of the

5. See Bibliography.

unpleasant results to be experienced from that sort of kamma. Fear of blame is rather the restraint imposed by fear of others' censure or by the thought that honorable persons whom one respects, such as parents or teachers, might get to know of such evil. Being "of few wishes" is another word for contentment (*santuṭṭhi*), a very valuable quality for a Bhikkhu. The other most prominent factor in this scrupulosity and modesty is mindfulness (*sati*), which is indeed at the root of all Buddhist training at whatever level. When there is mindfulness, however many precepts one keeps, it is likely that they will be well and carefully guarded. Mindfulness makes one careful and skillful even in mental kamma, not to mention those involving body and speech! It makes possible that all-round restraint often described by the simile of the turtle, which creature is immune from danger after having withdrawn its legs and head inside its shell. Of the Bhikkhu it is said:

> Beneficial is control of eye,
> Control of ear is beneficial too,
> Beneficial is control of nose,
> Control of tongue is beneficial too,
> Bodily control is beneficial,
> Control of speech is beneficial too
> Beneficial is control of mind,
> Everywhere restraint is beneficial.
> The Bhikkhu here restrained in every way
> Free utterly is he from every ill.
>
> (Dhp vv. 360–361)

All the various rules of the Vinaya might indeed be summed up in these verses. Further we have the famous exhortation of Lord Buddha to the Bhikkhus: "Be perfect in virtue (*sīla*), O Bhikkhus; be perfect in the Pātimokkha. Dwell restrained according to the Pātimokkha. Be perfect in conduct and (place of) resort *seeing danger even in the slightest faults,* and train yourselves by undertaking rightly the rules of training." It is from such exhortations as this that the scrupulousness of a good Bhikkhu is born. He resolves to make effort to train himself thus: "I shall be perfect in virtue. I shall be perfect in the Pātimokkha. I shall dwell restrained ... perfect in conduct and (place of) resort, seeing danger even in the slightest faults...."

Unscrupulousness, if we consider it in the light of these passages, will obviously indicate the presence of unrestraint and lack of mindfulness, to say the least, and probably the lack of shame and fear of blame (*ahiri, anottappa*). Quite often strong currents of craving (*taṇhā*), possibly unrecognized, may be involved, pride (*mana*) may have a hand (not wishing to submit to the whole Discipline), and false views (*micchā-diṭṭhi*), so often allied with pride, may tangle matters further by throwing out a smoke-screen of "reasons."

However this may be, the rules of training are praised by Lord Buddha in words which must prevent anyone from regarding them as "mere external rules": "Now all these rules combine together to make up the three trainings. What three? The training in supreme morality, the training in supreme collectedness, and the training in supreme wisdom. Herein are combined one and all of these rules.... Thus, O Bhikkhus, one who partly fulfills these observances experiences attainment partially, while one fulfilling perfectly comes to experience the complete attainment. Not barren of results, I declare are these rules of training" (AN 3:860).

Or we have this verse:

The Bhikkhu who delights in heedfulness
And looks with fear on heedlessness,
As a forest fire advances fast,
Burns up all fetters, great or small.

(Dhp v. 31)

Reason enough, if a Bhikkhu has set his heart upon Nibbāna, to keep the training rules strictly! Now the path of one who has gone forth from home to homelessness and who sincerely tries to train in those rules which he has undertaken is reckoned to lead directly to Nibbāna. It is therefore a great evil to obstruct one who has set himself upon this course, while it is great *puñña*[6] to aid such a one.

In the Buddhist dispensation there is mutual help given by Bhikkhus to laypeople in the form of Dhamma suitable for their

6. *Puñña* ("u" as in "put") is the benefit of increasing purity of mind derived from skillful actions such as generosity, virtue, helpfulness, etc. "Merit" is an inadequate rendering.

practice and by laypeople to Bhikkhus when they offer the four supports: robes, food, shelter, and medical necessities. In this way householders support the community of Bhikkhus from among whom those with knowledge and experience support the laity with Dhamma. Just as no Bhikkhu worthy of the robe would cause trouble among laypeople but only wish to help them, so devoted and knowledgeable householders think only to help Bhikkhus and *sāmaṇeras* (novices). In order to do this they must, of course, have at least some idea of what is and what is not allowable for Bhikkhus as laid down by Lord Buddha in the Vinaya.

It happens that Bhikkhus are now traveling more widely and able to visit and live in countries where formerly it was not possible for them to go. Also many people from non-Buddhist lands now travel to and stay in those countries where there is a living tradition of Dhamma, some of them becoming interested and wish to know what should and what should not be done in respect of Bhikkhus. There is consequently a need for knowledge among lay-supporters and others of some points of Vinaya. In this small book, the only points dealt with will be those where laypeople are somehow involved, while Vinaya matters of concern to Bhikkhus alone may be investigated in more comprehensive works.[7]

The Training Rules

As the Bhikkhu's life generally gives many occasions for contact with laypeople (except for the Bhikkhu engaged in meditation practice), and as erring Bhikkhus were not absent from the Sangha even in the days of Lord Buddha, so there is quite a large body of legislation relating to just these occasions. Because of the wrong conduct of various Bhikkhus, Lord Buddha had cause to lay down large numbers of training rules which, if infringed, would become offenses for the guilty Bhikkhu. It sometimes happened that a rule had to be modified, and sometimes various allowances proved necessary to qualify the range of the original rule. In this way many of the training rules were tested in the light of experience until they became perfectly practical.

7. See Bibliography.

All these rules fall into seven classes according to the seriousness of the offense involved when they are broken. Briefly, these seven classes with some of their characteristics are as follows:

1. *Defeat (pārājika)*. The first four training rules of the Pātimokkha, if broken, become offenses by which a Bhikkhu is defeated, no longer able to live in communion with other Bhikkhus, never able in the present life to be ordained Bhikkhu again; and being no longer "a son of the Sakya" (or the Buddha), he should disrobe immediately. These four offenses are:
    a. sexual intercourse of any description;
    b. taking what is not given with intention to steal;
    c. depriving purposely a human being of life in any way;
    d. falsely claiming superhuman states of attainment.

2. *Formal meeting (saṅghādisesa)*. Thirteen "heavy offenses," the second group in the Pātimokkha, for the commission of which there is a special disciplinary procedure designed to humble and purify the offender, who must, however, first confess to being guilty (as with all other offenses). Of special interest to the laity are numbers two, three, four, and five, which concern:
    a. engaging in bodily contact with a woman with lustful intent;
    b. addressing a woman with lewd words;
    c. speaking to a woman in praise of sexual intercourse;
    d. acting as a go-between for a man or a woman.

In the more detailed considerations below, we shall return to some implications of the first and last of these.

3. *Grave offenses (thullaccaya)*. These are numerous but not found in any one part of the Vinaya. Sometimes they are the types of offense resulting from partial commissions of acts which, if completed, would entail defeat or formal meeting. They may, in common with the other classes of offenses below, be cleared up by making a confession to another Bhikkhu who has not committed the same offense.

4. *Expiation (pācittiya)*. Ninety-two in number and all found in the Pātimokkha, these training rules cover a very wide range of subjects, some of which it is useful for lay-people to know.

5. *To be confessed (pāṭidesanīya).* Only four rules in the Pātimokkha, which find little application today.
6. *Wrong doing (dukkata).* A very numerous category, for the avoidance of breaking which care is needed. The 75 trainings *(sekhiya)* found in the Pātimokkha and which contain numbers of points of interest to the layman, become, when broken, offenses of wrongdoing.
7. *Wrong speech (dubbhāsita).* This includes all unprofitable speech not found in the above classes, as for instance, the use of coarse words uttered in jest. While there are numbers of cases for offenses in the above classes, there is only one here.

The Value of Vinaya

We have already seen that Lord Buddha, in laying down the training rules for Bhikkhus, was much concerned with the well-being of the laity. He had in mind, for instance, "being in sympathy with householders," "the pleasing of those not pleased (and) the increase of those pleased" (with Dhamma) alongside more monastic considerations. In another passage of very frequent occurrence in the Vinaya-collection, Lord Buddha, whenever he rebuked some erring Bhikkhu, would say: "It is not, foolish man, for the pleasing of those not pleased (i.e., outsiders, those of other faiths), not for the increase of those who are pleased (by their practice of Dhamma-Vinaya, i.e., Buddhists), but, foolish man, it causes displeasure among those who are not pleased as well as in those who are pleased, and it causes wavering in some" (i.e., those who are interested in Dhamma but have not yet gone for the Refuge to the Triple Gem). The very obvious effects which bad conduct by one in robes has upon laypeople, is here very strongly emphasized.

The converse is also true, since a Bhikkhu who has been well-trained under good teachers and learned thoroughly the theory and practice of Dhamma and Vinaya is indeed a great recommendation to the excellence found in the Conqueror's dispensation. A picture of such a Bhikkhu is awakened in the mind's eye by this verse:

Calm in body, calm in speech,
Tranquil and composed of heart,

Whoso has spewed out worldly wants
"Serene" is such a Bhikkhu called.

(Dhp v. 378)

The Dhamma, which all Buddhists revere as most precious and which is practiced by all who are truly followers of Lord Buddha, has been preserved for the people of the present by the Sangha. This community of Bhikkhus, those who (so to speak) have specialized in Dhamma, has been preserved by close adherence to the training rules laid down in the Vinaya. That this sequence is true may be seen from several instances in history when Bhikkhus no longer paid heed to the Vinaya and so lost the respect and support of the laity. Not having this support, they drifted towards being householders themselves and having become priests with families, they could give less time to learning and practice of Dhamma. Books got lost and were not replaced and the tradition became steadily more degenerate until no teaching at all remained—only "protection-ceremonies" and the like, often performed in a language not understood even by the priest, let alone by the people. The present time, alas, could also show some "Buddhist" traditions of which these words are true.

This preservation of the Dhamma by Vinaya and hence by the Sangha to whom the Vinaya applies finds expression in a simile in the Vinaya-introduction where it is said: "Flowers loose upon a flat piece of wood, not tied together by thread, are scattered about, destroyed by the wind. What is the cause of that? Since they were not held together by thread...." This is said to apply to the teachings of some former Buddhas who gave little of the Dhamma to their disciples and who did not lay down the Vinaya or make known the Pātimokkha. It is a cause for rejoicing that Gotama the Buddha *has* explained the Dhamma in detail, made known the Vinaya and pointed out the fundamental training rules of the Pātimokkha. "It is as if, Sāriputta, various flowers placed on a piece of wood, tied together by thread (as a garland), are not scattered, whirled about, or destroyed by the wind. What is the reason for that? They are well tied together by thread." This means simply that the winds of impermanence cannot so easily destroy the various aspects of Dhamma when these are secured by the thread of the Vinaya.

This brings us to appreciate the reverence which the Vinaya-collection is accorded by all true Bhikkhus as well as by knowledgeable laymen. This collection is given first place among the three collections (*piṭaka*) of Buddha Word, a fact which indicates that it is the support and mainstay of the other teachings. As it was said at the First Council or Saṅgāyana: "The Vinaya is the very life of the Teaching (*Sāsana*); so long as the Vinaya endures, the Teaching endures; therefore let us rehearse the Vinaya first."

"Reform of Vinaya"

If one appreciates that the Vinaya is indeed the mainstay, it will not be difficult for Buddhist laity, even in non-Buddhist countries, to realize that ideas of changing (sometimes called "reforming") the Vinaya, in order, as it is said, "to suit modern conditions," find no favor with the Sangha as a whole. There are many objections to such a course of action, in which indeed there would be almost no advantages. In what follows, the writer wishes to examine these objections and to show plainly their dangers and disadvantages.

Firstly, if one reads through the Vinaya, while there are a number of points that apply specially to Eastern countries, some even being limited to conditions peculiar to ancient India, none of these relates to the main principles of the Bhikkhu-life. The workings of the Vinaya in the life of the Bhikkhu of the present day is not made difficult by obsolete training rules. Those no longer having any application are very few and are really not of great importance.

All the main principles of the Bhikkhu-discipline are as valid now as they were when instituted by Lord Buddha two and a half millennia past. This is indeed a marvelous proof of the wisdom of Lord Buddha, who has so well formulated these rules. Nor is the structure of the Vinaya absolutely rigid and it does therefore permit necessary adaptations which are still within the spirit of the training. The use by Bhikkhus of modern methods of transport might be taken as an example. This would not have been possible for them if Vinaya was taken as a completely rigid code.

Secondly, there are the words of Lord Buddha himself: "So long, O Bhikkhus, as you appoint no new rules, and abolish not the existing ones, but proceed according to the training rules as laid down, so long will Bhikkhus be expected to prosper, not to decline" (AN 7:12). This statement of the Teacher is always to the fore whenever there are gatherings of senior Bhikkhus meeting to determine some Vinaya questions arising out of modern conditions. Or there are such exhortations from sources outside the Pali Canon as these words attributed to Lord Buddha: "O Bhikkhus, after my Parinibbāna you should revere and honor the precepts of the Pātimokkha. Treat them as a light which you have discovered in the dark, or as a poor man would treat a treasure he had found. You should know that they are your chief guide and there should be no difference (in your observances of them) from when I yet remained in the world" (the opening words of the "Discourse of the Teaching Bequeathed by the Buddha").[8]

Then there is a consideration based upon the events of the First Saṅgāyana (Council). In this great gathering of Arahants, Venerable Mahākassapa, who was its president, put forward this motion: "If it seems right to the Sangha, the Sangha should not lay down what has not been laid down, nor should it abolish what has been laid down. It should proceed in conformity with and according to the training rules which have been laid down. This is the motion. Your reverences, let the Sangha listen to me. If it seems right to the Sangha, the Sangha should not... (thrice repeated). It is pleasing to the Sangha; therefore it is silent. Thus do I understand." All those who are accepted as (Theravada) Bhikkhus in the present day follow this tradition as laid down in the First Saṅgāyana. This is Theravada tradition; it is based upon the decision of those great elders who were ennobled with the highest nobility. Who are we, indeed, to go astray from their way?

Although the Teacher before his Parinibbāna spoke thus: "After my passing, Ānanda, let the Sangha if it so desires abolish the lesser and minor rules of training," no Sangha anywhere actually ventured to do this, partly because of the uncertainty in defining "the lesser and minor rules" and partly because they were constrained out of respect to preserve that which had been instituted by the great Teacher. Acariya Nāgasena explains that "the Tathāgata spoke thus testing the Bhikkhus: 'Will my disciples on being left by me adhere to the passing, or will they

8. See "*The Buddha's Last Bequest*," The Wheel No. 112.

repudiate them?'"[9] There is also the consideration that those of other sects might say, "While the Teacher (Gotama) was alive, his disciples respected and honored his precepts but now that he is no more, they throw off the training." But principally the reason was devotion arising from the successful practice of Dhamma-Vinaya.

Supposing that someone proclaimed that he wished to "reform" the Vinaya, in doing this or in trying to do this, he would depart from Theravada tradition and place himself apart from others following Theravada and would in fact only start a new sect, and who is in honor of sectarianism? If he were a Bhikkhu, by his departure from the training laid down in the Vinaya he would only bring upon himself offenses, being burdened with which and failing to confess them, he would be precluded from making much progress on the practice path of Dhamma.

Again, *who* will change the Vinaya? As the Vinaya is the province of Bhikkhus, laypeople obviously cannot do so. One Bhikkhu cannot effect any changes since Vinaya-decisions are arrived at after the consultation of a Sangha. A Sangha of young Bhikkhus is not qualified to do so since decisions arrived at by them might well be swayed by preferences, or be based upon both lack of learning and lack of purity of heart. A Sangha of senior Bhikkhus competent to decide upon Vinaya-questions will scarcely undertake such a task since their training has imbued them with a deep sense of respect for the Vinaya. Any decision arrived at by a meeting of less than all Bhikkhus in the world (!) would be sectarian in character and be the cause of Sangha-schism (an offense of formal meeting and therefore very serious). Even if such a gathering could be contrived, not only would respect for the traditions of the Arahant elders easily triumph, but also the dissident voices would be found to represent somewhat unbalanced individuals. Actually, *no one at all* can be found who would be competent to undertake "changing the Vinaya." (But there is, as pointed out above, provision for decisions on the Vinaya-questions by a council of senior Bhikkhus well versed in Vinaya and the Commentaries as found in Thailand.)

Another point to consider is that even if changes were agreed upon by all competent authorities and the Sangha, therefore

9. *Milindapañhā* text, PTS, p. 143.

unanimous, how far are such changes to go, and when will this changing ever stop? This question, among all other considerations here, has always deterred Theravada Elders from effecting any changes. Ven. Chao Khun Sāsana Sobhana, writing in Thailand recently, says: "The argument of the Theravada Buddhists against the revision of the Vinaya is that while it is true that towards the end of his life, the Buddha did give permission to his disciples to suspend the minor rules, the First Council was not able to reach an agreement as to what 'minor rules' signified." They have thus remained in the Pātimokkha until the present time and have thus ensured that the standard of conduct and the direction of the training have remained the same (for those undertaking the training seriously) as they were in the Buddha-time. Ven. Paññavaddho, in his review of the Bangkok edition of "The Pātimokkha," has written: "It has been said by some people that in this modern day and age, some or many of the rules are archaic, restrictive, or otherwise undesirable in the greatly altered circumstances of modern civilization. But it must be remembered that the Vinaya, with the Pātimokkha as its basis, has maintained stability in the Sangha since the time of Lord Buddha."

Finally, there is a consideration based upon the nature of the training and the end which it has in view. From the Buddha-time down to the present it has been found that a careful application of the Vinaya's principles by a Bhikkhu in his life promotes his practice and understanding of Dhamma: "Vinaya leads to restraint; restraint to the absence of remorse; absence of remorse leads to joy; joy to delight; delight to tranquility; tranquility leads to happiness; happiness to collectedness; collectedness to knowledge and vision of the truly existent; knowledge and vision of the truly existent to revulsion;[10] revulsion to dispassion; dispassion to freedom; freedom to knowledge-and-vision of freedom; and knowledge-of-vision to freedom leads to Nibbāna free from (clinging to) substrata (for rebirth)" (Vinaya, Parivāra, 169). When Vinaya has been so formulated as to guide a Bhikkhu to the goal of Nibbāna, who shall entertain thoughts altering it? It is we who

10. *Nibbidā*, a word impossible to render into English, as it encompasses meanings such as: revulsion (but without hatred or dislike); weariness (but without physical tiredness); and means literally "turning-away from."

have to change by our practice of Dhamma-Vinaya, to come up to its level and not to expect it to change for us. In this connection, there is a little fable:

At one time there was a great and flourishing tree standing as it had stood for many, many hundreds of years. It was so beautiful that men and women bringing their children would come from scores of miles about to gaze in wonder at its perfect and majestic shape. Under its mighty spread of branches multitudes could sit down enjoying its cool shade. Even animals would come and delight themselves according to their several habits, some upon the grass beneath and some sporting amid the profusion of leaves, flowers, and fruits. And such flowers of such fragrance—no one knew where else their like might be found. And such fruits as this tree bore and in such abundance! No wonder that they are called best, highest, foremost, and supreme among all fruits produced by other trees. So the seasons and the years rolled by and still the mighty tree stood hardly changed, for where one branch died off, another grew to replace it. The delight of many beings, visible and invisible, was in the health and long life of this ancient tree. Then, in accordance with the change inherent in things, fashions changed and trees in their natural vigor were no longer praised but trimmed, and artificially-shaped trees were thought more beautiful. Agitation began among some men for the tree to be shaped up according to modern taste. Eventually, due to debased ideas of people by that time, loppers and clippers tried their hands upon the millennial giant. Branch after branch fell loaded with flowers and bearing fruits. "Never mind," they said, "it will look much better when we have finished." Before long, the tree was pruned into the form of a perfect cube and this was regarded by almost everyone with satisfaction. Only a few ignorant people regretted the sawn-off limbs and bare branches with a few clusters of leaves left here and there. These ill-educated persons were heard regretting the lack of any shade. How stupid of them!

It is needless to say that the venerable tree flowered and bore fruit no more and due to shock, died shortly afterwards, leaving only its great, but dead framework which then became an object for the speculative theses of numerous men of books.

Thus it is that most Bhikkhus generally would not talk of "changing" but of "tampering with" the Vinaya. After all, when closely examined many proposals to bring about changes in the body of Vinaya are found to be based upon the roots of unskill. A simple case will illustrate this: A Bhikkhu experiences pangs of hunger in the evening (in spite of allowable drinks!), which cause him to announce that he does not believe in strictly following Vinaya in this respect, since this would be an extreme of self-torture (!); the climate is too cold; modern times demand a change; "I follow Mahāyāna" (!)—or one of a thousand such excuses. He accordingly proposes that the training rule regarding not taking food after noon and before dawn be abolished. "After all," he reasons, "it is only a *pācittiya* offense— nothing much." Meanwhile, he has a good supper every night; not only his belly but also his greed, that root of unskill, are thoroughly satisfied. If the former is a little distended, the latter is certainly greatly increased, while the spirit of renunciation has fled from his dwelling. And of course, where greed is increased, so automatically are aversion and dullness... and so on....

Anyone—whether Bhikkhu or layman—who holds such a view or reasoning concerning his training rules as the imaginary Bhikkhu above, actually makes for himself a real stumbling block upon his own path. The mental attitude of thinking, "Oh, it does not matter; it's only a little thing!" is one to watch, since it appears at the gate of the wide and easy path leading downwards. Such slack ways of thinking, really urged on by some hidden craving, are just the reverse of the disciplined scrupulousness upon which so much stress is laid in the Vinaya.

Slackness and strictness in regard to the Vinaya are not to be associated in any wholesale fashion with this "*yāna*" or that "*vāda*" (vehicle or way). In Theravada, as in other Buddhist traditions, there are those Bhikkhus who are strict as well as those who are slack. Wherever there is a good Teacher who is concerned with the practical application of the Dhamma, there the Vinaya will be carefully followed. But where neither such a Teacher nor a good Vinaya-tradition are found, there undisciplined behavior will result, with a victory for not-Dhamma (*adhamma*).

Standards of Discipline

One important principle to remember about the Vinaya is that a life based upon its principles is very different from the ordinary life. The Vinaya guides a Bhikkhu in conducting himself so as to "go against the stream" (of craving) and his life and way of doing things is often opposed to the ways of one who "enjoys the five strands of sense-pleasures." Take food again as an example. An ordinary person not undertaking any religious discipline may eat, his mind delighted by sense-impressions of taste, smell, color, and so forth, and probably therefore overwhelmed with greed. He may chatter with others and, if the food is delicious, overeat. Restraint and mindfulness, by contrast, are the marks of a good Bhikkhu taking his food, which he regards as medicine to keep his body going and, should greed arise, he uses the meditation upon the loathsomeness of food to dissolve it. He talks but little, has his senses under control and eats only moderately.

The reason for this difference of attitude is not hard to see. One who is blown about by the winds of craving throughout his life, not understanding kamma and its fruits, and therefore not grasping the meaning of dukkha, is set on no sure course and wins little advantage in his or her life as a human being. One who wishes to become a Bhikkhu, on the other hand, has determined upon a definite course of action which is given guidance by the Vinaya and his practice of it, after his acceptance (*upasampada*). The Dhammapada emphasizes this:

> One is the way to worldly gain,
> Another to Nibbāna leads.
> Clearly comprehending this
> The Bhikkhu-follower of the Buddha
> Should not delight in honor and gain
> But devote himself to solitude.
>
> (v. 75)

It may be that some of the training rules to be dealt with below will seem strange and complicated—even unnecessary. They *are* unnecessary for a layman, but they have a definite part in the life of a Bhikkhu and help him generally in developing that scrupulousness which is so essential to Bhikkhu-life. For this reason, laypeople who are so fortunate as to be able to invite a good Bhikkhu to their towns should be truly pleased to help him keep the Vinaya. Those who do this, which is the doing of what is a little difficult and therefore requires effort but bears splendid fruit, are themselves undertaking the training rightly. A Bhikkhu such as the verses below depict is really worthy of help and support:

> For a Bhikkhu wise who practices this Sāsana,
> Control of senses and contentment too.
> And by the Pātimokkha well-restrained,
> And company of keen and noble friends
> Who follow purity of livelihood–
> Such things as these being the holy life.
> The Bhikkhu who has in the Buddhasāsana
> Serenist joy and faith that satisfies,
> Surely he can reach unto the State of Peace,
> The bliss of pacifying all conditioned things.
>
> (Dhp vv. 375, 381)

Some Aspects of the Vinaya

In the following Vinaya-information useful to laymen, most emphasis will be upon the offenses incurred in certain situations by Bhikkhus and how laypeople can help them avoid these, together with remarks upon the customary conduct of laypeople in the presence of a Bhikkhu. As, in Buddhist countries, the laypeople's code of manners and conduct is much influenced by the seventy-five trainings, a group of rules kept by both Bhikkhus and *sāmaṇeras*, it seems appropriate to include this matter here. The writer has, for the sake of easy reference, gathered the various points, some suggested through the kindness of others, under five headings: Greetings, Living-quarters, Food and Drink, Travel, and General Conduct. In the Conclusion are set out some observations upon the way Bhikkhus are regarded by the laypeople of Thailand at the present time.

Greetings

It is generally felt in Buddhist countries that the common Western form of greeting, the handshake, is unsuitable when greeting Bhikkhus. The point here is that a Bhikkhu must avoid all body contact with women. Since if lust arose in him, he could be embroiled in a heavy offense, entailing formal meeting. For these reasons it is obvious that the handshake is not a suitable greeting and, in the case of a Bhikkhu, if one has invited him knowing that he has knowledge and experience of Dhamma which is not one's own, then greeting by handshake will not express one's willingness to learn as well as do the traditional gestures.

In a public place, a Bhikkhu is traditionally welcomed and parted by "action of *añjali*," inclining the head and sometimes the body. This position of the hands is associated in theistic religions with prayer (one thinks of Dürer's famous "Praying Hands") but its use and meaning in Buddhist tradition is rather different.

Here, given space, one might elaborate a little upon relationships of mentality (*nāma*) with materiality (*rūpa*) and the reverse. Suffice it to say that there are certain gestures and positions of the body which lead to the arising, maintenance, or increase of skillful and concentrated mental states. We are concerned here with two of them: "action of *añjali*" and what is usually called "prostration," but which we prefer to call the "five-point-rest" or "lowering" the body.[11] Of these, "action of *añjali*" is commonly seen when laypeople greet Bhikkhus at stations, in the streets, within a hall, or other public place. The amount of respect thus accorded to a particular Bhikkhu tends to be expressed by the height at which the hands are held (from the heart up to the forehead) and the angle at which the head and body are inclined. However, any exaggerated form of *añjali* is disliked and not encouraged, since it usually expresses some mental strain in the mind of the persons making it (such as flattery, stupidity, conceit, etc.). What has been said here also applies to all novices and junior Bhikkhus when respecting their seniors in the Sangha. It is also widely used by Buddhist laypeople when greeting each other.

11. See Preface.

Another point which should be mentioned and which applies both to "action of *añjali*" and "five-point rest" (see below) is that the action of respecting one who knows Dhamma by one who wishes to learn *is for the benefit of the latter*. Through associations with prayer which will be present on many Western minds, it is often assumed that these actions when performed by Buddhists are acts of propitiation or are somehow for the benefit of whoever is "on the receiving end" (i.e., a Buddha image, or a Bhikkhu)! This is indeed very far from the truth, since even when Lord Buddha was teaching, he said: "But also, Bhikkhus, if others should speak in praise of me, in praise of the Dhamma, or in praise of the Sangha, you should not on that account be filled with pleasure and gladness, or be lifted up in mind... (for if that happened) that also would become a danger to your own selves" (DN 1, ¶ 6).

This is certainly true of good Bhikkhus of the present who will know that to have a mind that is stuck in the desire of praise and honor, which is one of the eight worldly conditions, is also one of the marks of an ignorant, worldly person and far from the ideal of the Noble Disciple (*ariyasāvaka*) to which he aspires. Thus a Bhikkhu does not teach the advantages of "the action of *añjali*" and "five-point rest," because he wants to be honored but because these things are skillful ways of conduct and increase the *puñña* of those performing them. According to a famous verse, this *puñña* increases in four ways:

> He of respectful nature who
> Ever the elders honoring,
> Four qualities for him increase:
> Long-life and beauty, happiness, and strength.
>
> (Dhp v. 109)

Just as a Bhikkhu will "honor the feet" by the five-point lowering before his preceptor, teacher, or any elder Bhikkhu, or at shrines and in temples where there are Buddha-images, so do laypeople lower themselves to their Bhikkhu-Teacher of Dhamma. This they generally do in a relatively quiet and enclosed space such as temple, Bhikkhu's lodging, or in their own houses where they may have invited Bhikkhus for teaching, chanting, or making *puñña* by giving gifts. At the time when they respect a Buddha-image, their Teacher, or other Bhikkhus in either of these ways, they encourage their children to do likewise, thus early inculcating a sense of respect which is bound to bear good fruits in the future. Happiness and peace characterize the faces of those who perform these acts of reverence with care. After all, is not happiness associated with an absence of mental strains?

Some laypeople, however, do these things carelessly, so that they become unmindful of their meaning and benefits; but those who really aspire to make progress on the Path never do so unmindfully, however often they have cause to greet with the *añjali* or lower the body in the five-point rest.

In the West, where these customs are not established among Buddhists and where Bhikkhus are in any case very few in number, carelessness is not likely to be a hindrance, although there is another one which deserves a little attention. Among some people one finds what amounts to a strong aversion to the practice of lowering the body. It may be that they hold some wrong view, perhaps an unconscious trait persisting from Protestant Christianity (idolatry, the bowing down to idols, etc.). Perhaps it may be connected with the idea dealt with above, that the other requires or expects to be worshipped; or perhaps compounded with some "view" which is like a smokescreen put out to conceal the true cause for objection—which is *pride*. It is the head which contains the eyes, ears, nose, tongue, many touch organs, and that agglomeration of nerve tissue called the brain, a circumstance which powerfully reinforces the idea of ego. That this topmost and splendid piece of apparatus should be lowered to the ground at the feet of another will naturally cause the mental strain of pride to object and perhaps to put out a smokescreen: "It's not part of our culture," "It's only an Eastern custom," etc.

The modern world manages most successfully to stimulate all the mental stains in man. Among them, the mental stain of pride is fostered by such notions as, "I'm as good as any man." As far as the training in Dhamma-Vinaya is concerned, such ideas do not apply and it is the humble man who goes forward, not he who is stiff with pride and therefore has no chance to learn. A Tibetan work "Trees and Water" puts it like this: "Just as the branch adorned with good fruits is bent down beneath their weight; so a wise man's mind adorned with all qualities is bent downwards with humility and calm and knows no pride. (But) just as the fruitless branch of a tree has the nature to grow aloft, so the head of the haughty man is always held high for his heart is not humble."[12]

The traditional position of lowering the body cannot be excelled for encouraging humility. It is known as the five-point lowering (*pañcaṅga-vandanā*) since in making it, five points are on the ground: (1) the forehead, (2–3) the two forearms, (4–5) the two knees.

It is common for Bhikkhus to acknowledge respectful salutation in either of these ways by saying (in Sri Lanka) "*Sukhi hotu*" ("May you be happy") and in Thailand often "*Āyu vaṇṇo sukhaṃ balaṃ*" ("Long-life, beauty, happiness, and strength"). In English, "May you be happy" seems very suitable since all Dhamma-practices undoubtedly bring happiness.

What has been written here has only been set down with a view that laypeople should understand, as Bhikkhus and *sāmaṇeras* have been taught to understand, what is truly beneficial. Neither Lord Buddha nor any teacher in Buddhist tradition has ever prescribed that this or that sort of greeting for Bhikkhus *must* be made. There is actually no rigid formality about this at all and much the same course of individual conduct applies in a Buddhist country like Thailand, as commonly applied in the days of Lord Buddha: "Having approached (Lord Buddha) some lowered themselves before the Lord and sat down to one side: some greeted the Lord politely and, having conversed in a friendly and courteous way, sat down to one side; some by their 'action of *añjali*' to the Lord, sat down to one side; some proclaimed their name and clan and sat down; while others without saying anything just sat down likewise." The commentary upon this frequently recurring passage in the Suttas makes it quite clear, however, that those who greeted him with humility reaped ample fruits, while those who "just sat down" were people with minds beset by pride, false views, and the rest.

The information gathered here and elsewhere in this book is, the writer believes, very difficult to come by in other works. Yet this is standard practice in the East, where it never has to be

12. See *The Wisdom Gone Beyond*, Social Science Press of Thailand, Phaya Thai Rd., Bangkok.

explained since people are in contact with living tradition. As and when readers also make contact with a living Buddhist tradition, it will also be useful for them.

Living-quarters

In a Buddhist country, when a Bhikkhu has cause to go to some place where there is no *vihara* (monastic dwelling), he will probably stay in a house with laypeople. If they are reasonably wealthy, a small room will have been set aside by them as a family shrine and in this the Bhikkhu will be invited to stay, study, meditate, and sleep. It is customary that only Bhikkhus are invited to sleep in a shrine-room, no member of the family doing so, that room being reserved at other times for *pūja* and meditation.

If Buddhists in other lands are able to set aside such a room for their own special devotion and practice, it may prove very useful when they are able to welcome a Bhikkhu. Its position in the house must of course be decided by circumstances, but relative quietness is a consideration and it is preferable to have it upon an upper floor. In houses where gardens contain a small detached outbuilding, this will be even more suitable.

There are some offenses into which a Bhikkhu may fall regarding his place of lodging. The first is that he cannot sleep in the same room with one who is not fully ordained as a Bhikkhu, except for a limited period of three nights; while a second training rule states "should any Bhikkhu sleep along with a woman, this entails expiation." The commentary takes this to mean "under the same roof" but as this will cause much inconvenience, it should rather be taken that he should have a room to himself away from one in which a woman sleeps.[13] There is here the consideration seen in many places in the Vinaya that not only should a Bhikkhu

13. This interpretation may not be acceptable to the strictest Bhikkhus for whom some small self-contained residence (as an apartment without women residents) would be needed. In respect of the different interpretations possible in some points of Vinaya, it is worthwhile for laypeople to enquire beforehand regarding particular points about which an individual Bhikkhu, or the tradition to which he belongs, holds to strictly. Another case is in the handling of money, discussed below.

be able to maintain his special mode of life with ease, but also that his repute, the reputation of the Sangha as a whole, and of course the good name of the Dhamma, should in no way suffer, not even from those who might invent and spread malicious gossip. For these reasons, strict Bhikkhus are most circumspect in their meetings with women (as the Vinaya leads them to be), while well-informed women in Buddhist lands help a Bhikkhu, by their modest and careful behavior, to keep to his code of discipline.

In the handling of certain things, there are offenses for a Bhikkhu; these, therefore, need not be left about in his place of residence. In this list there are both animate and inanimate. Thus women and girls, however small,[14] are included here, it being an offense for him to touch one, even though his mind is quite free from sensual intentions. Thus women keep their distance from the Bhikkhu and avoid actions which could lead him to come into contact with them. It may be emphasized once again, that this is simply for the good of the Bhikkhu concerned, who, since Arahants are not easily met with, is still capable of experiencing lust. Lord Buddha's teachings, as one soon sees, are always realistic. Women's clothes and articles of jewelry and cosmetics also cannot be touched by him. Neither can female animals, dolls, or money.

Money

Regarding money, there are some Bhikkhus who are of the opinion that this training rule cannot be kept in the modern world: they are willing to handle it for their own transport. (The use of money by Bhikkhus is certainly not a new thing, since the original cause for the holding of the Second Saṅgāyana at Vesālī, in Buddhist Era 100, was the acceptance of gold and silver by them.) Laypeople are also heard to criticize Bhikkhus who do not agree to handle money, on the grounds that this impedes the work of spreading Dhamma. On the other hand, there are traditions where Bhikkhus bear in mind that this is an offense of expiation with forfeiture, while Lord Buddha has said: "I do not say, O Bhikkhus, that *in*

14. It is one of the wrong ways of livelihood for a Bhikkhu if he fondles children, boys or girls — such tactics to increase gains in popularity being left to politicians!

any way may gold or silver (= money and valuables, according to the Commentary) be consented to, may be looked about for." The Second Saṅgāyana ruled that it was inadmissible for Bhikkhus to possess money and referred to the training rule in the Pātimokkha (Vinaya, Nissaggiya Pācittiya 18).

Where this rule is fully adhered to, laypeople do not therefore give money to Bhikkhus, nor expect them to carry it. Money can be made available for the use of a Bhikkhu but not given to him. Such money, which is called after that which it purchases, the "four supports,"[15] *remains the property of the donor* but is kept by the Bhikkhu's steward or attendant (who is often a lay-disciple in training) to be used whenever this becomes necessary. At the time when such "four supports" are made available, the donor may say to a Bhikkhu (or Bhikkhus), "I invite you, sir, with this sum of... for the four supports," at the same time handing that amount to the Bhikkhu's steward. Or a Bhikkhu may receive from the hand of a layman a slip of paper reading: "I invite you with the four supports equal in amount to the sum of ... which has already been handed to the steward. As you have need of it, please request it from him." Whatever is needed is then bought by the steward from that money. In this tradition, a Bhikkhu has no money troubles and may leave such affairs to his steward. He is thus free from thoughts on having only a little, and not troubled by thoughts of what he will buy if there be much money. He can therefore concentrate on the work of Dhamma and Vinaya which he has chosen as his life.

Other items which it is not allowable for a Bhikkhu to touch include: fruits (when still growing on trees), weapons, poisons (unless as prescribed as medicines), nets and snares, seeds, and musical instruments. Generally he will have no need of radio or television either!

Food and Drink

Perhaps one of the best-known training rules of the Bhikkhu concerns his not eating between midday and dawn: it is an offense for him even to touch food—let alone eat it—during this period,

15. See above.

which is called the "wrong-time." Laypeople keeping the eight precepts upon Uposatha days or at other times have basically the same discipline. As the sixth precept they recite: "I undertake the training rule refraining from eating at the wrong time." A *sāmaṇera* (novice) has also to keep this precept every day while he commits himself to observe the ten training rules for novices. It has many advantages both for the Bhikkhu and *sāmaṇera*, as well as for laypeople. The former benefit since they have free time, thoughts not concerned with food, and lightness of the body, which is suitable for study, meditation, and so on. As for the latter, they are not burdened by having to prepare food for Bhikkhus at night.

Although not included among the heavy offenses, this training rule (an offense of expiation) will not be broken by the scrupulous Bhikkhu (unless ill), since its breaking implies giving way to craving, losing the spirit of renunciation, encumbering the stomach, and hence making mind-development more, not less, difficult.

The "right time" for Bhikkhus (and *sāmaṇeras*) to eat begins when the day is light enough to see the lines on the palms of one's hand and ends at noon. During this time a Bhikkhu may eat once[16] or twice. If the former, then an adequate quantity of food is needed to last for twenty-four hours, while if he eats twice the second meal is usually served about quarter past eleven so as to finish well before noon.

There are very few dietary restrictions and these are reasonable, ruling out the consumption of certain animals' flesh (for instance, dogs', snakes', tigers', bears', hyenas') and also that of human beings. Here we may briefly consider the question of meat in relation to the Bhikkhu. The word Bhikkhu is derived from the root *bhikkh* = "to beg" (this English word is from the same Indo-Aryan root). Although a Bhikkhu, when he goes out to obtain almsfood, does not beg (he collects what is offered), since he is not allowed (unless ill) to ask for food, still he is largely dependent upon whatever is put into his bowl. After he has returned to the *vihara* he may if he wishes select whatever vegetable foods he has been

16. See *The Blessings of Piṇḍapāta* and *With Robes and Bowl*, The Wheel Nos. 73 and 83/84.

given and eat only that. In this respect it is proper to remember that when Devadatta requested Lord Buddha for a ruling that Bhikkhus should abstain from flesh, the latter did not agree to rule thus, saying: "And the eating of flesh that is pure in three respects, that is to say, that the eater has not seen, heard, or suspected that it has been killed (specially for Bhikkhus) is allowable." (Flesh and fish allowable must, however, be cooked, as Bhikkhus cannot eat any kind raw or uncooked.) There is also the discourse to Jīvaka on the same subject and the oft-quoted Āmagandha Sutta, in which the evils of ill-conduct in so many ways are pointed out as much more harmful than the eating of meat.

We may summarize by saying that as far as his almsround is concerned a Bhikkhu receives whatever is offered without discrimination (except the unallowable meats, which he is not very likely to be given nowadays). If he wishes to be a vegetarian, he may choose from among the food placed in his bowl, although where he receives only little, this will be very difficult for him. In any case, whether almsfood or that brought to the *vihara* by lay-supporters, he cannot ask for this or that kind of food unless he is ill, when it is allowable to do so. In countries where the almsround is not possible, a Bhikkhu or a Sangha of Bhikkhus will be dependent upon laypeople who agree to give support. Where a number of Bhikkhus are staying, laypeople will organize the buying, cooking, and offering of food in the way most convenient to them and in accordance with the Vinaya. There is no need for food offered by them to be special but it should be nutritious. Therefore, laypeople should not ask, "Do you like...?" or "What shall we cook for you today...?" The Bhikkhu tradition is to accept whatever laypeople wish to offer from the food they have themselves, in this way being as little trouble as possible to householders, of whom it is as true now as it was in Lord Buddha's days, that they have "a lot to do" (*bahukicca*).

A Bhikkhu cannot go to a restaurant or shop and buy or order food (or anything else for that matter). Nor can he personally store food overnight. Once food has been formally offered (see below) to him, it must be consumed by him before noon, or else left for laypeople to finish. Again, a Bhikkhu cannot cook for himself (although he is allowed to reheat food cooked already). Storing or cooking may, however, be done by a *sāmaṇera* or by a lay-disciple in the *vihara*. The principle underlying these three training rules is that greed, ever-ready to spring up where food is concerned, should of course be discouraged, while the Bhikkhu's dependence upon laypeople is greatly stressed. He is taught to reflect every day: "'My life is dependent upon others'—this should frequently be reflected on by one gone forth" (AN 10:48).

We should now deal briefly with the formal offering of food and other items to a Bhikkhu. It is a slight offense for a Bhikkhu intentionally to touch—let alone consume—food or drinks which have not been offered. The reason lying behind this rule is not difficult to see. A Bhikkhu is always very careful to avoid any act which could even be interpreted as approaching an offense of defeat. Taking what is not given with intent to steal is a defeat-offense and, even if he has not fallen completely into this, he may have a grave offense to confess. Hence the importance of formal offering. This offering is done by placing into his hands every item to be consumed, except these things be on a tray when this may be offered. A layman raises from the table, plates, and dishes (or tray) bearing food *with both hands*, or with the left hand touching the right wrist when the item concerned is a small one (as salt-cellars, etc.), and gives each one into the hands of the Bhikkhu. If there are a number of Bhikkhus, the most senior is offered food first and the others in due order afterwards. It is not necessary to offer food into the hands of *sāmaṇeras* as this training rule does not apply to them. Having completed the offering (to each Bhikkhu) a layman will usually salute with *añjali* and then take a seat a little to one side, waiting to see whether he can be of any further help. He should not, after having placed the food into the hands of Bhikkhus, touch it again; if he does so, that food or drink must be re-offered, Should he *receive* anything from the hands of a Bhikkhu, whether it is food or such things as paper or books, etc., it is again skillful training for the layman to salute with *añjali* before taking it.

Due to the training rules above, Bhikkhus cannot share food from the same dishes as those being used by laypeople and it is customary to give them their food apart. In a family this could be just one end of the table, while in any lay-assembly where many are dining, Bhikkhus should have a table specially set aside for them. *Sāmaṇeras*, since they do not have the acceptance into the Sangha as Bhikkhus, cannot share food with the latter and should be given separate food; they traditionally eat sitting elsewhere. As honored guests in the houses of lay-people, Bhikkhus are offered their food before the family sits down to eat or, when there is not time for this, their food is first formally offered to them before the others eat. Since it is an offense for a Bhikkhu to eat or drink standing, he should always be offered a seat. He cannot therefore take food buffet-style, since eating is for him a serious matter, a meditation and not an occasion for delight or gossip.

So far we have referred to a layman offering the food but the case is different when a laywoman makes the offering. A Bhikkhu does not receive anything directly from the hands of a woman, but she may place whatever is to be offered upon the small receiving-cloth which a Bhikkhu carries. Once she has placed it upon this cloth, it is considered to be offered into his hands.[17] In formulating such ways of conduct as these the *theras* of the first Saṅgāyana (Council) have been most careful to guard against physical contact between the sexes so that no possibility of slander or of infatuation might arise. One may here remember the opening suttas of Aṅguttara Nikāya: "O Bhikkhus, I do not perceive at all any other form which thus stands taking hold of the mind of man as does this: the form of woman ... sound... scent... taste... the touch of woman. O Bhikkhus, I do not perceive at all any other form which thus stands taking hold of the mind of woman as does this: the form of man, sound, scent, taste, touch of man." These words of Lord Buddha find practical expression in the Vinaya training rules for both Bhikkhus and Bhikkhunīs (when they existed).

As regards placing food into a Bhikkhu's bowl which is in his hands, whether he is standing, as on the almsround, or sitting in a layman's house, there is no difference between the way it is done by a layman and a laywoman. Nor does the bowl have to be offered to him since it is in his hands.[18]

---

17. Custom in Sri Lanka and Burma does not use this receiving-cloth and women may offer Bhikkhus *dāna*, provided that their fingers do not come into contact.

18. In Sri Lanka, his bowl may be taken from him by a laywoman for placing food in it, and placed into his hands by her, both actions so performed that there is no physical contact.

Other articles besides food and drink which should be offered to him include anything which will go inside the body, such as medicines. Also, his bowl, robes, and other requisites, if they are touched by laypeople, as these are then considered to be out of his possession. Upon occasions of making *puñña* when Bhikkhus are invited, the gifts which are offered to them by the laity such as flowers, incense, candles, medicines, and any other items useful for their lives, may also be formally offered. If such an occasion is during the "wrong-time" and laypeople wish to offer food in tins or jars (milk is included) these things cannot be placed into his hands or accepted by him, but intimation is made to the Bhikkhus of its offering and it is put aside to be kept by a *sāmaṇera* or lay-disciple. Such small points as these constitute not only a discipline for Bhikkhus but also for the laity, who may thereby grow in carefulness.

It was emphasized above that offering, whether by a layman or laywoman, is made with *both* hands. This is not simply some sort of ritual but has a very good reason behind it. When one gives something in the ordinary way, the giving is done with one hand if the object permits it. This kind of giving may as a fact become habitual in the sense that one is not aware any more of "giving" and from a Buddhist point of view this shows slackness of mind and lack of care. Now, Bhikkhus who are striving on the Path of Dhamma-Vinaya are said to be a "good field for *puñña*"—that is, the results to be expected from giving to them as they strive towards Nibbāna, leading a pure life, are great indeed, and will result in clarity and peace increasing in the hearts of the donors. Thus it becomes important when making offerings to Bhikkhus, whether of their daily food or upon some special occasion, to make the offering consciously, with a strong intention of giving. The stronger the intention, which is here skillful kamma, the greater the fruits of happiness reaped by the donors. So that laypeople are reminded to make this giving-intention strong, they are instructed to offer with both hands—an act which requires more forethought than the usual ways of giving. Respect is also expressed in this method of offering and it is also used by new Bhikkhus and *sāmaṇeras* when presenting anything to their teachers or preceptors.

The meal having been consumed, a Bhikkhu chants briefly (and a number of Bhikkhus for some time) verses of well-wishing for the laity. It is actually an offense of wrongdoing for him (them) not to do so if laypeople are present. The least which is done will be for a senior Bhikkhu to say a few words such as: "Long-life and beauty, happiness, and strength" (*Āyu vaṇṇo sukhaṃ balaṃ*). Whether laypeople have also finished eating, or whether they have not yet begun, at least the donor will sit quietly with folded hands listening to these words or verses of well-wishing. Every word of the Pali verses may not be understood but it is more important that the mind should be concentrated upon the chanting to the exclusion of everything else. A mindful and concentrated mind is always full of skillfulness. Frequently, such chants as are translated below form the core of well-wishing:

> Just as the rivers full of water
> Fill the ocean full,
> Even so does that here given
> Benefit the dead (the hungry-ghosts, *peta*).
>
> Whatever by you wished or wanted
> May it quickly be,
> May all your wishes fulfilled—
> As the moon upon the fifteenth day (the full moon),
> Or as the wish-fulfilling gem.
>
> May all distresses be averted,
> May all diseases be destroyed,
> May no dangers be for them,
> May (they) be happy, living long.
>
> He of respectful nature who
> Even the elders honoring,
> Four qualities for him increase:
> Long-life and beauty, happiness and strength.

At the close of the chanting it is the custom in many places to say "*Sādhu, sādhu...*" and then to raise the hands in *añjali* to the forehead, to lower the body. "*Sādhu*" means "it is well," and is an expression of delighted approval heard everywhere in Buddhist countries when a deed of *puñña* has been done, such as giving, helping, listening to Dhamma, and so forth.

As regards drinking, a Bhikkhu may not drink distilled or fermented intoxicants (*sura-meraya-majja*) (except minute quantities contained in necessary medicines). Before noon any other drink may be offered to him, with or without milk. After twelve o'clock noon it is not allowable for him to take milk (or any drink containing milk), cereals, eggs, etc., nor any kind of soup. He may be offered any fruit juice (uncooked but strained and free from particles of fruit), or any of the bottled soft drinks which are now common. The five medicines allowable over a period of seven days may also be taken by him if he is indisposed. The first of these, ghee, is generally not available outside India, but the other four are common: butter (but not cheese), vegetable oil (such as margarine), honey, and molasses (including all sorts of sugar). If more of these is accepted by him than he can consume in one evening, it may be kept by him for seven days at most. Any remaining after this time he cannot consume without falling into an offense. It is thus common for these "medicines" to be kept by a *sāmaṇera* or lay-disciple to be offered as they are needed. Tea, coffee, and cocoa (all without milk) are also allowable during the afternoon and evening. With these allowable drinks and fortified in any case by having few desires and some ability to endure, Bhikkhus (and *sāmaṇeras*) sustain themselves for study, practice, or teaching.

Travel

Since a Bhikkhu keeping strictly to the Vinaya will not handle money, if he is being invited to teach or to stay, it is customary in Buddhist countries for a layman to come and fetch him. Where distance prevents this, train tickets may be bought and sent to him. If the journey is a long one, he may be accompanied by a lay-disciple who will buy tickets and the Bhikkhu's food at the right time. When he is traveling alone, it is usual to meet him at the station.

A Bhikkhu commits an offense if he makes an arrangement to go on a journey with a woman, so that if he is accompanied, his companion must be a man (though where a male companion is present, women may also be in the party as well). This is another provision to prevent offenses and to stop the wagging of slanderous tongues. When the Bhikkhu travels by car, a woman should not sit beside him, though of course a man may do so. It is preferable that he does not travel in a car with only a woman who is driving.

There are also several places to which it is not proper to take Bhikkhus, such as the following, which are called the "wrong resort" for Bhikkhus: namely, crowded places or places of entertainment, theaters, concert halls, cinemas, stadiums, games-fields, exhibitions, fairs, casinos, nightclubs, brothels, army parades, and even fields of battle. It is common sense that Bhikkhus have no need for the various sorts of sense-stimulation provided by such places.

General Conduct

In Buddhist countries such as Thailand, the general conduct of laypeople in the presence of Bhikkhus is molded upon the discipline followed by Bhikkhus and *sāmaṇeras* when they are in the presence of *theras*. Much of this code of good conduct is contained in the articles of the seventy-five trainings (*sekhiya*) found in the Pātimokkha. Rather than comment upon all these, we may select the most important groups of points for outline explanation.

Buddhist laypeople living in Thailand have a good chance to acquaint themselves with the details of this conduct since they can at any time go to a Wat where Vinaya is well observed and see for themselves how Bhikkhus do things. They have another chance also not available to most Western Buddhists, for the custom here (and in Burma, Laos, and Cambodia) is that most young men (and a few young women) ask for temporary ordination over periods of time ranging from one to four months. While they are in the robes they learn, among other things, how to conduct themselves in the manner proper to those who have gone forth. Every day they receive instruction in the Vinaya (and much else) which includes, of course, the seventy-five trainings. Not only that, for these trainings, while they constitute only small offenses when broken, actually are very important since they cover events of everyday occurrence, such as walking, sitting, wearing robes, eating, teaching, and listening to Dhamma. When these temporarily-ordained monks (often called "rains-Bhikkhus") disrobe and return to their homes, they take with them experience of a good discipline and it is this which becomes the basis for lay conduct in the presence of Bhikkhus. As this training in good conduct applies to contact between laypeople and Bhikkhus almost as much as it does between junior Bhikkhus and *theras*, there is a considerable basis for common understanding and hence concord.

What sort of things are included in this training? First, we may mention regulation of the body in the four positions, the first of these being *walking*. When walking in company with a Bhikkhu, a layperson will walk somewhat behind him rather than immediately at his side, and certainly not push in front, always giving way to him where this is necessary. This is particularly important if the Bhikkhu is talking Dhamma, when it will be an offense for him to follow behind a layperson, or to walk to one side of the path while doing so. The ancient Buddhist tradition from India prescribes that one should as a mark of respect, "keep one's right side towards" one's teacher, the right side of the body being symbolically that associated with conscious effort and general skillfulness in conduct. If a Bhikkhu is sitting and a layman has occasion to pass in front of him (a laywoman will observe a stricter decorum and not come very near a Bhikkhu), it is good training in mindfulness to stoop the body and head and perhaps say something like "Excuse me, sir."[19] Again, if a layman or woman should enter a room where a Bhikkhu is sitting and perhaps talking Dhamma with others, he or she usually performs "the action of *añjali*" or lowers the body, according to what is suitable, before sitting down.

In *standing*, one should not stand upon a higher step or level than a Bhikkhu and talk to him. We have in the English the phrase "to look up to" implying respect, and if one is learning Dhamma that is what one should do, literally as well as figuratively. Standing, one does not stand too near or too far but at the "right" distance. One's hands should be clasped in front and one's body controlled while talking to a Bhikkhu. In Buddhist countries agreement or questions are accompanied by "the action of *añjali*" in the case of talking to a senior Bhikkhu. All these bodily actions help one to correct the mind and ensure that it is functioning in a way proper for the reception of Dhamma.

Should the Bhikkhu be barefooted, as is often the case in the East, a layperson with shoes on will not talk to him but remove

19. The traditional mode of address used for Bhikkhus in the time of Lord Buddha, and still used in Sri Lanka, is "*Bhante*" (venerable sir).

his or her shoes first. This is because it is an offense for him to talk Dhamma to one who is wearing shoes when he is not, though this situation is not likely to occur in the cold countries of the West.

When *sitting*, especially if Dhamma is the subject of a Bhikkhu's speech, one should sit attentively and not sprawling in a chair. It is also against the spirit of the Vinaya for a Bhikkhu to teach Dhamma to one who is smoking. (It is not against the letter, as this custom was not known in Lord Buddha's days.) However, smoking is bound to distract from listening to Dhamma and is often a sign of unmindful or tense states of mind. All such conditions are opposed to the profitable and attentive hearkening with which Dhamma should be received. Dhamma is so important, so valuable, that it becomes an offense for a Bhikkhu to teach it to anyone who shows by his bodily position that his mind is not concentrated to receive it.[20] The body should be controlled when sitting such that the feet are tucked in under a chair (or inconspicuous if sitting on the ground), with the back reasonably erect and hands placed comfortably in the lap. In sitting down a layperson is careful to notice whether the chair he is about to sit upon has a Bhikkhu's robe upon it. If so, he will sit elsewhere or else remove the robe, offering it to the Bhikkhu. As the robe is a symbol of pure life in Dhamma, it is never sat upon or leaned against by laypeople. A seat taken by a layman or woman should not be higher than that used by the Bhikkhu, and if several people are seated on the ground, a Bhikkhu should be given a separate mat to sit upon. All these sorts of things are also observed by good Bhikkhus in the presence of their teachers and other *theras*, and make for a spirit of respect and harmony.

Then in *lying down*, laymen if they do so in the same room as a Bhikkhu, will never point their feet at him. Nor for that matter will any Buddhist, whether in robes or "wearing white" (a layperson), lie down with his feet pointing towards any respected or sacred object in a room such as Buddha-images, stupas, pictures of the Buddha or of any teacher alive or dead, Buddhist scriptures, and so on. The head is always placed in their direction and usually

20. Under "nonsensical chatter" (*samphappalapa*), Tibetan tradition counts it "true" nonsense to teach Dhamma to one who is unprepared. There is also worldly nonsense (animal-talk, see below) and untrue nonsense (tales).

before lying down, a triple lowering is made to any shrine, etc., which happens to be in the room.

On the same principles as those set out above, if a Bhikkhu is sitting, a layperson does not talk to him standing but, after lotussing or lowering the body, sits down to talk; while if a Bhikkhu is standing, a layman will stand to talk with him. It is part of the reasonableness of this training that almost none of the usual lay conduct mentioned here is performed if a layperson is ill.

If one approaches a Bhikkhu to give something while he is sitting, one's head should not be higher than his own, and better lower. This avoids leaning over him and also helps the donor to give with a humble mind, which in itself will bear good fruits.

Generally in talking to a Bhikkhu one should try to avoid unsuitable subjects of discussion. Bhikkhus were several times rebuked by Lord Buddha for engaging in "animal-talk," which is defined by this quite common passage in the discourses: "Talk about kings and robbers, ministers and armies, danger and war, eating and drinking, clothes and dwellings, garlands and scents, relations, vehicles, villages and markets, towns and districts, women and heroes, street talk, talk by the well, talk about those departed in days gone by, idle chatter, talk upon the world and the sea, and also on gain and loss" (AN 10:69). When one comes to think about it, this list covers most of the subjects to be found in our newspapers! A layman may also remember that right speech, the third constituent of the Eightfold Path, is defined as: restraint from lying, slander, rough speech, and chatter. Nor is it suitable to ask a Bhikkhu what food and drink he likes, unless he is ill. Again, it is not proper to ask about the attainments which he has won through his Dhamma-practice. It is an offense of expiation for a Bhikkhu to tell a layman even the truth regarding his own attainments, and an offense of Defeat should he be tempted to lie, saying that he has won what has not been won by him. Also among requests which are improper, as they could embroil a Bhikkhu in what is not-Dhamma, are questions upon luck, signs, stars, and palms. All this is called animal-knowledge by Lord Buddha and he has made it an offense of wrongdoing for a Bhikkhu to learn or to teach it.

In this section also, one might mention some special provision regarding the conduct of laywomen. For instance, when coming to a Bhikkhu for instruction in Dhamma, it is proper if a man or boy accompanies the laywoman. Where this is not possible, provided that there is another Bhikkhu or *sāmaṇera* in the room when the teaching of Dhamma takes place, there will be no offense for the Bhikkhu. But he should not find himself alone with a woman in a room, especially one into which others cannot see. Again, women desirous of Dhamma-instruction should not visit a Bhikkhu after dusk but do so during the day. All these provisions are to guard individual Bhikkhus against their own mental stains and so help them in their training, thus being for the well-being of the Sangha and therefore, since the Sangha guards and maintains the Dhamma, for the good name of Dhamma too.

Laywomen when visiting a *vihāra* are therefore very modest whenever they have cause to speak to Bhikkhus. Their dress should be modest and their persons devoid of ornaments, while they address themselves to Bhikkhus with humility. In so doing, they help both themselves and the Bhikkhus: themselves by following the way of Dhamma which is to realize the impermanent, unsatisfactory, and unbeautiful nature of the body; and the Bhikkhus by remembering that most of those in the yellow robe have not yet conquered the mental stains (*kilesa*).

Those laypeople who are very well practiced and who have seen for themselves the immense value of Dhamma will, in the presence of their teacher or other respected Bhikkhus, sit keeping their hands lotussed all the time. Faith (*saddhā*) and serene clarity (*pāsāda*) of mind do, after all, increase in proportion to one's experience of Dhamma. Laypeople having this sort of deep appreciation of Dhamma after "the action of *añjali*" and the triple lowering are also seen to recite when their teacher or other Bhikkhus are departing: "Excuse me, venerable sir, for all the faults I have committed through the three doors (of mind, speech, and body); for these please forgive me. A second time, venerable sir.... A third time, venerable sir... please forgive me."[21] Only those who have had the blessing of a personal teacher and who feel great reverence for him will feel like making this opening-up

21. *"Okāsa ahaṃ bhante, dvārattayena kataṃ sabbaṃ aparādhaṃ khamata me bhante. Dutiyampi, ahaṃ bhante... Tatiyampi, ahaṃ bhante ... khamatha me bhante."*

of faults. It has been included here just because it is a very good practice. All who are not Arahants have the stain of pride and will therefore grow in the Dhamma as this is lessened and genuine humility increased. This practice can sometimes be beneficial. *The conduct of Buddhist laypeople in the West towards Bhikkhus who are their teachers may in these matters vary somewhat with the customs of the country which are accepted as polite. It may be stressed once again that such behavior, governed by mindfulness and wisdom, is for the welfare of all who practice Dhamma.*

Finally, a word may be said upon what a Bhikkhu may do in connection with lay ceremonies and what he may not. Where there are numerous Bhikkhus as in Thailand, they are frequently invited to the house of people for teaching, chanting, and upon occasions of making *puñña*. For instance at the time when a new house is occupied, as well as the various anniversaries of birth and death. Their chanting of the words of Lord Buddha to the listening laypeople who sit with "action of *añjali*" and minds concentrated upon the chanting, brings, in this case, peace and happiness. But it should not be thought that, without the effort of hearkening on the part of the laypeople, blessing automatically results. Indeed, Bhikkhus and their chanting are in no way a vehicle for the bestowal of "sacraments" or blessings. What are sometimes written about as "blessings" in connection with Bhikkhus' chanting would accurately be called well-wishings (see the stanzas translated above in the section on food, etc.). In other words, a Bhikkhu's work is not that of a priest.

Bhikkhus may be invited to chant stanzas of well-wishing before or after a marriage, an occasion when the engaged or married couple jointly make *puñña* to ensure the success of their new life. However, a Bhikkhu cannot "marry" laypeople as do priests in other faiths. Should he do so, he stands in danger of falling into a heavy offense, the fifth of the formal meetings (*saṅghādisesa*), where, acting as a go-between either for a man to a woman or a woman to a man, quite rules out the possibility of Bhikkhus marrying others. Marriage in Buddhist countries is purely a lay-contract between the parties undertaking it, the ceremony being conducted by a senior layman, this being ratified in various ways through some government agency.

Conclusion

It now remains only to say a little about how Bhikkhus are regarded by laypeople in Thailand at the present time. In this matter, as in so many others, one may perceive two extremes and a profitable middle course. One sort of extreme attitude which is sometimes found (more often in the West than in Thailand) is that of unqualified praise of certain Bhikkhus. In the eyes of those laypeople who follow him, he can absolutely do no wrong. It is as though they are bewitched by the yellow robe and, out of faith (or sometimes from less noble motives), will hear no word against their idol and see no imperfection in him. He is an Arahant, a Bodhisattva or by whatever other name they like to glorify him! Some amongst them, out of delusion, imagine that all those who wear the yellow robe are automatically Arahants and so lavish a Bhikkhu with praise such that if his head is not turned and his heart not corrupted by such flattery, it will be a great wonder. Such sweet doses of "spiritual" praise are very liable to cause a personality cult, rather than devotion to the Triple Gem.

The other extreme, which is much less common, is the sort of drain inspector's attitude to a Bhikkhu's life. It is the very critical, probing examination of a Bhikkhu and his way of doing things which springs out of the root of hatred. Slander is often employed as well so that small offenses of omission and commission by a Bhikkhu become magnified into mountains of iniquity. Untrue stories are eagerly chewed over and added to the unwholesomeness, and perhaps the people pride themselves upon the benefits which they are bringing about by making public what they regard as hidden crimes.

In Thailand, neither of these two extremes is prevalent. People tend to be respectful of Bhikkhus and *sāmaṇeras* but, unless particularly devoted to a teacher, do not lavish devotion upon those they do not know. There are, after all, about a quarter of a million men and boys wearing robes in Thailand; the quality of Bhikkhus in such a large Sangha, very naturally, varies considerably. On the other hand, laypeople generally shut their eyes to small faults of Bhikkhus and rarely criticize. This is quite proper since criticism is of no avail unless it can raise the other from unskill to skill. A teacher has much power over both his monastic and lay disciples, but a layperson rarely possesses such ability. It is well to reflect about kamma and how each person is—"owner of kamma, heir to kamma, born of kamma, bound by kamma, determined by kamma"—for such reflection cultivates equanimity. Each person trains himself, a Bhikkhu according to his knowledge and ability and a layman likewise.

Thus, we have all, Bhikkhus and laity alike, a great debt of gratitude to Lord Buddha, who has made known the training rules for Bhikkhus founded upon these ten reasons:

For the welfare of the Sangha,
For the comfort of the Sangha,
For the control of unsteady men,
For the comfort of well-behaved Bhikkhus,
For the restraint of the pollutions in this present life,
For the guarding against pollution liable to arise in a future life,
For the pleasing of those not yet pleased (with Dhamma),
For the increase of those pleased (with Dhamma),
For the establishment of True Dhamma,
And for the benefit of the Vinaya.

"Ayaṃ dhammo ayaṃ vinayo idaṃ Satthu-sāsanaṃ."

"This is Dhamma, this is Vinaya, here indeed is the Teacher's Instruction."

Bibliography

The Pātimokkha, 227 Fundamental Rules of a Bhikkhu with an introduction by Phra Sāsana Sobhana (Suvaddhano) and the Pali page by page with English translation by Ven. Ñāṇamoli Thera, Social Science Association Press of Thailand, 1966.

The Book of the Discipline, Volumes 1–6, complete translation of the Vinaya-Collection, translated by Dr. I.B. Horner, President of the Pali Text Society, 1939–1966 (all volumes in print). [See www.palitext.com.]

Vinaya Texts, Sacred Books of the East volumes 13, 17, 20, a selection from the Vinaya-Collection translated by T.W. Rhys Davids and H. Oldenberg, Oxford University Press, 1881, reissued by Motilal Banarsidass (Jawahawarnagar, Delhi 7, India), 1965.

Ordination Procedure, by His Royal Highness, the late Saṅgharāja of Thailand, Prince Vajirañāṇavarorasa. Pali texts in roman script with English translation of the higher ordination (or acceptance, *upasampadā*) and chapters explaining the basis of the Vinaya (Discipline), some rules necessary for the Bhikkhus, passages for chanting, etc. King Mahāmakuta's Academy (Phra Sumeru Rd., Bangkok), 2506/1963.

Sāmaṇerasikkha: The Novice's Training, compiled from Pali Texts and Commentaries with explanations by His Royal Highness, the late Saṅgharāja of Thailand, Prince Jinavarasirivaddhana. Pali Texts in roman script with English translation. With a "Brief biography of the Venerable Rāhula, the first Sāmaṇera," by Bhikkhu Khantipālo. King Mahāmakuta's Academy (Phra Sumeru Rd., Bangkok), 2509/1966.

Early Buddhist Monachism, by Sukumar Dutt, Bombay, 1960.

Early Monastic Buddhism, by Nalinaksa Dutt, Calcutta, 1960.

ABOUT PARIYATTI

Pariyatti is dedicated to providing affordable access to authentic teachings of the Buddha about the Dhamma theory (*pariyatti*) and practice (*paṭipatti*) of Vipassana meditation. A 501(c)(3) nonprofit charitable organization since 2002, Pariyatti is sustained by contributions from individuals who appreciate and want to share the incalculable value of the Dhamma teachings. We invite you to visit www.pariyatti.org to learn about our programs, services, and ways to support publishing and other undertakings.

Pariyatti Publishing Imprints

Vipassana Research Publications (focus on Vipassana as taught by S.N. Goenka in the tradition of Sayagyi U Ba Khin)

BPS Pariyatti Editions (selected titles from the Buddhist Publication Society, copublished by Pariyatti)

MPA Pariyatti Editions (selected titles from the Myanmar Pitaka Association, copublished by Pariyatti)

Pariyatti Digital Editions (audio and video titles, including discourses)

Pariyatti Press (classic titles returned to print and inspirational writing by contemporary authors)

Pariyatti enriches the world by

- disseminating the words of the Buddha,
- providing sustenance for the seeker's journey,
- illuminating the meditator's path.

www.ingramcontent.com/pod-product-compliance
Lightning Source LLC
Chambersburg PA
CBHW020346170426
43200CB00005B/69
* 9 7 8 1 6 8 1 7 2 4 9 5 9 *